Ambrose Macaulay

PATRICK DORRIAN

Patrick Dorrian

Bishop of Down and Connor 1865-85

Ambrose Macaulay

IRISH ACADEMIC PRESS

The typesetting for the book,
in 11 on 12 pt Plantin,
was output by Textflow Services Ltd, Belfast
for Irish Academic Press Limited
Kill Lane, Blackrock, Co. Dublin

© Ambrose Macaulay 1987

BRITISH LIBRARY CATALOGUING IN PUBLICATION DATA

Macaulay, Ambrose
    Patrick Dorrian, Bishop of Down and Connor.
    1. Dorrian, Patrick   2. Bishops—Ireland
    —Biography
    I. Title
    282',092'4   BX4705.D65/

    ISBN 0-7165-2406-6

Printed by Antony Rowe Limited
Bumpers Farm, Chippenham, Wilts., England

Sub ductu Episcopi virilis Belfastia cito foret inter longe florentissimas hujus magni imperii Britannici ecclesias.[1]

Joseph Dixon, Archbishop of Armagh

I would gladly go ten times as far as from here to Belfast to serve or gratify His Lordship of Down and Connor, whom I am proud to reckon amongst the most valued of my friends, and whom all Ireland regards as a model Bishop as well as a staunch, fearless and uncompromising Irish patriot.

T.W. Croke, Archbishop of Cashel[2]

At the beginning of your ministry Catholicity among us wore a pale and troubled aspect and the temples of God were few and far between in the land ... in that comparatively brief interval there have sprung up on all sides, as though at the touch of the enchanter's wand, churches, presbyteries, convents, schools, monastery, reformatory, hospital, lecture hall, each of goodly proportion and prolific of benefit.[3]

---

1 Under the leadership of an energetic bishop Belfast would soon be one of the most flourising churches of this great British Empire.

2 Writing from Ramsgate to apologize for his absence from the silver jubilee celebrations of Bishop Dorrian's episcopal ordination.

3 From the address of the Catholic laity of Down and Connor at the silver jubilee celebrations.

Contents

PREFACE		9
ABBREVIATIONS		11
1	Student and seminarian	13
2	Curate in Belfast	19
3	Parish priest of Loughinisland	65
4	Coadjutor bishop of Down and Connor	87
5	Pastoral care and problems of authority	113
6	Political problems 1860-70	163
7	The struggle for a Catholic press	193
8	Home Rule gathers momentum	219
9	Primary and secondary education	243
10	The university question	301
11	Politico-religious issues and Roman reactions	323
12	Celebrations and close	369
BIBLIOGRAPHY		377
INDEX		387

Map by Ian Alexander

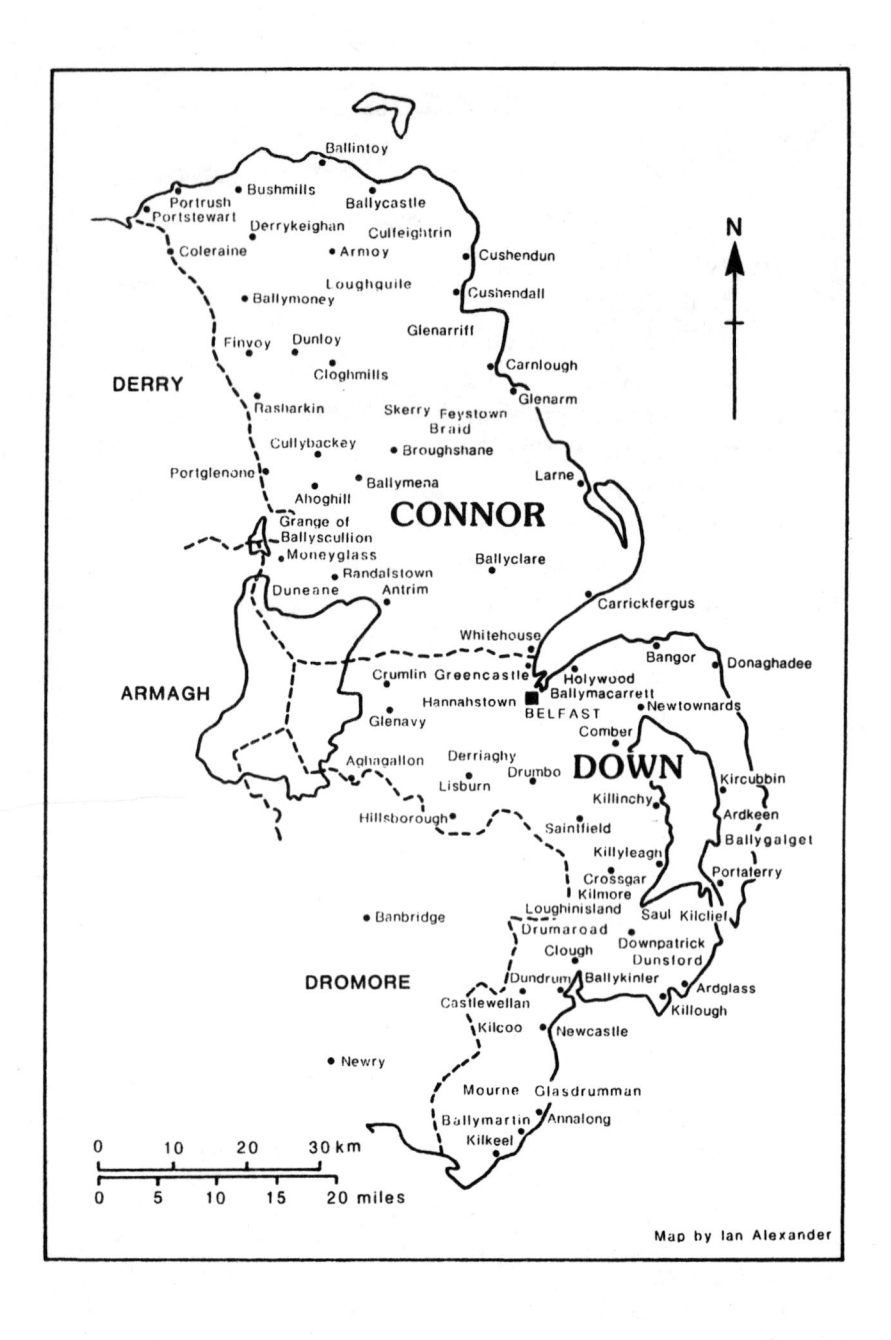

Preface

Patrick Dorrian was appointed coadjutor bishop of Down and Connor in 1860, succeeded to the see five years later, and held office until his death in 1885. He presided over the diocese during a period of intense development of ecclesiastical structures, when new churches, schools, convents and presbyteries arose to serve the needs of his people, especially in the expanding town of Belfast. The growth rate of Belfast during the nineteenth century was spectacular — from approximately 20,000 in 1800 to 350,000 in 1900 — and, apart from the first decade, was faster in the 1860s, when Dorrian's episcopate began, than in any other.

This swift urban development brought many problems in its wake. Immigrants from the countryside, whose experience was limited to rural life, were suddenly uprooted and forced to adapt to a very different and, in most cases, bleak and harsh environment. Driven by poverty and need, they were compelled to accept whatever accommodation was available, and often found themselves living in cramped, unhealthy and unhygienic houses in narrow streets, entries and courts, where resistance to diseases and epidemics was weak. Inevitably such conditions spawned a host of social evils and demanded a response from the church at many levels.

Bishop Dorrian devoted much time and energy to the provision of homes, orphanages and institutions for the sick, the poor, the elderly and the abandoned. He adjusted parish boundaries, instituted new methods of pastoral care and encouraged the extension of Catholic education. An able and diligent administrator, who was never daunted by the magnitude of the task ahead of him, he tackled all the issues and difficulties that confronted him boldly and directly, if at times with scant patience for opposition.

And not least of these difficulties were the sectarian tension and strife between Protestant and Catholic in Belfast. Throughout the period of Dorrian's connection with the town, both as curate and bishop, denominational distrust and hostility grew. Serious rioting occurred in 1864 and 1872, and in 1886, a year after the bishop's death, disturbances that followed the introduction of the Home Rule Bill claimed some thirty lives.

Dorrian's episcopate is important, therefore, not only for an understanding of the Catholic community of Down and Connor but also for the history of Belfast. And since the religious, economic and social divisions of Belfast to a great extent shaped the political climate of Ulster, the role played by its ecclesiastical leaders was ultimately significant for the general course of Irish history.

I have pleasure in acknowledging my indebtedness to all who have helped me in the preparation of this book. For permission to make use of archival material I am grateful to the following: Cardinal Stickler, Librarian of the Holy Roman Church; Cardinal Rossi, former Prefect of the Congregation for the Evangelization of Peoples; Cardinal Ó Fiaich, Archbishop of Armagh; the late Archbishops Ryan and McNamara of Dublin; Bishop Cahal B. Daly of Down and Connor; Bishop Laurence Forristal of Ossory; Bishop Francis G. Brooks of Dromore; Bishop Colm O'Reilly of Ardagh and Clonmacnois; Abbot Joseph Nardin, St Paul's Basilica, Rome; Monsignor John Hanly, Rector of the Pontifical Irish College, Rome; Monsignor John Kennedy, Rector of the Venerable English College, Rome; Revd Peter McCann, St Malachy's Presbytery, Belfast; Revd Bernard Magee, Parochial House, Loughinisland; Revd Simon Clyne, St Patrick's Training College, Dublin; Brother Gerard McHugh, Superior General of the Christian Brothers, Rome.

I wish to thank the librarians and staffs at the National Library of Ireland, the Public Record Office of Northern Ireland and at the City Hall, Belfast. I am especially indebted to Fr Joseph Metzler, former Archivist of the Congregation for the Evangelization of Peoples and present Prefect of the Vatican Archives; to Monsignor Charles Burns, Archivist at the Vatican Archives; to Mr David Sheehy, Director of the Dublin Diocesan Archives.

For their kindness in reading my typescript and giving me much helpful advice, I am glad to record my gratitude to Professor Patrick J. Corish, Professor John H. Whyte, Canon Michael Dallat, Mr Jack Magee and Fr Joseph Gunn. Finally, I should like to thank Bishop Cahal B. Daly for granting me a year's study-leave to carry out the research in Rome on which much of this work is based.

Ambrose Macaulay

Belfast
13 June 1987

Abbreviations

A.C.B.G.R.	Archives of the Christian Brothers' Generalate, Rome
A.C.D.A.	Ardagh and Clonmacnois Diocesan Archives
A.D.A.	Armagh Diocesan Archives
A.I.C.R.	Archives of the Pontifical Irish College, Rome
A.P.F.	Archives of the Sacred Congregation for the Evangelization of Peoples (formerly Propaganda Fide), Rome
A.S.P.B.R.	Archives of St Paul's Basilica, Rome
A.S.P.T.C.D.	Archives of St Patrick's Training College, Drumcondra
A.S.V.	Vatican Archives
A.V.E.C.R.	Archives of the Venerable English College, Rome
B.M.N.	*Belfast Morning News*
B.N.L.	*Belfast News-Letter*
D.C.D.A.	Down and Connor Diocesan Archives
D.D.A.	Dublin Diocesan Archives
Dr.D.A.	Dromore Diocesan Archives
D.R.	*Downpatrick Recorder*
F.J.	*Freeman's Journal*
I.P.	*Irish People*
M.N.	*Morning News*
N.L.I.	National Library of Ireland, Dublin
N.S.	*Northern Star*
N.W.	*Northern Whig*
P.R.O.N.I.	Public Record Office of Northern Ireland, Belfast
Ul.	*Ulsterman*
U.Ex.	*Ulster Examiner*
U.Ob.	*Ulster Observer*
V.	*Vindicator*
W.V.	*Weekly Vindicator*
Lyons, *Parnell*	F.S.L. Lyons, *Charles Stewart Parnell* (London, 1977)

Moody, *Davitt*　　T.W. Moody *Davitt and Irish Revolution 1846-82* (Oxford, 1981)

O'Laverty, *Down and Connor*　　J. O'Laverty, *An historical account of the diocese of Down and Connor, ancient and modern*, 5 vols. (Dublin, 1878-95)

1
Student and seminarian

Tradition ordains that St Patrick, the national apostle of Ireland, awaits the resurrection in the county town of Down which bears his name. Though the early Celtic sources may differ about the saint's last resting place, the Anglo-Normans, who created a new lordship in the ancient kingdom of Ulidia, greatly strengthened the claims of Dun Lethglaisse, which they re-christened Downpatrick, to have the privilege of guarding Patrick's mortal remains. John de Courcy, who developed the town as a powerful ecclesiastical centre in the late twelfth century, firmly anchored it in Irish religious sentiment and identified it not only with Patrick but also with Brigid and Columcille. Ever since then the residents of Downpatrick have been proud of their Patrician connections and of their cathedral church of the Holy Trinity. Destiny could choose no more fitting spot for the birthplace of a future bishop of the diocese of Down and Connor.

And it was in Downpatrick that Patrick Dorrian was born on 29 March 1814. His parents, Patrick and Rose, née Murphy, ran a general store in Irish Street. The name Dorrian is a variant of Doran and is found especially in Counties Down and Donegal. According to family tradition the Dorrians held land of the Forde family of Seaforde at Magheralone, which was then part of the parish of Loughinisland. Though information on the family background is scant, one may surmise that Patrick Dorrian *père* left the family home to earn his livelihood in Downpatrick when that town was sharing in the increased prosperity of the latter decades of the eighteenth century or in the early years of the nineteenth.

The improvement in the tillage of Lecale as a result of the beneficent interest of the local landlord, Judge Ward, led to the development of the small sea ports on the east coast of Down as trading centres. Exporting corn, potatoes and farm produce, and importing farm equipment, groceries, salt and some 'luxury' goods, the towns of Lecale enjoyed a boom for about forty years until the end of the Napoleonic wars brought a slump. Downpatrick experienced a share of this prosperity, and the opportunities for a general store providing foodstuffs, hardware, and household utensils to the farmers and townspeople of the area were good.

Patrick Dorrian may not have become wealthy but he certainly achieved modest prosperity, for he was able to provide his family with the best education available. Revd James Neilson, a member of a distinguished and liberal Presbyterian family, conducted a classical or secondary school in Downpatrick, and for a short time had the assistance of his son, Samuel, who was later ordained for the ministry in Dromore and ultimately succeeded his father in Downpatrick. Small classical schools, conducted by one or two people, existed in many Irish towns. As their name suggests, their principal purpose was to teach Latin and Greek at secondary level, but some of them also taught English, French, a little mathematics and other subjects. William Crolly, who became bishop of Down and Connor in 1825, his successor, Cornelius Denvir, and several priests of Down and Connor had attended this school and retained happy memories of the Neilsons' tolerance and broadmindedness.[1] Access to it for the Dorrian boys was easier than it had been for some of the future clergy of the diocese who had been obliged to travel a few miles daily on horseback. Though the fees were not large, they were beyond the means of the majority of Catholic families. Bernard and Edward Dorrian attended the Neilson school. Bernard achieved a sufficiently high standard in classics to enable him to join the logic class in Maynooth in 1828. Edward passed on to medical school in Dublin. The other brother, William, may also have attended this family school; he subsequently became a farmer and held property at Cumran near Clough. Patrick *fils* followed the example of his brother, Bernard; after his studies with Dr Neilson, he also enrolled at Maynooth.

Later, when he had become a stout champion of Catholic education, Patrick was questioned about his experiences at this school in Downpatrick. He had claimed that the safeguards afforded the faith of Catholic children in private schools where the teachers belonged to the established church were much better than in model or diocesan schools, and admitting to being taught by a Presbyterian clergyman in such a private school, was asked if this teacher had ever interfered with his faith and morals. He insisted that the contrary was the case; this Presbyterian divine in fact interfered 'with those who were of an

---

1 When James Neilson's son, Samuel, was called to the Presbyterian congregation in Dromore, William Crolly wrote to the parish priest: 'Your much esteemed character and his own liberal disposition have induced him to solicit an introduction to you, which, I hope, will be attended by your lasting friendship and sincere esteem for each other. His father is one of the most liberal and respectable clergymen in County Down, and I am persuaded that his son will establish his title to those hereditary virtues'. (Crolly to Hugh McConville, 11 Mar. 1825, Dr.D.A.)

opposite way of thinking'. He mentioned two Greek authors whom they used translate — one was the Gospel of St John — and, referring to the doctrine of the Blessed Eucharist, recalled that the Protestant boys translated the Greek η as 'and', and 'got a knock on the head for so doing'. The Catholic boys had the correct translation 'or' from the Douay version which 'blotted out the Protestant doctrine on the question of the two species'.[2] Like his elder brother, Bernard, Patrick also attained a high standard in Latin and Greek at the Neilson school.

The course of studies in Maynooth then lasted seven years; for the first four years the student read classics, philosophy and general science, the two years in classics being divided up into humanity and rhetoric. After having completed the equivalent of a general degree at a university, the seminarian then spent three years reading theology. But the entry system was not fixed and rigid; a candidate could sit the examinations at various levels and, if successful, join the next stage of the course. At the age of nineteen years Patrick set off for Maynooth, intending to sit the entrance examination for the rhetoric or second year. By mistake his name was placed on the list of candidates for admission to the third or logic year, and he was successful. He later admitted that his study had until then been confined mainly to Latin and Greek and that he had no knowledge of mathematics. And he also regretted that he was allowed to spend only four years in Maynooth; consequently he could not 'lay up a very great store of literature, and had no opportunity of going into Philosophy'.[3] He spent, in fact, one year reading general philosophy and the following year reading natural philosophy or science, before passing into theology. At the beginning of his second year of study his father died.

Maynooth had been established in 1795 to provide the education for the secular priesthood that had hitherto been available for the most part only in seminaries on the continent. It was built and endowed at public expense and received an annual grant of some £9,673, which was supposed to provide two hundred and fifty free places. But, as the population of Ireland increased rapidly during each decade in the first half of the nineteenth century, the pastoral needs of this more numerous people required more clergy. In 1834-5 the trustees of the college increased the free places by almost one hundred and determined that these additional places would last as

[2] *Royal Commission of inquiry into primary education (Ireland)*, hereafter cited as *Powis Commission*, [C6-II] H.C. 1870, xxviii, pt iii, 364. Presumably, the reference he had in mind was not to St John but to 1 Cor. XI,27. The Douay version reads: 'therefore, whosoever shall eat this bread, or drink the chalice of the Lord unworthily, shall be guilty of the body and of the blood of the Lord'.
[3] U.Ex., 20 Aug. 1885.

long as their strained finances permitted. But the limited funds available to the administrative staff could not be stretched to such an extent for long. By 1838 the college was forced to borrow money and in the following year almost half the additional free places were removed. The exact number of students attending Maynooth during Dorrian's student days is not known; in 1832 the figure was 388 and in 1839 it was 425.[4]

The chief consequence of this increased enrolment for student life was overcrowding and the deterioration of general facilities. There had been little capital expenditure on the college since its erection forty years previously and normal depreciation, added to the burden of numbers, produced bleak and comfortless accommodation. Students were forced to share rooms, and visitors to Maynooth commented on the miserable conditions under which the seminarians lived. Lord Clarendon, the Lord-Lieutenant, later remarked:

> I saw the rooms of which we heard so much in England. They have three or four beds in them and are wretched comfortless and ill ventilated, such as no one in England would ask a servant to sleep in for a night . . . The single bedded rooms are not much larger or better than those at Pentonville Prison.[5]

The Irish Church had no central system of funding its seminaries. Its principal resource — parochial collections — was mostly consumed in paying off parish debts incurred in erecting or repairing churches. Consequently, the bishops were forced to appeal to the government for an increased grant to help them out of their difficulties.

The pattern of life in the college followed very closely that of the seminary system which emerged from the Council of Trent. The regime was strict and austere, the food spartan, and the timetable virtually an unbroken round of prayer, class, study and recreation. The standardized courses of philosophy and theology favoured in the continental seminaries were followed, and many of the principal text books in use in the 1830s had been written by the first professors, *emigré* French priests who had themselves studied at the Sorbonne. Dorrian, unlike his friends, Charles William Russell and George Crolly — both of whom came from Lecale — did not distinguish himself academically. Russell, who was two years older, had gone to Maynooth in 1826 at the very early age of fourteen and by the time Dorrian enrolled had completed his first year of further

---

4 Donal A. Kerr, *Peel, Priests and Politics* (Oxford, 1982), pp 252-3.
5 Ibid., p.250.

studies in Dunboyne House, the post-graduate department. George Crolly, who was one year older, entered the college in 1829 and completed his course in 1835. He too enrolled as a postgraduate and spent two years in Dunboyne House before ordination in March 1837.

At the commission of inquiry into Maynooth in 1826 the president calculated that the cost of maintaining a student was £50 during his first year and £12 in subsequent years, if he enjoyed a free place; if not the cost was £70 for the first year and £33 in subsequent years. Even with the help of burses, on the college foundation or otherwise, these fees were beyond the means of many Catholic parents, and, not surprisingly, the president observed on that same occasion that the students generally came from the 'middling class', whom he took to include farmers who were comfortably off, tradesmen and shopkeepers.[6] Until 1845 Down and Connor had seven free places and diocesan burses which paid the pensions of three students and a half pension for a fourth. With a population in excess of 150,000 and no convenient way of finding more money, or students who could pay their way, the solution to the problem of clerical manpower was to reduce the course of studies of the seminarians.

At the beginning of Dorrian's third year at the college Cornelius Denvir, a former professor of natural philosophy there, who for the previous nine years had been parish priest of Downpatrick, became bishop of Down and Connor. His predecessor, William Crolly, had given a fillip to the expansion of the diocese by encouraging the construction of churches and by establishing a diocesan seminary or Catholic college for the education of boys who might aspire to the priesthood. More priests were needed to staff parishes which had been rejuvenated and to cater for an increasing population. Consequently Patrick Dorrian was chosen for ordination before the completion of his course in theology, an occurrence that was not infrequent because of burgeoning pastoral needs.

The ordination ceremony, which was performed by Archbishop Daniel Murray of Dublin, took place on 29 September 1837 in the Pro-Cathedral in Dublin. On his return to his native diocese, Dorrian was appointed a curate in Belfast and took up residence with Bishop Denvir and two colleagues in St Patrick's Presbytery, Donegall St.

6 *Eighth report of the commissioners of Irish education inquiry*, H.C. 1826-7 (509), xiii, 593.

2

Curate in Belfast 1837-47

I

The parish of Belfast embraced the entire town apart from the district of Ballymacarrett on the south side of the Lagan, which then lay outside the boundary, and extended as far north as Ballyclare and Greencastle. It was served by two churches, St Mary's in Chapel Lane and St Patrick's in Donegall St., and small chapels in Ballyclare and in Greencastle catered for the sparse and scattered communities living as far as twenty miles further to the north. Since 1825 the bishop of Down and Connor was the parish priest of Belfast and since his episcopal ordination in 1835 Cornelius Denvir had been assisted by three curates.

A census carried out by the Commissioners of Public Instruction in 1834 revealed that the population of the parish of Shankill, which was somewhat more extensive than Belfast, was 67,224 of which 22,078 were Catholics. By 1837 the Catholic share of the population of Belfast had undoubtedly passed the figure of 20,500 but, as the censuses of 1841 and 1851 did not include questions on religious affiliation, accurate statistics of the denominations are not available until 1861. By then the Catholic population stood at 41,407 which was almost exactly one third of the entire population, and so it is reasonable to assume that between the years 1834 and 1861 the Catholic percentage remained fairly constantly at this level; by 1841 it would have been about 23,500 and by 1851, 29,000. Ballymacarrett was incorporated into Belfast in 1840 but its Catholic community continued to form a separate parish. The combined Catholic populations of the Ballyclare and Greencastle areas may have been more than a thousand. So, though they consistently overestimated the size of their flock in the 1840s, the priests of Belfast had pastoral care of an extensive community, which must have exceeded 22,000 by the beginning of the decade and reached 28,000 by the end. In 1837 the Catholics of the town represented about one seventh of the total population of the diocese of Down and Connor; ten years later that proportion was approaching one fifth.

The national census of 1831 had omitted questions on denominational allegiance. In 1834 the Commissioners of Public Instruction re-employed the enumerators of 1831 and asked them to update their returns by distinguishing the religious persuasions of the persons whom they had already listed. When the returns for the parishes were complete, the commissioners left them open for public inspection by clergy of all denominations and invited corrections where necessary. To estimate the population in 1834 they augmented the figures obtained in 1831 by the rate of increase that took place between the census years of 1821 and 1831. And they claimed a high degree of accuracy for their final computation. They also asked each clergyman to report on the number of those attending his church services on Sundays, and the accuracy of these returns depended on the interest in and importance attached to the exercise by individual priests or ministers. It is in this area, however, that the figures have been disputed. For it is not clear in many cases whether these returns refer to those attending only the principal Mass in each church or both Masses, when there were two.

The unit used for the census was the ecclesiastical parish of the established church.[1] In the case of Belfast the ecclesiastical parish of Shankill embraced not only the Catholic parish of Belfast, which included Greencastle, but also Hannahstown, which was part of the parish of Derriaghy. The total number of Catholics given for Shankill was 22,078; they were served by five priests who, presumably, included Bishop Crolly, the parish priest of Derriaghy and three curates in the town. The clergy returned the average number attending church on Sundays as 1,500 at each Mass in St Mary's, 2,000 at the first and 4,000 at the second in St Patrick's, 175 at Greencastle and 350 at Hannahstown.[2] The Belfast figures look suspiciously rounded and give the impression of a hasty and inexact estimate, but assuming that the Catholic population of the town was 21,000, these returns indicate that the percentage of practising Catholics was low. Making allowance for the non-attendance of the aged and incapacitated, the sick and infirm, and the children of five years of age or under — perhaps a fifth of the whole — it would seem that the attendance rate at Sunday Mass, if the figures submitted by the clergy are reasonably accurate, was of the order of 55 per cent.[3]

1 *First Report of the Commissioners of Public Instruction, Ireland*, H.C. 1835, xxxiii, 5-12.
2 Ibid., 268-9.
3 Some 15 per cent of the Catholic population of 21,000 would have been children of five years of age or under. Of the adult population an average of 6 per cent would have been incapable of going to church on any Sunday because of illness. That leaves an attendance rate of 9,000 out of a possible 16,500, or 55 per cent.

St Mary's Church had been built in 1784 and St Patrick's in 1815. The construction of churches had not kept pace with the rate of increase of the Catholic population of Belfast. Bishop Crolly's episcopate, (1825-35), witnessed an impressive resurgence of church building throughout the diocese. Some thirty churches were either erected or substantially reconstructed and it seems surprising that he did not provide for the needs of his own parish. In his later years his energies were engaged on the construction of St Patrick's schools in Donegall St. and the acquisition of Vicinage House as the diocesan seminary and college for boys; the Commissioners of Public Instruction reported that on 22 February 1835 there were 1,045 children attending the Sunday school in St Patrick's and that the average attendance was nearly 1,000.[4] Most likely the difficulty of acquiring a suitable site and the limited resources of the Catholic people, already overstrained by school building, delayed the erection of a third church.

The number of priests serving this Catholic population was too low. While there is no agreement on the correct proportion of priests to people, as distance, mobility and special needs dictate local requirements, and while there are parishes today in traditional Catholic countries where one priest serves five or six thousand people, the proportion of priests to people in Belfast throughout Bishop Denvir's episcopate was much too small. In 1834 there were 54 priests in Down and Connor serving a population of 152,337,

I am indebted to Sir Peter Froggatt, former professor of epidemiology, and (later) vice-chancellor of Queen's University, Belfast, for the estimate of a 6 per cent morbidity rate which is based on his researches into similar rates in comparable British industrial cities during the nineteenth century. It is more difficult to calculate the attendance rates for the other parishes of the diocese, partly because the borders are not coterminous with those of the Church of Ireland and partly because it is not clear in some cases whether the figures refer only to the principal Mass, if there were two. Assuming that young children, the aged, the ill and those forced to remain at home to look after the sick or infants constituted one fifth of the population (a conservative estimate), the attendance rates vary considerably from parish to parish. Rathlin Island had a rate of 66 per cent whereas that of Ballycastle and Cushendall was about 33 — a difference large enough to cast doubt on one or other set of figures. Ballymena and Portaferry had a 50 per cent rate; the united parishes of Antrim and Randalstown had also about 50 per cent though the Antrim part is given as 70 and the Randalstown part as 35. A similar confusion is evident in the figures for Dunsford and Ardglass (50 and 20 respectively).

In assessing the standard of practice at the time it must also be remembered that stations for Masses and confessions took place in private houses usually in Lent and Advent (Revd William McMullan had 40 such in Loughinisland each year).

The census is discussed in P.J. Corish *The Irish Catholic Experience* (Dublin, 1985), pp 164-9 and D.W. Miller 'Irish Catholicism and the Great Famine', *Journal of Social History*, ix (1975), 81-93.

4 *Second report of the Commissioners of Public Instruction, Ireland*, H.C. 1835, xxxiv, 295.

which meant that the proportion, 1:2,821, was only slightly less favourable than that for the province of Armagh as a whole, 1:2,805.[5] When Dorrian was appointed to Belfast, there were only three priests for the entire parish. This meant not only that the ratio had fallen to below one to six thousand but also that, since these three priests were responsible, in addition, for the Catholics at Greencastle and Ballyclare, their full attention could not be concentrated on Belfast. Dorrian was later to recall that during his time as a curate he had to take his turn on Sundays hearing confessions and celebrating Mass in Greencastle before going on to do the same in Ballyclare; on those occasions he breakfasted at 3.00pm!

The pastoral needs deriving from the shortage of church accommodation and paucity of clergy were further exacerbated by the social and economic conditions under which very many of the Catholics were compelled to live. The rapid growth of Belfast in the 1840s transformed the town into a booming commercial and industrial centre but brought serious social and civic problems in its train.

In 1839 a rail link between Belfast and Lisburn was laid down; three years later the line was extended to Portadown. This connection opened up the whole Lagan valley to the trade of the town and Belfast became the magnet for thousands of Ulster people who, left without opportunities on the land because of the rapidly increasing population, or without employment in weaving or spinning because of the establishment of steam-powered mills, came in search of work. The 1840s witnessed a boom in the linen trade as huge mills were constructed to take advantage of new methods of linen production. Increased supplies of coal, raw materials, foodstuffs, and luxury goods were needed, and the tonnage of shipping entering and leaving Belfast grew enormously. The new corporation elected in 1842 after the extension of the town boundary soon bestirred itself to obtain loans from parliament to widen the streets of the town, to regulate and improve standards of housing, to provide gasworks and lighting facilities and to contain the Blackstaff River, which had caused pollution and become a health hazard. To provide adequate shipping facilities a new dock was completed in 1841, private quays were acquired by the Ballast Board, and the Belfast Harbour Board, which was established in 1847, soon gave evidence of its energy and

---

5 S.J. Connolly, *Priests and People in Pre-Famine Ireland* (Dublin, 1982), p.36. According to the report of the Commissioners of Public Instruction there were 58 priests in the diocese of Down and Connor. But the two attached to Lisburn and Hillsborough are mentioned twice, the same one served Ballymacarrett and Holywood, and the priest attached to the Grange of Ballyscullion, belonged, as did the Grange, to the diocese of Derry. The figure for the laity was obtained by subtracting the population of Ballyscullion from that given for the two dioceses.

foresight by opening the Victoria Channel and extending the Donegall Quay, thereby enabling much larger ships to tie up in Belfast. Though the growth rate of the town before 1840 had been much slower, it had always enjoyed a significant degree of prosperity through its trade, and its inhabitants were justly proud of its status and reputation. Catholics, debarred from acquiring land until the late eighteenth century, had been late entrants into the race for property, and, partly because of smaller numbers and the lingering effects of penal legislation, lagged behind in wealth and social status. A few had become prosperous as merchants and contractors, and a somewhat larger, though still small, number achieved comfortable middle class status as shopkeepers, provision suppliers or in the professions.

But the majority of Catholics were unskilled workers who had migrated or whose parents had migrated from rural Ulster and who were glad to take any job on offer, however menial. Poor and uneducated,[6] they also found themselves at the end of the race for housing accommodation. Consequently they huddled into densely overpopulated streets and courts, and the interaction of poverty, malnutrition, bad hygiene, fevers, tuberculosis and various other forms of sickness produced the worst kind of suffering and misery associated with Victorian industrial cities. The conditions obtaining both in their residential quarters and in the mills and factories contributed enormously to disease and ill health; millworkers were especially prone to lung disease which was caused by inhaling flax or cotton fibres. The link between dirt, overcrowding, bad hygiene and fevers, especially typhus, was recognized and acknowledged. In the 1830s some forty five per cent of all deaths were attributed to epidemic, endemic and contagious diseases. According to figures released in the census reports of 1841, the mortality rate in Belfast exceeded that of all other civic districts and of all rural districts of Ireland except for the age group from 46 to 55 years. In the younger age groups the mortality rate was over twice that of the country as a whole.[7]

6 When St Patrick's school applied for aid in 1832 to the recently appointed commissioners of national education, Bishop Crolly and his fellow applicants stated that 430 boys and 325 girls attended it on weekdays, and 480 boys and 380 girls on Saturday for religious instruction. The applicants explained that the school had hitherto depended on subscriptions and on pupils' fees of one penny per week but because of the poverty of the parents the fees amounted to less than £20 per year. Some Catholic pupils probably attended some other schools in the town but the majority of them as indeed the majority of migrants must have been illiterate. (P.R.O.N.I. ED 1/1/3).

7 P. Froggatt, 'Industrialization and Health in Belfast in the early Nineteenth Century' in *The Town in Ireland*, ed. D. Harkness and M. O'Dowd (Belfast, 1981), pp 156-73.

Andrew Malcolm, a public spirited physician attached to the Belfast General and Fever Hospital, who devoted his life to improving the lot of the poor both medically and culturally, was bitterly critical of the housing conditions in which they were condemned to live. Addressing the British Association in 1852 on the sanitary state of Belfast, he pointed out that upwards of 1,800 houses in stinking, unpaved courts and entries were accessible only by covered archways, and that the majority of them were accessible by only one outlet and could not be ventilated. And he added scornfully that it seemed to be a law of nature that the indigent did not require as much fresh air as the wealthy, finding corroboration in the fact 'that of a total of 579 streets, lanes and courts, 331 of the residence-ways of the poorer classes are under twenty feet in breadth'. Upwards of 3,000 houses were without yards of any description. The great majority of the poorer class of houses consisted of four rooms in two storeys of seven to ten feet square, with often as many as eighteen or twenty people sleeping in them. Belfast was deficient in public parks and pleasure grounds, and in the suburbs the great number of open ditch sewers, the vast extent of damp, undrained common, the carelessness in removing vegetable and animal remains in the poorer localities, and the hasty construction of labourers' tenements without provision of adequate sewerage increased the danger to health and well-being. Fever was endemic in the ill-ventilated, highly congested, damp and dismal quarters where the lowest paid and the unemployed were condemned to live. Malcolm noted that the standard figure of mortality in the United Kingdom was 1:50 while in Belfast it was 1:35, and complained that infant mortality was absolutely excessive, with the average age at death being as low as nine years. While the proportion of fever deaths to total deaths throughout Ireland was 6 per cent, in Belfast it was 16.2 per cent.[8]

Another observer who painted a horrific picture of social conditions in the town was Revd W.M. O'Hanlon, a Congregational minister. His descriptions, like those of Malcolm, were written in the early 1850s but doubtless depict with accuracy the misery experienced by many of the poor even before the famine. O'Hanlon's letters, first published in a newspaper, were designed to jolt the consciences of the rich and powerful by drawing their attention to the misery, vice and squalid poverty prevailing in the 'obscure dens' off the principal thoroughfares of the town. O'Hanlon wondered how few had ever visited or even heard of the numerous rows, entries and courts in the district bordered by Donegall —

8 'The sanitary state of Belfast' in *Problems of a Growing City, Belfast, 1780-1870*. P.R.O.N.I. (Belfast 1973).

Academy — Great Patrick — Corporation and Waring Sts., thronged by human beings in the lowest stages of degradation where, he supposed, one tenth of the inhabitants of the town lived. He drew attention to the dense overcrowding obtaining in these back streets and to the moral dangers arising from lack of privacy; the frightening wretchedness of the conditions obtaining there were compounded by drunkenness, quarrelling and prostitution. The abundance of spirit stores, most of which were open even on the sabbath, provided a constant temptation to intemperance and all its accompanying evils.

O'Hanlon also noted that few of the people in these neighbourhoods attended religious worship and explained this carelessness or indifference by reference to their extreme poverty: 'the want of decent clothing would form an almost insuperable barrier, even if there existed the inclination to attend any of the regularly established Churches of the city'.[9] And he believed that neither the Protestant nor the Roman Catholic clergy penetrated these haunts of poverty and vice except when the priest was summoned on special occasions (presumably to attend the sick or dying).

While he did not spare prim Victorian feelings in describing either the unhygienic conditions he encountered or the hovels where 'thieves and prostitutes all herd together . . . as in a common hell and shouts of mad debauch, and cries of quarrel and blood are heard through the livelong night',[10] he remarked tartly that 'if a tithe of the energy which is spent in theological warfare were expended in this species of practical religion — the improvement of the domestic circumstances and relations of the poor — in bettering their sanitary and social condition — in promoting the means of their remunerative employment — in redeeming them from gross ignorance and instilling into their hearts the lessons of our holy and divine faith — we should be better men and happier Christians ourselves'.[11]

Though he did not claim that the condition of the 'lowest poor' indicated a greater state of destitution and neglect than was to be found elsewhere in the British Empire, he maintained that the contrast between the extremes of wealth and poverty was greater than he had seen elsewhere, and, remarking that the commerce and fine buildings of Belfast were superior to those of Cork and Dublin, he claimed that the wretchedness, physical, social and moral, was, if not absolutely, at least relatively larger and more appalling.[12]

O'Hanlon, however, put his finger on an important factor which

---

9 W.M. O'Hanlon,*Walks among the Poor of Belfast and suggestions for their improvement* (Belfast, 1853), p.10.
10 Ibid., p.16.
11 Ibid., p.50.
12 Ibid., p.12.

modern sociologists of religion accept as an explanation for non-practice among the desperately poor and marginalized in any society: extreme poverty can so degrade and dehumanize people that they lose hope and trust in man and God. And undoubtedly reduction to this state, perhaps accompanied by alcoholism, or perhaps by the cultural shock of transferring from rural to urban life,[13] explains some of the non-attendance at Mass of the Catholics of Belfast. What proportion of the indifferent is explained by this degree of dehumanization or what proportion might have attended had it not been for the shame of appearing in dirty rags cannot, however, be known. That priests were summoned in cases of serious illness and that the attendance rate increased significantly when economic conditions improved and more churches were built seems to indicate, perhaps, that most Catholics were not dechristianized or seriously alienated from the church. And as the Catholic ghettoes grew stronger and could cushion their members, especially the migrants, against the harsh new realities of urban living, and as Catholic charitable organizations made more effective provision for the destitute, the obstacles to practice diminished. In 1838 the St Patrick's Orphan Society was formed when a group of ladies set up a committee to rescue orphans and abandoned girls. Two years later non-residents from poor families and broken homes were admitted to the school established by the society and the numbers receiving aid rose within a decade to almost 200.

II

Two years before Dorrian's ordination, William Crolly, the bishop of Down and Connor, had been transferred to Armagh. Both the priests of the diocese and the Catholics of Belfast greatly regretted the loss of Crolly. He had been appointed parish priest of the town in 1812 and succeeded to the bishopric in 1825. A caring, energetic and zealous pastor, he had continued to move freely among his people when he became bishop and throughout his episcopate enjoyed their respect and esteem. Conciliatory in political matters, he numbered several prominent Protestant churchmen among his friends. His contribution to public life and his eirenic advocacy of Catholic Emancipation enhanced the esteem in which both he and

---

13 The French sociologist, Gabriel Le Bras, has noted the deleterious influence which migration to cities often has on the religious practice of country folk. (*Études de Sociologie Religieuse*, (Paris, 1956), ii, 480-1.)

his assistant clergy were held by their people. Indeed, on his appointment to Armagh, the clergy of Down and Connor took the very unusual step of drawing up a petition to Rome asking that he be allowed to remain with them,[14] and in later years on his return to Belfast he was often lauded by his former subjects on public occasions. None was more laudatory than Patrick Dorrian who declared in the presence of his successor, at a St Patrick's Day dinner in 1840, 'I know none (and I must say it, My Lord, even in your Lordship's presence), I know no other to be put before Dr Crolly'.[15]

His successor, Denvir, had not enjoyed the advantage of having pastoral experience in Belfast before becoming bishop. Appointed to the staff of Maynooth shortly after ordination in 1814, first as a lecturer in music and then as professor of natural philosophy, he had remained there until he became parish priest of Downpatrick in 1826. While holding that office he had helped establish St Malachy's College in 1833, returning each weekend from Belfast to Downpatrick for his parochial duties. A clever and scholarly man, who maintained a life-long interest in science, and later impressed general audiences in Belfast with illustrated lectures on electric light, he did not have the same common touch as Crolly. Partly because of the increasing Catholic population of the town and partly because of the deteriorating relationships between Catholics and Protestants from the 1830s, he did not achieve the same status or esteem either within the Catholic or in the wider general community as Crolly had done.

Throughout his episcopate he served on the board of management of the General Hospital, was elected chairman from time to time, and was always willing to make what contribution he could to the civic progress and common welfare of all the citizens of Belfast. He continued Crolly's practice of sponsoring publications of the

---

14 Denvir subsequently explained to Paul Cullen, the rector of the Irish College and agent of the Irish bishops in Rome, that on Crolly's appointment to Armagh the clergy of Down and Connor assembled in Belfast and voted unanimously to ask the pope to allow Crolly to decline as they feared 'religion might be injured by his departure'. However, they accepted the advice of Archbishop Murray of Dublin, Bishop Blake of Dromore and others and did not forward the petition. Denvir added his own eulogy of Crolly on this occasion: 'I can and do testify that I do not believe there exists a more zealous, just and mild Bishop subject to the Holy See than Doctor Crolly, nor one who possessed more the cordial affection of his clergy than he possessed the love and veneration of the clergy of the Diocese from which he has been translated'. (Denvir to Cullen, 28 Jun. 1836, A.I.C.R.)
15 V., 18 Mar. 1840.

bible,[16] especially the New Testament, at moderate costs and he bought out the lease on St Malachy's College. But he seemed unable to realize how great were the challenge and problems posed by the rapid expansion of Belfast and he lacked the administrative skill and determination to cope with a situation of swift urban growth, that was, admittedly, rare in Ireland. He did not neglect any of his routine duties, carried out his diocesan visitation assiduously but was devoid of the pioneering spirit and the courage to take risks, when serious situations called for them.

In his report to Rome in 1845 on the state of his diocese, Denvir claimed that in sixty years the Catholic population of Belfast had grown from 50 to 30,000, and that on average there was at least 'one adult convert from Calvinism, or Protestantism received into the bosom of the Catholic Church for each day in the year'. He went on to explain:

> In other parts of the Diocese also many adults were converted with their families but here the conversions are in proportion the most numerous. Several of these converts being poor migrate to Scotland and other places remaining steady in the faith and diffusing so to the best of their ability wherever they go. This rate of conversions having been steadily in progress for many years will account for the great increase which the Catholic population has received within the past half century in this immediate neighbourhood.[17]

16 When a controversy arose in 1839 over the accusation that the bible did not circulate among Catholics, the *Vindicator* quoted three letters from booksellers, (none of whom were Catholics), to Bishop Denvir testifying to the outstanding sales of the Catholic editions of the scriptures to which Crolly and Denvir had given their patronage and support. Thomas Mairs of Greenisland testified that he 'stereotyped' 7,000 copies of the Douay Bible, receiving nearly £1,400 from Crolly alone for copies of it; later, with the approval of Crolly and Denvir he 'stereotyped' a very cheap edition of the Douay Testament, printing 2,000 copies and planned yet another edition. James Smyth of Belfast testified that at Crolly's request he had printed 18,000 copies of the Douay New Testament, and Simms and McIntyre of Belfast declared that they had printed and circulated 15,000 copies of the New Testament and were currently publishing a pocket edition of the bible, of which they hoped to sell 3,000 copies. (V., 21 May 1938).

17 According to a note made by the distinguished church historian, Johann Döllinger, in Munich after a conversation with C.W. Russell, the professor of humanity at Maynooth, Crolly was credited with many conversions, especially from Presbyterianism. Döllinger wrote: 'diese ausserordentliche Vermehrung schreibt R. dem Eifer und den grossen Talenten des gegenwärtigen Primas E.B. Crolly von Armagh zu, der viele Jahre (seit 1815) dort durch seine treffliche Predigten wirkte. Überhaupt find es in nördlichen Irland die Presbyterianer die am häufigsten zur katholischen Religion sich bekehren. Weit seltener sind dort und in Irland überhaupt Bekehrungen der Anglikaner'. (J. Friedrich *Ignaz von Döllinger*,

That some Protestants, especially at marriage, became Catholics was undoubtedly true but even at the rate Denvir suggests, and he did not claim that that rate was constant, thirty years of such conversions would not have accounted for much more than a third of the population, and that is assuming that the Belfast converts did not emigrate. Indeed, elsewhere in his report he alluded to the real source of the increase of his flock when, in explaining that he had confirmed almost 18,000 people in his last triennial visitation of the diocese, of whom he claimed many were adult converts, he added that Belfast was a manufacturing town where the operatives were mainly Catholics and that 'some thousands in number of all ages from 10 to 50 years old collected from surrounding counties, superadded to the natives, causes the number of persons to be confirmed to be so great'.[18]

Dorrian was later to present a very different picture of the growth of the Catholic population of the town. In 1865 he commented in a private letter that a thousand per year had been lost to the church during the previous twenty five years, and, though he was obviously using rounded figures, he clearly implied that the rate of lapsing had been serious from about 1840.[19] Given the shortage of churches and clergy, and his own intimate experience of the parish as curate and later as coadjutor bishop, there is little reason to question his view that losses had been occurring on a significant scale.

But Denvir was inclined to paint a rosy picture and many of his claims were justified. Paying tribute to the zeal and diligence of his clergy, he referred to the confraternities of Christian Doctrine and of the Blessed Virgin Mary which they had established in many parishes. These gave instruction on Christian doctrine to the young and the poor on Sundays and holy-days, and Denvir, who was himself impressed by their success in Belfast, had encouraged his priests to establish them everywhere, with the happy result that

---

(Munich, 1899-1901), ii, 525). Bernard McAuley, who was a curate in Belfast from 1812 to 1819, claimed in a defence of the archbishop in 1847 that during those years and subsequently Crolly had converted at least 300 Protestants each year. (McAuley to Propaganda, 1 Nov. 1847. A.P.F., S.C. (Irlanda, 29), f 388rv)

18 In a letter dated 29 June 1839, John Green, the parish priest of Coleraine, replied to a comment made by Henry Cooke at a meeting of the Ulster Synod. Cooke had claimed that the increase of Popery in Coleraine was due to mixed marriages; Green did not deny that this factor played an accidental part but insisted that it was merely one of many. (V., 3 July 1839) In a note in the Vindicator on 18 Sept. 1839 it was stated that the number of converts in Belfast exceeded the total Catholic population of twenty five years previously. The Catholic population in 1825, if Henry Cooke's guess is accurate and perhaps it is an underestimate, must have been 11,000.

19 Dorrian to Dixon, 12 Jan. 1865, A.D.A.

great numbers of both sexes had joined these sodalities.[20] The members of these confraternities were also committed to communal prayer and the diffusion of Catholic reading material, especially of an apologetic nature. And, though on this occasion he did not refer to it by name, the Rosarian Society,[21] based in St Mary's Church in Belfast, also contributed to this apostolate.

So when Dorrian joined the staff at the bishop's house in 1837 he found himself in a difficult and delicate situation. The Catholic population was so outgrowing the accommodation available in the two churches that a short time later Bishop Denvir could lament that 'on Sundays you will find the chapel-yards, nay the streets for a considerable space, covered with a kneeling throng who have no roof over their heads during divine worship'.[22] The social problems of his parishioners were immense and appropriate action was not taken to deal with them. The number of priests was inadequate to cope with the routine obligations of Masses, confessions, sick calls, direction of confraternities and house visitation, let alone deal with the peculiar problems of poverty and marginalization in a growing industrial town. But there were many positive sides to the picture. Among the Catholic population were many generous and committed people, who were willing and anxious to contribute both spiritually and financially to the Church, despite the difficulties confronting them.[23]

Moreover, they were mostly very well disposed to their clergy, though by 1837 many Catholics were settling in suburbs quite distant from the parochial house. As his colleagues Dorrian had his friend, George Crolly, and Hugh Hanna. Two years later Thomas Kearney replaced Hanna and he and Crolly remained until 1844 when he became parish priest of Coleraine and Crolly joined the staff of Maynooth. Their board and accommodation were provided by the

20 Denvir to Cullen, 20 Dec. 1845, A.I.C.R. There were about 1,000 Catholics in Belfast in 1785. Denvir may have intended to write 500 instead of 50.

21 The Rosarian Society was established in Belfast in 1794. Originally consisting of twelve men who met weekly to recite the Rosary and to subscribe a small sum of money towards honoraria for a monthly Mass for their own welfare and the repose of souls of deceased members, it widened its activities in 1819 to establish a circulating library of Catholic books for the parish of Belfast and later to provide contributions to local Catholic charities. Shortly after the erection of St Patrick's Church in 1815 the members took charge of the new Sunday school. (P. Rogers, 'The Minute Book of the Belfast Rosarian Society' in *Down Hist. Soc. Jn.*, viii (1937), 17-24.) The Christian Doctrine Society was founded in 1834. In 1839 a room was built at the back of St Mary's Church to house the library of the Rosarian Society, which then contained 800 volumes. This society was probably regarded as the confraternity of the Blessed Virgin Mary in Belfast.

22 V., 6 Nov. 1841.

23 According to a statement prepared for tax purposes in 1857, Denvir then paid his clergy £45 per year (D.C.D.A). Curates in other parishes in Down and Connor received a similar income at that time.

bishop and they probably received an income of about £40 per year. Their work was hard and demanding — when Thomas Kearney was leaving the town in 1844 he remarked that he had spent time in the confessional every day except when sick — for they were often called on to deal with welfare problems in addition to their more immediate spiritual duties. They had also to organize and supervise the courses of religious education conducted by the various confraternities and, after 1845, to give courses of instruction at the Sunday vespers in the churches during the winter months. And the politico-religious friction which could at any time erupt into communal strife created an atmosphere which made pastoral activity more difficult.

III

Catholic Emancipation had been a tremendous psychological boost but it had not been followed to any significant extent by the gradual opening of public offices to Catholics; on the contrary, a majority of Ulster Protestants chose to regard the extension of civil rights to Catholics as a challenge to their own influence and position. When the Catholic percentage of the population of Belfast was small (less than fifteen per cent in 1800), relations between the Protestant and Catholic communities were warm and friendly, and many Protestants contributed generously to the erection of St Mary's Church in 1784; the sovereign (mayor) of the town donated the pulpit, and the Belfast Volunteers, who were mainly Presbyterian, paraded on the occasion. But as the Catholic population increased and began to compete for jobs and houses, especially at the lower income level, antipathies developed and the first sectarian riot occurred in 1813.

In 1832 four people died violently when mobs stoned each other as Emerson Tennent, the Conservative victor in the general election, was carried off in triumph. When Tennent was unexpectedly defeated three years later, several Orange lodges, which had assembled to celebrate his victory, were so angered by the result that they went on the rampage, breaking the windows of every Catholic house they recognized. The commissioners appointed to investigate the state of municipal corporations in Ireland reported in 1835 on the total distrust of the Conservative magistracy they had found not only among Roman Catholic inhabitants but 'among other classes' (Liberals) who 'joined their Roman Catholic brethren in seeking for the protection of a fair and equal administration of the laws'. Though the commissioners were not prepared to pronounce on the justice of these complaints, they stressed the importance of the issue. 'As many serious and lamentable occurrences accompanied by bloodshed and loss of life' had taken place, they drew particular attention to:

the melancholy particulars of the "Sandy-row riots" arising out of the unchristian practice of hooting at, insulting, and attacking persons attending the funerals of deceased Roman Catholics; of the Brown-street riots which grew out of a custom of annually erecting an "Orange arch" across a public thoroughfare on the 12th July, by the Orange party; and of the Hercules-street riots which took place upon the collision of the exasperated parties on the occasion of the chairing of the Members for a borough after the general election in December 1832.[24]

Some liberal Presbyterians, encouraged and inspired by the example of Revd Henry Montgomery, had campaigned energetically for Catholic Emancipation. But Revd Henry Cooke, Montgomery's arch-opponent, who was an active conservative both in politics and theology, shared the alarm of his Tory friends at the measures taken by the Whig government in 1833 to prune the established church of some of its privileges. In the following year he proclaimed the banns of political marriage between the Presbyterians and the Church of Ireland at a great public rally at Hillsborough, and thereby symbolically confirmed the support of a majority of Presbyterians for Toryism. This link with the established church and landlord power involved, by definition, resistance to any and every extension of Catholic political influence and created a solid alliance of Protestant interests for the rest of the century. The Presbyterians who cast their lot with Montgomery and liberalism remained a minority but a tough and tenacious one and, though in the main anti-repeal, continued to resist Toryism.

The *Northern Whig*, founded in 1824, spoke for these liberal Presbyterians and advocated wider measures of parliamentary reform and the extension of the franchise. But the alliance between the Catholics and the liberal Presbyterians was always uneasy. The Catholics regarded the support of the Whig group as too weak, selective and mealy-mouthed: they wanted more robust advocacy of their legitimate claims.

To this end a group of the wealthier Catholics decided to establish their own newspaper and invited a young Monaghan man, Charles Gavan Duffy, who had some little experience of journalism in Dublin, to become editor. The *Vindicator* which was launched on 1 May 1839, and published twice weekly at what was then the relatively expensive price of four pence, soon boasted the second largest circulation in the province of Ulster. In his first editorial

24 *Appendix to the first report of the commissioners appointed to inquire into the municipal corporations in Ireland*, H.C. 1835, xxviii, pt 1, 259

Duffy proclaimed that the 'rational and practical reformers of Ulster have felt the want of a representative of their interests', and pledged his paper to earnest advocacy of the people's rights and to zealous combat against open enemies and pretended friends! Defining, in effect, these terms and admitting that his assignment would oblige him to highlight particular grievances, he went on:

> If we shall at any time address ourselves more especially to the Catholics of the Province, let no reader of ours suppose us activated by sectarian tendency; we shall do so chiefly because a sectarian prejudice, most unjust to them, does, unfortunately, exist among many *soi disant*, and, perhaps some sincere Reformers. The false and foolish spirit which, in '82, excluded Catholics from Volunteer corps which petitioned for their emancipation is still in operation in Ulster. A section of Protestant Reformers appear to feel that they condescend when they patronize their poor Catholic fellow countrymen, forgetting in the memory of what this government made them, that which they have made themselves; and some alas! recollecting it hate them for growing prosperous and powerful . . . The Catholics of Ulster — of Ireland have shook off the numbness of years, and grown strong again.

A decade after Emancipation the anticipated improvement in their social and political standing had not taken place. Conscious that their second-class citizenship was virtually unaltered, that they were regarded contemptuously, if not despised, they were determined to fight with all the means at their disposal to remedy the situation. Claiming that some of Belfast's Catholics were very opulent and highly respectable merchants, that many were extensive traders and that several were skilful professional men, the editorial insisted that not five of the former held any public appointment or honour, and of the latter not five held any of the five hundred petty offices to which people of their station were entitled.[25]

Not all the Catholics were perpared to crusade for equality; some few felt it more prudent to keep a low profile and avoid causing antagonism by drawing attention to their lot. Duffy caught their mood exactly when he wrote six months later that 'to be a Catholic in Ulster is not merely to be the object of Orange hatred and Tory enmity . . . but the despised, ill-treated and disregarded political dependant of Protestant Reformers'. Few of them would have disagreed with his analysis when he declared that to be a Catholic merchant in Belfast, Derry and other towns was to be invariably

25 V., 1 May 1839.

overlooked in all honorary or emolumentary civic appointments, to be a Catholic trader of a lower grade was to be distrusted in banks and to stand in every respect after a Protestant dissenter of every class, to be a professional man was to forfeit the public honours to which his station entitled him, to be a Catholic farmer was to be considered unfit to be a poor law guardian, a county collector or to hold any other local office of trust or emolument.[26] Duffy, who was not personally sectarian, was obliged to give his paper a polemical edge as it stood up to Orange swagger and upheld the claims to equality of what was undoubtedly the politically and socially underprivileged section of society.

In his autobiography Duffy later remarked that during his three years in Belfast — he retired from the editorship of the *Vindicator* in 1842 — he had made few intimate friends. Among the exceptions he mentioned the two curates — Crolly and Dorrian — both of whom he obviously respected as able, intelligent and perceptive men. And he rightly diagnosed their political sympathies and aspirations, finding Crolly, like his uncle, the primate, a Whig and Dorrian 'a steadfast Nationalist'.[27]

And Dorrian did indeed share Duffy's political sentiments and aspirations for the Catholics of Ulster. He firmly believed in the justice of Catholic claims for fuller representation in public life, and in the active, persistent and peaceful pursuit of these claims at all times. Disregarding the timidity or prudence of that minority among Belfast Catholics, who judged it inopportune to press their demands too vigorously for fear of provoking a Protestant backlash, he never hesitated to assert the rights of his people when opportunity offered. And he never placed any real trust in co-operation with the Whigs or expected the Whigs to undertake or pursue with a genuinely serious purpose a campaign for the achievement of real equality for Catholics. Holding these views it was not surprising that he threw himself with enthusiasm into the repeal movement.

After a decade of co-operation with the Whigs in the 1830s O'Connell restarted his agitation for repeal in 1840. A few months later the Tories returned to power, and however critical of and disappointed they had been by the Whigs, Irish Catholics tended at first to view the Tory government with great apprehension. To them it presaged more scope for Orange magnates, less check on Orange-minded magistrates and less opportunities for obtaining justice in the lower courts. The *Vindicator* expressed this attitude succinctly and powerfully when it wrote of 'the barbarously cruel or

---

26 V., 2 Nov. 1839.
27 C. Gavan Duffy, *My life in two hemispheres*. (London, 1903), i, 53.

barbarously ignorant government of de Grey'.[28] The scene was set for polemics, if not conflict, between the determined Orangeism of the north of Ireland and the advocates of repeal.

The Tory landlords and their henchmen of the ilk of Henry Cooke chose to regard repeal as a disloyal movement and its adherents as treacherous rebels. In fact O'Connell was devoted to the British connection, personally attached to the sovereign and, as he subsequently proved, unshakeably committed to constitutional methods of agitation. Before the repeal movement began, the Catholics of Belfast had frequently given clear and unequivocal proof of their loyalty to the British throne. At various annual celebrations they had toasted not only the queen but also her mother, the duchess of Kent, and other members of the royal family, and had expressed their sentiments fulsomely. [29] But these expressions of loyalty did not avail against the ultra 'loyalism' of the Tory party, which cast repealers in the role of rebels. Though O'Connell had co-operated with the Whigs and though their Belfast representatives could admire and support his work for parliamentary reform and improvements in the position of tenants, the Presbyterian liberals, with a few exceptions, stayed aloof from his campaign for repeal.

The threat of the return of the Tories to power had galvanized the leading Catholics of Belfast and, joined by a few Presbyterian reformers — chiefly James Thomson Tennent, John Sinclair and Robert McDowell — they held a meeting to restate their loyalty to the crown and to insist on their entitlement to the full rights of equality and citizenship. Prominent among the speakers was Patrick Dorrian, who pointed out that Emancipation was incomplete until religion was no impediment to Catholics obtaining civic or legal honours. He bewailed the desire of the intolerant Tories and of some equally intolerant milk-and-water Whigs to enjoy all positions of power and proclaimed the determination of Catholics to let the Tories know that their privileged system could not continue. Referring to the political doctrine of the English constitutional lawyer, Blackstone, which laid down that the 'civil law' was to be obeyed only when it could not be avoided, he

---

28 V., 2 Mar. 1842.
29 V., 4 Jan. 1840. At the annual dinner of the Christian Doctrine Society on 30 Dec. 1839 toasts were drunk to the pope, the queen, Prince Albert, the duchess of Kent, Lord Melbourne and his ministers, the Lord-Lieutenant, O'Connell, the *Vindicator* and the liberal press of Ireland, the town and trade of Belfast, the Catholic school committee and collectors and to their 'truly Liberal Dissenting Brethren, with Civil and Religious Liberty all over the world'. This last evoked loud cheers for Henry Montgomery, John Sinclair and James Thomson Tennent. Most of the toasts were proposed by Denvir.

contrasted these lax views with Catholic teaching which insisted that laws designed for the interest of the people and the state obliged even in secret, and went on to argue that this proved how suited the Catholic was to being a good citizen. And recalling that the code of laws and form of government by which the kingdom was guided was of Catholic provenance, he concluded by declaring that Catholics would insist on their rights. Meetings of a similar nature, attended almost exclusively by Catholics and emphasising their defence of the priests, whom the Tory press often called 'surpliced ruffians', were held at a few other venues throughout the diocese.

Many Belfast and Ulster Catholics soon became dedicated and enthusiastic repealers. Archbishop Crolly, while not committing himself in public, was convinced that repeal was not attainable and, indeed, that O'Connell's agitation was 'injudicious and unfortunate, a desperate and dangerous infatuation'[30] from which he hoped he had protected his priests, but Bishops Denvir of Down and Connor, Michael Blake of Dromore, Peter McLaughlin of Derry and Patrick McGettigan of Raphoe were all convinced repealers. Similarly, an overwhelming proportion of priests favoured the movement. In Down and Connor Bernard McAuley, parish priest of Downpatrick, stayed aloof and among the prominent laity who remained uncommitted were Hugh Magill, the ex-Presbyterian businessman who was widely regarded as the leading Belfast Catholic layman, and Edward O'Rorke, a lawyer and landlord from Portglenone.

Before the repeal movement gathered momentum Catholics and liberal Presbyterians found a common platform in 1840 in opposition to Lord Stanley's Registration Bill. At a large representative gathering on 30 April at which Sharman Crawford, a reforming landlord, Edward Hincks, the liberal-minded parson of Killyleagh, the earl of Gosford, Henry Montgomery, and Bishop Denvir spoke, and at which Dorrian and other clergy were present, firm objections were raised to proposals for methods of controlling the registration of electors which non-Conservatives feared would give too much power and influence to Conservative supporters. The Ulster Constitutional Association, born from this resistance to an extension of Tory aggrandizement and pledged to campaign for wider constitutional liberties and for the same system of registration and voting as obtained in Britain, drew support from both Protestant and Catholic reformers. Cornelius Denvir attended some of its meetings but Patrick Dorrian, obviously pessimistic about its chances of winning any serious reforms, did not. The *Vindicator* praised the association, lauded Lords Charlemont and Gosford for their advocacy of the extension of the vote to the working classes and expressed the hope

---

30 D.A. Kerr, *Peel, priests and politics*, p.77.

that the leading Liberal reformers — Sharman Crawford, Thomson Tennent, Henry Caulfield — would take up repeal. Crawford however drew the conclusion that repeal originated from the frustration of unfair parliamentary representation and was unwilling to support it.

The absence of other than token support from a small number of Presbyterians ensured that the repeal movement bore a distinctly Catholic image. O'Connell's defence of Catholic interests, as in his public letter to the Catholics of England in 1839, heightened the distrust of those who identified him exclusively with the successful struggle for Catholic Emancipation. Religious polemics between the papers representing Protestant interests — whether the Conservative *Belfast News-Letter*, and *Ulster Times* or the Liberal *Northern Whig* — and the Catholic *Vindicator* exacerbated the politico-religious divisions. Some controversy was inevitable: in the interests of reform and justice the *Vindicator* felt obliged to attack the compulsory payment of tithes by members of all religions to the established church. But attacks on the *Regium Donum*, the subsidy paid to the Presbyterian clergy, and the occasional innuendo that this was a political bribe, which had seduced the clergy from their proper role, deepened antagonisms further.

When news broke that O'Connell was coming to Belfast to rally the forces of repeal, the Tories chose to regard the visit as an assault on their sacred citadel, even though there was no likelihood of any advice being given other than an exhortation to campaign for political change by peaceful and constitutional means. Henry Cooke, the ambitious, power-hungry, anti-Catholic demagogue, challenged O'Connell, whom he derided as 'a great bad man engaged in a great bad cause',[31] to a public debate and the Orangemen of North Down planned to prevent him travelling to Belfast. O'Connell eluded them by arriving earlier than expected and was joined at dinner in a specially built pavilion by some eleven hundred men. Though the chairman, Robert McDowell, was a Presbyterian, and a few Presbyterian liberals — John Sinclair, a director of the Provincial Bank, John Houston, president of the Master Mariners' Society and a few mill owners and manufacturers — turned up to honour O'Connell as a reformer (Sharman Crawford refused the invitation), the atmosphere on the occasion was predominantly Catholic. Bishops Denvir and McLaughlin of Derry, thirty two priests from Down and Connor and sixteen from other dioceses were present. After the customary toasts to the queen and members of the royal family, to which there were no replies, were drunk, a toast was given to 'the people' and Patrick Dorrian, widely regarded as a very competent

31 N.W., 7 Jan. 1841.

and effective public speaker, was called on to reply to it.

Tendering thanks to their guest for his untiring exertions in advocating the rights and liberties of mankind in general and of themselves in particular, he remarked that they had been opposed not only by their open political foes, who had taunted them with their inability to muster in sufficient numbers, but also harassed by base attempts to thwart them, made by those who should have been their political friends; still they had succeeded because of the strength of the people, the source of all human power. He further explained that they had gathered to pay respect to one who had taught men that 'in themselves lay dormant a spark of moral strength, a thousand times more powerful and indomitable than the physical force to which they had alas too frequently resorted'. Recalling O'Connell's past achievement through peaceful, loyal and constitutional means, he noted that the flame then kindled spread to the sister isle, and when the foes of the people's rights had thrown the Reform Bill out of the House of Lords, two hundred thousand men assembled constitutionally in Birmingham and made their enemies quake within the strongholds of their bigotry. If so many Englishmen could peacefully bring about the Reform Bill, what might not be achieved by eight million Irishmen equally unanimous for their country's good? It was the duty of people to obey their sovereign but it was no less incumbent on their rulers to govern them on principles of impartiality and justice. Dorrian concluded by urging repealers to persevere in pressing by constitutional means for the removal of grievances and the granting of legitimate demands:

> The people have enemies to contend against and rules to obey — convinced of the latter on the authority of the creator himself, in society there must be different grades; determined to preserve this order it is your duty, a duty which cannot be too deeply impressed on your minds, convinced of your moral right and consequent inability of witholding from you your own just and constitutional demands, to leave no opportunity of pressing on your rulers the grievances under which you still labour and to make them sensible that they rule but for the people's good. Let people be unanimous and unceasing in upholding the champions of their cause and they may hurl defiance at their enemies and see their manufacturers unrivalled, commerce extended and old Erin great among the nations of the earth.

Prolonged cheering greeted this address.

Though McDowell toasted 'civil and religious liberty all over the world', few but the adherents of one religion were in evidence during O'Connell's sojourn in Belfast. The chairman also toasted Cornelius

Denvir and the Catholic hierarchy of Ireland. George Crolly replied to the toast of the clergy of all denominations who were present, and Daniel Curoe, the parish priest of Randalstown, replied to the toast of the Lord-Lieutenant. O'Connell received an address from members of the committee of the Christian Doctrine Society and, on the evening following the public dinner, he was entertained at a soirée held by the ladies of the St Patrick's Orphan Society in the Music Hall.[32] Rioting broke out during the visit and the windows of the Music Hall and the offices of the *Vindicator* were broken by stones thrown by Orangemen. Though the *Vindicator* boasted of the success of the occasion and undoubtedly repeal was given an enormous boost which was reflected in the growth of the membership, the increase in interest and adherents came almost exclusively from the Catholic community.

On the Protestant side the effect was negative; while it was unlikely that many Protestants would have joined the movement, Cooke's exploitation of the visit redounded to the advantage of the Tory party. Three leading liberals — Robert James Tennent, Robert Grimshaw and James Macnamara (a Catholic) — called on O'Connell to appraise him of 'the impropriety and impolicy of the course which he had been pursuing', to point out that not all Catholic reformers were repealers and to alert him to the harm done by his attacks on the Belfast liberals.[33] Interpreting O'Connell's mission as an invasion of their territory and a challenge to the constitution, the Tories held a public meeting largely attended by the aristocracy, gentry and clergy to reassert their resistance to repeal. There was a whiff of menace in the air. One speaker declared that they had the wealth, the intelligence and the nerve to meet their opponents, and, if Catholics chose to point to the differences between themselves and Protestants, they should remember Aughrim, the Boyne, Derry and 'No Surrender' and know that every river in Ireland would be made another Boyne. Henry Cooke, taking up the ultra-Protestant line that repeal would lead to the replacement of a Protestant by a Catholic ascendancy, claimed that O'Connell's black-coated backers were looking for the moment when they would be lords of every parish, and predicted that the mass of Presbyterians would never join the present conspiracy against the queen, the country and the constitution.[34]

The *Vindicator* replied by accusing Cooke of contributing to the rioting by not following the example of the Catholic bishop and clergy in begging his people not to cause a breach of the peace and

32 V., 20 Jan. 1841.
33 N.W., 19 Jan. 1841.
34 N.W., 21 Jan. 1841.

trying to persuade them to remain indoors.[35]

Denvir and some prominent Catholics, such as Gavan Duffy and Edward O'Rorke, continued to meet the leading Protestant liberals at meetings of the Belfast Reform Association but Patrick Dorrian did not attend. He had lost whatever slender faith he had had in the Whigs' seriousness of purpose regarding reforms leading to full and genuine equality.

Though the *Vindicator* hailed O'Connell's plan to make the land question a leading issue in the national association and spelt out the basic conditions for a settlement[36], and though Sharman Crawford, a keen enthusiast for land reform, accepted these general principles, the land question did not provide a common platform for united action between Whigs and repealers. Nonetheless, the Belfast repealers and Catholics in general had, perforce, to vote for a Whig at elections. They were too small a minority to put up a candidate of their own with any chance of success, and to deny their support to the Whigs was to contribute to the election of their inveterate enemies, the Tories. David Ross, the Rostrevor landlord, who stood for Belfast in the election of August 1842, enjoyed the reputation of being a sincere, committed reformer and with the aid of enthusiastic Catholic support topped the poll.

As O'Connell's movement gathered momentum throughout Ireland during what he promised would be the year of repeal, 1843, its Belfast supporters — including the clergy — contributed generously and membership continued to increase. The repeal reading rooms were located in Chapel Lane beside St Mary's Church and this was a further factor in strengthening the links between the local leaders and the clergy. O'Connell, the astute politician, was very aware of the value of clerical support and the role of the clergy as organizers and leaders, and knew how to apply the blarney to priests when opportunities arose. On receipt of a generous number of subscriptions from the repealers, both clerical and lay, of Belfast, he remarked that he knew Denvir and some of his domestic clergy personally and others by character, and there could not be a more useful, zealous and highly informed body of priests. Belfast itself, or rather the repeal section of it, came in for its fair share of praise; there was, he affirmed, a manliness about Belfast, for it faced the enemy and always told the truth.[37]

At the St Patrick's Day dinner in 1843, Dorrian, whose strong political loyalties were widely known and appreciated among his

35 V., 27 Jan. 1841.
36 V., 3 Apr. 1841. The paper argued that rent should be a fixed proportion of the produce of the land and that an evicted tenant should receive a fair compensation for his expenditure of labour and capital.
37 V., 15 Mar. 1843.

parishioners, was called on by popular acclamation to respond to the toast to O'Connell. Starting off on a robust note, he admitted that repealers were often taunted with being ultras, and insisted firmly that he was quite prepared to face that sneer rather than 'like some timid, mean, and, as the chairman very appropiately styled them, crawling bipeds be seen veering about from point to point accordingly as the baser motives of worldly interest or inordinate vanity may influence them'. Rejecting the admonition to the Catholic clergy, gratuitously and inconsistently given them by both Whigs and Tories, to steer clear of politics, he pointed out that the speeches of Orange parsons were carried by their own newspapers. There was no reason, he went on, why a priest should not hold and express his political views clearly, firmly and vigorously: 'I have always been taught to look upon tepidity in the religious life, as disgusting, and I can't see what should make it charming in the political; for my own part I hate it cordially in both'.

Recalling that scripture furnished numerous examples of just and saintly people who took an interest in politics, which he defined as questions connected with the temporal happiness of the community, he proceeded to argue that priests were capable of forming more correct opinions on politics than most other people, because they were less likely to be influenced by sinister or unworthy motives. He favoured discreet behaviour, however, on the part of the clergy: politics should not be discussed on the altar or pulpit and priests should go along with rather than take the lead in political movements. He proclaimed himself an ardent admirer of O'Connell's and, in extolling the liberator's gifts, even went to the extreme of saying that he had 'the magic of being always in the right'. Reminding his audience that O'Connell worked indiscriminately for Protestant Orangemen, Presbyterian liberals and Catholic radicals, he referred to the statement of his friend and colleague, George Crolly, at a previous St Patrick's Day celebration, that O'Connell had brought civil liberty to Ireland just as St Patrick had brought the Christian faith, and asked with innocent pride what country but Ireland could boast of two such luminaries?[38]

The cheerful optimism and exuberance of these sentiments were understandable and pardonable at the time. Irish Catholics in large numbers were coming to believe that O'Connell's massive constitutional campaign, which was gathering momentum weekly if not daily, would terminate as successfully as did that for Catholic Emancipation fourteen years earlier. Both movements were conducted on similar lines, the goals of both were reasonable and just, and as the British government had been forced to surrender to the moral

38 V., 22 Mar. 1843.

will of a determined people peaceably, powerfully and persistently expressed, many Catholics assumed that a favourable outcome was again as inevitable as in 1829. O'Connell carried the hopes and aspirations of Catholic Ireland, his methods were beyond any taint or suspicion of violence and the clergy naturally shared the instinctive enthusiasm of their people for a Dublin-based legislature, which would investigate and try to cope with the particular problems and peculiar difficulties of Ireland. Dorrian's views were typical of those of the majority of the clergy. They had invested immense confidence and trust in O'Connell and could not foresee the determined resistance of the British government and the inability of a constitutional movement to make further headway once that resistance was clearly and forcefully manifested.

An aspect of the repeal movement that appealed to many Catholics, especially clergy, was the close association of priests and people for a common objective. The firmer the bonds between the laity and the priesthood, they argued, the more effective would be the pastoral activity of the church. In Belfast these bonds were strengthened by the particular politico-religious situation which obtained in North East Ulster. A minority that feels itself virtually excluded from office and influence by a powerful majority can rarely afford the luxury of division and diversity of views. Consequently, Belfast's Catholics tended to close ranks behind their priests, especially as they believed that the clergy fully shared their political aspirations and social ambitions. Dorrian was very conscious of this warm and happy relationship and of the pastoral wisdom of developing and fortifying it. In reply to a toast to the clergy of Belfast at a dinner of the Christian Doctrine Society in 1842, he remarked that next to the internal satisfaction of having conscientiously discharged their duties, the priests were proud of acquiring the good will of the people, and he forecast that, as long as that healthy situation existed, the best results would flow from it. And he assured his hearers, and doubtless with more seriousness than is normally associated with such customary courtesies, that he believed 'in Ireland there was not a more thorough affection for their bishops, priests and religion than that which prevailed among the Catholics of Belfast'.

But he was not prepared to court popularity by churning out popular, warm-hearted compliments on all possible occasions. In fact, he was quite ready to issue a rebuke when he felt it necessary to do so. On that occasion, when paying tribute to those who took up the weekly collections for a new church, then in the course of erection, he commented that 'the wealthy classes were those who made the best hand at refusing'. And it was undoubtedly in a mood of half-fun-whole-earnest that he added that the poor, to whom the gospel was preached, had the best right to it, as they were among the best contributors to the good work. The collectors had received most encouragement from the poor but the rich Catholics had given them little reason for gratitude by their subscriptions. Though believing that it was 'better to tell the truth plainly than to put a hypocritical face on it', he nonetheless regretted to have to say that the wealthy Catholics of Belfast were not as liberal as those of other towns, and he expressed the hope that they would co-operate more generously and cordially in the future.[39]

The repealers of Belfast shared the anger and frustration of O'Connell's supporters everywhere at the ban imposed by the government on the mass meeting planned for Clontarf. They always resented the charges of their local political opponents that support for repeal involved disloyalty to the queen and government. They had gone out of their way to give public voice to their sentiments of loyalty to the sovereign when opportunity offered, as it did in the previous December, when they took an active part at a meeting called to address her on the success of British arms in Afghanistan and China. And in local politics, despite their exclusion from the town council and other public bodies, Catholics had always been anxious to identify themselves with the industrial, commercial and even artistic achievements of Belfast, which they frequently saluted with the grandiose and inflated title popularly conferred on the town in earlier years — the Athens of the north. So this enforced ending of peaceful public meetings was a severe blow to believers in legitimate constitutional politics and, while still rocking from this bruising denial of what they had regarded as a modest right, the behaviour of the law officers in tampering with the juries which were to try O'Connell intensified their excitement and, indeed, their fury. On 10 January 1844 a group of concerned Catholics hastily met in the diocesan seminary in Belfast to discuss their reaction to the deletion of all Catholic names from the jury list. Hugh Magill, the leading businessman who, as was customary, occupied the chair, proposed that the question for decision was whether to send a deputation to protest to Dublin or to organize a large public protest in Belfast. Patrick Dorrian argued that they could do both, and conveyed to the meeting the bishop's wish that he should be associated with a deputation to Dublin and that the Catholics of the town should express their views boldly and vigorously. Dorrian's suggestion was accepted, arrangements were made to hold a general meeting in Belfast and six representatives were chosen to present their views in Dublin.[40]

39 V., 7 Jan. 1843.
40 V., 13 Jan. 1844.

A few days later a huge gathering, mainly of Catholics, assembled in the Theatre Royal to petition the queen and address parliament about the officers' jury packing. Bishop Denvir presided and the prominent non-repealers, Edward O'Rorke and James Macnamara, spoke. Patrick Dorrian, the first priest to speak, proposed the third resolution which averred that trial by jury was a bulwark of the British constitution and that a fair trial was a simple act of justice. Claiming that the express provision made by the constitution for dealing with persons charged with criminal offences had been violated in this case, he pointed out (with partial accuracy) that the constitution itself was 'the offspring of the forethought, prudence and patriotism of their Catholic ancestors', and that the proud birthright of every British citizen had been the privilege of a fair trial. Dealing with the second part of the resolution which called for the fullest and most searching parliamentary investigation, he asked indignantly what theological factor contributed to making a Protestant oath better than a Catholic oath? He claimed that every Catholic believed that an oath needed to be fair, necessary and true, and that, if it lacked any of these basic qualities, a person committed perjury by taking it. No Catholic, however illiterate or however possessed of preconceived opinions, would acquit a prisoner, if the evidence told against him; to act otherwise would be in opposition to the principles of the Catholic religion. A deep insult, Dorrian continued, had been offered to the Catholics of Ireland and 'unless they took a bold and virtuously indignant step there was no knowing where aggression might stop'. He concluded by referring to an observation of Lord Morpeth (the former Lord-Lieutenant) that there was no nation under heaven containing men of more virtue and females of more purity, and thereby won applause for both his own and Morpeth's views.[41]

Dorrian's keen enthusiasm for repeal and criticism of the system by which O'Connell was jailed continued to draw warm applause at repeal meetings. At a large meeting called to draw up an address to O'Connell in June, the mention of Dorrian's name among the list of subscribers was, according to the *Vindicator*, 'received with all that acclamation it so justly deserves'.[42] And when Liberals and repealers came together in large numbers on 7 June to protest against O'Connell's imprisonment, Dorrian was the only priest invited to propose a resolution. He moved that an address be presented to O'Connell conveying their acknowledgement of past services and praying that he would emerge from prison in full health. Expressing satisfaction at being called to address a meeting

41 V., 20 Jan. 1844.
42 V., 5 June 1844.

composed of representatives of all shades of political opinion, including Tories, he emphasised that O'Connell was the consistent supporter of civil and religious liberty, and the friend of every slave of every creed or clime, which proved incidentally that there was nothing in the Catholic faith inimical to liberty. Though recognized as the particular liberator of Irish Catholics, he challenged anyone to point to any action in O'Connell's life that contributed even in the slighest degree to depriving anyone of the right to worship his God. And he instanced, as an example of O'Connell's openmindedness and fairness, his support for the claims of the Unitarians, even though he differed more widely from them than from the Trinitarians. When the Presbyterian, James Grimshaw, left the chair, Cornelius Denvir in proposing a vote of thanks explained that he had not taken part in the proceedings as he was anxious to prevent a hostile press from labelling the meeting a purely Catholic occasion and so left the main expression of sympathy to the Liberals and reformers.[43] The union of repealers and reformers was of short duration; Sharman Crawford, a leading reformer, recommended a federal relationship between Britain and Ireland and, though O'Connell briefly flirted with the idea, it never won acceptance among the repealers of Belfast. The *Vindicator* at first welcomed co-operation with the federalists in the hope of somehow undoing the act of union but the anaemic nature of federalism and the feeble advocacy of its supporters soon disillusioned the repealers.

Further grounds of separation between Catholics and liberal Presbyterians were provided by the government's new programme of legislation for Ireland.[44] Peel's cabinet decided to kill repeal by kindness and the obvious way to do this was to remedy serious grievances which the Catholics had been airing. The first item on their list was the Charitable Bequests Bill of 1844. Until then bequests were controlled by a highly unrepresentative board of which only one member out of fifty was a Catholic. It was now proposed to establish a board to deal with all bequests to charity of which half the appointed members (five out of ten) would be Catholic; provision was made for three ex-officio members. Two serious defects attached to the bill: no alteration was made in the terms of the Catholic Emancipation Act which prevented religious orders from inheriting property and a legacy made within three months of the testator's death was invalid. Catholic reaction was generally very hostile. Archbishop John MacHale of Tuam spearheaded the opposition and at the annual meeting of the bishops in November 1844 a majority supported his views; the minority,

43 V., 8 June 1844.
44 D.A. Kerr, *Peel, priests and politics*, pp 73-92.

however, led by Archbishop Crolly of Armagh and Archbishop Daniel Murray of Dublin, was prepared to try to co-operate with the government on the grounds that such remedial legislation was an improvement on the previous position and the best offer likely to be made to them. Among the eight bishops who formed the minority was Cornelius Denvir, Crolly's lifelong friend. Crolly and Murray agreed to serve as commissioners and, though the bishop of Killaloe at first joined them, he was forced by pressure of public opinion to withdraw, and his place was taken by the bishop of Down and Connor.

The excitement caused by the bill was intense. Catholic Ireland was not in a receptive mood in June 1844 since, in the wake of O'Connell's imprisonment, it tended naturally to suspect the government of double-dealing and dishonesty. MacHale struck this mood forcefully and eloquently; to him, and to those who thought with him, the government was engaged in a massive and subtle conspiracy to damage if not destroy the Catholic faith in Ireland; where the cruder means of persecution had failed, more devious methods were now being employed to seduce Catholics from their allegiance to their faith and due obedience to their bishops. The friars, though not touched by the bill, became a symbol of the policy of discrimination and injustice which the MacHale-minded associated with government policy. Throughout Ireland public meetings were called to denounce the bill and in those dioceses — the majority — where the bishops were in opposition there was no conflict of allegiance. But where priests and laity felt strongly against the bill and the bishop of the diocese belonged to the minority among the hierarchy, an embarrassing and indeed painful situation arose. To the more moderate opponents of the bill a bishop who co-operated with the government was misguided but to the more extreme he was an insufferable, dangerous and perhaps even an untrustworthy West Briton who was prepared to foresake the interests of his people for the dubious favours of Dublin Castle. Two of the eight minority bishops were northerners and both were intimately connected with the Catholics of Belfast. Hitherto they had both stood high in the esteem and affection of the people of their former and present dioceses — though Crolly's silence on repeal did not go unnoticed — but the Charitable Bequests Bill and the Queen's Colleges Bill of 1845 drove a wedge between these bishops and their people and never again was the former relationship of loyalty and trust rebuilt.

At their meeting at the end of November the majority bishops appealed to Rome. The government, afraid of a possible condemnation from the Vatican and anxious to move quickly before opposition hardened further, completed arrangements about the appointments of commissioners. In mid-December the names of the three bishops — Crolly, Murray and Denvir — appeared in the official gazette. Within a week a group of prominent Catholics, professional and business men, met at the rooms of a solicitor in Belfast to consider what action to take. Denvir was present and explained that he had accepted office on the understanding that the clauses in the Charitable Bequests Act which were unacceptable to the bishops would be amended in the next session of parliament; if this were not done, he promised to resign. He pointed out that the Catholics of Belfast were fully entitled to draw their own conclusions about the Act and this they proceeded to do, after Denvir had withdrawn from the meeting. They made arrangements to hold a large public 'unqualified protest' against the 'iniquitous measure'.

Since the Music Hall was too small to accomodate the expected crowds, the Theatre Royal was chosen as the venue, and even it was wholly inadequate. No building in Belfast, it was reported, could contain one quarter of the people who were anxious to protest. Hugh Magill, the chairman, expressed regrets that the bishop had permitted his name to go forward for membership of the 'abominable' Commission of Bequests, had not consulted with his priests and laity about such a step and was now being praised by a journal, presumably the *News-Letter*, which had formerly abused him. The first resolution proposed by Peter Magouran, a barrister, and seconded by Henry Murney, a well-to-do tobacconist and spirit merchant, stated that, notwithstanding the regard and esteem in which the bishop was held by the Catholics of Belfast for his learning, piety and unblemished character, they deeply deplored the 'ill-advised course he has recently adopted in allowing himself to be nominated a Commissioner for carrying into effect the provisions of that very objectionable anti-Catholic enactment, the Charitable Bequests Act'. Magouran lamented the change in their condition; hitherto, in their difficulties, they had been cheered by the guidance, counsel and advice of Bishop Denvir but now they were obliged to depend on their own exertions, as their clergy had deserted them. Referring to the past he remarked that they had often heard William Crolly speak in 'proud and eulogistic terms' of the Catholics of Belfast and no one had ever dreamt of the possibility of his separating himself from them on such an occasion. But this had occurred — Magouran feared from 'a want of grace' — and his hope that nothing would ever mar or eclipse the career of Crolly had been shattered; Crolly had no further claim on them and in a moment of weakness Cornelius Denvir was induced to accept office under an Act which was totally condemned by almost every Catholic clergyman or layman in Ireland. Magouran emphasised — and most speakers reiterated his view — the wisdom of following the advice of O'Connell, 'the father of his country', who had indignantly rejected the measure both as unjust and unconstitutional. But speakers also highlighted the MacHale argument that the Act was a Tory device to destroy if possible the Catholic faith of Ireland, and cast suspicion on the motives of any Tory Government bringing forward legislation allegedly beneficial to Catholics. James Magouran accurately represented the views of the meeting when he declared:

> The more I examine the act, the more I am borne out of my hostility to it. It is the dark tempest that sits lowering over the Catholic Church. It must be dispelled. It must be thrown back on its originators (continued cheering) or when the storm bursts in its violence over our heads, and the small cloud no larger than a man's hand, that portends its advent, is now visible in our horizon, we may be found, clergy and people, unable to resist its power, and fall one common ruin before its devastating progress.

Denvir escaped direct attacks and indeed tributes were paid to his personal qualities but was accused of foolishly following the lead of Archbishop Crolly. One speaker, Charles McDonnell, felt obliged to refer to painful facts about this association and revealed that Crolly was 'of Conservative principles'. He instanced Crolly's notable absence from a repeal meeting at Dundalk on one occasion and noted that not only had he been noticeably absent but had chosen that day to hold a conference of clergy a few miles away, thereby preventing his priests also from attending. And then driving home most effectively his point about Crolly's political wrong-headedness, McDonnell remarked that the archbishop had taken the opposite side to the liberator on every question in which the rights and liberties of Irishmen were concerned. Bernard Lennon, another speaker, was prepared to claim that, while Crolly had few peers as a bishop, he was an indifferent statesman.

Significantly the speaker chosen to propose the resolution denouncing the maltreatment of the friars was Dr Edward Dorrian, Patrick's brother, who was a general practitioner in Belfast. His case atoned in strength for what it lacked in accuracy. He argued that the position of the friars was worse than before the bill was introduced by reference to O'Connell's view that the commissioners would be obliged to recall all the bequests misapplied since 1829 and that this might involve suing and receiving evidence from people, which would hurt the friars. He drew a very questionable analogy between this element in the Act and a poisonous element in a medical prescription; if he were to draw up for a patient a prescription containing many good elements but one poisonous one, the patient would indignantly reject it, just as the bishops should have done with the Act. And he fell back on his classical knowledge — indeed he was not the only speaker to refer to Grecian guile — to recall the image of the Trojan horse and point the moral of the government's machiavellian intent.

Other speakers stressed the absolute right of a donor to bequeath to charitable causes at any time of his life, however late; paid tribute to Daniel O'Connell for his defence of the rights, liberties and privileges, political and religious, of the Catholics of Ireland and for 'his lucid exposition of the ambiguous anti-Catholic provisions of the insidious Charitable Bequest Bill'; thanked MacHale and his episcopal supporters for alerting Irish Catholics to the dangers in the bill and in particular the parish priest of Kilmore (Crossgar) for his public letter to Archbishop Crolly on the anti-Catholic tendencies of the proposed legislation.[45]

No priests took part in this meeting, but the likelihood is very strong that the views expressed at it represented those of many of Denvir's priests. Subsequently a few of them — Edward McGreevy and John Cunningham of Duneane, and Luke Walsh of Culfeightrin — aligned themselves publicly with lay opponents of the Act. And at the meeting reference was made to the fact that while only a few bishops and two priests — the mention of one of their names was hissed — publicly supported the government, some twelve hundred had publicly opposed it. Almost certainly Patrick Dorrian was among the opponents. His brother's presence and prominence at the meeting would be difficult to understand, if Dorrian had supported the Denvir line. Dorrian's strong political views, his keen support for and admiration of O'Connell, and his readiness to distrust and resist the Whigs, let alone the Tories, point to the strong probability that he differed from Denvir in his approach to the Act.

Though the Belfast protesters were careful to distinguish between their respect for and allegiance to Denvir as their bishop and their reaction to his behaviour in relation to a political issue, which had particular repercussions for Catholics, the difficulty of maintaining the distinction was great. The Act came to be widely regarded as a form of positive discrimination against Catholics and Denvir was judged by some of his flock as an advocate of a policy that damaged his own people.

At a public meeting in Coleraine this interpretation of the situation was voiced in a resolution which declared that 'the prelates who had accepted office had inflicted a deep wound on religion', and had placed themselves 'in a state of ill-omened antagonism to the great majority of their co-religionists and brought them into dangerous and suspicious alliance with the inveterate enemies of the Catholic

45 V., 8 Jan. 1845.

faith'.[46] The strength of feeling against the measure and the determination to fight it were illustrated by the number of meetings of protest in the dioceses of the prelates who co-operated with the government. Priests, who out of loyalty to their bishops or because of their own politico-religious interpretation of events, tried to withstand the tide of lay hostility to the Act, found themselves overrun and defeated. Daniel Curoe, the parish priest of Randalstown, only learned from a notice in the *Vindicator* that a protest meeting was to be held in the grounds of the parish church. He immediately wrote an indignant public letter of protest in which he justified his work for the Catholic people by a list of his services to education, parochial development and repeal, described the planned meeting as a 'direct intended insult' to his 'clerical station' and announced that it would not be held.

Curoe had a temporary victory. The meeting was not held at Randalstown but two months later on grounds adjoining the church at Antrim his parishioners gave vigorous voice to their misgivings. A large crowd strongly approved of the resolutions against the Act and, though hearty cheers went up when warm tributes were paid to Curoe's character, zeal and achievements, 'a wild burst of enthusiastic cheering' greeted the mention of the name of Edward McGreevy, the parish priest of the neighbouring parish, who was a firm opponent of the new law.[47] Whether for diplomatic or health reasons, Bishop Denvir did not attend the annual St Patrick's Day dinner in 1845 and so he was spared public embarrassment, but he must have noticed the omission of his name from the list of toasts. Significantly, Hugh Magill proposed the health of the Catholic laity of Belfast and, perhaps it was a further sign of the increasing solidarity of the beleaguered Catholic community that Magill, who had hitherto kept his distance from political agitation, announced that he had joined the Repeal Association.

IV

This division among Belfast's Catholics had unfortunately come in the wake of a praiseworthy if overdue achievement — the dedication of their long awaited third church. But the termination of this worthy undertaking was also marred by the problems of fundraising encountered during the last few months of construction and the disputes which arose over the sale of pews after its completion.

The frustrating search for a suitable site for another church ended

---

46 V., 15 Jan. 1845.
47 V., 19 Feb. 1845.

in July 1839 when Adam McClean, a Protestant businessman, generously donated ground free of charge. According to the minute book of the building committee,[48] the congregation of Belfast in accordance with the wishes of the bishop and his clergy decided to build a cathedral with accommodation for seven thousand people. Committees were appointed to translate this decision into bricks and mortar, and advertisements placed in the press offering a prize of £50 for the most acceptable plan. The competition, which attracted almost thirty entries from Britain and Ireland, was won by a Glasgow architect. But the committee then had second thoughts about the nature and purpose of their enterprise and decided that the urgent need for providing church accommodation took precedence over the other but less pressing need of having a large and architecturally meritorious cathedral; or as the minute book rather quaintly recorded, 'the Committee by applying to some scientific Gentlemen, found (from the length of time that would be necessary to make the projected Cathedral a shelter for those who were at present excluded from divine Worship) that the object to which they aspired (namely the present accommodation of their people) would rather be frustrated than accomplished'.[49] This proposal was then submitted to a general meeting of all parishioners, at which not only the bishop and clergy but also Archbishop Crolly were present, and having obtained approval for the building of a church on a reduced scale, with accommodation for 5,000, a subcommittee was empowered to employ a local architect, Thomas Jackson, with a view to a speedy commencement of the works. Proceeding democratically it presented Jackson's plans to the general parish committee and then submitted them 'to the inspection and perusal of seatholders, heads of families & householders belonging to the Congregation' in St Patrick's Church. This meeting unanimously agreed to Jackson's proposals and on 23 July 1841 an advertisement inviting tenders appeared in the local press. Dorrian was present with Denvir when the parish committee appointed a permanent building committee of seven members and chose the lowest tender, that of Campbell and Ross, at £5,679.[50] The foun-

---

48 The minute book, which is preserved in St Malachy's Presbytery, covers the years 1841-5.
49 This committee was empowered to co-opt other members at its discretion. Those selected on this occasion were: Hugh Magill (a linen merchant), who became treasurer and often acted as chairman, Alexander Turney (a coachmaker), Captain Delargy (a retired seaman), John Connor (a builder), James Connor (also a builder), who was appointed secretary, William Lennon, Arthur Aicken, Patrick McAuley and Henry Maguire. Bishop Denvir attended its meetings regularly and occasionally acted as chairman or secretary.
50 Minute book.

dation stone was laid on 3 November 1841, which was the feast day of St Malachy, the titular of the new church and patron of the diocese.

The ceremony was preceded by a procession of clergy and people from St Mary's Church and the crowds which assembled at the site were so great and the pressure exerted by them on the thick rope which was affixed to the beam to raise the foundation stone was so strong that the rope snapped. With great difficulty and after the repeated requests of the bishop and his clergy, the crowd withdrew to allow the ceremony to proceed. Dorrian was not among the speakers at the dinner afterwards for the clergy and leading laity of the town; his usual slot, on this occasion a toast to 'the People, the source of all political power', which immediately followed those to the royal family, was taken by George Crolly. The chairman, Hugh Magill, observed with regret that they would not have the financial support of every wealthy Protestant both Conservative and Liberal, which they had enjoyed when St Patrick's was being built, but, reminding them of their obligations to their liberal Protestant brethren for the generous assistance they had received, proposed a toast to 'Adam McClean and the Liberal Protestants of Belfast'.[51]

A deceased benefactor, Captain Thomas Griffith, had bequeathed £3,000 for the new church.[52] Apart from some other private subscriptions, the main source of revenue was a weekly collection of a penny from each household. The response to this collection seems to have waxed and waned in accordance with the rate of progress on the building. And progress at times was slow and unsatisfactory. The contractors obtained permission to withdraw when they had finished 'the skeleton of the house', and after a frustrating interlude when another contractor could not produce the two bonds of £500 each which he had promised the building committee, a third contractor, Peter Lundy, was employed to complete the interior of the building, the wood work and stucco work. Lundy, on the other hand, carried out his part of the contract with such speed that the finances available to the building committee could not keep pace with his demands and he was requested to employ less men and operate less swiftly. In the few months both preceding and following completion the financial position seems to have become desperate. The bishop was forced to appeal to all the parishes of the diocese and, though all except one or two, which had serious financial problems of their own, responded very generously, the minute book noted that he was obliged to 'call on his Protestant &

---

51 V., 6 Nov. 1841.
52 A plaque in the portico of St Malachy's Church commemorates this bequest of Griffith, 'a native of this town' who died on 30 Mar. 1838.

Presbyterian Brethren, several of whom made liberal promises, which when fulfilled, will meet the object of our first inquiry'. Other guarantors including members of the committee were also pressed by the bank, and though the minutes make no mention of the bishop's own predicament, James O'Laverty, the diocesan historian, who was a near contemporary of the event, claimed that he was arrested for the heavy debts which remained after the church was dedicated. O'Laverty also related that Denvir was greatly annoyed by the opposition which arose to the sale of pews, and seems to imply that class feeling entered into this friction.[53] The total cost of the church was about £7,000, which meant that after the Griffith bequest £4,000 had to be raised. About £900 was collected during the solemn dedication ceremonies. The building committee drew up plans for dividing the pews into four classes to be sold at sums ranging from £45 to £20 each, which would yield a total of £2,870 for 102 pews, and though the minutes end without recording the verdict of the general committee of the Catholic parish of Belfast, it seems likely both in view of O'Laverty's remarks and of the debt problem that few if any were actually sold.

St Malachy's Church was solemly consecrated by Archbishop Crolly on 15 December 1844. Bishop Denvir, who had travelled to Paris to acquire suitable vestments, celebrated the Mass, Bishop Kennedy of Killaloe preached and Patrick Dorrian was Master of Ceremonies. Among the collectors were some of the leading figures of the business and commercial life of Belfast — the liberal Protestants whose generosity Hugh Magill had praised — including James Grimshaw, Sharman Crawford, James Tennent, Adam Duffin, William McCance, Robert McDowell, Thomas Coates and Thomas Dunville. The *Vindicator* enthused over the presence of so many distinguished Protestants, which it interpreted as a sign of conciliation and progress. And in reply to the Presbyterian *Banner of Ulster* which asked how Protestants could justify their attendance even for one day at a Catholic church, it referred with pride to the role played by the Presbyterian Volunteers at the opening of St Mary's in 1784.[54]

V

But the ecumenism that could survive at the level of financial contributions to church building found the going tougher when confronted with the new political remedies being applied by Peel's

53 O'Laverty, *Down and Connor*, v, 601.
54 V., 21 Dec. 1844.

Conservative government to Irish problems. In fact Peel's response to the repeal agitation created further division and disharmony. The increased grant to Maynooth pleased the Catholics but displeased the Protestants; the Queen's Colleges bill, designed to make tertiary education available to Catholics and Presbyterians pleased the Presbyterians but displeased most Catholics.

When the terms of the bill became known in May 1845 the *Vindicator* immediately expressed reservations and suggested changes very similar to those later recommended by the bishops. The three colleges envisaged in the bill, which were to be located in Ulster, Munster and Connaught, were designed to be non-denominational, though provision was made for the churches to endow religious instruction in them. When the bishops, in response to William Crolly's designation of them as 'pregnant with danger to the Faith and morals of the youth of this country', assembled to discuss the proposals, they offered co-operation if the government would guarantee that a fair proportion of staff be Catholic, that bishops would be members of the appointments boards, that chaplains under their jurisdiction and paid by the state be appointed and that the professors of history, logic, metaphysics, moral philosophy, zoology and anatomy, whose lectures Catholics would attend, would be Catholics.

These were sweeping changes and went far beyond what the government was prepared to concede. The Home Secretary would only promise that a fair proportion of the professors would be Catholic and that there would be protection against proselytism. The bill, without any significant alterations, became law at the end of July. By then a tremendous furore had arisen throughout Ireland. O'Connell and his followers denounced it vigorously, taking up the criticism levelled against the colleges by the Tory MP, Sir Robert Inglis, as 'godless' but the Young Ireland wing of the party welcomed combined education as a means towards the reconciliation of different denominations and traditions in Ireland. The Young Ireland element, however, was never strong among the repealers of Belfast and consequently resistance to the Colleges Act was firm and widespread both in the town and throughout the province.

Great then were the surprise and confusion when William Crolly lent his support to the advocates of Armagh as the site of the northern college. The chief contenders for that honour were Armagh and Belfast, and Crolly, believing that Armagh would afford a less obvious Presbyterian and more neutral religious atmosphere, joined his Anglican colleague and the Armagh Presbyterian clergy at a public meeting on 14 August to canvass the suitability of Armagh. He justified his support for the primatial city by claiming that the government had made such arrangements as were calculated to afford general satisfaction but did not identify them or produce convincing evidence that this was so. The *Vindicator* was nonplussed by this *volte-face* and referring to the bishops' resolutions of May, which it reprinted, concluded that the primate had been misreported. Other newspapers took a much less charitable view of his change of attitude; O'Connell's repeal paper, the *Pilot*, suggested that Crolly had gone insane and the *Tablet* picked up this innuendo. The bewilderment expressed by the *Vindicator* undoubtedly represented the views of most concerned Ulster Catholics, and its contemptuous support for the claims of Belfast was consistent with its dismissal of the education offered by the colleges as 'infidel'. Remarking scornfully and sardonically that, if it were possible to claim a school of infidelity as of use to any town, Belfast could justly claim its warmest support, it went on to defend its principled refusal to support Belfast's claim: 'Let those who are willing to see the people degraded, under the irreligious, demoralizing effects of such institutions, petition for the introduction of one of them into Belfast; so shall not we'.[55]

Cornelius Denvir, however, did not feel inhibited by his reservations about the government's plans from supporting those who wished to have a college sited in Belfast.[56] In fact he attended a public meeting called to point out the advantages of the town and he was selected as a member of a delegation to present an address to the Lord-Lieutenant justifying the right of Belfast to a new college. His fellow delegates represented both Liberal and Conservative opinion and included Henry Mongtomery and Henry Cooke, D.R. Ross, the Liberal MP for Belfast, and Andrew Mulholland, the Conservative mayor. Since the overwhelming body of the priests and interested Catholic lay people were strongly and bitterly opposed to the colleges, bishops who countenanced them in any way drew down fierce criticism and hostility on their heads. When the hierarchy assembled in Dublin for its annual meeting in November, the debate over the colleges was argued passionately and sharply. On this occasion a substantial majority supported MacHale's line of total opposition to the colleges, and petitioned Rome for an outright condemnation of them. Only eight bishops, headed by Archbishops Crolly and Murray, were prepared to defend the general policy of the government in making provision for university education for Catholics and Dissenters, and they wrote to Rome asking that a condemnation be avoided, in the hope of their obtaining improvements in

55 V., 30 Aug. 1845.
56 Denvir believed that Belfast offered better facilities for student accommodation and medical teaching, and had an excellent system of communications with the interior of Ulster. (Denvir to Thomas Andrews, 15 Sept. 1845, quoted in Moody and Beckett, *Queen's, Belfast, 1845-1949*, (London, 1959), i, 86).

the whole system. Though Rome delayed an answer for nearly two years, it came down firmly in favour of the majority, declared the colleges to be dangerous to the faith and morals of Catholic students, warned the bishops to ensure that their people avoided them and counselled the establishment of a Catholic university.[57]

Bishop Denvir had chosen not only the side of the minority among the bishops but probably also that of the minority among his own priests and among the educated and articulate members of his people. His stand on the Charitable Bequests Act confused and antagonized, if it did not estrange, many of his Catholic subjects; his stand on the Queen's Colleges increased the confusion and the mistrust. 1845 marks a turning point in his relations with his people; for the first ten years of his episcopate the relationship had been characterized by warmth and trust and shared sympathies. After 1845, partly as a result of these differences and partly in response to the heightened sectarian feeling in Belfast and some of the larger towns of the diocese, most notably Lisburn, Denvir withdrew more and more from public meetings and public affairs. He kept up his interest in and contribution to the Belfast General and Fever Hospital by attending the meetings of the board of management and playing his part on sub-committees; he travelled to Dublin regularly to attend the meetings of the Commissioners of Charitable Bequests and (after 1853) of the board of national education, but his contacts with his own Catholic people diminished. Even his public liturgical activities decreased and, as acquaintances later explained, his increasing nervousness and timidity in the face of politico-religious bitterness turned him more and more into a recluse.

VI

Differences of opinion — but of a much milder nature — existed between the bishop and some of his flock over the question of Fr Theobald Mathew's temperance crusade. The Capuchin began his total abstinence movement in 1838 and very soon he was travelling throughout Ireland administering his pledge to huge numbers. Upwards of eighty thousand people were said to have taken the pledge at meetings in some Irish provincial towns, and tributes to the social improvements brought about by the diminution of drunkenness were paid both by perceptive observers of the Irish scene and by senior government officers. But Fr Mathew also acquired a less enviable reputation. Among the simple and credulous he was soon

[57] Fergal McGrath, *Newman's university: Idea and reality*, (Dublin, 1951), pp 43-83.

hailed as a wonder worker and the sick and handicapped were brought along to him to be cured. Not all the Irish bishops welcomed him into their dioceses; some bishops were worried and frightened by aspects of his movement. They shared the fears of those who disliked much of the emotionalism and excitement evident at the public meetings and who believed that the temperance campaign was a transitory, ill-planned affair, which depended on a wave of almost hysterical reaction.

The formidable archbishop of Tuam, John MacHale, attacked the policy of taking a life-long pledge of abstinence from alcoholic drink as too severe and impractical: a five year pledge, he argued, would be more in keeping with the frailty of human nature. He questioned Fr Mathew's passing from diocese to diocese as tending at least indirectly towards a diminution of episcopal jurisdiction and, referring to the tokens and badges given out to the pledged abstainers, he claimed that this was a form of mercantile manipulation.[58]

Bishop Denvir did not publicize his objections to the crusade but it can be safely assumed that he shared the misgivings about the emotionalism, excitement and extent of the pledge. At any rate he did not give the Capuchin crusader permission to enter his diocese. Gavan Duffy, when editor of the *Vindicator*, organized a deputation from Belfast to meet Fr Mathew in Moira in 1841.[59] And on one occasion as Fr Mathew arrived in Belfast from Glasgow, he was persuaded to administer the pledge to a group of people who had assembled at the docks to meet him. But another preacher of total abstinence did not have the same scruples about entering a diocese without an invitation to preach total abstinence. John Spratt, a Dublin-based Carmelite, who had long been among the most active advocates of total abstinence, came to Belfast in January 1846 and administered the pledge to some five thousand people. Some Protestant clergy strongly supported total abstinence from drink and the temperance movement had useful ecumenical dimensions.[60] But Spratt's intervention was regarded by Catholic clergy as improper and discourteous, and Patrick Dorrian, who shared his bishop's misgivings, stung by a criticism in the *Whig* of the Catholic clergy absenting themselves from Spratt's public meeting, wrote a lengthy letter in reply.

Responding to the general charge that no priest was found to 'countenance this brother in his high moral work', Dorrian maintained that this stricture implied that priests were under a duty to do

58 P. Rogers, *Father Theobald Mathew*, (Dublin, 1943), pp 42-77. A few priests, notably Daniel Curoe of Randalstown, formed branches in their parishes of the Cork Total Abstinence Association.
59 C.G. Duffy, *My life in two hemispheres*, i, 53.
60 Rogers, op. cit., p.116.

so, and then asked in frustration where was the precept. He then proceeded to say that he would leave aside the question whether Spratt was 'right or wrong in thrusting his sickle into another's corn' (though the implication that Spratt should have left the Down and Connor corn untouched was clear), he wondered whether a newspaper could be the 'proper and authorized party whose privilege, as well as duty, it is to pronounce when a clergyman is guilty of neglect of duty and when not'. Then, on the assumption that the *Whig* possessed the knowledge which its condemnation of the clergy seemed to suggest, he went on to ask it a few basic questions about the total abstinence movement. Was the obligation of the pledge human or religious? If religious, the violation of it would be sinful and, if so, should it be imposed on all indiscriminately, old or young, ignorant or learned? How often could a pledge, if broken, be renewed? Insisting that every one should be left to make up his own mind on the subject, he then put in a strong plea for freedom of conscience: 'if teetotalism be even sure of removing drunkenness, but willing to substitute this forcing of conscience to its own views, I think it might fairly be questioned if the old state, with all its faults, would not be preferable to the new one, and a less scourge to society in the long run'. Declaring that as yet he did not understand teetotalism, he expressed confidence in the proper use of the sacraments as a means of reclaiming the most abandoned sinner.

This was indeed a curiously long-winded response to the *Whig's* comment about the absence of Catholic clergy from Spratt's meeting, and the tactic of involving the *Whig* in questions of conscience and of expecting it to show wide knowledge of the total abstinence movement was certainly blunt and ineffective. By straying into side issues Dorrian sacrificed the effect which a simple, direct reply to the *Whig's* comment could have had. The *Whig* was not slow to spot the weak flanks which this mode of argumentation exposed and promptly rejoined by claiming that Dorrian's 'dialectic craft runs away with his judgement'. Disclaiming all intention of coercing anyone's conscience, it noted that it had simply stated that the clergy had kept aloof, and then driving home the advantage, added that it, in common with some Catholics, was glad that the good work could go on without the parsons. The *Whig* scored another point by observing that drunkenness had gone on despite church and sacraments, and so, drawing the conclusion that the church had not done its duty or was not suited to coping with this evil, went on to say that, if anyone were to be assaulted for arguments on these grounds, it was Fr Mathew or Fr Spratt. But it overstated Dorrian's argument that all were not called to the same degree of perfection when it concluded that, unless a man could be sure that God had designed him for greater perfection, he could tipple and smile away. In conclusion Dorrian was given the backhanded compliment of being described as 'a respectable clergyman and intelligent man, though with greater subtlety than judgement'.

Dorrian's reply filled almost two columns, but, as the *Whig* refused to print it, it appeared in the *Vindicator*. He scored a good point initially by attacking the *Whig* for labelling its reply 'the Rev. P. Dorrian RCC against teetotalism and Dr Spratt'. This he characterized as 'a sophism steeped in the bitterest mis-representation' and in defence pointed out that he was not against teetotalism but intolerance. He disclaimed all intention of introducing conscience to prevent the advance of temperance and with regard to the comment about the church neglecting its duty or not being suited to dealing with the evil, he rejected such a conclusion. Referring to the efficacy of the sacraments, he maintained that should the elysium of teetotalism be obtained there would still be other sins. Then presumably revealing his real reservations about the methods used in the temperance campaign, especially the giving of the pledge, he noted that there could be another species of pledging besides that of giving it to postulants, some of whom might be totally unconscious at the time, and that a way could be found that would be more sensible and would possess a greater likeliness of establishing it on the solid 'basis of human respect'. He ended this rambling, diffuse and at times hard-hitting defence by declaring that he was no enemy to the cause of temperance and would be glad to see it prosper, if the system could be defined and explained so that all could understand what it was and thereby be solidly fixed on the basis of religion and of conscience.[61]

The *Whig* explained its refusal to publish his letter by reference to its length and content: 'it is just that sort of stuff which no gentleman would write, and none would wish to read'. This was certainly a severe and extreme judgement but since the *Vindicator* also published all the correspondence, Dorrian's final letter at least reached the Catholic public. What that public made out of the controversy, beyond discovering the simple fact that Dorrian had reservations about the total abstinence movement would be difficult to guess. It seems likely that much of the ink was wasted.

VIII

By the autumn of 1846, however, problems much greater than the presence or absence of clergy at temperance meetings concerned the people of Belfast. A year earlier diseased potato leaves in Waterford and Wexford heralded the arrival of the great hunger. Belfast and the

---

61 V., 26 Sept. 1846. This letter was dated 21 Sept.

surrounding area were not to suffer the misery, devastation and death which marked the progress of the famine in Cork, Kerry, Clare, Mayo and Donegal but they did experience hunger and fever on a scale hitherto unknown.

In the first winter after the failure of the potato crop, 1845-6, deaths did not occur from famine. But the signs were ominous; reports of fever in many parts of Belfast and of particular distress in Ballymacarrett were carried in the newspapers. The failure of the potato crop in 1846 led to real distress, suffering and deaths during the following winter and severe cold increased the risks to which the vulnerable were subject. Fever soon caused anxiety to the health authorities in Belfast and the management of the Fever Hospital felt obliged to call on the Board of Guardians to provide extra accommodation in the infirmary attached to the workhouse in view of the alarming increase of typhus.[62] Already the workhouse had more than a hundred extra inmates and the Guardians were forced to erect additional buildings. The typhus epidemic became serious early in 1847 and smallpox and dysentery added to the health hazards. By April the workhouse alone was dealing with almost 350 fever patients.

Before the end of 1846 soup kitchens had been established in Belfast by voluntary charity workers. Clergy of all denominations attended the meetings of the subscribers to the Belfast Relief Fund and Belfast contributed generously to the provision of relief for the distressed throughout Ireland. Although Thomas McClure, the secretary, remarked at the beginning of January that Counties Down and Antrim had been made by a gracious Providence exceptions to the widespread destitution, that situation was very shortly to change.[63] Soon nearly 1,200 families representing 6,500 people were receiving gratuitous relief and the number of applicants was daily increasing. Each week 15,000 quarts of soup and 22 cwt. of bread were doled out.[64] At a public meeting on 15 January Bishop Denvir, appealing for aid for the distressed in the worst hit districts of Ireland explained that a few days previously he himself had seen terrible affliction in parts of Down and Armagh, and went on to say that, though Belfast was better provided for, it was under daily siege from the hungry.[65] Denvir and Dorrian were appointed honorary members of the committee set up to administer the relief funds and both regularly attended its meetings.[66] It donated money to Ballymacarrett, Skerry, Racavan, Randalstown, Cushendun, Cushendall,

62 P.R.O.N.I. BG 7/A/5, 20 Oct. 1846.
63 N.W., 5 Jan. 1847.
64 V., 9 Jan. 1847.
65 V., 16 Jan. 1847.
66 N.W., 28 Jan 1847.

Ardclinis, Mourne and Rasharkin as well as to the worst hit areas in Donegal, Armagh, Cork, Mayo and other places. By the end of January, Ballymacarrett was reported to be experiencing scenes of frightening destitution, as at least three fourths of its 6,000 inhabitants were in a state of terrible poverty.[67] The Relief Committee decided to carry on after the announcement of government intervention and official financial help. The Belfast Soup Kitchen committee which estimated that 15,000 people were dependent on public charity reported in April that at least 1,000 families in the town had no other form of bed than a heap of filthy straw on a wretched floor.[68] Shelter was provided in converted buildings for the homeless poor and arrangements were made to provide industrial training for some unemployed youth. Following the harrowing scenes of hunger came the dread spectre of fever.

One of the victims of typhus fever was Dorrian's elder brother, Bernard, who was parish priest of Lisburn. Aged thirty eight, he had been ordained priest in 1832, had taught in the diocesan seminary and been parish priest of Ardkeen, before his appointment to Lisburn in 1840. In the course of his pastoral work he succumbed to the epidemic and died on 27 March 1847. Another death that was to affect the course of Dorrian's life had occurred in the previous month. William McMullan, the parish priest of Loughinisland, had died on 19 February but the vacancy was not filled for some time. Presumably Bishop Denvir did not wish to promote his experienced and energetic curate in the midst of such distress, when the pastoral demands on the Belfast clergy had been immensely increased.

The fever epidemic worsened in April 1847. By the end of the month there were 250 fever patients in the General Hospital, and the workhouse infirmary, which had been extended by the hasty erection of extra sheds, had a further 500.[69] In response to a public petition from the leading citizens of Belfast, the Lord-Lieutenant gave permission for the establishment of a Board of Health. Bishop Denvir declared at a public meeting that, apart from the patients being treated in the hospitals, there were 200 or 300 others suffering from fever.[70] Urgent appeals were made to the committee of the General Hospital to put up more sheds, but despite their best efforts, the speed with which fever spread outstripped the provision of emergency services. Temporary accommodation was provided in Barrack St. and at the Belfast Academical Institution. By mid-June there were 1,700 cases of fever being treated in the Belfast hospitals.[71]

67 N.W., 30 Jan. 1847.
68 N.W., 10 Apr. 1847.
69 N.W., 1 May 1847.
70 V., 5 May 1847.
71 N.W., 22 June 1847.

Writing to Archbishop Crolly, Denvir described the heart-rending scenes of suffering:

> Disease and destitution are prevailing here at present to an appaling [sic] extent. In the Hospitals of this Town there are not less than 1,400 patients labouring under fever, dysentery and small pox; whilst for want of accommodation, there are about 600 extern patients, all paupers, labouring under the same infectious disease . . . No sooner has the Board of Health finished a new wooden shed to contain 100 to 150 beds than it is crammed to suffocation, and yet there are poor creatures in fever to the amt. of from 10 to 25 stretched outside the porters' lodges daily seeking admission. The sheds require several days for their erection and therefore in order to keep pace with the progress of the increasing epidemic we have to admit 400 additional cases. The accounts from the seaboard portion of this Diocess from Mourne around to Coleraine, Ards excepted, are afflicting. Much of the interior also suffers severely.[72]

The fever peaked in mid-July. The hospitals reported 2,118 cases but thereafter there was a steady decline. A month later the number had dropped to 1,647,[73] but before the year ended more than 13,500 people had been admitted to the hospitals suffering from fever,[74] and perhaps one out of every five people in the town had been attacked by it.[75] Even in death the victims of the epidemic posed serious difficulties for the citizens of Belfast; the cemeteries were full and there was difficulty in obtaining suitable burial ground. On 13 July the mayor called a public meeting at the request of the Board of Health to decide what measures to take for the interment of the poor; the equally serious problem of how to cope with the destitute and fever-ridden who were being repatriated from Liverpool was also discussed. Bishop Denvir reported that he had visited Friar's Bush cemetery that morning and found that a corpse brought for burial could not be interred for eight or ten days because space was not available. Both Shankill cemetery and the grounds of the Belfast Charitable Society were also full.[76] A memorial was drawn up for presentation to the Poor Law Commissioners informing them that 'all the places formerly used have been so recently refilled and

72 Denvir to Crolly, 11 June 1847, D.C.D.A.
73 N.W., 20 July and 17 Aug. 1847.
74 During the years 1847-8 there were 14,975 cases officially reported as suffering from fever and dysentery and of these 2,487 died. In the cholera epidemic of 1849 there were 2,282 cases and 997 deaths. *Problems of a growing city*, p.175.
75 J. Bardon, *Belfast: an illustrated history*, (Belfast, 1982), p.99.
76 V., 14 July 1847.

crowded that it will be impossible by any vigilance to prevent the exposure of the bodies of persons dying by contagious diseases, to the great detriment of the public health', and asking the commissioners to allow ground which they were about to purchase to be used for the interment of those dying in destitute circumstances, at least during the present epidemic.[77]

It was under these sad and inauspicious circumstances that Dorrian took his leave of Belfast. On 29 July he was appointed parish priest of Loughinisland. Unlike his former colleagues, Hugh Hanna, George Crolly and Thomas Kearney, he did not receive a public presentation on his departure. He later explained that he did not like accepting personal gifts,[78] but he doubtless felt that to take money from parishioners when such urgent demands for the most necessary of causes were being made on their charity would be selfish, heartless and unchristian. His popularity with his people was not in doubt; they had given frequent proof of their esteem for him and of their trust in his judgement and ability. It was he whom they had chosen as treasurer to oversee the erection of a monument to Kieran Buggy, the popular young journalist who had succeeded Gavan Duffy as editor of the *Vindicator*, and who had died prematurely. They had long recognized his gifts as a public speaker as evidenced by the frequency with which he was called on to reply to toasts on formal occasions; as early as 1839, the *Vindicator* referred to him as a preacher 'eminently distinguished for his piety and glowing eloquence'.[79] They had for the most part shared his strong support for O'Connell and, when the chairman of the repeal movement in Belfast wanted to reassure the faithful, the great majority of whom had remained loyal to O'Connell after the split with Young Ireland, he chose to emphasise the example given them by Dorrian; he pointed out at a crowded meeting in September 1846 that the first subscription they had received was from 'a gentleman of the noblest dispositions' who would not contribute if he felt O'Connell was wrong, and then to loud cheers identified the donor as the pious, religious and exemplary clergyman, Revd Patrick Dorrian.[80] O'Connell had died on 15 May. His death in the midst of the famine seemed to mark for many Irish Catholics the collapse of their hopes and to induce a sense of numbness, defeat and near despair. With his political hopes blasted, Belfast in the midst of fever and much of Ireland experiencing the worst suffer-

77 P.R.O.N.I. BG7/A/6.
78 U.Ex., 25 Aug. 1870.
79 V., 23 Nov. 1839.
80 V., 23 Sept. 1846.

ings of the famine, Dorrian must have left for his new appointment in a sombre and melancholy mood. His transfer, however, brought him back close to Downpatrick and to his mother, who lived in the family home until her death in 1849.

3

Parish priest of Loughinisland

I

As its name suggests, the parish of Loughinisland derives its origin from a church built on an island in a lake. In fact three small churches were in existence as early as the thirteenth century — they were included in the taxation rolls of Pope Nicholas IV in 1306 — on this island, which is attached by a stone causeway to the shore. According to tradition an ecumenical arrangement survived the reformation settlement: both Catholics and Protestants continued to worship in the largest of the three churches until 1720. In that year Protestant worshippers were angered by being made to wait outside in the rain until Mass ended, and in a fit of pique built their own church with the help of their landlords, the Fordes, at Seaforde, and roofed it with the slates of the Loughinisland church.[1] For some twenty years the Catholics had no church; in 1740 they put up a very simple and unadorned building which lasted until the present church was completed in 1787.

Today Loughinisland wears a verdant, pastoral, almost lush appearance and its gentle, undulating hills enclosing the dark waters of the lake convey to visitors a sense of tranquil beauty and restful peace. But in the early nineteenth century the landscape presented a more varied picture; a much larger population strove to eke out a living from a patchwork of small farms, which were heavily tilled to provide food and rent. According to agricultural returns for 1850 the electoral division of Rosconnor, which embraced about half the townlands of the parish (which were also predominantly Catholic) contained 6 holdings not exceeding one acre, 43 holdings exceeding one but less then five acres, 166 holdings of between five and fifteen acres, 126 of between fifteen and thirty acres and 63 with more than thirty acres.[2] Though the vast majority of these farms are small, the number exceeding thirty acres is significant, and may reflect the

---

1 O'Laverty, *Down and Connor*, i, 25-6.
2 *Returns of agricultural produce in 1850*, H.C. 1851 (1404), 1, 108-9.

consolidation of holdings which had begun to take effect after the famine. A further study of these returns shows that cultivation was intense: among the 43 holdings ranging from one to five acres, 109 acres were under crops; wheat accounted for ten acres, oats for fifty, potatoes for seventeen and other crops — turnips, beans, cabbage, flax, barley and clover for the remainder. Similar proportions prevailed in the other smaller holdings, but, as the size of farms increased, the proportion of pastureland increased with them; of the 166 farms between five and fifteen acres 927 acres were given over to crops, and of the 126 between fifteen and thirty acres 1,431 acres were tilled. Among the largest group of farms the area under tillage was 1,862 acres. Heavy cultivation and the maximum use of all available land were essential to sustain the needs of a large dependent population.[3]

But the population of the parish had been falling slightly, even before the famine. The register[4] of marriages and baptisms shows a gradual decline from 1832. In that year there were 109 baptisms but in 1835 the number had fallen to 89 and although it rose again to 99 in 1839, it had fallen four years later to 65. After the famine the numbers never again reached their former level and for the decade of the 1850s remained at about forty. According to the 1861 census the parish contained 2,700 Catholics,[5] and it had probably declined to this level a decade earlier.

And indeed Loughinisland had been regarded as one of the largest and most prestigious parishes of the diocese from the late eighteenth century. In 1800, in the submissions of clerical incomes made to the government when the possibility of state payments of the Catholic clergy was being considered, it was placed alongside the bishop's parish of Downpatrick and five others at the top of the diocesan list.

It lay within the barony of Kinnelarty, which until the wars of religion in the seventeenth century had been ruled by the ancient Gaelic family of McCartan.[6] In 1737 a member of that family, Theophilus McCartan, was appointed parish priest of Loughinisland on his return from Paris, where he had studied at the Sorbonne. Ordained bishop of Down and Connor in 1760, he retained the parish of Loughinisland along with his mensal parish of Downpatrick and continued for the most part to reside in his former home. He died in 1778 and was interred in one of the island churches in the same vault as the last representatives of the heads of the ruling

3 Ibid., 109-11.
4 This register, which is preserved in the parochial house in Loughinisland, was begun by Revd William McMullan in 1805 and is the oldest of its kind in the diocese of Down and Connor.
5 O'Laverty, *Down and Connor* i, 9.
6 The name is variously spelt MacArtan, MacCartan and Macarten.

family. On his death William Stafford McCartan, his nephew, claimed the right of presentation to the parish of Loughinisland and submitted the names of two diocesan priests, both called John McCartan,[7] to Bishop Hugh McMullan for appointment. McMullan, who resisted this claim and argued that the right of appointment to an office vacated by the death of a bishop devolved on the Holy See, appealed to Rome for authority to settle the issue by a concursus among the candidates and, pending the Roman verdict, gave the administration of the parish to another McCartan, Patrick, who had been parish priest of Kilclief. Though the claimant to the right of presentation also appealed to Rome,[8] Patrick McCartan remained in possession of the parish until his death in 1805.

When the diocese of Dromore became vacant by the death of Bishop Patrick Brady in July 1780, the name of Patrick McCartan was among those mentioned for succession to the see. The guardian of St Isidore's Franciscan Convent in Rome, in supporting his candidature, tried to reassure the Holy See that the opposition McCartan had shown to the appointment of Hugh McMullan to Down and Connor derived from zeal and love of peace rather than from a lack of respect for the Roman authorities.[9] Though not appointed himself on this occasion, McCartan did not lose his taste for interference in others' appointments. When Hugh McMullan petitioned Rome for the nomination of his namesake, Patrick, as coadjutor in 1793, McCartan formed a caucus of priests who were opposed to this postulation, and these irreconcilables led by six McCartan priests under the nominal leadership of Paul McCartan, the last dean of Down, appealed to Rome against the appointment and the subsequent succession of Patrick McMullan. Ignoring Patrick's right of succession, they elected Paul McCartan vicar capitular after the bishop's death.[10] Archbishop Richard O'Reilly of Armagh had got wind of this opposition to the election of a coadjutor and promptly alerted Rome to the episcopal ambitions of Patrick McCartan, whom he classified as the ringleader and organizer of the dissidents.[11] Persisting in his refusal to recognize the new bishop, McCartan and two of his fellow rebels were disciplined for their

7 They were parish priests of Kilkeel and Saintfield respectively. Presumably they were cousins of William Stafford McCartan but the degree of relationship is not clear.

8 Hugh McMullan to Propaganda, and William and Orsola Stafford McCartan to Propaganda, A.P.F., S.C. (Ibernia), 15, ff 131r -132r. These letters are not dated but a note on the back indicates that replies were sent in March 1781.

9 Ibid. ff 393r-394r

10 O'Reilly to Propaganda, 31 Jan. 1794, S.C. (Irlanda, Fondo di Vienna),28, ff 141r-143r; clergy to Propaganda, 28 Oct. 1794, ff 170r-171r and 27 Nov. 1794, ff 172r-175 & 180r-181v.

11 O'Reilly to Propaganda, 23 June 1793, Ibid., f.83rv.

violation of canonical obedience, but Archbishop O'Reilly sought permission from Rome to remove the censures imposed on them, when they promised him that they would submit fully to their bishop.[12]

After Patrick McCartan's death in 1805 Bishop Patrick McMullan appointed his own nephew and namesake, William, parish priest of Loughinisland. William, unlike his uncle, had not been born in the parish but had moved there, to the townland of Seavaghan, when he was very young. Towards the end of his life the bishop himself returned from Downpatrick to live in Seavaghan, and it was there that William spent almost his entire ministry, a total of forty two years. Not long before his death Bishop McMullan applied to Rome for the title of dean for his nephew and also for permission to cede part of the parish of Downpatrick to Loughinisland.[13] But when death intervened without any decision being taken on either of these requests and William McMullan sought the intercession of Archbishop Curtis of Armagh, he was told to await the appointment of a successor through whom he could submit his petition.[14] In fact the succession to Down and Connor had caused Curtis considerable concern from the first mention of the appointment of a coadjutor in 1823 until William Crolly, the parish priest of Belfast, emerged as the clear choice of the clergy. Before the election took place Curtis confided to Archbishop Murray that the 'ostensible candidates' were William McMullan, whom he called the '*fav.te nipote*' and Crolly, and went on to remark (wrongly, in fact) that the diocese had been held and handed down from uncle to nephew by the McMullans for the last half century and was 'much exposed to continue so as the greater number of the parishes are actually in possession of the Bp's nephews or other near relatives, who will preponderate, probably, in the choice'.[15] Crolly, who eventually succeeded, also believed that McMullan had ambitions on the see, even though he had not figured among the three whose names emerged from the votes of

12 Ibid., 21 Dec. 1794, f.194rv.
13 In an undated draft of a letter presumably to Crolly, William McMullan stated that the application for the deanship of Down and 'another request' had been made by his late uncle on 28 Oct. 1823. A reply from Rome, dated 20 Mar. 1824, had explained that the requests were not granted because the name of the late dean had not been included in the petition. (D.C.D.A.)
14 Curtis to William McMullan, 5 Nov. 1824, D.C.D.A.
15 Curtis to Murray, 28 July 1824, D.D.A. Bishop Patrick McMullan was a distant cousin of his predecessor, Bishop Hugh. John McMullan, Hugh's nephew, was parish priest of Duneane; Edward McMullan and James McMullan, who may have been relatives of either bishop, were parish priests of Ballee and Glenavy, respectively. Daniel McMullan, a native of Loughinisland, was a curate in Kilmore.

the clergy.[16] McMullan remained parish priest of Loughinisland but was not appointed dean.[17]

Dorrian could only have felt honoured by being selected to fill a position long held by priests who had played such a prominent role in the diocese of Down and Connor. Either in a constructive or confrontational way, the incumbents of Loughinisland had been centre stage for nearly a century; the parish had been firmly stamped on the diocesan map. Though the administrative centre of the see had moved to the growing town of Belfast, Downpatrick and the neighbouring parishes were regarded as important appointments, since they were better equipped with churches than many other parishes. Dorrian's most immediate problem on arrival was the acquisition of a parochial house. The house in which William McMullan had lived was his own personal property and he had also owned about eleven acres of land. McMullan had bequeathed a sum of money to his executors to be invested for charitable purposes. He had also left £200 to be invested by them to provide an income for purchasing clothing for the poor of the parish and, adding £21 to a bequest he had already received, bequeathed £40 towards the improvement of the parish church.[18] Dorrian made an urgent appeal for a loan of £200 from McMullan's trustees to help him provide a parochial house, and apparently with success.

The summer of 1847 was a dismal and depressing time for a parish priest to take up office. The famine was then in its third year and, though places like Loughinisland had not witnessed the fearsome scenes of hunger, fever and death associated with the western parts of Ireland, they were far from immune from this dread visitation. If the resort of the starving to the local workhouse is a reliable index of the misery of an area, the hinterland of Downpatrick bore its share of misery. The Downpatrick workhouse had been opened in 1841 to cater for one thousand paupers (as the poor were then officially described); by the end of January 1847 it was still not full, unlike those of the neighbouring unions of Banbridge, Newtownards and Newry. But it had 790 inmates, of whom 100 were confined to bed in the hospital section.[19] The numbers were destined quickly to increase as the famine fevers, especially typhus and relapsing fever, which were rapidly spread by the malnutrition and weakness of the

---

16 After Crolly's election as vicar capitular he informed Cornelius Denvir in Maynooth that his 'former competitor and the most of his friends' had given him their votes. When Crolly called with William McMullan for the official papers belonging to his late uncle, he was received with great kindness. (Crolly to Denvir, 6 Nov. 1824. D.C.D.A.)
17 The chapter of Down and Connor was not restored until 1920.
18 P.R.O.N.I. D 2223/18/29.
19 D.R., 30 Jan. 1847.

poor and hungry, who were thrown together in workhouses or huddled around soup kitchens, began to claim victims alongside hunger. By early March the workhouse had almost reached its quota, with 938 inmates, and fever accounted for 36 cases.[20] The fever hospital in Downpatrick had been hastily enlarged by the addition of wooden buildings and by the beginning of May 142 patients were being treated in it.[21]

In January 1847 the government had introduced new relief measures. Divisions of the poor law unions were formed into units to administer funds, which were collected partly at local level and were augmented by grants from the Treasury. These committees were empowered to establish soup kitchens to feed the starving, and the *Downpatrick Recorder* reported on 13 February that the local relief committee had begun selling soup on alternate days at a halfpenny per quart, and bread and fuel at reduced rates. It claimed that 355 families, which it estimated at 2,000 persons, were receiving aid. Though Loughinisland was not specifically mentioned in the newspaper descriptions of local misery at this time, the situation there cannot have been much different from that of neighbouring Crossgar, where '240 persons' were reported in 'an utterly destitute condition',[22] and it must have produced its share of the 'miserable spectacles, greatly emaciated and reduced in strength'[23] who flocked to the workhouse in Downpatrick.

As the death rate began to increase in the Downpatrick fever hospital, the Board of Guardians decided to erect screens to prevent patients seeing the dead being removed. By the end of May 1847, however, the fever epidemic had begun to subside and, though it carried off the matron and five nurses, the number of patients had decreased to 114 and during the summer the epidemic ended. The summer months also brought a welcome decline in the numbers seeking refuge in the workhouse; by September less than half the places in it were filled but with the approach of winter and a further failure of the potato crop the poor and hungry seeking asylum in it increased again. During the nine months from January to October 1847 there were 864 cases treated in Downpatrick and of these 122 died; a further 102 died from dysentery, tuberculosis and other causes, giving a percentage mortality in fever cases of more than 14. About one half of those who died had travelled distances varying from seven to fourteen miles, only to find that the overcrowded wards actually increased the dangers of mortality. Before the

20 D.R., 6 Mar. 1847.
21 D.R., 1 May 1847.
22 D.R., 30 Jan. 1847.
23 D.R., 13 Feb. 1847.

temporary wooden sheds were erected as many as 120 were squeezed into accommodation fitted only to take 40 and two out of every three were forced to lie on the floors.[24] It would be wrong to assume, however, that these statistics represent the sum total of local misery. When one considers the emigration to Britain and America and the migration to places like Belfast of many who were already in the grip of fever, the need to augment these figures becomes apparent.

Though what Dorrian encountered in Loughinisland must have been a lot less frightening than what he left behind, the famine was still far from over. Throughout Ireland three million were still being fed from public soup kitchens and a further two years of the terrible visitation were still to come. Towards the end of the year the government pressed the Poor Law commissioners in Dublin to instruct their local agencies to make arrangements for the distribution of outdoor relief. But some Boards of Guardians, including those at Downpatrick, Newtownards and Lisburn, resisted this bitterly until compelled to yield. Representing as they did the property of each union, and bound by the *laissez-faire* economics which then prevailed, their views and reactions illustrate the frustrating difficulties that clergy and other socially-conscious workers must have felt at the time. This harsh mentality was typified by the Downpatrick Guardians who, in a petition to parliament, described outdoor relief as a mode of administering to the wants of the poor, totally subversive of and antagonistic to the spirit and essence of the Poor Law as first instituted, which constituted the workhouse the proper and only test of individual destitution. The practical operations of outdoor relief, they argued, involved as a necessary consequence increased sloth, idleness and profligacy — a breakdown of that spirit among the working class which should seek for support in the exercise of honest and independent labour.[25] They were ready to make any change of policy unnecessary either by increasing the size of the workhouse or by hiring larger buildings.

Though unsuccessful, the Downpatrick Guardians continued to fight a rearguard action against outdoor relief and to complain of the inability of landed property to bear the expenses of providing for increasing numbers of able-bodied paupers.[26] During the winter of 1847-8 the workhouses filled up again. By the end of 1847 there were 750 inmates in Downpatrick; three months later that number had increased to 804.[27] A similar cyclical pattern was experienced in

24 D.R., 30 Oct. 1847.
25 D.R., 11 Dec. 1847.
26 D.R., 18 Mar. 1848.
27 D.R., 1 Apr. 1848.

the summer of 1848 and in the winter of 1848-49. In the spring of the latter year fever struck again in the form of cholera and carried off hundreds of victims throughout the country. In Downpatrick its toll contributed to the burial problems of the town, and a committee had to be formed to acquire more cemetery space.[28]

The famine and the emigration which it provoked probably cost Ireland the loss of about two million of her people. Rural parishes with many small holdings and little employment to offer their sons and daughters except work on the land were particularly vulnerable. The rapid decline in the numbers of marriages and baptisms registered in Loughinisland points to the effects of emigration. During the three years 1849-51 an average of thirty five baptisms took place; ten years earlier, from 1839 to 1841, the average was ninety one. For the remainder of Dorrian's pastorate the figure did not increase much beyond the average. The population of the parish stabilized at about half or less of its pre-famine size.

Among the immediate consequences of the famine was a marked deterioration in the relations between landlord and tenant. During the terrible years of starvation and disease many tenants could not pay their rents, and some landlords seized the opportunity to amalgamate holdings which they regarded as too small, uneconomically farmed and overpopulated, and began to evict tenants who could not pay. The most extensive clearances took place in Connacht, but parts of Munster and Leinster were also affected. As a result tenants began to band together, either illegally to intimidate the landlords or their agents, or legally to form societies for self-protection. In Ulster the land system afforded more favourable terms to the tenant; by virtue of a long established custom he could sell his 'goodwill' (the contribution he had made to improving the value of the property) if he chose to leave his farm, and, as long as he paid his rent and fulfilled his terms of the agreement, he could not be evicted. The Ulster tenants did not feel that their grip on their homesteads was as precarious as those of their fellows in the other provinces, since few landlords tried to violate the custom. But ultimately this privilege was guaranteed only by custom and not by law, and the famine provided the opportunity for hostile landlords to test it. A failure to carry a bill to legalize this tenant right in 1847 indicated the weaknesses of the custom and the resistance of several landlords to it.[29]

Made aware of their vulnerability and angered by high rents and evictions in Monaghan and Donegal, tenants throughout Ulster began to agitate for greater security and protection. The movement

---

28 D.R., 1 Sept. 1848.
29 J.H. Whyte, *The Independent Irish party, 1850-9* (Oxford 1959), pp 4-12, 84-5.

was spearheaded by Dr James McKnight, the editor of the Presbyterian journal, the *Banner of Ulster*. The dominant element in it was Presbyterian but Catholics joined, and from several platforms clergy of both denominations spoke. The Ulster Tenant Movement joined forces with that of the south of Ireland in the short-lived, if hopeful, League of North and South in 1850; but three years later the League fell apart in the midst of recriminations over the policy of independent opposition in parliament.

Public meetings to defend tenant right were held throughout Ulster from 1848. At one held in Dungannon in April of that year letters of support were read from Archbishop Crolly and from the bishops of Clogher and Derry, and at another in Belfast in June 1850 several priests were present but none of those listed was from Down and Connor.[30] Two of the most prominent leaders in the south, Archdeacon Fitzgerald from Limerick and Fr O'Shea from Kilkenny, attended some of the rallies. But one Down and Connor pastor took a very active interest in the campaign. George Maguire, parish priest of Crossgar, often shared platforms with the prominent Presbyterian clergy, who supported the movement, John Coulter of Gilnahirk and John Rogers of Comber. At the great meeting for the farmers of Lecale and Kinelarty in Downpatrick on 1 January 1851 Maguire, who was accompanied by Peter Denvir, parish priest of Killough and Roland Magill, parish priest of Saintfield, made a stirring speech demanding an end to the landlords' abuse of their power, and the legalization of tenant right as a right, not as a favour, as Sharman Crawford's bill would have implied, nor as a boon from the landlords' bounty as Lord Londonderry had suggested.[31] A year later Maguire was one of the principal speakers at a large rally in Belfast, where he pointed out that he understood the harsh economic problems facing tenant farmers as he himself ran a farm which had not shown a profit for years.[32]

Bishop Blake of Dromore lent his support to the movement and Catholic clergy in the dioceses of Armagh, Dromore, Clogher and Derry shared platforms with their Presbyterian colleagues at local meetings. In Down and Connor the movement also counted the parish priests of Portaferry (James Killen), Ballee (Patrick Starkey), Duneane (Samuel Young), Loughguile (Henry McLaughlin), and the curates of Belfast (Francis McKenna and John Gallogly) and Randalstown (William McAuley) among its active supporters. Though Dorrian must have been aware of the gravity of the problem and must have experienced at first hand in Loughinisland the harsh

30 W.V., 15 June 1850.
31 D.R., 4 Jan. 1851.
32 W.V., 13 Mar. 1852.

necessities of emigration, he did not take an active part in the campaign. Apart from attending a meeting in Crossgar[33] to rally support for Sharman Crawford's candidacy for parliament, his name is not listed as being present at other local venues. Perhaps he thought the campaign was destined to fail or foresaw its collapse under the strain of sectarian tensions which were then building up. In later years he placed very little, if any, faith in the Whig/Liberal party and it seems likely that this distrust, evident during the repeal campaign, had been fortified by the recent Whig legislation and by the behaviour of the party during the famine.

The relations of the Ulster Catholics, especially those in Antrim and Down, with the Whigs became more uneasy after 1840. The Catholic minority was too small and insignificant to put up a candidate with any chance of success in Belfast or in Antrim and Down and so was compelled *faute de mieux* to support the Whigs. The Whigs in turn courted the Catholic vote at elections but, realizing that the Catholics had little political muscle, did not feel obliged to repay this support at other times. The tenant right movement in the north was dominated by Presbyterians and Whig supporters, and very likely because of Whig policy in other fields, which caused pain and embarrassment to Catholics, clergy like Dorrian held aloof from this particular agitation. For not only had Lord John Russell and his party antagonized Catholics by their inactivity during the famine and by their firm advocacy of mixed education at university level, but they had outraged Catholic feelings by their response to the establishment of the hierarchy in England in September 1850. Russell's letter to the bishop of Durham denouncing the mummeries and superstition of Rome gave great offence and his Ecclesiastical Titles Bill added a stupid insult to an unnecessary injury. Co-operation with local Whig/Liberals who had baulked at repeal, if they did not actively oppose it, and who were linked in broad ideological terms to Russell's party, may have been too much for an ardent repealer of Dorrian's ilk to take.

To exacerbate matters sectarian tensions were intensifying in Co. Down since a resurgent Orangeism claimed the right for its members to march in public. Ribbonism, which was primarily an agrarian secret society for the defence of tenants but had nationalist overtones, grew more sectarian in response to Orange demonstrations and the Orange assertion of Protestant supremacy. Its revival in the famine and immediate post-famine years had been confined mainly to Louth and Monaghan but lodges existed also in Co. Down. A skirmish between Ribbonmen and Orangemen in February 1849 at Katesbridge produced one fatal casualty and much

---

33 W.V., 8 May 1852.

bitter recrimination.[34] On the following St Patrick's Day a body of nationalists describing themselves as 'sons of shamrock', who had assembled in Downpatrick from the surrounding parishes to march on to Crossgar, was prevented from doing so by opposing Orangemen, and in the ensuing fracas a policeman and a woman were killed.[35] But an affray at Dolly's Brae near Castlewellan a few months later, when a pitched battle between Orangemen and Ribbonmen took place, terminated with three deaths, many serious injuries, damage to a Catholic church and parochial house, and the destruction of a number of Catholic-owned houses.

As the investigator appointed by Dublin Castle to inquire into the incident reported, the inexplicable element in the whole affair was the action of magistrates in tolerating a march of armed Orangemen through a district known to be decidedly hostile to them, and their refusal to disperse an armed mob of Ribbonmen who had gathered nearby to prevent or attack the march. That violence would occur in such circumstances, irrespective of who fired the first shot, was inevitable. Magistrates, in their capacities as Orangemen, had accompanied the procession and one of them had made no effort to dissuade the Orangemen from returning by the route where trouble was likely to flare up. There was no doubt about the victory; the investigator referred to the 'work of retaliation both on life and property by the Orange party . . . in a most brutal and wanton manner, reflecting the deepest disgrace on all by whom it was perpetrated or encouraged'. And he deplored the insensitive action of another magistrate, who was present on the occasion and who subsequently spoke at an Orange dinner in the presence of the high sheriff of the county, 'in very unfeeling terms, expressive of exultation at what had occurred, as a triumph achieved by the Orange body over an enemy deservedly punished'.[36]

The refusal of magistrates in South Down, all of whom were Protestant, to take informations against some of the participants in this strife induced a cynicism and disrespect for the law among many Catholics.[37] And though the chairman of these magistrates, Lord Roden, and the two others who emerged with little glory from the inquiry, were dismissed shortly afterwards, the refusal of the Lord-Lieutenant to respond favourably to a memorial from Belfast bearing the signatures of some 60,000 laity and 165 clergy for the dismissal of 'those who had rejected the informations' was regarded by many of those who had looked confidently to Dublin Castle for

---

34 W.V., 17 Feb. 1849.
35 W.V., 24 Mar. 1849.
36 *Papers relating to an investigation at Castlewellan into the occurrences at Dolly's Brae on 12 July 1849*, H.C. 1850, [1143], li, 331.
37 W.V., 22 Sept. 1849.

redress as bringing the law itself into disrepute.[38] Immortalized in balladry, the 'battle' of Dolly's Brae contributed a powerful emotive element to rising sectarian tensions in the Down countryside.

Illustrative of this feeling was the reaction to the establishment of a convent by the Sisters of Mercy in Downpatrick in 1855. The *Downpatrick Recorder* greeted the Sisters' arrival with the comment that 'they are greatly misrepresented if proselytism be not the chief task to be undertaken' and called on the Protestant ladies of the town to ensure that 'if Romanism is to be taught in all its strength . . . let scriptural religion be enforced more and meet the agents of Rome' and match their 'zeal, vigilance and activity' by visiting, comforting and relieving the poor with greater dedication.[39] A few months later the governors of the Down Infirmary and Fever Hospital explicitly forbade nuns to visit patients under their care[40] and by a unanimous verdict the Board of Guardians, who had charge of the workhouse, extended this prohibition to their inmates a year later.[41]

Though these tensions damaged good relations generally, they did not impinge on Dorrian directly. His parish was essentially rural and to some extent isolated from the trouble brewing in the towns. The chief and overriding concern of most of his parishioners was to eke out a living on their small holdings. In a situation dominated by such a basic issue there was little room for spectacular pastoral initiatives or innovations of any kind. The administration of the sacraments and the care of the sick and dying were the principal clerical activities. The parish itself was compact: from the church to the boundaries with other parishes was never much further than five miles. For some years before his death William McMullan had been assisted by a curate; for most of his sojourn in Loughinisland Dorrian had similar assistance and, though the Catholic Directory lists none from 1849 to 1851 and from 1859 to 1860, the signatures of other priests' names during these years on the baptismal and marriage registers suggest that he enjoyed the help of temporary assistants. Indeed, the presence of two priests for a relatively small parish of perhaps 3,500 reflects the increased proportion of priests to people consequent upon the enlargement of Maynooth, its increased grant and the decline of the population in the wake of the famine. Compared to Belfast, where the clergy were serving some 8,000 people each, the situation obtaining in Loughinisland was luxurious.

38 W.V., 19 Jan. 1850.
39 D.R., 5 May 1855.
40 D.R., 12 Apr. 1856.
41 D.R., 12 Dec. 1857.

The problem of poverty among his parishioners was still with him, but Dorrian had little or nothing of the social malaise of an expanding industrial city to contend with in Loughinisland. The one obvious outlet for his social apostolate lay in the field of education; there were many children to be saved from the handicap of illiteracy.

Since the 1830s primary schools were being erected throughout Ireland with the aid of state grants for building and equipment, books and teachers' salaries from the commissioners of national education. Though the original plan was to encourage mixed education of children of different religions and the commissioners were instructed to look more favourably on applications from the combined representatives of the Protestant and Catholic denominations rather than from the members of one church only, by the 1850s the system had virtually become denominational. Parish priests could appoint the teachers and, if they adhered to the rules of the national system which imposed certain inconvenient but not serious restrictions in the interests of supposedly combined schooling, could effectively control their local schools. Before the national system came into operation in 1832, landlords and clergy of all denominations had established schools. While many of them were not inadequate in the circumstances then obtaining, others survived in a very uncertain and precarious way. Some of those already existing applied for grants from the newly erected national board.

One of the early applications from Co. Down for aid to the board of national education came from Loughinisland. A school attached to the church at Tievenadarragh, which had been opened in 1800, was connected with the board in 1833 at the request of eight local Protestants and ten Catholics. Its enrolment stood at 60 boys and 36 girls and the parish priest, William McMullan, was the official correspondent. Like many such rural schools the equipment was minimal and the comments of the inspector on the teacher were unfavourable; he was described as intelligent but ignorant of the national system. McMullan felt obliged to hold classes in the church when additions were being made to the schoolhouse in 1839, but was reproved by the board for doing so.[42] Another school, established at Annadorn in 1829, was also connected to the board. Though Catholics outnumbered Protestant applicants for aid for it by sixteen to fourteen the correspondent was a prominent Protestant. But an inspector reported in 1836 that it seemed 'so badly kept that it is almost worse than useless'. Within a few years it was struck off by the commissioners after it had ceased to exist; the teacher had actually sold the school house in an attempt to pay off his debts.[43]

42 P.R.O.N.I. ED 6/1/3/1/35. The inspection was held on 25 April 1837.
43 Ibid., ED 6/1/3/1/47.

Dorrian decided to improve the facilities at Tievenadarragh school. He had a second storey built to it to form a separate school for the girls and in 1856 applied for aid to the board for the teacher's salary and books.[44] Provision was made for a small cloakroom and for partitioning off a part for a second room for a monitress, should that ever become necessary. The average attendance of girls was given as 80, though Dorrian indicated that he did not expect this figure to remain so high; the average attendance of boys in the lower part of the school was 59. The board accepted the application and awarded the young twenty-year-old teacher £17 as an annual salary in accordance with the grade given to her by the inspector. The teacher was assured of a further income of £24 yearly from the school, which was derived partly from school fees and partly from parish subscriptions. As in all schools at the time, when attendance was not compulsory, the numbers present varied greatly. When the inspector carried out his inspection on 2 December, there were only 42 girls present but he reported that of the 85 on the rolls, 71 had been attending daily during the previous month. He further pointed out that the school was badly needed and he expressed his confidence that it would be well conducted.

With the enrolment increasing Dorrian applied for a salary for an assistant teacher in the following summer. As promised he had laid out an additional classroom and claimed that he had counted 93 children present on one occasion. But the inspectors reported unfavourably on the size of the average attendance. A further application, however, was successful. When an inspector called on 26 October he found 64 girls out of the total enrolment of 148 in attendance, and the average figure for the previous six months had been 72. He added that the average attendance over the previous four months had been 76, and recommended that the request be granted. From 1 November 1857 the board recognized an assistant paid teacher.[45] So when Dorrian left Loughinisland in 1860 it was well equipped educationally by the very limited standards of the time.

The isolation of the parish had also been greatly reduced by the extension of the railway network. In 1859 the line connecting Downpatrick to Belfast was completed. The journey took one and a half hours and three trains ran daily. This not only facilitated passenger travel but also benefited commercially the countryside around Downpatrick. Grain, pork and butter which had formerly

---

44 Ibid., ED 1/16/196. The letter is dated 5 Nov. 1856. The dimensions of the school room are given as 26 feet long by 22 feet broad. There were three windows on each side and it was heated by a fire.
45 Ibid., ED 1/16/215.

been carted to Belfast could now be transported by train.[46]

In the same year Loughinisland acquired the dubious privilege of having the notorious rabblerouser, Thomas Drew, as its Anglican rector. Drew, a native of Limerick, who had been attached to Christchurch in Belfast for twenty six years, arrived in Seaforde in May 1859. During his sojourn in Belfast he had established an unenviable reputation as an eloquent preacher of the most extreme, lurid, anti-Catholic polemic, and had entertained and inflamed ever-increasing congregations with the most blood-curdling accounts of the cunning, diabolical and murderous designs of the Catholic priesthood. Immensely popular with the Protestant proletariat, he had embarrassed his superiors by disobeying the requests of the civil authorities to desist from preaching his provocative sermons in the midst of riotous situations, and the expected promotion that his popularity seemed to promise never came his way. A more hostile colleague Dorrian could not possibly have encountered, though, doubtless, they never had to experience the embarrassment of a personal meeting.[47]

II

Since Dorrian's departure from Belfast sectarian tension and animosity had continued to grow. Catholics were angered by the public protests made by Protestants against the rebellious spirit in the south in 1848, protests which spanned the Whig-Tory divide. The advocacy of mixed education by newspapers which reflected Protestant attitudes or the criticism of the endowment of the established church or the *Regium Donum* by those representing Catholic views widened the divisions. The *Whig's* support for what it regarded as liberal causes, whether in education or in the bill to inspect convents which it extolled as a laudable means of saving young women from 'the possible oppression and coercion of parents and priests', widened the

---

46 The prices of the fares were: first class single 3s. 6d., first class return 5s. 3d; second class single 2s. 4d, second class return 3s. 6d; third class single 1s. 6d; third class return 2s. 3d.

47 The variety and versatility of Drew's charges against Catholics bear witness to his colourful imagination if not to his judgement. On one occasion he bade his audience 'contrast the Protestant and Romish physiognomy, and say where you will find such depressed, saddened, drooping-looking men, as the poor, opressed, mentally aggrieved Romanist? Look at this scene around you, each of you. Look at the generous, cheerful, intelligent, and determined faces of the men — look at the faces of their lovely ladies — who have honoured us in such numbers at this great feast and say, where in Romishdom are such men, such women to be found? (Ul., 6 June 1855) After the outbreak of the riots in Belfast in 1857 Drew was forbidden by his bishop to preach in the open air.

gap further between Catholics and Presbyterians.[48] Theological differences and their insensitive, if not polemical, expression on such issues as the dogma of the Immaculate Conception, which was declared in 1854, heightened misunderstandings. Institutions either with a direct proselytizing aim or at least a planned side-effect such as Henry Cooke's Belfast Mission, which appealed to more than the Presbyterian working class, created constant misunderstandings and hostilities.

As the Catholic community increased in numbers and the economic strength of the leading shopkeepers, building contractors and merchants who serviced it grew, their demands for greater representation in public life heightened accordingly. Even the few Catholics — John Hamill, the landowner of Trench House, and Bernard Hughes, a prosperous baker, whose wealth matched that of the leading Presbyterian industrialists and businessmen — were excluded from the Harbour Commission, and the Port and Docks Authority. And despite his support for the Tories, Hamill was obliged to fight for any public office which came his way. Other rich Catholics — William Watson, who had made a fortune as a merchant in London and who owned much house property, and George Murney, a shopkeeper and tobacco importer — became Poor Law Commissioners by winning seats in the heavily Catholic Smithfield ward. The very low Catholic representation in the magistracy was the most deeply felt grievance. The strong suspicion and fear existed that a preponderant Conservative magistracy could not be trusted to administer the law with full impartiality. At a public meeting in 1856 of Catholics in Belfast it was disclosed that only two out of the thirty two magistrates were Catholics and a demand was made for a fairer proportion. The relevance of this request was soon verified by the commissioners appointed to inquire into the riots of 1857 who, when commenting on the disproportion (there was then only one Catholic magistrate), strongly recommended the appointment of others.

In July 1857 Belfast experienced the worst riots in its history to date. During the general election in April the windows of St Malachy's Church and of the non-subscribing Presbyterian Church in Rosemary Street, presumably to represent the religious poles of Liberalism, had been smashed by a Tory mob. But this was a small affray of no significance in comparison with later developments. On the evening of Sunday 12 July, Orangemen marched to Christchurch, which was situated at the interface between the Catholic Pound and the Protestant Sandy Row districts, to hear a provocative, anti-Catholic tirade from their Grand Chaplain, Thomas

---

48 A large representative meeting of Catholic laity took place in Belfast on 8 May 1854 to protest against the bill to inspect convents. (Ul., 10 May 1854).

Drew.[49] While the congregation was still inside the church, a 'tipsy' Catholic youth mischievously sporting an Orange lily drove into the midst of the Catholic crowd, which had assembled outside. This dangerous prank not only brought him physical injuries but unleashed the anger of the Catholic mob. From that evening both sides exchanged bricks, stones and gunshots nightly for a whole week. Two Catholic boys and a girl were seriously injured by gunshot wounds from Sandy Row. A street of houses belonging to the property developer, William Watson, was wrecked by a Protestant mob, and minor forms of damage, especially broken windows, were suffered by both sides. The outburst ceased after a week but tension was maintained at a dangerous level by the open-air sermons of anti-Catholic divines, especially the fiery Presbyterian, Hugh Hanna. Further violence occurred in September.

Two commissioners were appointed by the government to investigate the origin and character of the riots, to study the local arrangements for maintaining law and order in Belfast and to report to the Lord-Lieutenant. They examined some hundred and twenty witnesses, and, though they came to the conclusion that the 'first outrages on persons and property were committed by the Roman Catholics', they pointed out that 'it was a matter of little moment by whom the first blow was struck, or the first stone was thrown, or by which party the greater degree of violence was exhibited'. They placed the blame squarely on the Orange Order, which, by its annual July commemorations, disturbed the normally peaceful relations existing among the different religious groups in Belfast. The whole spirit of the Order was destructive of communal goodwill since it provoked 'a feeling of dominancy and insult on the one side and of opposition to its display on the other'. The preparations for the celebration of the Orange festival led to the polarization of the working class communities in the densely packed streets of the Pound and Sandy Row and the consequent belligerency of both camps:

> The celebration of that festival by the Orange Party in Belfast is, plainly and unmistakeably, the originating cause of these riots. These districts in Belfast are circumstanced in a peculiar manner to show the effect on the public mind of the annual celebration of a festival which is used to remind one party of the triumph of their ancestors over those of the other, and to

---

49 The *Northern Whig* commenting on Drew's sermons remarked: 'we regard a Dr Drew as encroaching civilization in conquered territory admires the last of the aborigines, making a final stand for the disappearing savagery which he believes, with his barbarous prejudices, to be eminently suited to reverence'. (29 Aug. 1857).

inculcate the feeling of Protestant superiority over their Roman Catholic neighbours.

While exonerating the magistracy from partiality, the commissioners made no such defence of the town police,[50] the local unarmed force which was under the control of the town council. Explaining that Belfast had only thirty constables in addition to one hundred and sixty town police, all of whom, with six or seven exceptions, were Protestant, they maintained that the latter force was an embarrassment and an encumbrance; disliked and distrusted by the Catholics it could not venture into the Pound district without the danger of being attacked and so had to be defended by the members of the national constabulary. Expressing strong reservations about the composition of the local force, a great many of whom were Orangemen, the commissioners called for a total change in its mode of appointment and management. Though sympathetic to the burdens to be borne and the dangers faced by the very small regular force of thirty constables, they nonetheless made clear their amazement at the inaction of this body when, without any provocation from the Pound, a Sandy Row mob of between two hundred and three hundred men, women and boys went on a rampage of destruction against a row of Catholic-owned houses in Albert Crescent.

The commissioners also emphasized the explosive potential of public preaching in the main thoroughfares of Belfast. Where hitherto open air services had been discreetly geared to the non-churchgoing and conducted unostentatiously in quiet parts of the town, a new development had occurred; the sermons of William McIlwaine, a Church of Ireland rector, which were scheduled for July were directed in a controversial manner at Roman Catholics, who were invited to attend by placards worded in 'not very complimentary terms' to their religious beliefs. Though McIlwaine was commended for cancelling his sermon during the July riots[51]

---

50 A special commission subsequently exonerated the constabulary from the charge of partiality. Claiming that the local force was more a hindrance than a help, it maintained that the constabulary, though small in numbers, attacked the mobs without distinction.

51 The *Belfast News-Letter* bewailed 'the alas, successful attempt — to prevent the excellent ministers of the Established Church preaching in the streets — far from the dens of the Romish mobs — the simple doctrines of the Cross to the ragged and benighted poor' as 'a still bolder and more audacious part of the great Papal movement to strike down to the dust the interest of Protestantism, and to exalt Romanism in this, the great mart and metropolis of Ulster'. (5 Sept. 1857) The Tory magnate, Lord Downshire, had no such sympathy for Hugh Hanna. When he heard of Hanna's threat to resume his open air preaching, he wrote to the Lord-Lieutenant describing Hanna as a notoriety-seeking ex-porter, who could not be dealt with as a gentleman and who deserved drumhead treatment, were it not that he would become a martyr. (Downshire to Carlisle, 24 Sept. 1857, N.L.I. MS 7624).

and for the mild and Christian spirit in which he gave his evidence, nevertheless the timing of a public service by a 'denouncer of Popery' — 19 July — demanded 'some exercise of cool judgement . . . to disconnect this announcement altogether from being more than accidentally connected with the state of things then existing in Belfast'. Unlike McIlwaine, Hugh Hanna was determined to assert his right to preach in public, despite the advice of the magistracy and 'the almost certainty of a scene of conflict, violence and perhaps bloodshed'. In consequence on Sunday 6 September 'one of the most disgraceful riots . . . and one of the most alarming in its extent over the whole town' took place.

Undeterred by the bloodshed and indeed interpreting all opposition to street preaching as a violation of Protestant rights by 'the audacious and savage outrages of a Romish mob', Hanna had carried out his plans at the cost of serious disturbance. The commissioners clearly distinguished between the inoffensive forms of public sermons before 1857 and those which followed from Hanna's exercize of his 'abstract right', which was in effect the right 'to insult your neighbour, and to proclaim him of a degraded class'. Translated into a question of rights, Hanna's evangelism further polarized the religious communities: 'the pious and weak minded of the Protestant inhabitants were easily persuaded that the question at issue was whether Protestant worship was to be put down by violence, while those of the Catholic inhabitants were as easily persuaded that the question now was whether Belfast was henceforth to be proclaimed as a Protestant town, in which Roman Catholics could barely find sufferance to live in a state of degradation'.

The commissioners also regretted the creation of a Gun Club among the residents of the Pound and a Protestant Defence Association among those of Sandy Row, but both these developments were short-lived. They concluded by expressing the hope — unhappily destined to be unfulfilled — that the worst had been seen of such riots in Belfast.[52] In the event Belfast became the riot capital of Ireland but its pre-eminence in this field should not be allowed to obscure or conceal the similarly dubious if much less significant distinction achieved by other towns in the diocese of Down and Connor.

Already in June 1853 the arrival of two Rosminians to conduct a parish mission in Lisburn had led to unpleasant scenes of violence and disorder. Though John McKenna, the parish priest, included several prominent Protestants among those whom he entertained at a public dinner to mark the opening of the mission, this gesture did not mollify the working class Orangemen who chose to regard the presence of the missioners as a threat to the character of their town.

52 *Report of the Commission of Inquiry into the Belfast riots*, H.C. 1857-8, xxvi, 3-17.

As the mission came to an end on 1 July an Orange mob paraded through the town screaming abusive remarks at the visiting clergy (and, for good measure, at the absent pope) and hurling stones at the church. Despite the intervention of the police and two companies of soldiers, the parish priest and one of the visiting preachers escaped serious injury only by making a very quick dash from the church to the parochial house.[53] Bishop Denvir later reported that Orangemen from outside Lisburn had gathered there armed with daggers and loaded pistols determined to assassinate the missioners and destroy the church and parochial house but the wife of one of the conspirators, in a fit of remorse, communicated the plan to him, and the pastor, having become aware of it, sought the protection of a reluctant magistracy. The local landlord, taking his cue from the enraged Orangemen, then brought an ejectment order against the parish priest on the grounds that the lease of the church, school and parochial house had expired.[54] But this threat to deprive the Catholic community of its property, valued at £6,000, and leave it without even remotely suitable sites for re-establishing a church, home and school did not materalize. Missions in Downpatrick and Belfast had also provoked displays of Orange displeasure, though on a much reduced scale. The great Protestant religious revival of 1859, though it claimed a few Catholic converts, did not affect religious relationships significantly.

III

During Dorrian's thirteen years absence from Belfast the Catholic population there had grown in proportion to the expansion of the town. Interdenominational relations had, however, continued to deteriorate. Competition for jobs among the unskilled, the revival of Orangeism and the suspicions of Protestants about the growing strength of the Catholic Church in Ireland, as evidenced by the building of churches, schools and religious institutions, contributed to increasing misunderstanding. The land agitation which promised to bridge the religious divide by emphasizing the common problems and opportunities of the tenant farmers quickly declined and lost its unitive thrust. The limited co-operation that had existed in the 1840s decreased in the 1850s.

These developments did not directly impinge on Dorrian in Loughinisland. He was free to concentrate his energies on the immediate pastoral duties of his parish, though his reputation as an

---

53 Ul. 22 June, 6 July 1853.
54 Denvir to Kirby, 12 June 1854, A.I.C.R.

eloquent preacher ensured that he was invited from time to time to give special sermons elsewhere. The best testament to his success in the parochial ministry was of course the place accorded him by the parish priests of Down and Connor in their choice of candidates for the episcopacy. In the absence of any other evidence his selection indicates their awareness of his pastoral dedication and zeal. Loughinisland during his term as parish priest offered little scope for pastoral experiments; a rural parish with a declining population and many of its people living at subsistence level only afforded room for a modest consolidation of resources. The provision of improved standards of education facilitated a deeper understanding of religion, and the acquisition of skills at work by those fortunate enough to require them. Dorrian ensured in Loughinisland, as he was to do later in Belfast, that his people were given every possible chance to better their lifestyles. The parish was homogeneous and manageable, and presented no unusual challenges, and so the tenor of life for the parochial clergy must have been even and unruffled. The move as coadjutor bishop to Belfast, with its taxing pastoral, political and social problems, from the calm and placid atmosphere of Loughinisland was a challenge capable of testing the ability, stamina and courage of the most resolute priest.

4
Coadjutor bishop of Down and Connor

I

The invitation to the parish priests of Down and Connor to assemble on 29 November 1859 and select the names of three candidates whom they considered suitable for appointment as coadjutor bishop of the diocese was the culmination of a long and frustrating campaign conducted by Archbishop Dixon of Armagh, Archbishop Cullen of Dublin and the congregation of Propaganda in Rome (which had charge of Irish ecclesiastical affairs) to remedy the pastoral neglect of Belfast. As early as 1851 Cullen, then archbishop of Armagh, had, in the course of a letter surveying the state of his ecclesiastical province, drawn the attention of Propaganda to Denvir's neglect of his duties; he pointed out that, though Denvir was not old, he had not visited some of his parishes for five or seven years, that he provided only three priests to serve the 50,000 Catholics of Belfast, and that in consequence the Catholic people were very discontented. He suggested a remedy: the provision of a coadjutor.[1] Though this was not the first complaint Rome had received about Down and Connor, it carried enormous weight, coming as it did from one who enjoyed the confidence of the senior officials of Propaganda. And in fact, in this brief reference to Denvir — and the letter contained unflattering remarks about other bishops — Cullen put his finger on the charges that were to keep recurring for the remainder of the decade.

The estimate of the Catholic population of Belfast — 50,000 — was undoubtedly too high. The census of 1861 revealed that it was 41,000, which was one third of the total population of the town, and as the same proportion had obtained in 1834 the presumption is that

---

[1] Cullen to Mgr Barnabò, 20 Sept. 1851, A.P.F., S.C.(Irlanda), 30, ff 706r-707v. In response to a request for information consequent on previous charges, Denvir had assured the cardinal prefect that he had seldom been absent from his diocese without a just cause, that he had become a commissioner of Charitable Bequests at the request of the two primates and that thereby they had helped win an increased grant for Maynooth. (Ibid., Denvir to Fransoni, 2 Jan. 1846, S.C. (Irlanda), 28, ff 644r-645v.)

at the beginning of the 1850s it stood at about 30,000. Throughout the diocese the clergy had continued to erect churches in districts where none had hitherto existed or as replacements for older, decrepit or unsuitable buildings. But since the opening of St Malachy's Church in 1844 no further provision had been made for the Catholics of Belfast, and the three churches were grossly inadequate for the ever-increasing congregations. In 1850 Denvir had permitted the St Vincent de Paul Society to establish a conference at St Mary's Church. This body of laymen which collected money to help the poor and needy soon established a second branch at St Malachy's Church and proceeded to tackle the problem of education for the large number of children for whom schools under Catholic management were not available. In 1852 it set up schools at Chapel Lane beside St Mary's Church and at Ligoniel.[2] In 1855 it made provision for the children at the docks and for the expanding suburbs along the Falls Road. The Society undertook to pay the manager's share of the costs of running these schools, and to cover the fees of poor children, in addition to its more normal work of looking after the victims of accidents and sickness from the mills and attending to the myriad needs of 'the penniless and friendless' who gravitated to Belfast.[3] And it also sponsored the publication of translations of French Catholic tracts, claiming to have put 80,000 into circulation to counter the saturation campaign then being conducted by Protestant sects.

A Ladies Charitable Society did similar work for Catholic girls, and though it did not have the resources to establish schools, made arrangements for catechetical instruction for them. The Sisters of Mercy came to Belfast in January 1854 and a few months later established a school for girls at Callender Street, attached to their residence at Donegall Square North. However, only a minority of children were able to avail of these schools; lay voluntary efforts, however laudable, could not make adequate provision for the thousands requiring education.

Denvir either did not grasp the full magnitude of the pastoral problems of Belfast or he thought they should be solved slowly and gradually as finances permitted. He himself related how in the spring of 1845 he was laid low by 'an attack of nervous and bilious fevers . . . which had well nigh proved fatal'[4] and bouts of illness seemed to come his way frequently. Though he continued to attend the meetings of the board of the General Hospital and patronized the publi-

---

2 By Aug. 1853 the society had 1,000 pupils in its Sunday schools. (Ul., 3 Aug. 1853.)
3 *Society of St Vincent de Paul Centenary*, (Belfast, 1950) p.9.
4 Denvir to Cullen, 20 Dec. 1845, A.I.C.R.

cation of cheap Catholic versions of the bible, he tended to withdraw more and more to his study and his parishioners rarely saw him officiating in the churches. He was more effective as a public relations officer for the Catholic community with civic bodies than as its effective leader, and through a combination of general timidity and particular fear of Orange reactions was unwilling to take initiatives to cope with his pastoral problems.

In 1853 he accepted an invitation to join the board of national education. This step annoyed the bishops who were opposed to the national system, and especially Cullen, who commented testily to his confidant, Tobias Kirby, about Denvir's intervention in other people's affairs in Dublin despite the deplorable state of religion in Belfast. When Propaganda heard of this development it promptly sent him a warning letter, and to Denvir's justification of his decision to join the board on the grounds that his vicar general and clergy had advised him that Ulster should have at least one Catholic commissioner who could look after their interests in the appointment of inspectors and in the examination of text books, Rome replied sharply, reminding him that before taking this step he would have done better to consult more widely, especially among the prelates who were highly regarded for their pastoral zeal for the Catholic education of youth.[5] Rome could not understand all the nuances involved in the national system and so took its cue from Cullen who was decidedly hostile to it. Consequently Denvir did his own reputation there an immense disservice by accepting this office, and left himself more vulnerable to any charges that could be made against his administration in Down and Connor. And as a result of the adverse comments filtering through to Rome from Cullen and others, he was invited by a letter bearing the authority of the pope to respond to a set of particular accusations about the maladministration of his diocese. In reply he wrote a long apologia to Tobias Kirby, the rector of the Irish College and agent of the Irish bishops in Rome, to be translated or passed on to the appropriate channels.

Taking up the various points that had been relayed to him and beginning with the allegation that he had neglected the educational apostolate, he replied that schools existed in every parish of the diocese, that his diocesan seminary, on which he had spent much of his own personal money, was turning out sufficient students to fill the diocesan places at Maynooth and that shortly they would have enough priests for their own diocesan needs; there were schools for

5 Propaganda to Denvir, 31 Mar. and 12 May 1853 in A.P.F. *Lett.*, 343, ff 211rv and 358v, and Denvir to Cardinal Fransoni, 17 Apr. 1853, S.C. (Irlanda), 31, ff 431r-432v. Kirby had passed on Cullen's angry observation that Denvir's joining the board had given 'una specie di sanzione a tutte le birberie della commissione' and the suggestion that he should be advised to attend to his own affairs. Ibid., f. 425v.

the poor scattered throughout the town[6] and he had ground taken beside St Malachy's Church for another one, but the crushing debt of £6,000 which remained after the completion of that church (of which £500 had still to be paid off) had prevented him from building it; on Sundays and holy-days the various confraternities and the Society of St Vincent de Paul assisted the clergy in teaching religion to the children, and he himself, when examining the candidates for confirmation the previous year, had found 'the most satisfactory preparation' had been made for it. To the suggestion that he had consulted in every respect for his own convenience and not that of the people, he pointed out that after paying his ordinary living expenses he spent all his superfluous money on the upkeep of his curates, seminary and churches, in contributing to charities, and in helping to support two clergy, whose parishes could not adequately do so. Regarding his dilatoriness in inviting religious orders to the diocese, he referred to 'the diabolical spirit of antipathy prevailing here' against them and went on to explain the intensity of the Orange animus towards Catholics, pointing out that nearly all the great land owners in Antrim and Down shared this anti-Catholic hostility; he illustrated this antipathy by referring to murders of Catholics planned in Orange lodges and in particular to that of the missioners in Lisburn in the previous year, which was averted by information being secretly passed to him which enabled them to obtain the protection of the police and magistrates. Orangemen had also destroyed a school which was run by the St Vincent de Paul Society.[7] But despite the perpetration of murder by Orangemen, none of them had been hanged, because the sheriff, an Orangeman, selected the juries and thereby effected acquittals.[8]

Cullen, who was much more intrepid than Denvir and always ready to vindicate ecclesiastical rights, decided, almost certainly without Denvir's knowledge, to try to remedy one of the deficiencies of the Belfast pastoral scene. Accordingly he consulted his friend, William Monsell, a landlord, convert and generous benefactor of the church, about helping to finance a Vincentian foundation in Belfast. Expressing confidence in the generous response of the Belfast Catholic community, he observed that there were twelve Vincentians attached to their church at Phibsboro and added the hopeful but unrealistic prediction that 'Dr Denvir, as he is a very timid man, will look with coldness on this undertaking, but he will let others carry it

---

6 He stated that the Donegall St. schools had 1,200 pupils, the school near St Mary's over 400, and that large numbers attended the school attached to the orphanage and the one run by the Sisters of Mercy.

7 This was the school at Ligoniel. 500 Orangemen marched in procession to it and destroyed it. (Ul., 7 June 1854).

8 Denvir to Kirby, 12 June 1854, A.I.C.R.

out'. The project, however, did not materialize; the superior of the Vincentians decided that, if his order were to be established in Belfast, it would be restricted to parochial activities and prevented from carrying out its particular work of conducting parish missions, and so declined the offer.[9]

By 1855 no changes had been effected. Denvir was due to pay his *ad limina* visit to Rome in that year to submit his report on the state of religion in his diocese. But he excused himself from making the journey, partly because of legal commitments at home[10] and partly because of the beneficial effects his presence would have on public collections which at that time were being made throughout Belfast for a new convent, schools and orphanage for the Sisters of Mercy. The outlay, £6,000, was formidable and, as the initial appeal had brought in less than £1,000, the liquidation of the remaining debt threatened to be a slow, tedious and burdensome task.[11] In his report on the diocese which he forwarded to Propaganda, Denvir admitted that more than three years had elapsed between his current triennial visitation (begun in 1853) and the previous one. He again emphasized the difficulties of obtaining sites for churches and schools, noted that the clergy were diligent in conducting Sunday schools in association with lay members of confraternities, but as the report followed a prescribed pattern, he did not discuss the peculiar problems of Belfast.[12] However, his omission of the customary and indeed obligatory visit to Rome, meant that an opportunity for explaining his case more fully had been lost.

Anxiety about the situation in Belfast was mounting in another quarter as well as in Rome and Dublin. Joseph Dixon had succeeded Cullen as archbishop of Armagh in 1852. By temperament he was timid and diffident, but conscientious to the point of scrupulousness in fulfilling his duties. When he felt obliged to take action, he did not hesitate, and his impulsive, excitable nature tended at times to make him over-react. The recipient of many letters of complaint about the pastoral neglect of Belfast, he decided to pass on his apprehensions

9 Cullen to Monsell, 16 and 26 June 1854, N.L.I. MS.19337(7)
10 James O'Hagerty, parish priest of Ballymoney, had left money in his will for the upkeep of a curate in that parish and for the education of diocesan seminarians. His brother contested the will and a prolonged case in chancery followed. Denvir, as executor, was anxious not only to claim his just rights under the will but also by so doing to prevent others from being intimidated by fears of similar court action from leaving property for charitable purposes.
11 Denvir to Kirby, 20 Nov. 1855, A.I.C.R.
12 Referring to 'obstacles to the exercise of his office' he explained: 'Multa vero obstant ex parte Acatholicorum qui lethales inimicitias et odio foventes saepius pro posse impediunt ne v.g. loca commoda Ecclesiarum et scholarum comparentur'. (Denvir to Cardinal Fransoni, 19 Nov. 1855, A.P.F., S.C.(Irlanda), 32, ff 579r-582r.)

and worries officially to Rome. And he did so in a devastating way. Estimating the Catholic population more accurately than other critics at 40,000 and noting that only four priests served this multitude, he insisted that it was a physical impossibility for half this number to be confessed; indeed it was scarcely credible that a third frequented the sacraments. He added that one priest took his turn each week attending the dying and by day and night was rushing to sickbeds to prepare for death people who had not been to confession for twenty or forty years. His recommendation was that Cullen, or he and Cullen together, should be deputed to conduct a visitation in Belfast and suggest a suitable remedy to the Holy See.[13]

This picture was reinforced a short time later by Cullen himself; in fact he blackened it considerably for he informed Propaganda that he had been assured by the president of the St Vincent de Paul Society among others that the Catholic population of Belfast was 50,000, and he added a new charge, which had been relayed to him by a missioner, who had spent some time in the diocese, to the effect that the spiritual desolation of the countryside was no less great than that of the town.[14] Dixon followed up his intervention by seeking in effect to enlist Kirby on his side by referring to the public expression recently given by the *Ulsterman* (a Belfast Catholic paper) to the shortage of clergy in Belfast and by expressing the hope that Rome would soon end this enormous evil which must be occasioning the ruin of hundreds of souls.[15]

The Roman response to this barrage was to tell Denvir that the pope now wished him to make the *ad limina* visit, which he had already been allowed to postpone, as soon as possible.[16] Cullen and Dixon were invited to pass on any suggestions they might have for the good of the diocese. Denvir in reply pleaded the difficulty of the prolonged law suit, which was still unresolved but which he hoped would be settled about mid-February.[17] Two events intervened to cause further delay. The law suit went badly and he wanted to be present to salvage something when the disputed property came up

---

13 Dixon to Cardinal Barnabò, 16 Oct. 1856. Ibid., 33, ff 128r-129v. This jeremiad climaxed with the pained exclamation: 'Uno verbo, non existit in universo mundo, in quantum scire possum, oppidum vel civitas quae tanta egestate spirituali laborat ac Belfastia; et hoc in Hibernia; et in civitati opibus florente'. He exonerated Denvir from personal culpability. Timidity lay at the root of his problems: 'Doleo ex intimo corde hoc scribens: episcopus enim Dunensis est mihi amicissimus; est quoque vir bonus et pius sed timoribus plenissimus ubi non est timor'.
14 Cullen to Barnabò, 19 Nov. 1856, Ibid., 32, ff 947r-949r.
15 Dixon to Kirby, 5 Nov. 1856. A few days later the *Ulsterman* made further damaging comments, this time on the educational neglect of the Catholic poor of Belfast. (14 Nov. 1856).
16 Propaganda to Denvir, 2 Dec. 1856, A.P.F., *Lett.* 347, f.613r.
17 Denvir to Barnabò, 26 Dec. 1856, Ibid. S.C. (Irlanda), 32, f. 984 rv.

for sale, and he also wanted to place his newly ordained clergy and conduct some confirmation ceremonies before setting out. Consequently, he begged permission to postpone his visit till the autumn.[18] And Dixon reinforced this plea by passing on the information that the bishop had become seriously ill through 'exposing himself to wind and rain in an effort to save St Malachy's Church from the Orangemen'.[19] But the Holy See had grown impatient and would wear no further excuses. On receipt of the first request he was told to make adequate provision for the government of the diocese and proceed to Rome,[20] and, though Dixon's request was favourably received and a further delay was granted,[21] Denvir had set out before it reached him, and he arrived in the eternal city in May. But before leaving Belfast he had already received another sign of Rome's displeasure: he had been told to resign from the board of national education.[22]

When he presented himself at Propaganda he was at once confronted with the charges of pastoral neglect of his own parishioners. But he defended himself, disputing the figure of 60,000 for the Catholic population by producing the relevant volume of the latest census returns showing that the total population stood at 92,000 and claiming that the Catholic share did not exceed, did not indeed equal, a third of that figure.[23] He further maintained that, despite his previous shortage of clerical manpower, he had then nine priests in his parish, all of whom were under forty years of age, and as a consequence of the enlargement of Maynooth did not foresee any difficulties in that respect in the future. He also defended his position on the religious orders; he was the first bishop in the northern province to invite them to give missions, but the Protestants had tried to murder them in Lisburn, and only during the previous Holy Week they had tried to destroy his churches and schools, the nuns' convent and his own house.[24]

18 Denvir to Kirby, 14 Feb. 1857, A.I.C.R. He also referred in this letter to a severe attack of typhus fever which he had caught recently when attending a funeral.
19 Dixon to Kirby, 25 Apr. 1857, Ibid. St Malachy's Church was attacked during the general election which had taken place on 3 April. Dixon believed that this illness was so serious that it had brought him to the brink of the grave.
20 Propaganda to Denvir, 4 Mar. 1857, A.P.F., *Lett.*, 348, f. 127r
21 Kirby to Dixon, 23 May 1857, A.D.A.
22 Propaganda to Denvir, 21 Feb. 1857, A.P.F., *Lett.*, 348, f. 99rv. In view of the dangers to faith that could arise from the plan to introduce schools depending exclusively on the national board, Denvir was told he should resign. This was a reference to a plan to erect more model schools.
23 According to Kirby's letter to Dixon of 23 May 1857, Denvir claimed that the population was 27,000 and that he had 400 converts annually, but writing four days later he quoted Denvir as saying that the population was 30,000.
24 Denvir to Barnabò, 10 June 1857, A.P.F., S.C. (Irlanda), 33, ff 346r-347v.

During his sojourn in Rome he also tried to secure an honorary doctorate of divinity for George Crolly, a Down and Connor priest who was a professor of theology in Maynooth. Only two years previously Crolly's theological views had been condemned in Rome as gallican and, though Crolly was anxious to rehabilitate himself and also enjoyed Dixon's support in his quest for this honorary degree, Rome regarded the matter as injudicious, and Denvir's involvement in it was doubtless interpreted as an indication of his deficient judgement.

However, the immediate concern of Propaganda was to get at the truth about Belfast, and faced with the conflicting evidence about the population and the clergy serving it, the congregation wrote to Dixon requesting him to obtain accurate and reliable information and forward it before Denvir left Rome.[25] Dixon promptly did as requested, and duly reported that he had consulted a prudent and trustworthy parish priest of Down and Connor.[26] This confidant had no hesitation in estimating the Catholic population at a minimum of 50,000 and making due allowance for Denvir's shortage of clergy, insisted that only four were 'acting as recognized curates' in the bishop's parish. Only these four attended the sick calls, except in cases of necessity, and the others — there were then four of them — were just recently ordained and, as they awaited an appointment, said Mass and heard confessions but received no pay.[27] To Dixon's query about the possibility of establishing another presbytery with six additional priests, his correspondent replied that some solution of that kind was essential in the interests of religion,[28] and predicted that, if Belfast were divided into districts under the control of particular priests, the financial response of the people would be generous. Two further churches were required, one at the quays and the other along the Falls Road. Though he thought it not unreasonable to suppose that the faith of the children might be in danger, he had not heard of any case of neglect. Dixon accordingly recommended that Belfast should be divided into at least two districts, that Cullen and he should be empowered to see that within a year a presbytery was ready for four priests, with two others to join it within two years, and that Denvir and his clergy be exhorted to erect two more churches.

25 Propaganda to Dixon, 28 May 1857, Ibid. *Lett.*, 348, f. 284r.
26 Dixon to Kirby, 10 June 1857, S.C.(Irlanda), 33, ff 358r-359v.
27 Dorrian later confessed that he did not understand why some young priests were left so long without a charge. All he could say was that Denvir 'in modo agendi fuit valde tardus'. (Dorrian to Propaganda, 25 Mar. 1867. Ibid., S.C.(Irlanda), 35, ff 1063r-1068v.)
28 'I *know* that the words of the prophet are constantly being fulfilled: "parvuli petierunt panem et non erat qui frangeret iis"'.

Hot on the heels of this damaging missive came an equally damaging one from Cullen. Quoting a reliable source about the spiritual destitution of the diocese in general, he went on to contest Denvir's population estimates (which a prominent Belfast layman had told him were based on the number of baptisms) by pointing out that Catholic adults came into the town from the neighbouring counties in search of work. Repeating the facts about the small number of parish clergy serving a large parish, he remarked that Denvir had ordained four priests in Dublin before his departure for Rome but he thought these new priests were mere supernumeraries in Belfast, and that the increase in clergy was therefore only apparent. Giving substantially the same recommendation as Dixon about churches, but postulating an increase of clergy to fifteen and adding that something should be done about the country parts, he ended on a very pessimistic note: he feared that Denvir was so timid and easily frightened that he would do nothing.[29]

Propaganda wasted little time in acceding to this request. Denvir was told in effect that it did not accept his estimate of the population of Belfast, and was urged to increase the number of his clergy to fifteen, to build two more churches and to divide his single parish into three or at least two parts. Though this pill was sugared with an anodyne reference to his zeal for religion and good dispositions to the Holy See, the import of the instruction was clear and unmistakeable. Dixon and Cullen were appointed watchdogs of this operation and Denvir was requested to forward details of his response to this order.[30]

But, in the event, Denvir justified the pessimism of the two archbishops. A few months later Propaganda was obliged to commission them to prod Denvir into carrying out its last instruction.[31] They immediately wrote to him 'insisting on something being *actually* done by the first of May', and Denvir promptly went to meet Dixon in Drogheda and promised, despite complaints about the difficulty of finding priests, to establish a new presbytery in Belfast and to have two priests residing in it before 1 May.[32] By the end of that month Dixon had some cheerful news for Propaganda. Denvir

29 Cullen to Barnabo. 5 July 1857. Ibid. ff 612r-613v.
30 Propaganda to Denvir. 24 July 1857. *Lett.*, 348, f.420rv.
31 Propaganda to Dixon and Cullen. 13 Mar. 1858, Ibid. 349, ff 164r-165r. This order was probably provoked by a translation of another letter of complaint about the pastoral situation in Belfast, and in particular about the neglect of the Catholic children in the deaf and dumb institutions to which the *Ulsterman* had drawn attention. On 3 Mar 1858 the *Ulsterman* published a letter from an Irish convert resident in London declaring that in all his wanderings he had never visited a place where the Catholic population was so inadequately provided with churches.
32 Dixon to Kirby, 30 Mar. 1858, A.I.C.R.

had acquired a presbytery near St Malachy's Church and placed four priests in it. The number of clergy engaged in the daily visitation of the sick had been increased and the bishop had hopes of obtaining, or perhaps had already obtained, a site for a new church. Dixon suggested that Propaganda should encourage Denvir to invite the Vincentians to conduct a mission in Belfast in view of the fact that many Catholics had not been attending the sacraments because of the paucity of priests. But, despite the glimmer of hope in the first part of the letter, Dixon ended on a gloomy note; like Cullen, he had lost all faith in Denvir's capacity to cope with the pastoral problems of his diocese and foresaw no progress there unless an energetic bishop were in control.[33]

Propaganda in reply exhorted Dixon to maintain his vigilant observation of the Belfast scene and to continue encouraging the bishop to do what was necessary for his people. Then, finally accepting the need for more drastic action, it suggested that the time was opportune for the appointment of a coadjutor bishop and assured Dixon that he would make a contribution to the church in Down and Connor and please the congregation at the same time, if he would persuade Denvir to apply for one.[34]

Dixon obviously baulked at this suggestion. Presumably he just could not bring himself to give Denvir this painful advice, for nothing happened for nearly a year. Then an opportunity arose with Cullen's visit to Rome in May 1859. Dixon decided to take advantage of his presence there and asked him to make a formal proposal to Propaganda for the nomination of a coadjutor and, if possible, to bring home the authorization to initiate the process of appointment. But Cullen had left Rome before the letter arrived and so he was forced to ask Kirby to convey his plea to Propaganda. Kirby did so, again adducing the oft repeated laments about Denvir's failures and the reasons for them. When the secretary of Propaganda formally

33 Dixon to Propaganda, 31 May 1858, A.P.F. S.C. (Irlanda), 33, ff 621v-622v. Dixon concluded: 'Ultimo sperandum non est Ecclesiam Belfastiae grandes progressus facturum quamdiu regnat Episcopus Denvir. Vir quidem est optimus, sed procrastinatione insignis valde, plenus timore Protestantium ubi non est timor et constitutionis physicae tam debilis ut saltem per ultimos quattuor annos, haud bis publice celebravit Missam; et nescio si umquam praedicavit per eosdem quattuor annos, vix occasionibus sacramentum confirmationis administrandi. Sub ductu Episcopi virilis Belfastia cito foret inter longe florentissimas hujus magni imperii Britannici ecclesias'. Denvir, however, did not neglect his ordinary routine duties. The *Ulsterman* reported that he confirmed 343 boys in St Malachy's Church on 9 Nov. 1858 and between 500 and 600 the following day. On Sunday 21 Nov. he confirmed nearly 600 and on the following Sunday, when the ceremonies lasted from 11.15am to 6.30pm, he confirmed nearly 800 girls, young women employees from the mills and factories and adult converts.
34 Propaganda to Dixon, 18 June 1858. Ibid., *Lett.*, 349. ff 409v-410r.

submitted the request, the pope agreed at once and ordered that the usual machinery for an election be set in motion.[35] On hearing of Rome's judgement Denvir accepted it with good grace and was prepared to summon the parish priests straightaway but Dixon persuaded him to wait until after the national meeting of the hierarchy in October, when the bishops of the Armagh province could make arrangements about coming together to formulate their comments on the names chosen.[36]

According to the terms of the Roman rescript of 1829, the parish priests of the diocese where a bishop or coadjutor-bishop was to be appointed were obliged to assemble and choose in order of preference a *terna* or three names of candidates whom they considered suitable for appointment to the vacant office. The bishops of the province were then obliged to comment on the *terna* chosen, though they were at liberty to recommend none of the three candidates and, if they so wished, to make other recommendations. The Holy See was, of course, free to reject any or all of the names submitted to it, though if the recommendations of the parish priests and bishops coincided, especially on the first candidate, and if no strong objections came from any important source against him, he was normally chosen.

The parish priests of Down and Connor met in St Patrick's Church, Belfast on 29 November 1859. Of the thirty eight votes cast Charles William Russell, president of Maynooth, received sixteen and was placed first or *dignissimus* on the *terna*. Patrick Dorrian obtained nine and was placed second or *dignior* and John Fitzsimons, parish priest of Cushendall, obtained four and was placed third or *dignus*. The remaining votes were scattered among other priests whose names did not go forward.

Russell's dominant position in the *terna* came as no surprise. A scholar of international distinction, whose name had long been mentioned as a candidate for episcopal office, he was well known and highly respected throughout Ireland by many bishops and priests. Some of those who favoured him knew that he would be reluctant to move to the pastoral scene. John Lynch, the parish priest of Ballymena, explained to a close friend of Russell's that those who voted for him did so despite realizing that they were thereby asking him to make 'many, great sacrifices in many ways', because to have overlooked his great and varied merits would have been a slight on him and an 'unspeakable disgrace' to themselves. Lynch then went on to claim that Dorrian owed his votes to ties of kinship and to *sentimento campanalistico*:

35 A.P.F. *Acta*, 224. ff 159v-160v, 163r.
36 Dixon to Kirby, 31 Aug. 1859, A.I.C.R.

And I feel some pride in saying 13 of the 16 votes, or rather 14, were Antrim votes: and those given to Mr Fitzimmons & myself (I got 3) were neither asked nor desired. I should have been ashamed to see my name beside his, and as if in rivalry. The County Down did itself no credit and already the principal party (consisting of brothers cousins & so on), has got the soubriquet of 'The Loughinisland Lodge' even among themselves. Having vindicated ourselves I dare not go further than to say that if Dr Russell will use any influence to get out of it, the same influence will have a serious responsibility to supply his place. I need not tell you who know so well what is wanted the total & well-known inadequacy of the others, especially Mr Dorrian . . . If Dr Russell will come all is right. If not (which is the confident opinion) we were never bad till now.[37]

In this analysis of Russell's support Lynch must have been referring to the pastors stationed in Co. Antrim rather than to the Antrim-born clergy (who could not have mustered thirteen or fourteen votes). Those who supported Dorrian could not have represented a large proportion of the clergy born in Co. Down, and at the most only half of the parish priests of the county. This criticism of the Co. Down clergy must therefore have reflected disappointment at Dorrian's choice by the parish priests who presumably served in Co. Down and who would have had better opportunities for assessing his qualities than their confrères in Co. Antrim. The parish priests of Bright and Ballee were brothers, and there may have been cousins among the others, but Lynch's sneer reveals his own displeasure at the prospect of Dorrian's succession, in the event of Russell's withdrawal, rather than the existence of any kind of serious caucus based on blood relationship to Dorrian. Coincidentally the second and third candidates on the list were both scrutators, and they signed the official report to Rome, together with Denvir, who presided, and Lynch, who was secretary.

The archbishop of Armagh, the bishops of Down and Connor, Meath, Kilmore, Clogher, Ardagh, the coadjutors of Dromore and Raphoe and the apostolic administrator of Derry, representing all the dioceses of the Armagh province, forwarded their assessment of the candidates to Rome two days after the election. Their verdict was brief, decisive and unanimous: they concluded that both Dorrian and Fitzsimons on account of their learning, piety and zeal were worthy of commendation but declared that Russell, who was the equal of the other two in piety, prudence, zeal and administrative ability, was much to be preferred because he far surpassed them in

---

37 Lynch to Thomas O'Hagan, 5 Dec. 1859, N.L.I. MS 17874(3).

learning. Under normal circumstances such an emphatic choice by both parish priests and bishops would have led to Russell's appointment, but Russell, who believed that he lacked the strength of will and firmness of character required for episcopal office, was most unwilling to undertake a responsibility for which he felt himself unsuited.

But, apart from Russell's strong personal aversion to such a promotion, there were valid reasons for his seeking to avoid it. He had pledged himself to pay off substantial debts which an ailing brother had incurred, and, as he explained to the cardinal prefect, he feared that these serious financial obligations, not only 'would deprive me for many years and perhaps for ever, of that liberty and independence which is necessary to the ministry of a bishop, but would expose the episcopacy itself to the most serious danger of dishonour, and in the case (unfortunately likely) of the death of my brother, to lawsuits and court actions and perhaps even to worse humiliations'.[38] This plea which was confirmed by Archbishops Dixon and Cullen and further upheld by Cullen, when Rome invited him to reconsider it, effectively ruled Russell out.

That left only two others in contention. Cullen, whose knowledge of and contacts with Down and Connor were very limited, was unimpressed on first hearing of the inclusion of Dorrian's and Fitsimons' names on the *terna*; 'good parish priests', he observed, but 'I fear they are not up to the mark'. His first reaction, in the light of Russell's desire to be excluded, was to suggest the name of John Pius Leahy, the former Dominican provincial, in whose appointment as coadjutor bishop of Dromore he had played an important part.[39] But he does not seem to have pursued that suggestion fearing perhaps that it would create as many problems in Dromore as it might solve in Down and Connor. And, strangely, in view of the gravity of the situation in Belfast, there was remarkably little urgency shown about the appointment. Cullen, when replying to letters from Rome, excused his delay in forwarding information on the grounds of distance and paucity of opportunities for making contacts in the winter months. Presumably he contacted Dixon but no written evidence survives. What does survive and was undoubtedly of prime importance in influencing the archbishop of Dublin and, subsequently, Rome, is a letter from John Pius Leahy in answer to a request for his comment on Dorrian.

Leahy began his observations by noting that from his first acquaintance with Dorrian about five years previously he had formed a very favourable opinion of him ('he seemed so priest-like in all his

---

38 Russell to Barnabo. 5 Dec. 1859, A.P.F. *Acta*, 224. f. 165rv.
39 Cullen to Kirby, 3 Dec. 1859, A.I.C.R.

demeanour') and had even then regarded him as a suitable successor to Bishop Denvir. His spiritual commitment, his political views and his experience seemed to equip him for the coadjutorship, and the only question mark to be placed on his suitability concerned his possession of the requisite energy for the burdensome office in question:

> Your Grace is I suppose aware that the Clergy of Down and Connor never have had the benefit of a spiritual retreat within the Diocese, but Mr Dorrian to my knowledge used to go, occasionally at least, to Maynooth to make his retreat with the Dublin clergy, a sign that he is fully aware of the importance of that great means of inspiring Ecclesiastics with the spirit of their vocation. From his conversation I think it very unlikely that he would show any subserviency to Government or permit himself to be deluded by their plausibility. On the Education Question he is not, I believe much in favour of the National System, as at present administered, though as far as I know his views are as moderate as my own.
>
> There is only one matter about which I have any hesitation, and that is whether he has the energy and activity that would be requisite under the actual circumstances of Down and Connor. Not that I could not vouch for his possessing them. However his health was at one time seriously injured when he was Curate in Belfast, by his zealous discharge of the multitudinous duties laid at that time on the four priests who resided there.[40]

Cullen promptly forwarded the substance of this communication to Rome and suggested that further more precise information might become available within a few weeks.[41] Almost two months later he wrote again; he had been able to acquire little detailed knowledge but from the little he had acquired it seemed that there was no obstacle to Dorrian's appointment.[42] A letter favourable to Dorrian had gone to Rome at the end of January from George Pye, parish priest of Glenavy, who admitted that he had voted for Russell and who claimed that others to whom he had spoken, who had voted likewise, now believed that Dorrian was the only suitable candidate not only because of his ability, zeal, administrative skill and experience in Belfast but also because he was a distinguished preacher.[43] And at about the same time as Cullen's second letter in support of Dorrian arrived, a translation of a commendation from a former classmate,

40 Leahy to Cullen, 2 Mar. 1860, D.D.A.
41 Cullen to Barnabo, 4 Mar. 1860, A.P.F. *Acta*, 224, f.167r.
42 Ibid. 24 Apr. 1860, f.167v.
43 Pye to Barnabo, 24 Jan. 1860, Ibid., f.166rv.

the vicar apostolic of Hyderabad, who was then passing through Italy, was submitted to Propaganda. The importance of Daniel Murphy's intervention was that it scotched the doubt raised by John Pius Leahy about Dorrian's possessing the requisite energy for the coadjutorship in Down and Connor. Murphy insisted: 'he is intimately acquainted with the spiritual necessities of the diocese and he possesses not only the will but also the energy to remedy them'.[44]

As Cullen, whose advice on episcopal appointments in Ireland was often decisive in Rome, seemed to have no further suggestion to make and as no serious opposition to, or objections of any significance about, the candidates had emerged, it only remained for the cardinals of Propaganda to consider the advice they had received and recommend a name to the pope. The documentation on which such a recommendation was based normally consisted of an analysis of the situation prevailing in the diocese under review together with details of the voting and the more important letters on the subject received by the congregation. Cardinal Barberini drew up the analysis (*ristretto*) in this case and did not mince his words in describing the state of Down and Connor and the failure of Bishop Denvir to take appropriate remedial measures.[45] Recalling Russell's petition to be excused the appointment and Cullen's acceptance of it as justified, he noted that the information forthcoming on Dorrian was favourable, apart from the possible reservation about his possessing the requisite energy. This point was subsequently cleared up, and Cullen's views were fully confirmed by the letter of George Pye. All this testimony, which was supported by that of the vicar apostolic of Hyderabad, seemed to remove all doubt about the wisdom of nominating Dorrian, if the cardinals decided to leave Russell at his post in Maynooth. The nine cardinals present at the plenary congregation on 4 June 1860 accepted Barberini's conclusion and recommended Dorrian. Six days later the pope acted on their advice and formally appointed Dorrian titular bishop of Gabala and coadjutor with right of succession to Bishop Denvir.[46]

44 Ibid., ff 167v-168v. This opinion was prefaced by a note to the effect that Murphy submitted it at the suggestion of the cardinal prefect. The appointment to Down and Connor must have come up in conversation, and the cardinal, on discovering that Murphy knew Dorrian, must have suggested that he should make a formal statement. In 1846 Dorrian was present at Murphy's episcopal ordination in Kinsale, and five years later Murphy celebrated High Mass at the opening of the church in Bangor at which Dorrian preached.

45 Ibid., ff 159r-161r, 'La sua attività però e lo zelo nel promuovere il bene delle anime a lui affidate, sembra ben lungi dal corrispondere ai bisogni di quelle ed ai pericoli che corrono nei tempi e nelle circostanze presenti'. He also drew attention to the numerous reports made to Rome of Denvir's 'incuria' and 'poca cura'.

46 Ibid., ff 159v-162v. The ancient bishopric of Gabala in Syria became extinct when the Moslems overran the Middle East.

The episcopal ordination took place in St Malachy's Church, Belfast on 19 August. Archbishop Dixon, assisted by Cornelius Denvir and Charles MacNally, the bishop of Clogher and senior suffragan of Armagh, performed the ceremony. Five other prelates were present. In the course of his sermon, John Derry, bishop of Clonfert, explained the details of the rite and pointed out that a bishop's rule 'for the good of his flock was based on the soundness of his walk of life, and on his judicial and administrative powers'. The new bishop afterwards entertained many of his guests to dinner.[47]

II

As coadjutor Dorrian was attached to St Malachy's Church and lived in the presbytery at 2 Adelaide Place and later at 8 Howard Street; he retained the parish of Loughinisland, which was administered by a curate until 1866.

Since he enjoyed the right of succession he was assured of becoming bishop of Down and Connor immediately on Denvir's death or retirement. But Denvir retained full jurisdiction within the diocese. Apart from specific rights as laid down in canon law, a bishop has a large area, unclear, perhaps, and shadowy, of influence and indeed authority bordering on his strict jurisdiction, in which he can guide and inspire the work of his priests. As a future bishop of the diocese Dorrian undoubtedly possessed this kind of influence but he did not have any independent authority and so was only entitled to use his orders within the diocese as Denvir directed. The judicious delegation of authority by a bishop to his coadjutor so that they and their priests can work together happily and harmoniously occurs only in an ideal world. And Down and Connor in the early 1860s was not ideal terrain for effecting this delicate division of responsibility.

Denvir seems to have agreed to Dorrian's officiating at many of the confirmation ceremonies but otherwise to have excluded him from sharing in episcopal jurisdiction. Dorrian, for his part, was either unable to persuade Denvir to make any significant pastoral changes in the diocese, especially in Belfast, or more probably, was unable to communicate in any meaningful way with him on the serious issues which needed attention. Whatever kind of paralysing fear or destructive indecision afflicted Denvir at this stage of his life, he had become immune to proposals for new initiatives. And apart from any pastoral re-organization, positive action was urgently required on two projects: the construction of the new convent and schools for the Sisters of Mercy and the new church of St Peter on the Falls Road.

47 B.M.N., 20 Aug. 1860. Derry chose as his texts 2 Cor.II, 14-15 and III, 5-6.

To pay off the substantial costs of both these buildings would have required the co-operation of an energetic committee working to a systematic plan of house-to-house collecting. Perhaps, because of his less than happy experiences with St Malachy's Church or, perhaps, as one of Dixon's informants had surmised, his 'natural turn of mind would not relish what he considered dictation from the laity',[48] Denvir was reluctant or unable to adopt tough fund-raising methods. As a result, after the first financial response to the appeal for the Sisters of Mercy, the donations dwindled or dried up altogether. By the end of 1861 a crisis had been reached; the building contractor, who had committed a lot of money and a substantial work force to the scheme, found to his consternation that there were no funds from which he could receive payment. The very substantial sum of £2,500 was due to him and he felt unable to continue the work without reimbursement. In his predicament he consulted Archbishop Dixon, for whom he was then building the cathedral in Armagh, and Dixon asked Cullen, who, as apostolic delegate, enjoyed a special responsibility for religious orders, to use any influence at his disposal to obtain payment for the harassed contractor and thereby relieve him of the necessity of instituting legal proceedings to recover the money.[49]

The superioress of the community also sought Dixon's aid. Her main concern was to avoid a court case but she was also anxious not to be compelled to borrow money at a rate of interest which the convent could not pay back. She feared that 'Dr Denvir would just raise some money in the Bank, and, like the Church of St Malachy, the whole expense would be more than paid in interest and the principal still lying there', and consequently suggested that the bishop should assume the debt due on the schools and get the priests of the town to collect it. If this were done, she was confident that they would soon raise a large part of the money which was due and with the prospect of receiving the remainder soon, the contractor would be satisfied and the nuns would in time be able to pay for the convent building.[50]

Dorrian was forced to watch this development helplessly from the sidelines but as the processes of law were set in motion and the sheriff was about to take possession of the building, he bared his soul to the archbishop of Armagh. Deeply hurt by the public humiliation which the church in Belfast was being made to suffer and chafing at his own

48 Translation of Dixon to Kirby. 10 Jun. 1857 in A.P.F. S.C. (Irlanda), 33, ff 358r-359v.
49 Dixon to Cullen, 16 Jan. 1862, D.D.A.
50 Sr M.P. Maguire to Dixon, undated, A.D.A. Bishop Butler of Limerick preached a charity sermon on 19 Feb. 1865 in St Malachy's Church to raise money to pay off the remaining £500 which the convent still owed to the bank. More than £400 was collected. (B.M.N., 20 Feb. 1865)

impotence to prevent or undo the scandal, he explained that the schools attached to the convent had closed and that arrangements had been made for the Sisters to board with various families as soon as the sheriff took possession of the convent. Remarking that 'the spirit of the Catholics has been damped enough already', he gloomily observed that the 'effects on religion' were 'incredible' and predicted they would remain so. He then made clear, politely but firmly, where the blame and remedy for this painful contretemps lay, and did not conceal his frustration at the negative response which his own remonstration with Bishop Denvir had elicited:

> Dr Denvir is exerting himself by driving about but from what I see and hear, he will not do the only thing that can meet the crisis. Last night I went so far as to tell him that he himself was morally responsible, that he let the works go on when it was his business to have stopped them, and that any effort now was only putting off the evil without meeting it, unless some Catholics would join him and secure the money in one of the Banks, till time would have it paid, and that if *he* would do this, Catholics would join. But he answered 'I will not, I nearly lost my life before by that'. Now, of course, he alone can do anything. Nor ought anyone else to interfere, for he might and would be left in for it without any help.
>
> The Bishop has no committee and will have none. People hold aloof and will now say, as they do say, 'this is what comes of leaving our money affairs in the hands of the clergy who know nothing about business matters'. Whatever may turn up the effects must be disastrous to religion. The Bishop blames Mr Byrne, I do not.[51]

When the superioress informed Dixon officially of the vexatious loss of the convent and the consequent dispersal of the nuns, he advised her to consult Archbishop Cullen about leaving Belfast temporarily, but he was unable to give any practical, financial help. His dispirited comment that he thought this 'the saddest affair for the Catholics of Ulster' that had happened in his lifetime and his bleak forecast that 'the Catholics of Belfast especially will not be able to hold up their heads for many a long day to come' echoed Dorrian's sentiments in full.[52] But the public embarrassment provoked by the evacuation of the nuns from the convent spurred the wealthier and more generous Catholics of Belfast to come to their rescue and to ensure that sufficient money was forthcoming until the building was completed.

51 Dorrian to Dixon, 21 Feb. 1862. A.D.A.
52 Dixon to Sr M.P. Maguire, 27 Feb. 1862, D.D.A.

The same difficulties and delays also attended the construction of St Peter's Church on the Falls Road. The site was acquired and presented to the diocese in 1858 by Bernard Hughes, the proprietor of the extensive Model and Railway bakeries, whose great wealth was equalled only by his princely generosity to Catholic charities.[53] The foundation stone was laid on 1 August 1860, but when money dried up, work on the building had to be stopped, and after a change of architects and builders, was eventually completed in 1866.

These humiliating developments for the Catholics of Belfast began to force the archbishop of Armagh to the conclusion that the solution found in 1860 to the problems of Down and Connor had failed. Nothing seemed to have changed and the coadjutor was obviously precluded from interfering in situations where his administrative skill, vision and intrepidity were badly needed. In the wake of the convent crisis, he confessed to Kirby in Rome his regret that Dorrian did not have charge of the administration of the diocese and observed sadly: 'I see nothing making progress in Belfast'.[54] However, he seems to have borne his disappointment in patience for a further year before taking any action.

But towards the end of the following summer he obviously felt it was time to come to closer grips with the situation in Belfast. He wrote to Dorrian for information about the population of the town and the enrolment of children at schools managed by Catholics. Dorrian, champing at the bit at his prolonged and enforced inactivity, declared himself ready to make 'any personal sacrifice' to 'attain the end which the spiritual interests of others demand' and concluded his reply by hinting that Rome might be persuaded to inquire what he had done 'in order to open up the question'. The Catholic population of the parish which was served by eight priests — four in Donegall St. and four in Howard St. — he estimated, basing himself on the census of 1861, at 40,000. The Catholic school-going population he put at 12,000 but noted with regret that only about 2,370 of these were attending schools managed by Catholics, and suggested that a very large number of them — 'many hundreds' — were attending national schools under Protestant management.[55] The

---

53 Bernard Hughes came to Belfast from Blackwatertown, Co. Armagh in 1827 and found work as a young apprentice baker. He became a highly successful and prosperous businessman, and served on the Belfast Town Council for several years as a Liberal member for Smithfield ward. He died in 1878.

54 Dixon to Kirby, 8 Mar. 1862, A.I.C.R.

55 According to Dorrian's figures there were 600 girls at the convent schools, and at the other schools, the numbers were: Donegall St. (270), May St. (300), Chapel Lane (300), Alexander St. W. (300), Malvern St. (150), Earl St. (300), Smithfield (150). These figures correspond reasonably closely to those issued by the board of national education for the average daily attendance at these schools. The numbers on the rolls were often much higher.

position of many of these Catholic schools was insecure; half of them were managed by the St Vincent de Paul Society, received no aid and 'next to no encouragement' from the clergy and some were 'threatened to be given up and notice has been served for 1 November'. What exacerbated this situation was the intense missionary activity of numerous and well endowed proselytizing evangelists: 'what opposition we have to deal with may be surmised from the large swarm of dissenting Ministers, Bible readers, etc., that abound here, and who have the bulk of the wealth etc., of the town in their hands'.[56]

Armed with this information Dixon decided to act. He wrote to Kirby seeking his advice on how to approach the cardinal prefect, directly or indirectly, about the retirement of Bishop Denvir. Declaring that 'the state of things in Belfast is very little improved', he referred to the inability of eight priests, much of whose time was spent in 'organizing and superintending collections and various other works' to 'instruct such a multitude, hear their confessions, or prepare them for death' yet Denvir would not organize a mission lest it might provoke the Orangemen. He quoted Dorrian's statistics of the children attending schools under Catholic management and asked plaintively where were the other Catholic children:

> Dr Denvir's timidity cannot be overcome. Are we to allow a regard for the feelings of one man no matter how exalted and how good his intentions, to outweigh the salvation of a multitude of souls redeemed by the precious Blood of Our Lord? I am now thoroughly convinced that the only remedy for the state of things in Belfast is to remove Dr Denvir from the administration of the diocese; and that this ought to be done without delay.

Dixon then went on to disclose that he proposed to suggest to Rome that the 'young and vigorous co-adjutor' be given charge of the diocese, that the bishop retire to a more genial climate on an allowance of £200 annually and while expressing his hope that a request from Rome should be sufficient to achieve this goal, he suggested that, should this fail, Rome ought to insist on retirement. Though making clear his own readiness to act as intermediary, he indicated a preference for Archbishop Cullen's association with him in executing any commission from Rome.[57]

Kirby relieved Dixon of the need to make a formal request to Propaganda by translating this letter and, for good measure, adding

56 Dorrian to Dixon, 8 Sept. 1863, A.D.A.
57 Dixon to Kirby, 16 Sept. 1863, A.I.C.R.

that he could corroborate the case from his own experiences in Belfast in 1851. Cardinal Barnabò, he reported, seemed 'greatly struck by Your Grace's expositions of this sad state of affairs' and promised to lay the matter before the pope at his next audience a few days later. Kirby was optimistic that something, which he did not specify, would be done, though he thought it unlikely that 'they will in the first instance take the administration of Belfast directly out of the Bishop's hands'[58]

Kirby's prediction proved correct. Rather than present Denvir with a blunt ultimatum Rome chose to act more delicately and humanely; Cardinal Barnabò on the pope's authorization invited Dixon, in association with one of the other archbishops, to try gently to persuade Denvir to resign.[59] But the pope also wished Denvir to know that this advice was being given with his knowledge and that he could no longer remain silent in view of the frequency of the complaints relayed to the Holy See. Dixon could scarcely have been encouraged by this response; Denvir had already given irrefragable proof of his power of resisting persuasion, however insistent or persistent it might be.

Perhaps it was at this time that Dixon received another disturbing report from Dorrian, for though the letter is undated, it refers to the school problem, which was then being experienced. Dorrian had been told that the schools in Chapel Lane, which were run by the St Vincent de Paul Society, would probably be closed. But when he confronted Denvir with this depressing news, the bishop had complained about the schools being opened in the first place and then thrown on to the expense of the parish, and concluded 'well, let them go down'. When the subject turned to the nuns and their request for a collection from the public at a ceremony of profession, Denvir's comments were equally dismissive:

> What did these Nuns want now did I think, but he would not yield to them. This convent must go down. Wiser people than I have told me not to mind them. The way is to keep away from them . . .

When Dorrian persisted in explaining the financial anxieties pressing on the nuns, Denvir reluctantly allowed the collection, despite his fear that the nuns wanted to take all the parish funds. Dorrian was forced to draw the dismal conclusion:

58 Kirby to Dixon, 9 Nov. 1863, A.D.A.
59 'benevolis simul suasionibus atque argumentis R.P.D. Denvir adducere studeas ad supplicandum SS.mo ut renuntiationem accipiet Episcopi Dunensis et Connorensis reservata tamen ipsius favorem pensione congrua . . .' Propaganda to Dixon, 17 Nov. 1863, A.P.F. *Lett.*, 354, f.558r.

There is no satisfaction nor use in speaking to him about schools, convents or chapels. He seems to think that we have some design on him and that nobody understands anything but himself; nor will he let you explain unless at the risk of being perhaps too bold. I would rather never go near him.

I thought I would just let your Grace know this evening's incident. It is so characteristic that your Grace will forgive me.[60]

Encouraged both by Rome and by the disheartening accounts emanating from Belfast, Dixon moved quickly to execute the pope's will. He begged Cullen to join him in trying to persuade Denvir to resign,[61] and, though Cullen found the prospect of taking part 'not an agreeable business',[62] he could not refuse to do so. The meeting took place in Dixon's house in Drogheda and, though at first Denvir reacted badly to their suggestion of resignation, claiming that he had been defamed and calumniated at Rome, he eventually yielded to their persuasions or rather to his own sense of reverence for the pope and promised to resign, if he were allowed to delay the announcement until he could officially inform his clergy at their next meeting, which would take place shortly after Easter. He would then petition the pope for permission to retire and request a suitable pension from the diocese.[63]

Cullen thought this condition was a price worth paying and Dixon was happy to go along with it. And Cullen, who ought to have known how quickly promises of amendment could evaporate and might have been expected to postpone expressions of satisfaction until more positive steps had been taken, seems to have accepted Denvir's agreement as the final solution. He reported contentedly to Kirby that 'Dr Denvir's affair terminated very quietly'.[64] But Denvir, whether through what might have become, by then, pathological procrastination or through a desire to avoid the embarrassment of taking a step that was unusual in Ireland and therefore likely to be interpreted as an indication of failure, put the agreement into cold storage.

The conference of diocesan clergy took place as arranged in Belfast on 19 May 1864. But Denvir extricated himself from his commitment to announce his resignation at it by the simple expedient of absenting himself. The only announcement made referred to arrangements about confirmation; Dorrian was commissioned to advise some priests to be in readiness for confirmation and to let them

60 Dorrian to Dixon, undated, A.D.A.
61 Dixon to Cullen, 9 Dec. 1863, D.D.A.
62 Cullen to Kirby, 11 Dec. 1863, A.I.C.R.
63 Dixon to Barnabo, 18 Dec. 1863, A.P.F. S.C. (Irlanda), 34, ff 1019v-1020r.
64 Cullen to Kirby, 19 Feb.1984, A.I.C.R.

know that Denvir might not be able to officiate. A bewildered but unbowed Dorrian could offer no comment or explanation other than that Denvir complained of 'nervousness and debility'.[65] In reply to this discouraging news Dixon obviously told Dorrian that he was going to write to Denvir telling him that he had informed Dorrian of the agreement and promise of resignation. But Dorrian on reflection decided against the employment of these tactics. He suggested an alternative ploy: Dixon should write to Denvir two or three days before writing to him in order to give Denvir the opportunity of personally conveying to his coadjutor the news of his resignation. Dorrian had heard that money was being collected to buy Denvir a new carriage and he thought the presentation ceremony might afford a suitable opportunity for an announcement. But he was growing impatient. He felt that precious opportunities were being wasted; the summer months, when they should have been pushing forward with arrangements about establishing the Christian Brothers in Belfast, were passing and delay was damaging. Looking to the future, Dorrian suggested that when the resignation had been settled, Dixon would oblige him by judiciously hinting that the new bishop 'was expected to throw some vigour into this Mission' by establishing Christian Brothers' and other schools and increasing the clergy in town. And to illustrate the grave reason for this urgency he pointed out that the Presbyterians controlled seventy of the eighty national schools in and about Belfast, but depended in very many cases on Catholic children to bring up the levels of enrolment with the result that 'we have been absolutely thus giving a positive support to, not merely Presbyterian schools, but to the proselytism of our own'.[66]

On receipt of this letter Dixon wrote officially to Dorrian, ostensibly to find out if Denvir had carried out the agreement which he had made with the archbishop of Dublin and himself, namely to submit his resignation formally to the pope after announcing it to the assembled clergy at their Easter conference. If Dorrian conveyed this inquiry to Denvir, as he was obviously intended to do, it had no effect. So Dixon finally braced himself to execute his painful duty and wrote telling Denvir that Cardinal Barnabò wanted to hear if the terms agreed at their meeting at Drogheda about his resignation had been fulfilled. Enclosing the cardinal's letter,[67] he remarked that the information he had received from 'a respectable clergyman' of Down and Connor that no announcement had been made at the conference had given him 'great pain' and illustrated his displeasure by declar-

65 Dorrian to Dixon, 26 May 1864, A.D.A.
66 Ibid., 2 June 1864.
67 Barnabò had written to Dixon on 5 Jan. 1864 praising him and the archbishop of Dublin for their satisfactory handling of the issue of the resignation and leaving the details of the execution of it to their discretion. (A.P.F. *Lett.*, 355, f.2r).

ing that, after consulting Archbishop Cullen, he intended to ask Rome to be relieved from 'all further responsibility in this matter, as I am unwilling to be engaged in a fruitless affair'. But foreseeing that Rome would then enter into correspondence with his coadjutor, he had decided to let Dorrian know what had been agreed at Drogheda but was prepared to let three days elapse before resorting to this measure, in order to allow him to communicate with Dorrian first.[68]

Denvir replied promptly that he fully intended to adhere to the promise he had made at Drogheda. As he hoped to meet Dixon and Cullen at Maynooth in a few days time, he would then execute his promise in their presence — presumably to submit the official letter of resignation to Rome. Consequently, he felt sure there was no need to write to Dorrian or to take any further step until they met.[69] But he did not attend the meeting of the hierarchy in Maynooth and so escaped an encounter with the archbishops of Armagh and Dublin. He clung on tenaciously to office, and as the months passed and problems mounted Dorrian became more depressed.

At the beginning of 1865 he again unburdened himself to Dixon. Maintaining that the population of Belfast had increased by 10,000 or 12,000 within the previous three years, he contrasted unfavourably the response of the Catholic authorities to this development with that of other denominations, which were erecting new churches, meeting houses and schools in the suburbs. Faced with a crisis, he had assumed responsibility for authorizing the completion of St Peter's Church at a cost of £2,000. £4,000 was still owed for the fabric, and he was embarrassed at his inability to raise £1,000, which had then to be paid. Moreover, a chapel both for the sailors and the locals was needed near the quays, in addition to one for the 500 Catholics who resided at Ligoniel, two miles outside the town. Two or three smaller churches were required in other parts of the suburbs, as well as ten or twelve schools. Without these facilities a heavy leakage from the church would continue:

> In the meantime sad ravages are being made stealthily among our people, of *every* class and by *every* influence. It is very sad. We lost a thousand a year for 25 years.
> Dr Denvir has not been out of the house for three months. Yet, though he complains of his health, he is as sound as man can be. I think just he is most unwilling to take a certain step and is moping over it. He has not spoken to me on the subject

---

68 Dixon to Denvir (copy). 17 June 1864, A.D.A.
69 Denvir to Dixon, 17 June 1864, A.D.A.

but the once. And he speaks of the future to me and to others just as if nothing was to happen.

Another year's rent is now due on all the Vincent De Paul N. Schools, but no provision is yet made. Difficulties are daily met, with no satisfactory result.[70]

Without Dorrian's permission, Dixon promptly forwarded this letter to Cullen with the pessimistic observation that 'it was enough to break a man's heart, to think of the ruin that is falling on the mission of Belfast by Dr Denvir's delay in doing what he undertook to do'.[71] On receipt of this Cullen immediately communicated his disappointment to Denvir. Reminding him of their agreement at Drogheda a year previously, the result of which had been transmitted to Rome, he observed that the congregation of Propaganda must have since concluded that Dixon and he had tried to delude it and prevent it from taking the steps it had then determined to take. Consequently, he had decided to let Rome know that 'he had no wish to lead them astray and to request them to take the matter into their own hands'. He predicted that this information would cause displeasure and that the pope would give positive orders to have the arrangements made at Drogheda put into effect at once. Suggesting to Denvir that it would be better to settle the problem without delay, he promised to hold back his letter for a few days in the hope of receiving a favourable answer.[72]

Denvir began to realize that he could not hold out indefinitely against this pressure. He must have contacted the archbishop of Armagh about a suitable pension, for on 21 April 1865 Dorrian informed Dixon that he gave full 'assent to the requirements of Dr Denvir that £400 a year should and shall be paid his Lordship out of the revenue of the diocese'.[73] On the following day Dixon formally submitted to Propaganda Denvir's resignation.[74] At his next audience on 4 May, Barnabò placed the resignation before the pope, and Pius IX immediately accepted it and officially confirmed the pension of £400. Almost two weeks later, on 17 May, the prefect of Propaganda communicated the pope's acceptance of the resignation to Dixon, Denvir and Dorrian, and transmitted the full episcopal faculties to the new bishop.[75] Though Dorrian had known about the

70 Dorrian to Dixon, 12 Jan. 1865, A.D.A.
71 Dixon to Cullen, 16 Jan. 1865, D.D.A.
72 Cullen to Denvir (copy), 22 Jan. 1865, D.D.A.
73 Dorrian to Dixon, 21 Apr. 1865, A.D.A.
74 Dixon to Barnabò, 22 Apr. 1865, A.P.F. S.C.(Irlanda), 35, ff 240r-241v. The archbishop's relief is evident in the words he chose to begin this letter: *tandem aliquando*. Dixon expressed his concurrence with the size of the pension as the revenues of the diocese were ample, and went on to say that Denvir was anxious that the cardinal should know that he had never hesitated in carrying out his intention of resigning. The delay was due to causes which would take too long to explain.
75 Ibid., *Lett.* 356, ff 204r-205v.

resignation, Denvir never mentioned the subject to him until they both received the official letters from Rome; the retiring bishop then handed over the reins graciously.[76] A year later he died.

So nearly five years after his appointment as coadjutor — five years of enforced inactivity, frequent vexation and mounting frustration — Dorrian succeeded to the bishopric of Down and Connor. With the enjoyment of full episcopal jurisdiction he was at last free to put into effect all the schemes of organizational reform and pastoral *aggiornamento* that he had been hatching during his powerless coadjutorship.

---

76 Dorrian to Dixon, 25 May 1865, A.D.A.

5

Pastoral care and problems of authority

I

The new bishop of Down and Connor was no stranger to his clergy. Both he and they had had ample opportunities for getting to know each other. With the exception of the four years he spent in Maynooth his entire life had been spent within the confines of the diocese. Of his twenty eight years of priesthood, fifteen had been spent in Belfast at the centre of the diocese, where inevitably he came into contact with most of the clergy. As coadjutor on the confirmation circuit he must have met virtually all the parish clergy and built up a fairly comprehensive picture of the conditions and needs of the parishes.

Few priests could have had any illusions about what was expected of them. Dorrian had a clear vision of diocesan development and an acute sense of the effort needed to effect it. Not only was he very sensitive about the missed opportunities and, indeed, neglect of the past, but he also realized that the diocese, and especially its principal town, faced a period of great expansion. This necessitated the provision of structures that not only would satisfy present needs but would also anticipate the requirements of the future. Due to the hesitation, delay and inactivity of the previous episcopate a backlog of work remained to be tackled, and the sooner this was begun the more quickly would the people of the diocese be given what they were entitled to. Speed was essential.

Throughout his life, indeed almost to the end, Dorrian enjoyed robust health, which was copiously matched by vigour and energy. John Pius Leahy's anxiety about the new bishop's possessing sufficient energy for the task in hand could not have been more groundless. A taste for administration and the determination to tackle any and every problem boldly, fearlessly and perseveringly were among his most conspicuous talents. A capable organizer, he was gifted with business acumen, tenacity and optimism. Unlike Charles William Russell, who headed the *terna* at the election in 1859, and to a much lesser extent his predecessor, he was not a scholar, had not been allowed to complete his formal course and had given himself entirely to parish work. Though he continued his theological reading when leisure permitted, he did not have the scholar's hankering for study and could happily devote nearly all his time to administration and pastoral duties.

He was also fortunate, in view of the work that lay ahead, to possess a formidable and at times inflexible will-power. Once he was convinced of the need to take action on any issue, he did so with zest and determination. He was not prepared to tolerate fractious or captious opposition.

At the very beginning of his episcopate he showed his mettle when confronted by the querulous and refractory parish priest of Antrim, Henry O'Loughlin. Dorrian had sought and obtained permission from the pope to apply the collections taken up at the services connected with the jubilee or special indulgence of May 1865 to the funding of a hall or conference room for his clergy at the diocesan seminary.[1] O'Loughlin did not forward his contribution, using the excuse that he had not heard the announcement about this matter at the clerical meeting at which it was made, and explaining that he had already applied his collections to other purposes. Dorrian retorted that he should devise some means of making restitution, but O'Loughlin was unrepentant and even challenged the bishop's claim that he had any authority from the pope to allocate the alms in this way. Dorrian was not prepared to tolerate this insubordination as he realized its destructive potential for the exercise of his authority, and so consulted Archbishop Dixon about the reply he proposed to make to O'Loughlin.[2]

Fortified with information from the curate of Antrim that O'Loughlin's behaviour was deliberate,[3] he wrote to the truculent pastor reproving him for the disrespectful tone of his letters, and reminding him of his duty to comply with diocesan rules under pain of suspension.[4] Dixon had recommended that, if O'Loughlin proved contumacious, he be suspended for two months;[5] Dorrian gave O'Loughlin a week to come to heel under pain of suspension for six months.[6] O'Loughin, who had already transmitted to Rome a series of complaints against Bishop Denvir, most of which were groundless and fanciful, again appealed to the Holy See, and then extended his accusations at a personal level against Dorrian

1 Dorrian to Kirby, 2 May 1865, A.I.C.R.
2 Dorrian to Dixon, 29 June 1865, A.D.A.
3 Ibid., 12 July 1865.
4 Dorrian to O'Loughlin, 10 July 1865, A.P.F. S.C. (Irlanda), 35, ff 1057r-1058v.
5 Dixon to Dorrian, 2 July 1865, Ibid., f.1069r.
6 Dorrian to O'Loughlin, 10 July 1865, Ibid., f.1055rv.

himself.[7] When Dorrian carried out the threat of suspension and O'Loughlin withdrew his allegations of improper conduct, the suspension was lifted,[8] and Dorrian invited O'Loughlin to dine with him. However, O'Loughlin true to form continued to bombard Rome with a confusing mixture of complaints and forced Dorrian to answer a lot of complicated charges at great length; but the plaintiff achieved nothing, and, concluding that the better part of valour was discretion, eventually transferred to the diocese of Brooklyn.[9]

Dorrian, as a dedicated and energetic administrator, preoccupied with the establishment of all necessary aids to pastoral care — churches, schools, religious orders, institutes for the poor, the abandoned, the old and the infirm — represented a type of bishop which was by no means uncommon in the English-speaking world in the second half of the nineteenth century. His concerns, burdens and anxieties were paralleled by those of bishops in Britain, Canada, the United States, and Australia as well as in Ireland. These countries were all experiencing the rapid growth of urban centres — in many cases much of it due to the emigration of people from the Irish countryside — and of industrialization, with all its concomitant physical problems of housing, health, hygiene, unemployment and the equally grave problems of dislocation and deracination. In these urban settings, with their prospects of continuing expansion, the bishops were constantly searching for more clergy, both secular and regular, more orders of nuns to concentrate on education, welfare, social problems, and for money to raise and maintain the institutions which were essential to this form of pastoral care — schools, orphanages, homes, hospitals, asylums. Had Dorrian been appointed to Liverpool, Toronto or New York, he would have faced very similar problems to those he encountered in Belfast. Even sectarian hostility, though it did not assume the same political and virulent form as in Belfast, would have provided the same unwelcome and unchanging backdrop to his daily work.

Dorrian's first priority was an extension of the diocesan seminary. St Malachy's College, a secondary school for the education of Catholic boys (primarily for those aspiring to the priesthood) had been established in 1833 in Vicinage House on the outskirts of Belfast. The students who boarded there walked daily to join their day-boy colleagues for tuition in classrooms attached to St Patrick's national school in Donegall St. Since its foundation the seminary had not been enlarged, despite the increasing demand for

7 O'Loughlin to Barnabo, 17 July 1865, Ibid., f.1054rv.
8 Ibid., 4 Aug.1865. f.1070r.
9 O'Loughlin to Propaganda, 24 Oct.1865, and 18 Jan.1866. Ibid., ff 1071r-1072v, 1061r-1062v. and Dorrian to Propaganda, 25 Mar.1867 and 17 Aug.1867, ff 1063r-1068v, 1194rv, 1197rv.

education. Dorrian determined to extend it immediately. His purpose was twofold: he wanted to offer better opportunities to the increasing number of boys seeking secondary education, and to prepare more of them, if they so wished, to become priests; he also wanted to have a diocesan centre, a place where meetings of clergy could take place and especially one with residential facilities where his priests could assemble for retreats and religious exercises to deepen their spiritual lives. His first plan was to extend Vicinage House and he got this project off to a start with permission to use the funds collected at the jubilee in May 1865.

But he decided on a more ambitious scheme — the construction of a new college. A set of buildings to house both the residential and academic parts of the seminary was planned, and work began in the following year. By this means all his requirements would be met — a larger school and seminary, and a diocesan centre, were to be combined on the same site. The advent of the Christian Brothers to Belfast doubtless hastened this project. The Brothers, who provided both primary and secondary education to the poorer sections of society, which were often not able to afford the fees, however modest, that were charged in classical schools and diocesan colleges, had been establishing schools extensively throughout Ireland for three decades. Dorrian had intended inviting them to Belfast for some time, and when he called for help at a preliminary meeting in St Malachy's Church to enable 'those zealous and gifted men who devoted themselves to the education of the children of the humbler classes . . . to meet all the wants and requirements of this great rising town',[10] the response was enthusiastic and generous. A residence had to be provided for the Brothers and the grounds of Vicinage House afforded a suitable site. The formidable undertaking of erecting new collegiate and residential buildings went forward and the substantial sum of £4,000 for St Malachy's and nearly £3,500 for the Christian Brothers had to be found.[11] By the end of 1867 both buildings were complete.

The declaration of a jubilee (or extension of the holy year indulgence to the universal church) in May 1865 gave Dorrian an ideal opportunity to launch a general mission in Belfast. Where

---

10 U.Ob, 12 Dec.1865.

11 According to figures released by Dorrian in January 1868, St Malachy's cost £3,922, and the expenditure on the Christian Brothers' residence and repairs to the Donegall St. and Barrack St. schools amounted to £3,639. The bazaar in aid of the Brothers realized £2,290, from which £160 was paid out in expenses. All the parishes of the diocese were taxed to pay for St Malachy's. Belfast was assessed at £1,250, Kilkeel and Lower Mourne at £190, Duneane at £134, Lisburn at £117, Loughguile at £107, and all the others at less than £100. (Dorrian papers, D.C.D.A.)

hitherto the maximum number of priests available to hear confessions had been eight, twenty-four, including priests drafted in from other parts of the diocese, were assigned to this task and, apart from Sundays, were occupied for ten hours each day. Dorrian reported with deep satisfaction that 'persons who have not been at confession for years are coming in crowds and waiting for several sittings in order to get to confession',[12] and was greatly relieved when permission was given by the Holy See to extend the indulgences of the jubilee until the end of June. The bishop did not lead from behind a desk; he presided regularly at the morning Masses and evening devotions in the three churches and took his turn in the confessional. At the end of May he calculated that over 20,000 people, many of them for the first time, had confessed,[13] and his anxiety to obtain an extension of the jubilee was dictated by the desire to ensure that all who wished would be given an opportunity to do so. As it neared an end he reported exuberantly that the jubilee had been a 'wonderful success', that among those received into the church had been two Protestants who had been imprisoned for taking part in the riots of the previous year, and that many Protestants were included among the 1,200 adults whom he had confirmed.[14] His final estimate of the numbers of those who had been to confession and holy communion was 30,000.[15]

In the following year the Catholics of Belfast were given another welcome boost. St Peter's Church which had been started six years previously was finally blessed and opened. Since his accession Dorrian had speeded up operations and had improved the system of collecting throughout the town. As he looked forward to its completion he admitted that he was nearly £5,000 in debt, but expected to raise £2,000 at the opening; in the event £2,260 was lifted on that occasion.[16] The bishop was anxious to make the solemn ceremony of dedication splendid and memorable, one to give encouragement and pride to his people. Consequently, he invited Cardinal Cullen, who only four months previously had brought the red hat for the first time to an Irish see, to celebrate the High Mass and later to complete the ceremonies with benediction. Dorrian himself blessed the church and Bishop Ullathorne of Birmingham preached the

12 Dorrian to Kirby, 16 May 1865, A.I.C.R.
13 Ibid., 31 May 1865.
14 Ibid., 27 June 1865.
15 Ibid., 17 Sept. 1866.
16 Ibid., 19 Oct. 1866. (Dorrian was invariably gratified by the very generous response of the Catholic laity not only to parochial but also to diocesan collections. In 1865 Down and Connor contributed £312 to Peter's Pence. In the following year the collection had increased to £379, and throughout Dorrian's episcopate the average subscription per head of the population remained among the highest in Ireland.)

special sermon at the Mass, during which Haydn's No. 3 Grand Imperial was sung with full orchestral accompaniment. In the evening the bishop of Limerick sang vespers and the bishop of Dromore preached. In all, twelve bishops were present. Belfast had never witnessed such a magnificent and solemn religious spectacle, and after the frustrations of the Denvir era, this marked a symbolic change in the attitudes and expectations of the Catholic people. As church and school and convent rose side by side, they took pride in the possession of imposing religious institutions and willingly and generously contributed to them.

Taking advantage of this spirit of enthusiasm and of the facilities offered by the new church, Dorrian organized a general mission for the town. It began on 21 October, just one week after St Peter's opened, and ran concurrently in St Peter's, St Patrick's and St Malachy's for one month. Twelve Dominicans conducted it — four in each church — and they were assisted by diocesan clergy. He regarded it as launching a new spiritual era: 'it will with God's help thus lay the foundation for our future works'.[17] A total of forty priests officiated and the bishop was again happy to report complete satisfaction with the participation of the people and the general outcome. He felt that a start had been made. Though a religious order had preached a mission in Belfast in 1851, Denvir had been too timid, especially after the experience in Lisburn, to make this religious exercise a regular event. Dorrian had no such inhibitions. He was unconcerned about such eventualities. He did not believe that such fears should be allowed to interfere with his pastoral activities. He thought that there was no justification for refusing or putting off the valuable missionary contribution of the religious orders on the grounds of possible offence being given to Protestants. Catholics could no longer be deprived of a service to which they were entitled merely because Orangemen had a superstitious detestation of monks and friars.

In the same year Dorrian finally put into effect the scheme which Dixon had strenuously recommended to Rome and which Rome had insistently, if largely in vain, demanded that Denvir implement: the division of Belfast into smaller parochial units. Apart from Ballymacarrett which was attached to Holywood, the rest of Belfast formed the bishop's mensal parish. On the death of John Killen in 1866 Holywood was made a separate parish and Ballymacarrett became a part of Belfast. This meant that five churches served the entire Catholic community of the town. Each was constituted the centre of a quasi-parish under the direction of an administrator, who exercised most of the functions of a parish priest, but who did not enjoy full

17 Ibid., 17 Sept. 1866.

authority as such, was removable at the bishop's will and whose income was not much higher than that of a curate. For all general pastoral purposes the town consisted of five parishes and the clergy assigned to them were bound by the same rules and customs as in other parishes. The permanent staff attached to the five churches was increased by eight, bringing the total number to sixteen.[18] Not only did this arrangement make possible an increased number of services but it also gave to the different districts of the town a sense of religious *esprit de corps*, a pride in their own locality and a loyalty to their parish community.

The disruption of ecclesiastical life in Ireland during penal times had meant that the normal channels for enforcing clerical discipline and making regulations about the administration of the sacraments had been virtually non-existent. Some dioceses began to draw up their own legislation in the early decades of the century, and the Synod of Thurles in 1850 and the provincial synods which followed drew up extensive legislation for the whole country. Diocesan synods normally reinforced this legislation and added to it regulations about local issues. Statutes had been published by Bishop Crolly localizing Tridentine legislation in 1834 but Down and Connor had not held a synod since that time. One was announced for May 1867 and all the priests of the diocese took part in it.

The synod declared its acceptance of all legislation enacted at Thurles and Drogheda (the Armagh provincial synod of 1854) and abolished all exemptions which were not conceded by the law itself. Decrees were passed forbidding clergy to take up collections in churches, and prohibiting collections for the benefit of priests without the bishop's permission. Where a parish was served by two curates, each was to receive a fourth of the income; priests were prohibited from collecting outside their parishes without episcopal authority; collections by priests from other dioceses were permitted only with the bishop's permission; and the buying and selling of pews were ended.

These statutes were published along with those made by Crolly in 1834, which, among other regulations, had dealt with the administration of the sacraments, censures, preaching on Sundays, the maintenance of churches and parochial records, the visitation of the sick and decorum at wakes. These had also laid down that no priest could be absent for more than five days without the permission of the bishop or vicar general, and that no curate could be absent without consulting his parish priest. And vicars forane had been ordered to report four times annually on the observance of the diocesan statutes by the clergy of their districts and, in particular, on whether or not

18 Ibid., 16 Dec. 1866.

they imparted religious instruction on Sundays and holy-days, on whether or not they had commissioned suitable cathechists to teach religion to the aged, infirm and those who could not attend church, on the violations of statutes, on any scandals which had occurred, on the length of time for which priests under their surveillance had obtained leave of absence, on conversions, the reclamation of public sinners and all other details of significance.[19]

Side by side with these developments in canonical legislation the programme of church building proceeded apace. In his first two years as bishop Dorrian blessed and opened new churches at Rathlin Island, Cushendun, Ligoniel, Saul, Legamaddy, Cullybackey and Whitehouse. Some of these — Ligoniel, Cullybackey, Whitehouse — were built to serve communities which had grown in areas previously populated almost exclusively by Protestants, and others such as Legamaddy were erected to facilitate parishioners who lived at some distance from the main parish church. Rathlin, Cushendun, Saul and Glenavy (1868) were replacements for older buildings, as indeed were many of the new churches of Dorrian's episcopate. The diocese was in fact experiencing its second wave of church construction, as more substantial structures were being erected to replace the smaller, poorer and more inadequate buildings which had been put up in the latter years of the eighteenth century or the early years of the nineteenth.

On the initiative of the local clergy this work had gone on throughout Denvir's episcopate. But Dorrian gave a powerful fillip to it by his firm encouragement and constant support of the fund-raising efforts of his priests. He himself was directly responsible for the rebuilding of St Mary's in Belfast. This, the first Catholic church in the town, had been built in 1784, at a time of warm ecumenical co-operation, when Presbyterian Volunteers paraded at its opening and the Anglican sovereign of the town donated the pulpit. Not only did it hold a special place in the affections of Belfast Catholics, both for historical and ecumenical reasons, but it also served the dense Catholic community of Millfield and the lower Falls. Architectural examination revealed the fragility of the structure and so, despite the financial burden imposed by the construction of St Malachy's College and the residence for the Christian Brothers, the decision was taken to rebuild St Mary's completely. The new church was opened on 22 November 1868, when Dorrian, with greater hope than prescience, spoke of the flames of strife and bigotry in Belfast dying out. And while this building was in progress additional work

---

19 Acta et Statuta primae Synodi Dunensis et Connoriensis habitae die 15 Maii A.D. MDCCCLXVII; Statuta Dioecesana in Dioecesi Dunensi et Connoriensi obervanda et a RR.mo Gulielmo Crolly . . . edita et promulgata. Belfastiae, 1834.

costing more than £1000 was undertaken at St Malachy's Church: a further tower was built, the brickwork was repaired and the interior was painted. Ground was acquired beside the church as a site for a new parochial house.

In June 1867 Dorrian paid his first visit to the eternal city. Pope Pius IX invited bishops from all over the world to come to Rome for the eighteenth centenary of the martyrdom of Saints Peter and Paul, and many took advantage of the occasion to make their routine *ad limina* visit, and submit the official reports on the state of their dioceses. These reports usually conformed to a fixed pattern, detailing the number of clergy, churches, schools, religious institutions, the state of practice of the people and obstacles to freedom of religion. In his submission Dorrian expressed satisfaction with the standards of religious observance, regretted the shortage of clergy (eighty nine priests were then serving in the diocese), referred to the problems of acquiring sites for churches because of the reluctance of some landlords to lease them, and mentioned the dispute he had had with the indocile and 'Calvinist-minded' patrons of the Catholic Institute.[20] During his absence a meeting of prominent Catholics was held in Belfast to arrange the presentation of an address of welcome to him on his return. Ironically, one of those who was instrumental in calling and playing a leading part at the meeting was A.J. McKenna, the editor of the *Ulster Observer*, about whose role in the Catholic Institute Dorrian had complained to Rome. Other participants in this expression of respect and gratitude were Peter Keegan, a vintner, Dr Alexander Harkin who was prominent in the work of the St Vincent de Paul Society and Alexander O'Rorke, a solicitor. Their interest and enthusiasm certainly reflected the satisfaction of the laity with the measures being so promptly and courageously undertaken to provide Belfast with much needed pastoral structures. The address, couched in the orotund and ornate style which was then customary, referred to the great works which owed their advancement to the bishop's zeal and to the healthy and flourishing state of the religious institutions conducted by Brothers and Sisters.[21]

The Sisters of Mercy had completed their convent, schools and orphanage before Denvir's resignation in 1865, but they had retained control of a female penitentiary or home for delinquent girls at Bankmore House, whither they had moved in 1863 from the smaller home they had established three years earlier in Hamilton Street. They now wished to be relieved of this charge because of their increasing commitments on the Crumlin Road. In 1867 Dorrian invited the Good Shepherd Sisters, who, among other apostolates,

20 See pp 140-52.
21 U.Ob., 6 Aug. 1867

specialized in this work, to come to Belfast and take charge of Bankmore House. In the following year they moved to a more spacious and healthy site at Ballynafeigh in the suburbs. In 1870 the Irish Dominican Sisters founded a convent on the Falls Road, and set about establishing both a primary school for local girls and a secondary one, both for day-girls and boarders; in the same year a group of French nuns, belonging to the recently founded Sisters of the Sacred Heart, opened similar schools in Lisburn. In 1872 the Bons Secours, an order devoted to nursing and welfare work, opened a house in Alfred Street. In 1876 Dorrian handed over his own house at Ballynafeigh [22] to the Sisters of Nazareth, and this became the nucleus of their convent and home for the poor, orphans and elderly. In 1883 Bedeque House on the Crumlin Road was acquired by the Sisters of Mercy for £2,300, and at a further cost of £1,000 was equipped and opened as the Mater Infirmorum Hospital with residential, surgical and extern facilities. The social work carried out by the nuns was invaluable. And the Catholic community responded generously to the frequent appeals made to it for support for those who cared for the abandoned, aged and indigent, the waifs and strays of society.

In fact the munificent response of the Catholics of Down and Connor to the funding of these religious institutions is all the more impressive because of their many commitments at local, parish level. Very few of them were wealthy. In Belfast William Ross employed some 600 people in his flax mill, Bernard Hughes had 150 men in his bakeries and John Hamill was an extensive landowner. Apart from them there were a few who had become moderately wealthy as merchants and shopkeepers. Catholics increasingly dominated the liquor trade and butchery business. A small number were to be found in the professions as teachers, doctors, lawyers or architects, but the vast majority earned their livelihood as mill hands or labourers. Dorrian believed that in the mid-1860s some 70, 80 or 90 of them had capital ranging from £2,000 to £5,000 and so could spare £100 from their income for charitable purposes.

The decade of the 1870s was the period of church building *par excellence*, when the diocese was covered or re-covered with a coat of fine new churches. These were invariably substantial edifices usually gothic in style, built of solid stone, carefully finished, comfortably furnished, and far superior to the simple, bare, and generally impoverished buildings which was all that a less affluent and a more cowed generation could afford. The list includes Antrim (1870), Crossgar (1870), Portglenone (1871), St Columba's, Rasharkin

22 Dorrian lived in Holywood from 1867 to 1871, at Ballynafeigh from 1871 to 1876, and at Chichester Park from 1876 to 1885.

(1872), Downpatrick (1872), Comber (1872), Dunsford (1872), Saintfield (restored 1873), Holywood (1874), Ballycastle (1874), Rasharkin (1874), Glenarm (1875), Ballycran (1876), St Patrick's, Belfast (1877), Newtownards (1877), Ballymoney (1878), Ballintoy (1878), Feystown (1878), Ballygalget (1879), Kilkeel (1879), Ardglass (1879), Drumaroad (1879). Though the pace slowed down in the 1880s, five new churches were erected: St Joseph's, Belfast (1880), St Matthew's, Ballymacarrett (1883), Cloughmills (1883), Dundrum (1884), Castlewellan (1884) and after major renovations Killough and Rossglass were re-dedicated also in 1884. Two of these churches were the gifts of wealthy benefactresses. The first, at Newtownards, was erected solely at the expense of the dowager marchioness of Londonderry,[23] whose family had a seat nearby at Mount Stewart; the second, at Ballintoy, was due to the munificence of the local landlords, Alexander George and Georgiana Fullerton,[24] both of whom had become Catholics.

Not long after St Mary's in Belfast was rebuilt, it was discovered that the second oldest church, St Patrick's, was in a dangerous condition. In 1867 several people fell four or five feet when a floor collapsed, the congregation panicked and a few were injured in the rush to leave.[25] By 1873 Dorrian had decided to knock down the old church and replace it with a new one. Meetings were called to explain the plans and the people of the St Patrick's district were asked to be responsible for the costs. An editorial in the *Belfast Morning News* suggested that the new St Patrick's should be the responsibility of the entire Catholic population of the town. Dorrian countered this argument, incidentally revealing his strategy as well as his financial burdens. He pointed out that there was still a debt of £1,300 on St Malachy's Presbytery and that new schools were needed in that district. St Peter's had a debt of £1,600, was still not completed, had no organ and schools nearby were long overdue; St Mary's had a debt of £1,000 after it was opened, and the area it served badly required a presbytery and new schools. There had not been general collections for many of the schools which had been recently built, and the policy was not to tax the people by general appeals except for general objects.[26] A temporary church was established in converted sheds near the quays in 1872; in 1880 it was replaced by the present St Joseph's.

23 Elizabeth Frances Charlotte, daughter of the third earl of Roden and wife of the fourth marquis of Londonderry, had become a Catholic in 1855.
24 Lady Georgiana Fullerton, née Leveson-Gower, daughter of the first Earl Granville, became a Catholic in 1846. A distinguished novelist, she wrote on subjects relating to religious controversies, and to Ireland.
25 U.Ob., 18 June 1867.
26 U.Ex., 28 Apr. 1875.

Fund-raising was a constant difficulty for the clergy involved in this wave of ecclesiastical building. Apart from house-to-house and church collections, they relied on sales of work and bazaars, and occasionally some of them followed the emigrants to Britain or America in search of help. One popular form of appealing for money was through a charity sermon. Sums varying from one to ten shillings were charged for seats when prominent and distinguished preachers were invited to speak in aid of particular charities. Doubtless many attended as a method of contributing but some may have been attracted by the novelty value and the theatrical aspect of the occasion. Whatever they thought of the content of the sermons, the congregations could rarely have been disappointed by their length, as many of them lasted at least an hour, and the preachers must often have mystified as well as flattered their audiences by interlarding their sermons with texts in Latin.

The financial outlay of the diocese during Dorrian's episcopate cannot be calculated as few parochial accounts have survived. The collections lifted at the opening ceremonies of churches and at charity sermons were usually published in the press, but the details of expenditure on schools and church equipment rarely appeared. One striking exception to this practice was the publication of a booklet by John McErlain, the parish priest of Ballymoney, in 1881.[27] He had been appointed to the parish in 1856 when the Catholic population must have been less than 1,500[28] and during his pastorate repaired the main church, which had been built in 1832, enlarged the outlying church, built a parochial house and schools, and crowned his achievements by building an impressive gothic church (to seat 650) in 1878. McErlain's experiences were not untypical. In the course of his collecting tours he spent eighteen months outside his parish, and with 'great labour and fatigue' raised £4,360; of this he got £650 in Dublin, £350 in Belfast, £420 in London, £1,080 in other parts of Britain, £300 in various Irish towns and the remainder in places which he did not name. He mentioned a large subscription received from the duke of Norfolk, but did not specify the amount, and he paid tribute to the 'excessive generosity' of a number of Protestant friends.

His full receipts were:
Subscriptions from parishioners	£ 4,062. 2. 4
Proceeds of a bazaar	£ 1,202. 8. 3
Parish collections by cards	£ 459.15. 3
Subscriptions from non-parishioners at charity sermons	£ 1,419. 0. 0

27 *A statement of accounts and a few facts concerning Ballymoney and Derrykeighan*, (Ballymoney, 1881).
28 In 1880 the population was 1,552. Ibid., p. iii.

Twelve subscriptions for stations of the cross	£ 78. 0. 0
Contributions of the Royal Irish Constabulary for the high altar	£ 453. 0. 0
Collections in various places	£ 4,360. 6. 5
Allowance in contract for the old church	£ 250. 0. 0
TOTAL	**£12,284.12. 3**

His expenditure was:

Debt on the church in 1857	£ 46. 0. 0
Erection of a gallery in the old church	£ 100. 0. 0
Enlarging the church at Dervock and erecting a school	£ 702. 0. 0
Parochial house, offices and boundary wall	£ 1,466.18. 0
Ballymoney schools	£ 727. 3. 6
Houses bought in Ballymoney	£ 40. 0. 0
Erection of lodge, reading room, entrance gates and railing.	£ 332. 0. 0
Cost of the church	£ 8,870.10. 9
TOTAL	**£12,284.12. 3**

Most of the churches built in the 1870s and 1880s were not as large as Ballymoney and consequently their principal costs would have been less; also in proportion to their outlay the Catholic population in some parishes was larger, but in many cases, the debts and the methods adopted to reduce them were comparable.

St Peter's, Belfast, which Dorrian claimed could accomodate 3,000 — though he was obviously referring to its capacity for a mainly standing congregation — had cost, by the end of his episcopate, £36,000. The outlay on the original church and presbytery was £28,000, a further £5,000 was spent on completing the spires in 1884-5, and almost £3,000 on the organ and the carillon of bells.[29] This was the largest and most impressive church in the diocese, and by 1884 when the foundation stone of St Paul's Church on the Falls Road was laid, the parochial area must have had a population in excess of 20,000. The bishop undertook to pay for St Paul's — the cost was estimated at £4,000 — from his own money but he died before it was completed.

29 P. Rogers. *St Peter's Pro-Cathedral, Belfast, 1866-1966*, (Belfast, 1966), p.23. The *Morning News* on 7 Aug. 1880 reported that St Joseph's Church, which was due to open the following day, cost £10,000, but this figure probably included the cost of the presbytery. The estimate for Downpatrick Church (before the spires were completed) was £9,000, for Castlewellan £8,000, for Holywood £5,000 and for St Patrick's, Belfast £11,800,(which, with the reductions allowed for work that would be completed later, brought it to £8,700).

Dorrian also carried out an extensive re-organization of parish boundaries in the rural parts of the diocese. Shortage of clergy and poverty had dictated the size of many parochial units, especially where Catholics were proportionally small in numbers. To ensure more constant pastoral attention and to facilitate the provision of more schools, he divided some parishes and detached parts from others which, geographically and perhaps psychologically, were better suited to joining with neighbouring parishes. Some subdivision had been going on since Crolly's time, but a greater supply of priests and the greater capacity and desire of the people to equip themselves with churches and schools now facilitated more extensive rearrangements.

After the death of William McCartan, parish priest of Rasharkin, in 1864 the district attached to the church at Dunloy was constituted a separate parish. In 1869 when Henry McLaughlin, parish priest of Loughguile, died, several townlands which were convenient to Dunloy were added to that parish. In exchange Glenravel parish surrendered to Loughguile townlands which were closer to it. When, in 1873, the next parish priest of Loughguile died, the Cloughmills end of that parish was also added to Dunloy. In 1866 Ballygalget was cut off from Ardkeen or Lower Ards and Portglenone from Ahoghill and both became separate parishes; three years later Carnlough was detached from Glenarm and achieved the same status. Also in 1869 the districts attached to the churches at Ballyclare and Ballygowan were united to form the parish of Ballyclare and townlands were added to it from Ballymena. In 1872 the union of Armoy and Ballintoy was dissolved and a parish priest was appointed to Ballintoy; in the following year Armoy became a separate parish, as also did Randalstown, which became independent of Antrim. In 1877 Drumaroad, which had formed part of Dundrum parish, was joined to Clanvaraghan which had been part of Castlewellan, to constitute a new parish. In the following year the Braid and Glenravel became separate parishes. And from 1877 parish priests were no longer appointed to Rathlin; instead a junior priest, with the title of administrator, was given charge of the island for a short period and then transferred to a curacy elsewhere. In addition to the creation of these parishes and the transfers of territory involved, boundaries were adjusted elsewhere in the interests of convenient administration and parochial homogeneity.

Apart from church building Dorrian's episcopate witnessed the provision of an extensive network of national schools and the erection of parochial houses for the clergy. As with the second wave of church building these were usually solid and substantial edifices located, if possible, beside the parish churches and much superior in accommodation and comfort to the smaller, and in many cases, merely rented houses which they replaced. In Belfast a presbytery had been built simultaneously with St Peter's; commodious houses were constructed at St Malachy's and St Mary's in the 1870s and at St Joseph's and St Matthew's in the 1880s.

The provision of spacious and convenient churches facilitated a more sedulous cultivation of the spiritual and devotional life of the people. A general mission was held in Belfast about every three years. The first was occasioned by the jubilee of 1865; in 1869 another jubilee was proclaimed in anticipation of the Vatican Council; 1875 was a holy year and in 1879 Pope Leo XIII granted the jubilee indulgence to inaugurate his papacy. Ordinary missions conducted by members of religious orders were held between these privileged years. These missions usually lasted a month, beginning with Masses in the early morning, either at 6.00am or 5.00am, and ending with evening devotions. Throughout the day the confessionals were crowded. Dorrian was indefatigable in attending the mission services; he moved frequently from one church to another, presiding at Masses, preaching and hearing confessions. Adult confirmations often marked the close of the missions as those who had missed confirmation either by moving from the countryside, by personal or family neglect, or who had become Catholics, came forward to receive it; at the end of the mission in 1875 he confirmed more than three hundred, mainly adults.[30] The same pattern was followed in the rural parishes, and the case of Ballymoney may be taken as not untypical; John McErlain reported missions of two to three weeks duration in 1866, 1869, 1874 and 1881. Dorrian often attended missions in country parishes, especially when they were being held for the first time, to offer his support and encouragement.

This awakened spirit of devotion bore fruit in the proliferation of parochial societies and confraternities. These were either of a purely devotional kind, catering for groups who assembled for religious exercises other than Mass or who undertook to conduct Sunday schools to catechize children. The confraternities of the Blessed Sacrament encouraged Eucharistic devotion. The confraternities of Christian Doctrine played a vital role in evangelizing children and indeed young adults, who either did not attend the Catholic-controlled schools, did not go to school at all or attended very irregularly. In 1877 the St Vincent de Paul Society reported that the average attendance of boys at its Sunday schools was 2,020.[31] The parishes tried to provide sufficient books for catechetical instruction, both for teachers and pupils, and to make useful works on Catholic doctrine available to all. The Rosarian society attached to St Mary's

30 U.Ex., 1 Nov. 1875.
31 U.Ex., 15 Sept. 1877.

Church had run a lending library for many years; Dorrian encouraged the other churches in Belfast to provide a similar service. In his Lenten pastoral of 1867 he referred to the value of parochial libraries, remarked that Belfast had four, and suggested that all parishes establish one.[32]

In Belfast also a Catholic Young Men's Society flourished from the early 1870s. It was based in the classrooms in Donegall St. formerly used by the students of the diocesan college and, apart from having access to a library, members met to hear talks and lectures on subjects of general religious interest and on Irish history and literature; these ranged from ancient Irish monasteries to O'Connell and repeal. When its activities were transferred to St Mary's Hall, its rooms were taken by a club for St Patrick's parish, which was inaugurated in 1881. Ballymacarrett had its own Catholic Literary Association, and both St Matthew's and St Patrick's parishes sponsored lectures and debates in addition to providing centres for recreation and games. Rural parishes, and especially those in the country towns, often followed the example of Belfast in instituting clubs, newsrooms and literary societies. In Lisburn, for example, D.B. Mulcahy, who was interested in Irish history and antiquities, founded a Catholic and Celtic Society.[33] Some of the parishes in the town had penny savings banks and encouraged small wage-earners to invest their modest savings;[34] some had their own bands, which traditionally escorted the confraternities and societies on their annual outings, and there was a Belfast Catholic Musical Association, which was founded in 1866.

As the Catholic community in Belfast grew in size and self-confidence, it felt increasingly the absence of a centre where meetings of a social, cultural and broadly religious nature could be held. After four years of planning and preparation, spurred on by the generous subscription of £500 from Bernard Hughes, St Mary's Hall was opened on 23 February 1876. Built on the site of part of the former Catholic Institute, the hall was located near the central thoroughfares of the town, though it stood off a narrow side street. Equipped with a library and reading room, kitchens and offices in addition to the main halls, it was smaller than the Ulster Hall but larger than the Music Hall. In his inaugural address, which dealt with the right use of reason and its consonance with faith, Dorrian stressed the two-fold character of the hall: a centre for recreation and enjoyment and, more importantly, a place where Catholics would

32 U.Ob., 5 Mar. 1867.
33 U.Ex., 21 Apr. 1877.
34 The St Malachy's savings bank, which was established in 1868, reported three years later that since its foundation £4,249 had been deposited and £2,047 withdrawn. (D.Ex., 9 Dec. 1871.)

receive instruction in harmony with their faith and where they would acquire a more intellectual training in science, music, art and literature, and be thereby elevated in the social scale. He envisaged an enhanced atmosphere of refinement permeating the Catholic body from the social and cultural activities which the hall would provide, and emphasised that their desire to develop their knowledge of and loyalty to their faith sprang from 'not the slightest spirit of unkindness, not the slightest wish to be intolerant or uncharitable' and was particularly necessary in an age when their Catholic principles were being caricatured in literature, morality and history.[35] He concluded by announcing lectures to be delivered by the dean of Limerick and Isaac Butt; and mention of the latter's name drew vigorous applause for reasons other than spiritual or cultural.

Dorrian's plans for greater pastoral activity were often hampered by a shortage of clergy. When he became bishop, the diocese was understaffed, and though he succeeded in attracting students from the dioceses of Ossory and Cashel, who were subsequently ordained for Down and Connor, he never had extra clergy. Moreover, the financial problems of training seminarians increased considerably. As a result of the disestablishment of the Church of Ireland in 1869, grants both to the Presbyterian and Catholic churches ceased, and from 1871 Maynooth was forced to depend on the investments from the lump sum given to it in lieu of its annual grant. Before 1871 Down and Connor enjoyed sixteen free places; after that year the number was reduced to six. This was an additional financial burden on top of many other parochial and educational debts, and Dorrian was forced to make special appeals and institute special collections. He tried to reduce the costs of educating seminarians by retaining the students for a more lengthy course at St Malachy's College. Seminarians were then allowed to sit the entrance examinations at Maynooth at different levels, and Dorrian spared expense by having them complete their classics, and mental and natural philosophy courses at St Malachy's before entering Maynooth to read theology. His pastoral letters during the 1870s and 1880s testify to his anxieties about having a sufficient number of men preparing for the priesthood and providing adequate finance for their education.

His efforts met with success. In 1865 the diocese had 80 priests; in 1885 that number had risen to 130 (including four Passionists). The great majority of these were the sons of farmers, received their early education in St Malachy's College and were trained in Maynooth. The proportion of priests to people improved substantially during Dorrian's episcopate. The population of the diocese seems to have remained constant at about 150,000, as the enormous growth of the

---

35 B.M.N., 24 Feb. 1876.

Belfast Catholic community was offset by the decline of rural parishes.[36] And, though in his account of the diocese presented to Rome during his *ad limina* visit in November 1882, Dorrian claimed that Down and Connor had 160,000 Catholics, the highest figure reached during his episcopate did not exceed 155,000. But, as he reported on that occasion, the laity had been provided with an impressive array of religious institutions and six different kinds of sodalities existed for men and women everywhere throughout the diocese. The Catholics of Belfast, numbering 70,000, were served by 28 priests, confessions were heard daily in the seven churches, and his clergy had the assistance of 12 Christian Brothers and 70 nuns. An official of Propaganda commented favourably on the back of this document about the improvements made since the last report was submitted in 1867, and attributed them — not without justification — 'in great part to the zeal of the bishop'.[37]

II

Dorrian's reputation as a communicator had preceded his appointment as coadjutor. He had gone outside his parish to preach on special occasions and, in particular to assist colleagues in raising money for schools and churches. This work increased vastly when he became a bishop. He never shirked an opportunity of preaching a charity sermon to help a parish priest in any part of the diocese collect funds for his parochial needs. And when not preaching at them he often added to the solemnity of the occasion by presiding. Nor was this activity limited to the diocese of Down and Connor. He received and accepted requests to share his gift of eloquence, and the best tribute to his standing as an orator was paid by fellow bishops honouring him with invitations to deliver the homilies at their episcopal ordinations. This privilege was accorded him on no less than five occasions: at the ordinations of Nicholas Conaty (coadjutor of Kilmore in 1863), Thomas Nulty (coadjutor of Meath in 1864), George Conroy (bishop of Ardagh in 1871), James McDevitt (bishop of Raphoe in 1871) and

---

36 According to the census conducted by the commissioners of public instruction in 1834 the total Catholic population of Down and Connor was 152,000. In 1861, when the census returns gave a denominational breakdown of the population for the first time, Catholics in Down and Connor numbered 150,000. In 1871 that figure had increased to 154,000, but by 1881 it had fallen again to 150,000.

37 A.P.F. S.C.(Irlanda), 39, ff 658r-665r. This 'relatio status dioecesis' was dated 12 Oct. 1882. The official did not miss a slip which Dorrian had made about nearly all the churches being equipped with red vestments for benediction; he noted that it was necessary to tell him that the proper colour was white and that a priest was entitled only to wear Mass vestments when benediction was linked to Mass and vespers.

Michael Logue (bishop of Raphoe in 1879). Newspaper reports of such occasions were invariably florid and grandiloquent; the description of the sermon at Conaty's ordination — 'a model of apostolic eloquence' — was fully representative of that genre.

Within the diocese of Down and Connor he preached on every aspect of the Christian faith. He naturally followed the liturgical cycle in his choice of themes for the great feasts of the year. When the popes proclaimed a jubilee and attached indulgences to particular religious exercises, he explained the need to pray for the intention which the pontiffs had in mind. When giving charity sermons in aid of school building projects, he usually expounded the whole Catholic attitude to education, and at times of special prayer for some particular need, such as the restoration of the pope to his temporal possessions, or at a special event such as the definition of the dogma of the Immaculate Conception or the summoning of the Vatican Council, he dealt at length with these immediate issues.

His yearly pastoral letters followed a similar pattern. He frequently commented on developments in educational policy. When necessity arose, he discussed problems relating to local politics, always appealing to his people for restraint, for the avoidance of confrontation and the pursuit of political goals by constitutional means. Typical of this kind of exhortation were his remarks in 1867 when he vigorously condemned Fenianism:

> Our duty is clear: to abhor illegal and execrable confederacies of every kind . . . We can remove injustice by constitutional redress if we be in earnest . . . If we are obedient and dutiful children of the church, we shall be both good Christians and good citizens.[38]

At times he pleaded with his people not to respond to provocation under any circumstances, to forego their right to hold parades of any kind of political or national complexion lest they be turned into occasions of violence, and not to succumb to a tit-for-tat mentality. Remarking in 1873 that the blame for the disgrace brought on the town by riots lay with those who by even-handed justice could have prevented it, he made a strong appeal to Catholics not to take part in processions:

> We must not conceal our great dislike of public and bantering processions. We can see no good but much evil in them. They are neither religious nor patriotic . . . remember your promises at the close of the mission not to take part in the procession of 17

---

38 U.Ob., 5 Mar. 1867.

March. To do so in Belfast or in the country districts would be to throw down the gauntlet. No. Be Christians, give no provocation.[39]

Condemnation of moral evils, and especially of the abuse of alcohol, occurred frequently in the pastorals. Though the bishop did not believe in solving the problem of intemperance by severe civil legislation, and feared that compulsory closing of bars on Sundays would lead to the greater evil of an increase in illicit consumption with its attendant immorality, he was extremely anxious to encourage a spirit of restraint among his people with regard to the consumption of alcohol. The dangers and abuses associated with excessive drinking were frequently and powerfully described by observers of the condition of the working classes in Belfast; the contribution it made to the impoverishment of workers' homes, the destitution of families, quarrelling, prostitution and other social and medical ills was amply documented. Dorrian was very concerned to combat alcoholism as a moral, social and spiritual abuse. Through his encouragement the Belfast Catholic Temperance Association was founded and by the end of the 1860s a centre existed in each parish. By joining, members pledged themselves to abstain from all alcoholic drinks for one year, and at the expiry of that promise, were invited to renew it. He faithfully attended the annual meetings of the society and used all his persuasive powers to exhort his audience to total abstinence. In his pastoral of 1874 he summed up the dangers and consequences of over-indulgence in the dread words of St Augustine: 'drunkenness is the corrupter of the soul; it is a voluntary insanity; a storm shattering the body, the tempest of the tongue, the ship-wreck of chastity, the loss of time, the squandering of goods — the mother of all vice and the origin of all wickedness'.[40] It was a theme to which he often felt obliged to return, and like all other Irish reformers in this field, both clerical and lay, he could only claim partial success in combating excessive drinking.

He also gave warnings occasionally about the moral dangers attached to dancing houses. Belfast had its share of sleazy halls which attracted drunks and prostitutes, and the bishop was not alone in advising Catholic parents to ensure that their sons and especially their daughters did not frequent these unsavoury saloons. Nor was he alone in warning people to prevent wakes from becoming occasions of disgraceful conduct which dishonoured the deceased. Irish bishops had long begged for restraint at wakes, but, taking advantage of the hospitality that was *de rigueur* at such times, the local

---

39 U.Ex., 24 Feb. 1873.
40 U.Ex., 16 Feb. 1874.

exhibitionist and the village idiot invariably competed for attention and often turned the nights of mourning into occasions for quarrelling, heavy drinking or indulging in indecent conversation or behaviour. In 1869 he complained that wakes often resembled pagan orgies rather than vigils for the Christian dead, observed that 'persons of the lowest morals having no connection with the deceased invite themselves' and indulge in wickedness, and consequently he admonished all young females to keep away from such scenes of iniquity.[41]

Not surprisingly, Dorrian also found himself involved in religious controversy, though this was more accidental than deliberate. His opponent was no less formidable a figure than Revd William McIlwaine, the rector of St George's, Belfast, a prominent controversialist, who had already won notoriety for his polemical, anti-Catholic sermons. They did not intend to engage in a public dispute about their doctrinal differences. McIlwaine wrote to Dorrian, a couple of months after their correspondence had terminated, to say that because of erroneous impressions that had arisen about it he had been advised by friends to publish it. Dorrian was reluctant to have it published because of his 'insuperable distaste for religious polemics'. But he did not veto McIlwaine's plans and, when the *Belfast News-Letter* began to publish what McIlwaine released to it, Dorrian prepared a booklet with an explanatory preface and notes for publication.[42]

The correspondence had a curious origin. A discussion arose at the turkish baths in Donegall St. about a priest being burned in effigy in Skibbereen. One of those present, who turned out to be McIlwaine, commented that this was God's judgement on the Roman Catholics for burning the Word of God in the presence of their priest in that locality in 1847. Challenged by Dorrian about this claim that Catholics were deprived of scriptural reading, McIlwaine held his ground and later brought to Dorrian's house what he maintained was a fragment of the bible that had been rescued from the flames. But during this visit he admitted that the incendiarism had occurred at Kanturk rather than Skibbereen. Dorrian promptly wrote to the parish priest there and in reply received a firm disclaimer of the allegation; this he passed on to McIlwaine and the series of letters began.

McIlwaine then shifted the scene of the incident to Newmarket and the date to March 1848. Then turning to the wider issues behind such activities, McIlwaine diagnosed the real problem as the

41 U.Ex., 9 Feb. 1869.
42 *Correspondence between Rev. W. McIlwaine and Most Rev. Dr Dorrian*, (Belfast, 1865).

treatment of the scriptures by their respective churches and stated as an unquestionable fact that the Church of Rome had repeatedly displayed hostility to the authorized version of the Word of God. Then, referring to the assumption of the Roman Church to be the sole keeper and infallible interpreter of the scriptures, he pointed out how one pope had, in the preface to an edition of the bible, forbidden the slightest alteration to it, while a successor subsequently introduced changes, and corrected upwards of 2,000 errors. He offered these points, he concluded, for candid consideration and was prepared to discuss them further in a calm and friendly spirit.

Dorrian, before replying, again contacted the parish priest of Kanturk, who in turn raised the issue with his colleague in Newmarket. The pastor of Newmarket admitted that one of his curates 'finding several tracts and small works containing gross and insulting language to all Catholics, collected them in a heap and publicly burned them in the street' but denied that any bible or testament was among them. He conceded, however, that some pious lady from Newmarket could easily find some burned leaves of a bible. Dorrian quoted this letter in response to McIlwaine's and also dealt with the attitudes of their respective churches to the scriptures. He explained that Catholics depended on the authority of an infallible church for their belief in the inspiration of the bible; the Anglicans had no authority for claiming an inspired bible for by denying an infallible church they had left themselves without a bible, as Dr Colenso had proved.[43] The church, he argued, which allowed Colenso to reject the bible or any part of it as not being the Word of God but allowed McIlwaine to look upon it as the Word of God must be a false church. When the pope forbade changes in an authoritative version, he was merely forbidding individuals to make alterations; they were being asked to leave it in the hands of those to whom God had entrusted it.

A dozen letters followed in much the same vein developing these points and adding for good measure a few of the customary charges of contemporary religious polemic. McIlwaine refused to accept the designation of the tracts as filthy and stoutly maintained that the burned pages of the bible, which were in his possession, had been rescued from the flames in Newmarket. Dorrian with equal firmness insisted on the disreputable nature of these tracts. McIlwaine went on to discuss the foundations on which their faiths were built: his was established on the written Word of God; Dorrian's on scripture, unwritten tradition and the apocrypha. He poured scorn on the Council of Trent (which had determined the Catholic canon of

---

43 John William Colenso, the Anglican bishop of Natal, had then aroused much opposition by his studies of the Pentateuch and Joshua in which he challenged the accepted authorship and historical accuracy of these books.

scripture), denying it the title of ecumenical. That popular figure of religious controversy, Pope Alexander VI, duly made his appearance, with McIlwaine instancing his scandalous behaviour along with the confusion caused by councils deposing popes and popes deposing councils as illustrating the impossibility of papal infallibility; Dorrian retorted by distinguishing between the man and the office, between the personal lives and opinions of popes and their official teaching as the successors of Peter.

But the issue grew more confusing for general readers when quotations in Latin were bandied about. McIlwaine argued that Pope Liberius had subscribed to Arianism, citing the Catholic apologist, Cardinal Bellarmine, as his author; Dorrian repudiated the quotation pointing out that Bellarmine had used the name Hilarius not Liberius in the original, and McIlwaine subsequently admitted that he could have written down the wrong name.

The correspondence terminated through exhaustion. Both sides saw it was leading nowhere, and in fact tempers had been rising and the language growing more robust as it progressed. Because it was a private exchange, with both parties moving back and forward from the burning of bibles and tracts to the familiar arguments of theological controversy, rather than a planned, systematic statement of a case designed for general consumption, it did not make easy reading and must have been too condensed and opaque for the ordinary public. Indeed, it seems likely that Dorrian's own prediction was realized: 'the public will not likely derive any information from our lucubrations'.

III

Dorrian had always been a consistent supporter of papal prerogatives. He had welcomed the publication of the Syllabus of Errors in 1864 and believed that a clear and unequivocal condemnation of views opposed to Catholic doctrine reassured not only Catholics but also Protestants of good will. The prospect of a solemn and final definition of papal infallibility appealed to him, and though in 1869 he did not discuss the theological issues facing the council, when calling for prayers for its success before leaving Belfast, he set off in the confident expectation that this question would be satisfactorily settled. He had never been a professional theologian and did not lay claim to expertise on the subjects discussed at the council. He prepared a speech which should have been delivered at the beginning of July 1870, but, when the discussions on infallibility were cut short, it was submitted to the conciliar officials with the others which were not delivered and subsequently published in the official collections of the council. It was an unequivocal defence of the personal and independent infallibility of the pope when acting as teacher of the universal church.

Dorrian seems to have been provoked into making his contribution by a claim made by a Canadian and two American bishops that the definition would create difficulties for bishops who lived among Protestants.[44] This he repudiated because it contained the false insinuation that the Holy Spirit would not be the author of the definition and would not give help to the pope at the opportune time. He then went on to explain that he lived among Protestants and Orangemen of the most militant kind and claimed, surely not without justification, that, if any bishop living among Protestants were entitled to fear the definition, it was he. But on the contrary he warmly welcomed it and had a greater fear of bad Catholics of the gallican school who corrupted and deceived the simple faithful. In fact, it was his experience that even the most educated Protestants said that Catholics did not believe in infallibility because they did not agree on the subject in whom it adhered; if the doctrine were true, they would know where infallibility resided. He believed that controversy with Protestants would be facilitated by the definition, and he insisted that among Protestants there were many sincere lovers of truth who would happily accept the truth when presented without ambiguity.

He then went on to deal with arguments against the definition which were based on Irish traditions. He rejected the view expressed by Bishop Moriarty of Kerry that Irish pastors had never preached infallibility; he himself had done so and the clergy of his diocese assembled in conference had all agreed on infallibility. He then took on again the same North American opponents but this time linked their names to that of the redoubtable archbishop of Tuam (who had made a long and powerful speech against the opportuneness of the definition). The important historical fact to which he drew attention was the attempt of Peter Walsh, a Franciscan and friend of the Protestant viceroy, the duke of Ormonde, to obtain the signatures and support of the bishops and clergy of Ireland in 1666 for a loyal remonstrance testifying to their independence of papal authority in all matters of civil concern. Dorrian, interpreting Walsh's activities in a very dim light, explained that the friar presented to an assembly (which consisted of ten bishops, seven vicars general, and heads of

---

44 Thomas Connolly, archbishop of Halifax, Michael Domenec, bishop of Pittsburg, and Richard Whelan, bishop of Wheeling, had referred to Protestant opposition to papal infallibility and to the traditional replies of Catholic apologists that the belief in it was not *de fide*. They feared Protestants would accuse the church of adding to the rule of faith and of being deceitful, and as a result would become more hostile to it.

religious orders, and was morally representative of the whole Irish church) six propositions which had been passed at the Sorbonne in 1663. Despite all the intimidation and deceit three signatures were obtained for the first three articles but none at all for the other three. Those which were totally rejected related to the deposition of bishops, the supremacy of a council over the pope and the denial of papal infallibility; Walsh himself was forced to acknowledge that his opponents had been taught to believe that the pope was infallible. Consequently Tuam and his friends erred when they said that for thirteen hundred years the Irish had not held this belief. And he concluded by asking that the phrase *ex cathedra* precede the words referring to the pope in his capacity as supreme teacher, and that the opposite opinion be anathematized.[45]

By the time this speech was submitted the anti-infallibilists had been routed. The real discussion had come to centre on the terms of the definition and so Dorrian's intervention, had it been in fact delivered, would not have had any significant effect. The argument about the consequences for Protestants of the clarification of church teaching on the question of infallibility has never been, and could never be satisfactorily settled; the immediate reaction of the great majority of Protestants was far less benign than Dorrian anticipated, but as infallibility has come to be understood in the light of further conciliar teaching, its role in religious controversy has diminished. One of Dorrian's claims, however, could not be gainsaid: he certainly lived among the most determined of Protestants.

IV

Sweeping administrative changes and the vigorous prosecution of more active pastoral policies by a dedicated bishop were bound to produce friction with either clergy or laity. Dorrian was fortunate not to encounter much dissension, but he did meet opposition from a religious order and from an influential group of lay people; the tension with the clergy did not become public knowledge but the controversy with the laity landed him with some very adverse publicity at the beginning of his episcopate.

The Passionists owed their invitation to establish a foundation in Belfast to Dorrian's need for clerical manpower rather than to a policy on his part of giving his people a choice between secular and regular clergy. In 1868 he offered them a quasi-parochial status within his own parish, by assigning the suburb of Ardoyne to their care and selling them a site for a church and house. They were also

45 Mansi, *Sacrorum Conciliorum nova et amplissima collectio*, lxii, 1067-1070.

given charge of a small church at Ligoniel. They hastily erected a wooden church at Ardoyne, which was dedicated on 10 January 1869, and they began to minister to the people of the district. The bishop drew up an agreement with the order which may have been intended to safeguard his position should it decide to leave, but which contained clauses that were productive of future discord. The superior of the new community was recognized as a quasi-parish priest and, in the event of his removal, the superior general was to present his successor with commendatory letters to the bishop. The bishop was to enjoy the right of ordering collections in the church, of receiving the same proportion of income from it as from other churches in Belfast, and was to determine when and for what length of time the Passionists could 'quest' or seek alms. It was also understood that the bishop was to determine how many members of the community would have diocesan faculties to enable them to hear confessions, and that those with such faculties were to attend the conferences of the diocesan clergy.[46]

The relations of regular and diocesan clergy have defied all attempts by church law to prevent friction between them,[47] and the agreement between Dorrian and the Passionists was no exception. In fact its terms contributed to misunderstanding and tension, because the Passionists soon came to believe that they had allowed their canonical rights to be whittled away. They began to feel that the bishop regarded them in the same light as his own curates, and, though serious confrontation with the diocesan authority did not occur until after Dorrian's death, his interpretation and execution of the agreement continued to rile them.

They objected to deviations from the practice obtaining in their houses in Britain where the superior appointed the assistants for parochial work and where he alone or his substitute attended the diocesan conferences. But, much more seriously, they objected to the financial arrangements: they resented the bishop's claiming one third of their monthly and other collections for the upkeep of the clergy; they were annoyed at his refusal to allow them to quest on more than one occasion, and that for only one month; and they were angered by his constant postponing of permission for them to build a new church and start gathering funds for it. Dorrian argued that major collections and money-raising schemes had to be spread out and because of the expense involved in St Patrick's and St Joseph's

---

46 A.P.F. S.C.(Irlanda), 56, ff 251r-259r.

47 A dispute in England between the bishops and the regular clergy concerning the exemption which the religious orders claimed from episcopal jurisdiction was sparked off in 1877 when the Jesuits opened a school in Manchester without the permission of the bishop of the diocese. It was settled by the bull *Romanos Pontifices* in 1881 in which nearly all the points at issue were decided in the bishops' favour.

Churches other appeals had to be delayed.[48] In the event nothing happened during his episcopate and by the time of his death the Passionists' church was in a dangerous condition.

Dorrian's refusal to allow the Passionists to hold missions in Ardoyne was another painful irritant to them. In the early years he may have thought that the population they served was too small, but when he did not change his attitude they felt they were being insulted. His decision to rearrange the boundaries of their district and to re-assign a part of it to the secular clergy caused further offence. From the bishop's point of view he was free to make whatever parochial arrangements he wished in his own parish. The Passionists regarded this re-arrangement as a financial blow, for they lost some of their best contributors by it.

They subsequently claimed that they suffered in silence during Dorrian's episcopate for the sake of peace. But, though they made private remonstrances to the bishop, he was not prepared to alter his arrangements. They awaited, according to one of their provincials, the appointment of a 'more just and benign successor', but, when they were disappointed by the successor's refusal to change the regulations he had inherited, they protested at length to him and, obtaining no redress, to Rome. In his defence Bishop Patrick McAlister claimed that they accused both Dorrian and himself of oppressive, arbitrary and unjust treatment, and that the provincial had attacked Dorrian with particular vehemence about the arrangements for rebuilding the church in Ardoyne. And Dorrian, according to McAlister, regretted ever having allowed them to enter the diocese.[49]

In fact the differences between the bishop and the Passionists were not settled during McAlister's episcopate and probably had a significant bearing on the appointment of his successor.[50] But eventually most of the Passionists' claims were conceded.

---

48 Statement of some points of controversy between Bishop McAlister and the Passionists. A.P.F. S.C.(Irlanda), 43, ff 108r-133r.

49 McAlister to Propaganda, 20 Oct. 1888, Ibid., 56, ff 224v-246v.

50 In 1895 the two leading candidates for succession to the bishopric, Henry Henry and Daniel McCashin, obtained the same number of votes from the parish priests of the diocese. But the bishops of the province of Armagh expressed anxiety about Henry's 'Parnellism' and recommended McCashin. Under normal circumstances this would have ensured McCashin's appointment. But an ex-provincial of the Passionists pointed out to Propaganda that McCashin had been the constant counsellor of both Dorrian and McAlister in the rigorous measures they had taken against the order and that his hostility to it in Belfast was notorious; Henry's views were the very opposite and he wished the Passionists to have the same liberty as other religious orders in Ireland. Cardinal Vannutelli drew the attention of his colleagues to the long standing controversy, and this may well have been the deciding factor in Henry's appointment.

V

If the public did not become aware of the strained relations between the bishop and the Passionists, it was certainly made aware of the dispute between the bishop and the shareholders of the Catholic Institute. The controversy was widely reported not only in the Irish but also in the British press.

The Catholic Institute had come into existence in 1859. Considering themselves isolated and politically powerless in the predominantly Protestant town of Belfast, some leading Catholics decided that they needed a centre where they could associate, a base for meetings and discussions on issues that concerned them in business, politics, civic or religious affairs, and a place where activities of a cultural and educational nature could be carried out. Three prosperous merchants, William Watson, George Murney and Daniel Rogan Brannigan, acquired a valuable property consisting of a spacious house and grounds in Hercules Place[51] and formed a company to establish the Institute. Arrangements were made to find the capital by offering shares at £1 to any member of the Catholic public, and shareholders were entitled to elect a board of twenty directors, who, after a fixed period, were to be elected annually. According to the report of its inaugural meeting, the purpose of the Institute was to provide for the educational, study and recreational needs of its members; it proposed to give the less-educated opportunities of acquiring useful knowledge at charges so low as to enable the humblest man in the community to avail of them; the library and reading rooms were to be stocked with books, periodicals and newspapers, selected with prudence and wisdom; and the principal subjects to be taught in the large lecture hall were to be chemistry and mechanics.[52] The richer Catholics were selected as directors and the Institute tried — unsuccessfully — to cover its costs by charging small admission fees.[53] Some clergy became shareholders — the Institute was also envisaged as a place where they could stay, when in Belfast, 'without being obliged to go to a Protestant hotel where they run the risk of being insulted' — but the founders were generally disappointed at the level of support it attracted both from the clergy and from the Catholic middle class.[54]

It did, however, provide Catholics with the kind of social and literary centre which its founders envisaged. On special occasions

---

51 It had belonged to Robert James Tennent, a member of a leading commercial family, who was MP for Belfast from 1847 to 1852. The site is now occupied by the Allied Irish Bank, at 2 Royal Avenue and by St Mary's Hall, Bank St.
52 *Irishman*, 16 July 1859.
53 P.R.O.N.I. D1905/2/205A.
54 *Irishman*, 8 Oct. 1859.

such as St Patrick's Day formal dinners were held in it. The newsroom was abundantly stocked with papers and non-members were allowed to use it for a small fee. Lectures on a wide variety of topics from literature, history and music to science were given in it. Courses were organized on such diverse subjects as chemistry and art and design. But the problem of paying off the capital costs proved too difficult for the number of people who were willing to become shareholders.

Dorrian distrusted some of the leading figures of the Institute, believed that they were somehow trespassing on episcopal jurisdiction and was afraid that the rooms might be used by secret or seditious societies. Though Canon Law did not, and perhaps could not, clearly legislate for the requirement that all bodies laying claim to the official title of Catholic should have episcopal approval, many bishops interpreted their authority as embracing this requirement. The growing ultramontane movement certainly tended to enhance episcopal power in such areas. And the encyclical *Quanta Cura* and the Syllabus of December 1864 by demanding increased vigilance against all possible dangers to Catholicism, whether through the press, education or any anti-clerical forms of association, gave added encouragement to bishops to challenge bodies or associations which they regarded, however remotely, as dangerous to the purity of the faith.

Dorrian's chance to interfere came when legal difficulties arose over the company's right to sell property. In 1864 the Provincial Bank negotiated with the directors and agreed to purchase part of the site for a substantial sum — approximately double what the whole property had cost — which would not only have cleared the debt but would have left some money available for remodelling the premises. The directors notified the shareholders in February 1865 of their view that the offer of the bank should be accepted, but explained that this could only be legally done by winding up the company and vesting the property in a liquidator, who would then be empowered to sell it. Further consultations were promised as to the advisability of 'reconstructing and remodelling the plan of the Association' or applying its funds, in whole or part, to some other kindred purpose.[55] The directors decided that shareholders should be paid a dividend on their investment and were holding consultations to this effect, when Dorrian challenged their behaviour as uncanonical and improper. Arguing that the original prospectus of the company committed it to improving the moral, intellectual and religious condition of the Catholic people, he maintained that the Institute should be preserved as a permanent possession for the Catholic body rather than turned into a source of profit for investors.

55 P.R.O.N.I. D1905/2/208A.

A meeting of shareholders was called to discuss the issue on 13 April 1865. Though it fell on Holy Thursday, Dorrian in his capacity as a shareholder (though a small one) attended in the hope, as he subsequently explained, that he could be of use in arranging the matter to meet the views of the directors and gratify the ardent aspirations of the great majority of those who had bought shares. The chairman proposed a resolution about winding up the company without any allusion to the surplus property. Dorrian then submitted a series of resolutions: that the Belfast Catholic Institute Association be wound up, that liquidators be appointed for this purpose and that they execute the contract already made to sell part of the premises to the Provincial Bank; that the liquidators be authorized to sell to trustees part of the grounds of sufficient size as a site for a lecture hall, library and newsroom and that such hall, library and newsroom be conducted by, and in accordance with, such rules as would have the approval and sanction of the bishop of the diocese for the time being; that the remaining part of the premises be conveyed by deed to Bishop Denvir or Bishop Dorrian as a site for a Catholic church or religious institution; that the surplus funds, after the payment of all debts, be transferred to trustees to purchase the headrent of the premises, or to invest it to pay the rent of the premises or, if this were not possible, to apply it to the erection of whatever building the bishop of the diocese should approve of. The directors explained in response to these resolutions that they were legally constrained from putting any motion to the meeting other than that of winding up the association. The majority of the shareholders[56] present then rejected this motion of the directors, and Dorrian expressed the hope that the problem would be solved satisfactorily after some calm reflection.

However, some of the directors or shareholders were not disposed to forego the chance of earning the unexpected dividend which the sale of the Institute would have brought them. Word leaked out almost immediately that the case would be brought to the court of chancery.

In the light of this development, Dorrian sent a printed circular,

56 According to the *Belfast News-Letter*, (10 Nov. 1865), there were three groups among the shareholders: the first wanted the company to be wound up and the proceeds divided among the shareholders; the second group were the followers of Dr Dorrian and, though few in number and weaker in influence, were willing to vote with him; the third group wanted the concern to be wound up on condition that a new institute would be born. By combining this third group with his own Dorrian was able to prevent the resolution for winding up the company from being carried. At the Powis Commission in 1868 Dorrian himself referred to three parties, two of which corresponded to the first and third mentioned by the *News-Letter*. The other party, according to this version, wanted a site for a Christian Brothers' establishment, or perhaps for a church.

dated 27 April, to all the shareholders, acquainting them of his views and of his responsibilities in the whole issue. 'Long and universally was it believed that this property had been purchased for the purposes that could be approved of as calculated to advance the moral and intellectual standing of the Catholics of Belfast and neighbourhood', he wrote, astutely omitting the name of the person who was to give the approval and conveniently leaving his readers to guess who precisely held this belief. But he clearly implied that the wider Catholic public had assumed that the Institute was established with episcopal approval and went on to add that 'such was the import of the name assumed in the articles of association' and 'such was the object proclaimed in the reports published with official and authorized sanction'. When it was realized that to carry out the sale the association had to be dismantled, he was 'everywhere spoken to, asked and implored to initiate some movement' and so he felt in conscience bound 'to interfere in any reasonable and judicious way . . . to secure the realization of objects dear to the Catholic heart'. He had exchanged views with as many shareholders as possible, but the directors, with one or two exceptions, refused to attend meetings to discuss the situation, until the official meeting of 13 April, when the proposal was put to wind up the association. He then set down the series of resolutions he had proposed, the decision that had been taken at the meeting and the report that the question was to be brought to the court of chancery. Reminding them that he would remain faithful to the responsibilities of his office and support those who looked to pastoral superintendence for protection, he concluded his letter by pointing out the obligations in conscience of those who had given their money 'expecting no return but the moral and social improvement of their fellows'. They had no more right to withdraw it, he insisted, than they had to take stones from a church they had contributed to build, but he admitted, nonetheless, that those who wanted simply to make an honest percentage were at full liberty to claim it.[57]

This brusque declaration of his claims angered some of the directors and shareholders, who interpreted his intervention as a desire to confiscate their property. In May he succeeded to the see of Down and Connor and this gave his views increased weight and correspondingly lessened the likelihood of firm resistance to them. However, he received no official response from the directors to his letter. But in September he was invited to attend a meeting of a committee appointed to form a new company. Feeling that he could not attend without compromising the responsible trust he held, he wrote to the secretary of the company magisterially rebuking the

[57] B.N.L., 10 Nov. 1865.

directors for not responding to the proposals he had made in April and incidentally revealing that his increased authority had decreased his readiness to brook opposition.

Loftily dismissing the request to act on the committee, which he alleged 'might possibly compromise the duties of my office which makes me the proper judge in this diocese of everything pertaining to the moral and religious training and education of my people', he termed the refusal of the directors of the Institute to inform him whether his proposals had been accepted or rejected 'a departure from what is due by reverent intelligent laymen and docile Catholics to their Bishop'. Consequently, since no explanation had been given or reparation made, he had decided that the most effective way he could serve his people was by remaining free 'to approve, if it can be, or, if need be, to interdict this or any other association as the future may suggest to be my duty'. He then quite openly disclosed the roots of his suspicion:

> You will gather from this that my faith in the fitness of some parties to become approved guides of a Catholic Institute had been greatly shaken by the experience of the last few months — and that no men shall have my sanction for such office unless their practice of religious duties and general character be satisfactory to me.

And he concluded that conscience compelled him to be explicit since neither his mind nor his sense of duty would allow him to look silently on but would oblige him to bless or condemn, as the case merited.[58]

Presumably this letter to the secretary did not have the intended effect. Consequently, Dorrian addressed another letter to the shareholders, in which he reminded them of his last circular, and of the failure of the directors to respond to his proposals, and in which he quoted his recent reply to the secretary. Then he went on to say that, if the object of the Institute was to improve the moral, intellectual and religious condition of the Catholic people, the sanction and guidance of the bishop could not be dispensed with and would not be ignored. He could not be indifferent about its management or rest content with a mere honorary patronage and then leave it to its fate. Asserting that they could not regard themselves as Catholics, if they thought otherwise, he justified his views by an appeal to some propositions that had been condemned in the Syllabus of the previous year. He listed three of these propositions: the forty-eighth which forbade Catholics to approve of a system of

---

58 Dorrian to P McGivney, 19 Sept. 1865, in B.N.L., 27 Oct. 1865.

education unconnected with Catholic faith and which regarded the knowledge of merely natural things as the only or at least the primary end of social life; the fifty-seventh which condemned the view that philosophy, morality and civil law should or could be beyond the sphere of divine or ecclesiastical authority; the twenty-second which rejected the opinion that Catholic teachers and authors were bound only to believe and accept what was proposed by the infallible judgement of the Church. Without trying to prove how the condemnation of these propositions could be construed as giving him authority to interfere with the Catholic Institute — a task that would have been virtually impossible save by the broadest possible interpretation of their meaning — Dorrian went on to say that not to require proper safeguards from the Institute was to acquiesce in the errors prescribed in these three propositions. He therefore laid down four conditions for his approval of any new or adapted form of Institute:

1. The approval by the Bishop of such Articles of Association as he shall judge satisfactory, and their adoption as the basis of any new company to be formed.
2. The same right, on the part of the Bishop, of approving the rules of management of Lecture Hall, Library and News-Room.
3. A veto by the Bishop on any member acting on the Directory, whose morals, religious principles and habits of life, the Bishop may object to.
4. The approval by the Bishop, or one appointed by him, for all books and newspapers to be admitted for reading into News-Room or Library; and the like approval of any lecturer to be invited to lecture to members.

Then came the crushing alternative to the acceptance of these conditions for the establishment of any Institute or similar association:

I shall consider it my duty, for the protection of my people, to debar from Sacraments all and every one who may become a member, or aid in its construction, these securities for its proper management not being first provided.

And he reinforced the terms of surrender by an appeal to the assent of all good Catholics — implicitly suggesting that those who found the terms in whole or in part objectionable or unacceptable were bad Catholics — for the steps he had taken.[59]

59 B.N.L., 27 Oct. 1865. The letter is not dated but was probably written during October.

Doubtless this ultimatum fell like a bombshell on the leading members of the Institute and especially on those who regarded the bishop's charges and claims as unjustified. The *Ulster Observer*, presumably from a sense of delicacy and from a desire to avoid giving the appearance of quarrelling with the bishop, which many of its readers would have found distasteful, if not blameworthy, irrespective of the rights or wrongs of the situation, had refrained from all comment on the matter. But the columns of the *Belfast News-Letter*, once the details of Dorrian's intervention reached it from some aggrieved director or shareholder, positively dripped with *Schadenfreude*. This Tory and Orange organ, which was normally fiercely hostile to and dismissive of Catholic claims and interests, suddenly became concerned about the rights and freedoms of the Catholic layman, which it undertook to protect and defend against the encroachments of an obscurantist, ultramontane bigot.

Devoting an editorial to the conflict on 27 October the *News-Letter* chose to regard the bishop's claims as a symbol of the unchanging tyranny of Rome, recently exposed in the encyclical, and, as an example of the danger of 'making any, even the slightest concession beyond bare toleration of a system so infamous, so outrageous, so utterly discordant with the spirit of civil and religious liberty'. Claiming that Dorrian ignored the Institute while it was not paying and only stepped in when there was a balance to its credit, the paper drew out the conclusions of the dire threat to refuse the sacraments to disobedient Catholics, likened the bishop's conditions to those which 'a planter in Carolina might have offered to his slaves', and declared that it was publishing the text of Dorrian's letter 'as a duty to the Catholics of Belfast . . . many of them men of intellect and position' who, presumably, had no organ of their own which would dare to publish it.[60]

Not content with one lengthy manifestation of its new-found concern, the *News-Letter* returned to the fray the following day to express its sympathies with the Catholic laity, who were held by their bishops and priests in civil and religious bondage. It pointed out the danger of making concessions to episcopal tyrants on national and university education — the threatened surrender to a Catholic university college in Dublin being 'a rod in the hands of the clergy with which the laity will be scourged' — and congratulated itself on being privileged to reprint Dorrian's communication and on receiving from 'intelligent Roman Catholic gentlemen the warmest expressions of gratitude for our part in the transaction'.[61] And, on hearing that Dorrian, in his sermon on the following day (Sunday), had

60 B.N.L., 27 Oct. 1865.
61 B.N.L., 28 Oct. 1865.

referred to the publication of his letter and had remarked that he had not bothered to read the articles about him, being content to treat them with the contempt they deserved, the editor again returned to this promising theme, repeated again the four conditions, lambasted the bishop with renewed vigour and pointed out the incongruity of Dorrian's demanding a form of control over the Institute which was not permitted by the board of national education over schools conducted by Catholic patrons. Concluding scornfully that 'we are not surprised at any antics which a Romish prelate may please to play', the editorial declared that, if the laity submitted to the fundamental laws of the ecclesiastical system, they must needs be slaves.[62]

British papers and Protestant-owned papers in Ireland[63] picked up the controversy with enthusiasm and cheerfully lashed Dorrian's authoritarian ultramontanism. The editor of the *News-Letter*, to exploit the issue as a symbol of the danger of yielding to the Irish bishops' demands on university education, forwarded a copy of his edition of 28 October to Lord John Russell, the prime minister. Evidently pleased with this stratagem — though the letter elicited but the briefest non-committal acknowledgement — the editor published both letters on 10 November, along with the circular Dorrian sent to the shareholders after his failure to carry his proposals at the meeting on 13 April, and for good measure included another blast at the bishop and further melancholy ruminations on the 'grinding tyranny under which Rome holds her unhappy children'.[64]

Paradoxically, the *News-Letter* diminished the chances of resistance to the bishop among the shareholders of the Institute. For, by attacking him so wildly and venomously and dragging in the complex issue of Catholic education, it presented Dorrian in the eyes of most Catholics in the unassailable role of the persecuted prelate, and increased the likelihood that those Catholics who resisted his demands would be regarded disdainfully by their fellows as Castle lackeys or treacherous subversives. And, though Dorrian did not welcome the sudden and highly critical attention he received in the British and Irish press, it in fact strengthened his case in dealing with any refractory or potentially refractory members of his flock.

And, as the editor of the *News-Letter* was doubtless aware that they

62 B.N.L., 1 Nov. 1865.
63 According to the *Whig* 'hell or my dictatorship' were the alternatives offered by Dorrian to the directors of the Institute. (N.W., 8 Nov. 1865).
Reference was made to Dorrian's 'spiritual despotism' in a debate on the disestablishment of the Church of Ireland in the House of Commons in May 1867. (*Hansard* 3, clxxxvii, 175)
64 B.N.L., 10 Nov. 1865.

would, his strictures on the silence of the local Catholic press touched a very raw nerve in Andrew Joseph McKenna, the editor of the *Ulster Observer*, which was printed in premises rented from the Institute. McKenna was undoubtedly the leading figure in the Institute whom Dorrian least trusted, and who in turn strongly resented the episcopal intervention. Shortly after the crisis broke but before Denvir's resignation, Dorrian had written frantically to Rome to prevent McKenna from receiving a papal honour. He had learned that the editor of the *Observer* had been showing off a letter from an official in Rome, which intimated that all he required to obtain a papal award was a letter from his bishop, and that Denvir had postponed giving a decision until returning to Belfast. Evidently fearing that Denvir might succumb, Dorrian was determined to stop the honour at source and on Archbishop Cullen's recommendation wrote to Tobias Kirby in Rome to solicit his aid. He explained to Kirby:

> I wish, therefore, to appraise you that McKenna is a person *most unworthy* of any mark of confidence — he is without consistency, principle, or truth. Long ago I had to inform the Bishops of this province that I had lost all confidence in him as a person suited to continue at the head of a Catholic newspaper. He is the *Bunkum* Orator, to whom the Tablet alludes, at the Louth election lately.[65]
>
> For my sake, then, prevent Rome from being deceived by some officious person, unless it all be a forgery of his own, which is quite possible.[66]

Nothing further was heard of the honour.

McKenna, however, felt unable to take on Dorrian in the columns of a paper, of which some priests were shareholders, and many of whose readers would have automatically sided with the bishop. But stung by the hostile persistence of the *News-Letter* he replied in an editorial of furious eloquence, entitled *Impudence Extraordinary*, on 11 November. Rejecting with derision the attempt of their Orange contemporary 'to act the character of patron and defender of Catholics' who, McKenna insisted, 'required no instruction from the ignorant, no advice from the impertinent, no advocacy from the intolerant, no assistance from the hypocritical', he characterized its posture as aggressiveness and intolerable officiousness, and insisted that Catholics contemptuously repudiated its interference and

---

[65] The *Tablet* (8 Apr. 1865) had criticized a speech made by McKenna in support of the Liberal candidate in Louth.

[66] Dorrian to Kirby, 2 May 1865, A.I.C.R.

regarded with scorn its attempts to injure their interests.[67] The *News-Letter* replied deriding the cowardice of the *Observer* and sarcastically twitting the editor for his refusal to comment on the dispute charged that 'it has been a mattter of notoriety for the last fifteen months . . . that the Bishop and the journalist were at daggers drawn'. Then, plunging in the knife a little further, the editorial went on to claim that the *Observer* (and presumably McKenna) 'known to be dead against' the bishop dared not publish its views. Taunting the *Observer* with breaking its cowardly silence only to 'valiantly assail this journal', it concluded by self-righteously confessing that 'Roman Catholic gentlemen, despairing of seeing one line of honest comment on the subject in the *Observer* laid before us Dr Dorrian's letters and asked us to give them to the world'.[68] There was little the editor of the *Observer* could say in reply to such a painful public exposure of his relationship with the bishop and he had to content himself with reaffirming his statement that Catholics were the guardians of their own honour and the judges of their own duty.[69]

This public airing of the controversy and especially the revelation in print of McKenna's hostility to Dorrian ensured that at the meeting of shareholders called for 16 November little opposition to Dorrian's views would be expressed. McKenna, probably the most likely one to lead or galvanize the opposition, was compromised by the disclosure about him in the *News-Letter*. Only about forty shareholders turned up and they took the decision to terminate the association and to appoint liquidators to take control of and dispose of the property.[70]

A further meeting was held on 4 December to confirm this decision and to appoint the liquidators. It was resolved to complete the sale to the bank, and to value the remainder of the property and sell it to Dorrian to be used by him and his successors for Catholic purposes. The liquidators included two of the three original leaseholders, George Murney and Daniel Rogan Brannigan, two other highly influential directors, Bernard Hughes[71] and Dr James Cuming, and a couple of other prominent members. And, after the sale to the bank was completed, they wrote to Dorrian on 10 February 1866 offering him the remainder of the property for the sum which the whole had originally cost. He promptly accepted the offer, having already

67 U.Ob., 11 Nov. 1865.
68 B.N.L., 13 Nov. 1865.
69 U.Ob., 14 Nov. 1865.
70 P.R.O.N.I. D1905/2/205A.

71 Dorrian later commented to Kirby that Hughes 'unintentionally did harm by leading an attempt made here to put me under lay dictation, which I resisted, and, thank God, defeated. Some of our Catholics in the North of Ireland have been imbued with too much Presbyterianism'. (6 Apr. 1867. A.I.C.R.)

received from some of the shareholders' gifts of enough shares to enable him to do so, and, apart from the completion of legal formalities, the Catholic Institute disappeared into history.[72]

On the very day on which the shareholders agreed to the dissolution of the company — 16 November — Dorrian referred to the conflict in a letter to Tobias Kirby in Rome. He revealed that he regarded the very existence of the Institute, in the form in which it was then constituted, as a rejection of his legitimate episcopal authority:

> I am going through a little trouble here at present, and have the Protestant press in full cry against me as, perhaps, may fall under your notice. Some of my own people wish to have themselves entirely free from all Ecclesiastical control in what is called the 'Catholic Institute'. I have to make a stand to purge it from the Presbyterian leaven, & I hope to succeed. But McKenna, who was to have been honoured with a knighthood from Rome, is one of the prime movers against me. It was a great blessing that he was foiled, for had he got any distinction from Rome, my authority was gone. However he is now pretty well known here. I never read a word that the papers publish of my 'spiritual despotism', 'Ultramontanism' or my 'daring' to quote from or refer to the 'Encyclical' etc. etc. Indeed, I never felt more calm or more happy, as I trust good must come from it. The sore here wanted to be opened that our people might be cured of their Presbyterianism.[73]

Three years later he explained before the Powis Commission that the authorities in the Institute 'were letting rooms . . . for purposes which were very objectionable' and instanced an occasion when, on a Sunday afternoon, 'persons were got to meet in some rooms for political purposes, cheering was heard in the streets' and he was spoken to and had to interfere in that case. He added that he had found, what his predecessor had dreaded, that 'the place, if left uncontrolled, and without being duly watched, might become the nursery, perhaps, of some secret society'.[74] Significantly, he did not state that political gatherings of a reprehensible nature had occurred on more than one occasion, and did not indicate that he regarded the very existence of the Institute as it was then constituted as a challenge to his jurisdiction. Since 1865 Fenianism, which was never strong in Belfast, had become a matter of grave anxiety to the Irish bishops

72 P.R.O.N.I. D1905/2/205A.
73 Dorrian to Kirby, 16 Nov. 1865, A.I.C.R.
74 *Powis Commission*, p. 356, vol.iii, pt iii.

and perhaps Dorrian projected a little of his concern in 1868 back into his attitudes in 1865. In the four conditions, which he laid down for his approval of a new or reconstituted Institute, politics had not been mentioned and the only condition which could have applied to political use being made of the centre was the requirement that the bishop approve of all lecturers invited to speak in it. But, as he would have known, this was a feeble precaution against the native ingenuity of political activists who could easily have found ways and means of circumventing such a restriction. The omission of specific safeguards against the use of the Institute for political purposes indicates that anxiety on this score was not then a high priority in Dorrian's mind.

The conflict over the Institute doubtless left ruffled feelings among some of the prominent members of the Catholic community and could have seriously alienated the sympathies of precisely that class of Catholics, whose help Dorrian so badly needed in carrying out his programme of church and school-building in Belfast. Luckily, this danger was not realized and he received the willing and abundant support and co-operation of virtually his entire flock. Relations between Dorrian and McKenna grew cooler but Bernard Hughes, whom Dorrian also suspected, certainly did not allow his customary generosity to Catholic charities to be affected by any personal sentiments about the bishop. With the closure of the Institute the Catholic community lost a valuable centre not only where Catholics could have met socially but also where they could have improved their understanding of their religion, and learned something of its social and political implications. The directors and leading members were middle class and almost certainly opposed to revolutionary ideals and anxious to pursue their political aspirations by constitutional means. A base for the diffusion of such political views could have been invaluable to Dorrian later on, when local political rivalries or more extreme forms of nationalism threatened to entice some Belfast Catholics into violent ways. The absence of opportunities for respected constitutional nationalists to exercise the kind of influence which they might otherwise have exerted was part of the price paid for the closure of the Institute.

Dorrian himself never regretted his action. He remained convinced that in clashing with the Institute he was only fulfilling his responsibilities. In a letter to the press in 1869, provoked by a reference which Isaac Butt had made to his circular to the shareholders, he explained:

> The delicacy of feeling with me at that time was to do my duty, but not to wound, if possible not to expose, the ignorance of some who, in a moment of excitement, seemed to have quite forgotten the first principles of their religion, and who were

committing at least material sin by a course of action at variance with Catholic principles . . . the circular, I say, pointed out to those to whom it was addressed that the question was one in which unanimity was for us a matter of necessity and not of choice; that I was not the authority deciding so, but that the principle for which I was contending had been decided by the highest authority of our church.[75]

And even in his will, when making over to his successor some property which he had acquired after the dissolution of the company, he declared that his motive in his dealings with the Institute was to create a spirit of union and charity among Catholics.[76] It is unlikely that the founders of the Catholic Institute ever foresaw any conflict with their bishop over what they regarded essentially as a club for their co-religionists, and it was fortunate for the progress of the church in Belfast that the dispute did not lead to a serious estrangement between the bishop and an important section of his people.

VI

The conflict between the bishop and the shareholders of the Catholic Institute occurred within the Catholic community. A few years later Dorrian found himself in conflict with the Belfast town council, a body which proved much tougher and more obdurate. The dispute was caused by the need to provide more extensive burial facilities for the population of Belfast. As the denominational cemeteries were full and could not be further enlarged, the town council undertook to buy suburban land for a municipal cemetery. Controversy arose about the rights which the bishop claimed over the portion set aside for the graves of Catholics.

The shortage of burial space was one of the harrowing experiences of the famine in Belfast. Fears were expressed at a public meeting requisitioned by the Board of Health in July 1847 that the exposure of the bodies of those who had died from contagious diseases could not be prevented and would be a serious danger to the public.[77] Both the Shankill and Friar's Bush burying grounds were overcrowded. The situation did not improve after the famine had ceased. In 1863 the professor of Latin at Queen's College got up a memorial against Friar's Bush (which was used exclusively by Catholics) charging that

---

75 U.Ex., 25 Mar. 1869.
76 Copy of will. D.C.D.A.
77 P.R.O.N.I. BG7/A/6.

it was contributing to the spread of fever in the town.[78] The town improvement committee ordered an inspection of the cemeteries to be carried out. The inspector found the practices obtaining at Friar's Bush decidedly unhygienic: mounds of earth had been raised over bodies which were placed just below the surface, and the ground had not been properly drained, so that the soil gave off 'very noxious exhalations and the water charged with putrid matter is suffered to flow over the surface, and to pollute the atmosphere'. On the basis of the reports it received the improvement committee sought permission from the Lord-Lieutenant to close Friar's Bush and the older parts of the Shankill and of the Belfast Charitable Society's cemeteries. Permission was given, provided a new burial ground was available before the older graveyards were closed.[79]

The town council then bought 102 acres on the Falls Road and resolved to lay out 45 of them as a municipal cemetery. In December 1866 it was decided to mark off 10 acres for Roman Catholic graves. Over 17 acres were to be laid out for Protestant graves and the remainder was to be allocated to all other religious denominations. An official cemetery committee was appointed to carry out these proposals. As the plans were being prepared, Dorrian's solicitors contacted the committee about the arrangements and informed it that he would be satisfied with a straight division running from front to back, provided this enclosed a third of the ornamental grounds; if this were refused, he would be happy to purchase 15 acres, if the council erected a dividing wall. The estimate for the cost of the wall was £480.[80]

As the work on the cemetery neared completion, Dorrian wrote to the town clerk to inquire what power he, as bishop, would have over the ground set aside for the interment of Catholics, explaining that he was deterred by ecclesiastical law from consecrating ground for burial purposes unless he was guaranteed the right to protect it from desecration.[81] The council sent him a copy of their rules for the use of the new cemetery with a request that he forward any suggestions for alterations to them. Dorrian, in reply, further explained that a bishop was not free to consecrate ground 'unless he shall also be able legally to inhibit its being used for the interment of those to whom the Church refuses Christian burial and other things of a like nature'.[82] Pointing out that he raised this issue not

---

78 U.Ob., 22 Oct. 1863.
79 *Minutes of the Cemetery Committee of Belfast Corporation, 1867-87.*
80 Ibid.,
81 Ibid., Dorrian to James Guthrie, 20 Jan. 1869.
82 The rigidity of some Catholic churchmen on this matter is well illustrated by an incident that occurred in Nantes in 1855. A Protestant lady was buried in the

out of any desire to be controversial but to avoid possible future difficulties, he referred to the case of Liverpool where the Catholic bishop had blessed a part of the new cemetery on receipt from the Home Secretary of the same guarantees as those he had sought. He also drew attention to the situation obtaining in Limerick where the Catholic clergy leased the burial ground from the corporation which in turn paid them for conducting the funeral services of the poor.[83]

The cemetery committee, however, was unimpressed by these precedents. Its chairman insisted that, though Dorrian had not fully explained what he wanted, he had asked for rights at variance with those entrusted to the corporation as a burial board by an act of parliament. The claims put forward were 'antagonistic to the rights entrusted to the Corporation' and, representing as they did all classes, creeds and parties, they could not divest themselves of their rights. Should Dorrian wish to pursue the issue further, he could appeal to the Lord-Lieutenant and the Privy Council. One member suggested that a resolution be passed regretting the committee's inability to comply with Dorrian's claim, but another introduced a note of sectarian bitterness not only by opposing this proposal but also by explaining that he was glad to have the opportunity of doing so, as he 'was opposed to all ascendancy, and he would not give Dr Dorrian superiority over other denominations'. John Hamill, a Catholic member, rejected any such desire on Dorrian's part, and, well aware of the bishop's reputation for firmness, forecast that he would cling to his rights with as much determination as the corporation. A resolution was passed, with Hamill alone dissenting, instructing the town clerk to inform the bishop that the rules for the new cemetery had already been passed, and regretting that the council could not comply with his suggestions.[84]

Dorrian took counsel with his parishioners at a meeting in St Mary's Church on 4 April 1869, and won their approval for a plan to buy land for a Catholic cemetery, if he could not obtain the

---

Catholic cemetery but in response to local protests her remains were exhumed. According to the historian of the diocese of Nantes 'une ceremonie fût organisée à la demande de Mgr Jaquemet pour qu'une nouvelle bénédiction fut donnée aux lieux profanés,: "Chacun s'estimait heureux, les droits de l'Eglise étaient reconnus, les tombeaux des ancêtres étaient respectés; et comme le coeur vraiment catholique ne sait que pardonner et prier, au milieu de cette cérémonie touchante, des voeux ardents montaient vers le ciel, pour le retour des frères égarés". M. Launay, *Le Diocèse de Nantes sous le Second Empire*. (Nantes, C.I.D. Editions 1982), ii, 894-5.

83 Dorrian to Guthrie, 15 Feb. 1869, *Minutes of the cemetery committee*.
84 B.M.N., 2 Apr. 1869.

guarantees he sought from the town council.[85] But the council refused his offer to purchase 15 acres and the dispute went to the Privy Council in Dublin, where permission was sought to close all existing burial grounds in Belfast and where Dorrian asked for the control over the Catholic section which he felt was necessary to prevent it from being desecrated. Counsel for the corporation argued that every effort had been made to accommodate the Catholics, instancing the erection of a wall surrounding their burial area.[86] Isaac Butt, on behalf of the bishop, admitted that Friar's Bush cemetery, apart from the ground recently acquired for proprietary graves, ought to be closed but asked that closure be deferred until other satisfactory arrangements could be made. He referred to the central ornamental part of the new cemetery, which had been so arranged that only a very small part of it extended into the Catholic section and which, consequently, was regarded by Catholics as a badge of inferiority; and he observed that a suggestion had been made that this site should be so altered that a part of it should be in the Catholic section or that it should be divided in a different way. But the really serious problem concerned the bishop's control of the Catholic part of the new cemetery; rightly or wrongly, the Catholic population of Belfast had no confidence in the corporation and the bishop refused to consecrate ground that was to be under the control of that body unless it was made secure from the threat of desecration. When challenged by a Privy Councillor with the argument that the corporation was precluded by law from making an unfit use of the ground allotted to a particular denomination, Butt explained that it could sell a plot to a Catholic who on the following day could become a Protestant, or an excommunicated Catholic could seek a grave, and according to the rules of the church such persons should not be buried in consecrated ground. The bishop could not prevent such violations of ecclesiastical law unless he had legal authority to do so, and had therefore to provide for every contingency. The Privy Council deferred judgement and the hearing resumed on 3 July.[87]

Before this took place the bishop's solicitor presented the town council with five rules or conditions which Butt had drawn up to represent the terms on which Dorrian could agree to accept and bless the part of the cemetery which had been set aside for the Catholics of Belfast. These required that no part of the land which had been

85 U.Ex., 6 Apr. 1869.
86 The depth of ground dug for the construction of this wall became a matter of dispute. Some members of the cemetery committee later made the sardonic claim that twelve to fifteen feet had been excavated to protect all the soil affected by the consecration, but Dorrian denied that he had made any suggestions about the size of the wall.
87 B.M.N., 25 June 1869.

dedicated as a Catholic burial ground should ever be used for any purpose 'inconsistent with such dedication'; no part of that ground was to be used for any purpose without the consent of the bishop and no burial was to take place in it without a certificate from someone authorized by him; a sufficient number of officials and gravediggers were to be appointed, with the approbation of the bishop, to look after the Catholic part of the cemetery; the burial board of the corporation was to provide a suitable mortuary chapel for the celebration of the rites of Catholic burial, and to remunerate the Catholic clergy who officiated at the funerals; no soil was to be removed from the ground which had been blessed without the consent of the bishop.[88]

At its meeting on 30 June the cemetery committee declined to accept all these conditions but agreed that the portion allotted to Roman Catholics should continue for all time to be burial ground and no part would ever be used for any other purpose, and that no soil should be removed from the consecrated portion of the Roman Catholic ground without the bishop's consent in writing.[89]

On 3 July Butt petitioned for a postponement of the closure of Friar's Bush for a reasonable time to enable the bishop and his people to bring the town council to terms; or, failing this, to apply to the Queen's Bench for a *mandamus* to require it to accede to the bishop's rules; or, as a last resort, to give the Catholics time to purchase a cemetery for their own exclusive use. He contended that immediate closure would be regarded by the Catholics of Belfast as a defeat at the hands of the corporation. The Privy Council decided to allow part of Friar's Bush to remain open until 25 November so that the bishop might have sufficient time to apply for a *mandamus*, if it was thought advisable to do so.[90]

When the town council met to consider the report of its cemetery committee on 19 July, it remained adamant in its opposition to any concession to Dorrian. The report stated explicitly that the committee felt it could not give the bishop authority to inhibit interments and could not misapply cemetery funds by giving payment to Catholic clergy for their services. Though a Protestant member suggested that Dorrian be given the assurance he sought in the first of the five rules and that a delegation be appointed to confer with him, the proposal was not carried and the report was adopted.[91] By then, however, Dorrian had decided that he could not reach satisfactory terms with the corporation and when the new cemetery was formally

88 B.M.N., 5 July 1869.
89 *Minutes of the cemetery committee.*
90 B.M.N., 5 July 1869.
91 B.M.N., 21 July 1869.

opened on 1 August, it was already known that the bishop had purchased land for an exclusively Catholic graveyard at Milltown. On 7 November at a public meeting in St Mary's Church, he gave an account of his negotiations with the town council, his appeal to the Privy Council and his decision to establish a cemetery under exclusively Catholic management. He characterized his dealings with the town council as an invitation to 'make any proposal and we will consider it' only to be told no concession could be made. Recalling the satisfactory solution achieved in Liverpool where the bishop was not only given the assurances he sought about maintaining the character of the Catholic part of the cemetery but also the right to fix the fees that were to be paid to the Catholic chaplain, he expressed his regret that a similar arrangement could not be made in Belfast. He had therefore consulted some friends and decided to buy ground for a Catholic cemetery. They had found a site more suitable than that of the new cemetery, for they had acquired a brickyard covering fifteen acres from which the clayey parts had already been removed. He and two others had bought this land for £4,100 and, as trustees, they would pay the interest until the capital was paid off, and then the proceeds would be devoted to charitable purposes. This information was greeted with enthusiasm.[92] Privately Dorrian assured Isaac Butt that the ground of the new Catholic cemetery was much superior to that of the municipal one, since much of the clay had been burned away to make brick, leaving sand behind. Their failure to reach an agreement on the dispute was a blessing in disguise:

> And, whilst I much wonder that our Tory Town Council should have, through bigotry, lost a yearly revenue of several hundreds, I rejoice that they cast us off and forced us to the course we adopted and which is so great a boon as well as success for us.[93]

The controversy over the cemetery marked yet another phase in the growing alienation of the Catholic people of Belfast from their mainly Protestant corporation. Apart from the claim for fees for the officiating priest, which Dorrian was prepared to waive, the real points at issue were small, and it should not have been difficult to reach a formula which guaranteed Dorrian that only those who died in communion with his church would be entitled to burial in the Catholic section of the cemetery. This was the nub of the dispute but both sides based their cases on abstract rights which they could not

92 U.Ex., 8 Nov. 1869.
93 Dorrian to Butt, 26 Sept. 1870, N.L.I. MS 8692 (ii).

surrender and so a settlement which could have been reached without any violation of these rights eluded them. When Dorrian returned from the Vatican Council in 1870 an address was read by Alexander O'Rorke, a prominent solicitor, at a public banquet attended by some three hundred people, both clerical and lay, in which he was assured that if any one thing more than another entitled him to their heartfelt gratitude 'it is, that, by your action with regard to the new cemetery, you have manfully resisted the uncalled for restrictions which the Town Council would impose on us even in death. We are no longer exposed to the danger of being interred in desecrated ground, and having our bones disturbed by unhallowed hands'.[94] That a compliment couched in such extreme hyperbole should have been paid on such a happy occasion to the bishop is a sad indication of the unfortunate contribution to community misunderstanding and tension which the cemetery issue had made. In death as in life, the struggle for *Lebensraum* generated sectarian illfeeling!

VII

Another cause of friction between the Catholic church and the secular authorities was provided by the interpretation of the regulations relating to the exercise of religion in the workhouses. But in the ensuing strife the bishop did not take up his position on the front line.

Ultimate control of the poor law system lay with a body of commissioners in Dublin but the management of each institution rested with a Board of Guardians chosen by the ratepayers, of which justices of the peace were *ex officio* members. The character of these boards often reflected the puritan ethic of those who designed a scheme which was intended to be 'irksome' and to deter the 'idle able-bodied' from taking advantage of it; the harsh rules of the Poor Law Act of 1838 were generally observed in the strictest fashion, especially where ratepayers' money was concerned. In the north-east the Guardians were predominantly Protestant but because of the prevailing economic conditions they often had to deal with a disproportionately large number of Catholic paupers.

In 1861 Archbishop Cullen decided to challenge the discrimination and injustices of which he felt many Guardians were guilty, and began by making inquiries about the number of Catholics in the workhouses and the salaries of their chaplains. Bishop Denvir's reply was bleak: 'the Guardians in the Counties of Down & Antrim being almost entirely Protestant do just what they please both as regards

---

94 U.Ex., 25 Aug. 1870.

chaplains & paupers; but nothing in favour of the Catholic religion which they can avoid doing'.[95] Within the diocese there were eleven workhouses — at Belfast, Newtownards, Lisburn, Ballymena, Kilkeel, Ballymoney, Ballycastle, Larne, Antrim, Coleraine and Downpatrick.[96] During Dorrian's episcopate some of the Catholic chaplains attached to them challenged the management about facilities and pay for holding religious services; disputes also occurred about the registration of children of mixed marriages, particularly when one or both of the parents had died. Moreover, a narrow interpretation of the rules by a hostile official sometimes provoked clashes with the clergy.

Accusations were made that Catholic children were subjected to forms of proselytism. Henry O'Loughlin, the parish priest of Antrim, charged that the Guardians provided only the Protestant version of the scriptures for the inmates, and that in Antrim the Catholic children were forced to receive religious instruction from Protestant chaplains. Religious tracts of an offensive nature circulated freely in the Antrim workhouse.[97] Patrick McAlister, the chaplain to the Ballycastle workhouse, forced the Poor Law commissioners to hold an inquiry into the behaviour of a lady evangelist who directed her apostolate to all the inmates; her visits were deemed to be 'intrusive and aggressive' and stricter rules were then applied.[98] Michael McConvey, the chaplain to the Newtownards workhouse, complained that during the time set apart for separate religious instruction for the school children, the Catholics were sent into a cold room without any supervision as there was no one to teach them. The Guardians duly investigated these charges, found they were true and resolved to take steps to correct them. But they repudiated McConvey's other claim that the Protestant children received their religious education at the ratepayers' expense, for they pointed out that this instruction was given by the master and mistress of the school who were paid by the board of national education. McConvey made the further accusation that Catholic children were put outside the dormitories when the others were engaged in morning and night prayers. He also claimed, as did O'Loughlin, that despite his remonstrances, Catholic children were

---

95 Denvir to Cullen, 5 May 1861. D.D.A.
96 Since 1850 there were 163 workhouses in Ireland.
97 U.Ex., 26 Jan. 1869.
98 U.Ob., 30 Nov. 1867.

hired out by the Guardians to Protestant employers who either discouraged them or prevented them from practising their faith.[99]

Bernard McCann, the chaplain to the Belfast workhouse, maintained in 1879 that a porter not only did not bother to summon a priest to the death bed of an inmate but cursed the nurse who requested him to do so. A short time later he denounced the workhouse as 'a nest of drunkenness, immorality and vice' — a charge that had been made by a predecessor, James O'Laverty, and by Protestant critics as well.[100] The accusation that the staff at the workhouse in Larne prevented the 'casual paupers', who had just been admitted, from attending Sunday Mass was made by Daniel McDonnell, the local curate. The Guardians replied that the 'casuals' had to be washed and dressed at that time. McDonnell brought his complaint to the Poor Law commissioners and was assured that the casuals were entitled to the same religious rights as the other inmates. But the Larne Guardians replied by discharging the casuals on Sunday mornings before Mass time. When overruled from Dublin on this issue the Guardians countered by arguing that the casuals required medical inspection before admission to Mass, but this was not available as the doctor's visits took place later in the day.[101]

McDonnell's attempts to ignore the Guardians' chicanery led to an accusation of assault by him on a porter, but McDonnell insisted that the porter gave one of the casuals, an infirm old man, whom he was helping to Mass, a rude push causing him to fall on his back. When the Guardians considered the incident and the letters concerning it, which had been returned from the local governmnet board in Dublin, they were mollified by a letter from Francis McKenna, the parish priest of Larne, who expressed regret at his curate's conflict with the porter and referring to the good relations that had existed between the Guardians and the Catholic clergy, promised that there

---

99 M.N., 24 Mar. 7 Apr. 3 June, 28,29 July, 1884. McConvey and the Guardians of Newtownards were at loggerheads for years. In a dispute over salaries in 1876 the local government board requested a return of the numbers of each denomination in the workhouse, the number of visits paid by each chaplain and the number of hours he spent in the workhouse the previous year. The Presbyterian chaplain, whose salary was £40, had spent 260 hours attending to his congregation of 260. The Church of Ireland chaplain, whose salary was £35, had spent 48 hours attending to his congregation of 87. McConvey, who had received £25, had spent 137 hours attending 45 Catholics. When the Poor Law commissioners ordered the Guardians to increase McConvey's salary to the same level as that of his colleagues, they found a way around the problem: they decided that the heavy workload of the Presbyterian and Church of Ireland chaplains justified a further increase of £15 and £10 respectively for them.

100 U.Ex., 4 Mar. 17 Apr. 1879.

101 M.N., 1 Dec. 1882.

would be no repetition of the incident.[102] But an unrepentant McDonnell defended himself in an uncompromising and pointed public letter the following day, and insisting that it was 'ridiculous presumption' on the part of the Guardians to ask for an apology, explained their success in obtaining one such 'in any shape or form' as 'the work of a holy and foolishly wise man'. He then opened an attack on a wider front by pointing out that from the highest official to the humblest warder in the Larne workhouse there was not a single Catholic.[103] Other chaplains, including O'Loughlin of Antrim, also accused the Boards of Guardians of discrimination in employment.[104]

Another grievance which some of the Catholic chaplains levelled at the Guardians related to salary. Some of the boards paid the chaplains of all denominations, irrespective of the number served, the same salary. Other boards geared the salary to the number of patients or inmates whom a chaplain attended. A few Catholic chaplains, who claimed that they had to attend half the patients in the infirmary and fever wards of the workhouses, claimed an increase of salary, and on the Guardians' refusing their requests pursued the matter to the commissioners in Dublin.

Controversy over the religious denomination in which children were registered occurred not infrequently in many workhouses. The facts were often difficult to disentangle as the disputes centred on children of mixed marriages, where relatives disagreed among each other or with a surviving parent. Such situations permitted religious zealots on the workhouse staff to take advantage of legal ambiguities to enrol the children in their denominations. A further complication derived from a decision of the Attorney General in 1841 which laid down that children whose religion was not known should be brought up in the established church. The crux of the problem experienced by the Catholic chaplains with the workhouse authorities or Boards of Guardians lay in the readiness of some anti-Catholic officials to deny to the chaplain the benefit of the doubt in cases where they could have been more lenient or favourable. Though the commissioners in Dublin retained full authority for the implementation of the Poor Law, the local Boards of Guardians were responsible for the appointments to the staffs of the workhouses and for the details of their administration. This gave them scope for deciding on the times of religious services, the provision of religious literature for the inmates, and church requisites for the chaplains. Some of them were,

102 M.N., 7 Dec. 1882.
103 M.N., 8 Dec. 1882.
104 An editorial in the *Vindicator* on 11 Apr. 1846 claimed that of the 55 offices — master, matron, teachers, porters — in the workhouses in Down and Connor only 3 were occupied by Catholics.

at the very least, loath to make available to the Catholic chaplain any facilities other than the minimum required by law, and in the workhouses themselves some officials were prepared to turn a blind eye to the circulation of religious tracts which were offensive to the Catholic inmates. Consequently, tensions led to controversy and appeals to Dublin, and though from time to time the chaplains may have gained the immediate point at issue, the disputes probably contributed little to improving the atmosphere for their co-religionists in the workhouses.

6

Political problems 1860-70

I

Belfast was spared outbreaks of prolonged and serious rioting between 1857 and 1864 but minor incidents flared up nearly every year. In 1858 an attack by a group of people from Sandy Row on a party returning from a funeral at Friar's Bush cemetery led to heavy exchanges of stones between rival crowds. St Malachy's Church, Bernard Hughes' bakery and the offices of the *Northern Whig* were attacked. A few days after the trouble began, a request from Bishop Denvir to the people not to collect in crowds and to go home immediately was passed on at the Sunday Masses, and this advice seems to have been heeded.[1]

More troublesome outbreaks occurred in the wake of a great Protestant rally in Botanic Gardens on 17 September 1862. Heady language about the dangers of Romanism inflamed some of the participants. St Mary's Church, Hughes' bakery, the Royal Hotel and the homes of a few Catholics were attacked, and in turn Catholic rioters attacked Hugh Hanna's church in Berry St. In Bishop Denvir's absence, Dorrian presided at a meeting of concerned Catholics that was summoned to help calm the situation. A strong resolution was passed repudiating both the provocation and the retaliation:

> 'whilst strongly reprobating the insults and outrages so unsparingly levelled against the Catholics, we deplore and condemn the measures of retaliation adopted, or said to be adopted, by some of our people, inasmuch as those acts endanger the lives and liberties of those concerned in them, and involve a violation of the law from which punishment is certain to ensue. We therefore exhort the people to forbearance and to the most patient endurance of those wrongs which cannot fail to elicit the condemnation of the honest fairthinking men of every creed.

1 Ul., 31 May, 3 June, 7 June 1858.

We particularly reprobate attacks upon religious houses, and most earnestly conjure our people to allow no insults, in word or deed, to draw them into acts that are a slur upon their manhood, and, what is still worse, a refutation of their practical Christian tolerance'.[2]

This appeal for an end to the violence was interpreted by the *Belfast News-Letter* as an admission that the Catholics had been responsible for provoking the strife. Dorrian did not allow this conclusion to go unchallenged. He wrote to the *News-Letter* denying that their meeting had acknowledged that the Catholics were the aggressors and explaining that their purpose had been not to inquire into the origins of the confrontations but merely to throw oil on troubled waters. Remarking that it was no honour to any party to continue the unchristian exhibition, whoever might have originated it, he pointed out that he himself and a gentleman who was with him were insulted on the platform of one of the railway stations by 'some debris of the party who had been at the meeting on the 17th'. Consequently, he was scarcely likely to accuse the Catholics of having started the violence. He concluded by suggesting that all should agree to vindicate their principles 'by other arguments than fierce passions, exhibited in broken bones or shattered windows'.[3]

Hostile mobs engaged each other after the Orange celebrations of July in the following year. Dorrian's house in Howard St. and the homes of the proprietor of the *Whig* and the editor of the *Ulster Observer* (both papers were opposed to Orange demonstrations) were attacked. No significant amount of damage was done. But the situation changed drastically in 1864. In that year Belfast experienced its most savage politico-religious disturbances to date, which claimed eleven lives, more than thirty serious injuries and extensive destruction of property. As the population of the town had grown, communal violence had increased proportionally and in 1864 the riots not only lasted longer but proved more difficult to contain and resulted in damage being done on a much larger scale.

On 8 August 1864 the foundation stone of the O'Connell monument was laid in Dublin. A huge crowd, including many clergy and ten bishops, attended the ceremony. Though the Belfast contingent travelled to and from Dublin without offering any political provocation to opponents of O'Connell's political aims, some Protestant extremists chose to regard their presence at the commemoration, or perhaps the commemoration itself, as a provocation, and, to show their contempt for, and rejection of, O'Connell, arranged to

2 B.M.N., 22 Sept. 1862.
3 B.N.L., 26 Sept. 1862.

burn him in effigy on the Boyne bridge as the train carrying the Belfast representatives returned. Some four thousand people assembled for this symbolic cremation but, when prevented from crossing into the Catholic district of the Pound, dispersed quietly. This coat-trailing gesture did not draw the expected response and so the following evening a smaller mob of some fifteen hundred or two thousand decided to continue the symbolic exequies for O'Connell — though this time in the form of inhumation. To the accompaniment of a fife and two drums and uttering 'party cries and imprecations well understood in Belfast'[4] a procession followed a coffin to the Catholic cemetery of Friar's Bush and on arrival demanded that the caretaker open up 'till we bury O'Connell'.[5] On being refused admission the processionists stoned the caretaker's house and then withdrew, forced their way across the Boyne Bridge to the Catholic ghetto of the Pound but were eventually driven back by the police. On 10 August preparations were made in the Pound to resist incursions, stones were collected, and when the Sandy Row invaders broke through, an engagement took place but the police succeeded in breaking it up. But windows had been broken in the Methodist Church on the Falls Road and the first arrests of rioters were then made in the Catholic district in Milford St. Reinforcements of constabulary were called in and during the next week more police and troops were drafted into Belfast until the additional forces numbered over one thousand men.

Mobs fought each other across Durham St. on 12 August, millworkers passing through opposing camps were attacked on their way to work, and houses belonging to both Protestants and Catholics in several parts of the town were wrecked. On that morning there also occured 'an outrage than which nothing more brutal and unmanly was perpetrated throughout the riots'. A reformatory for girls conducted by the Sisters of Mercy at Bankmore St. was attacked and its windows were all broken. In retaliation the windows of Henry Cooke's church and of the homes of several Protestants were smashed, which in turn led to a second and more violent attack on the penitentary, which the constabulary could only suppress with difficulty. Dorrian had got wind of a rumour that the home would be attacked and had written to a magistrate seeking protection. The letter had been passed on to a sub-inspector of the constabulary and he had taken a party of men 'to the locality, but after about an hour, seeing no symptoms of disorder, withdrew and the wrecking then took place'.[6]

4 *Report of the commissioners of inquiry, 1864, respecting the magisterial and police jurisdiction, arrangements and establishment of the borough of Belfast* . . . H.C. 1865 [3466], xxviii, 9.
5 Ibid., 9.
6 Ibid., 10.

The next two days were relatively tranquil but on 15 August a group of Catholic 'navvies', who had not gone to work because of the religious holy-day, gathered near St Malachy's Church and, 'shouting and firing shots of defiance' marched off to attack the school in Brown St. (which was attended mainly by Presbyterian children). Windows were smashed, shots were fired and 'the attack equalled if it did not surpass in atrocity the outrage committed by the ruffians of the other party on the Bankmore Penitentiary'.[7] That evening a Protestant mob set off from Sandy Row to St Malachy's Church but, as it was amply defended, both sides then engaged in gunplay and several people were wounded.

On 16 August preparations were made to revenge the assault on Brown St. School. The day began with an encounter between residents of Sandy Row and a party of constabulary who were trying to protect workers on their way to the mills; two of the wounded subsequently died. Later in the morning a body of ships' carpenters or skilled workers at the shipyards left their work and with the support of other rioters, raided pawn shops, a gunshop and hardware shop in the centre of the town, and the plundering of shops in broad daylight in the centre of a town where there were 400 constabulary, infantry and a troop of horse was later adjudged to be 'amongst the most astonishing instances of lawless daring that had ever occurred in a civilized community'.[8] They went off in search of the 'navvies' but the troops prevented a collision.

On that day the *Ulster Observer*, angered by the response of the magistrates to the riots in general and by an assault on its deputy editor in particular, made a powerful appeal for concerted action on the part of Catholics, suggested the establishment of a defence association and announced that a meeting would take place at the Catholic Institute that evening to discuss these proposals. Dorrian was completely taken aback by this development. Two elements in the *Observer's* initiative galled him: the paper had claimed the right to give guidance to the Catholic community, and had thereby encroached on the exclusive rights of the bishop and clergy to the leadership of Catholics considered as a religious body; and he feared that under the guise of defence, agitators and demagogues would emerge to lead the Catholics more deeply into conflict with their Protestant neighbours, and this fear was enhanced by his distrust of the editor of the paper whom he had come to regard as dangerous and irresponsible.

Two days previously he had pleaded at the Sunday Masses in St Malachy's Church for an end to all participation by Catholics in the current strife and had begged them not to allow provocation of any

---

7 Ibid., 11
8 Ibid., 12.

kind or degree to induce them to retaliate. Now he issued a stinging rebuke to what the *Northern Whig* called the mischievous appeal made in the *Observer*. Reminding his people of the immense harm that could be caused by imprudent and indiscreet advice at such a time, he implored them to act with patience and forbearance and not to 'be carried away by self-installed advisers nor be influenced by any sayings or writings as authorized but what may come from your bishops or clergy'. Insisting that only they had the right to address 'the Catholics of Belfast', he declared that they were now calling on their flocks to be always in the right and to ensure that, if peace were to be broken, it would be on the part of others. He repudiated any suggestion of retaliation, scornfully dismissed all talk of foolish heroism and reminded them of the Pauline injunctions on charity.[9]

Bishop Denvir, nervous and fearful, was too timid to step into the arena and summon the combatants to withdraw from the conflict. Dorrian had no such inhibitions. He was determined that the full authority of the episcopal office would be thrown on to the side of peace. And for the remainder of his episcopate, firm denunciations of violence, coupled with strong appeals to his people to desist from any form of provocation, were to be repeated with wearisome and melancholy frequency. When the riots began he did not foresee the ferocity or extent of the strife, but they quickly proved how fragile peaceful coexistence in Belfast could be and how tenacious and deep-rooted politico-religious passions were.

On 17 August, while the army and police were searching for arms, a 'fearful conflict' took place between the Protestant ships' carpenters[10] and the Catholic navvies who were working at the docks. Guns were again used, the navvies were driven out on to the mud for refuge and one man later died from wounds received in the affray. On 18 August the funeral of John McConnell, a riot victim from Sandy Row, who had been shot by the constabulary, took place and, despite the pleas of the mayor to limit the mourners to immediate relatives and friends, as had been done for the Catholic victims, it was turned into a powerful political demonstration and became a gesture of defiance of political opponents. Between 2,000 and 3,000 people took part in the procession, some of whom carried guns, and as the cortège moved along, shots were fired by several of the mourners as well as by opponents nearby to provoke and annoy each other. The procession, despite the intervention of magistrates, deliberately chose a longer route which passed by a Catholic area and, on

---

9 N.W., 17 Aug. 1864.

10 The terms 'ships' carpenters' and 'navvies' were frequently used in the press at this time to describe the Protestant and Catholic workers at the shipyards and docks, and implied that the Protestant workers were skilled and the Catholics unskilled. Obviously, only a minority of the Protestant workforce was skilled.

returning from the burial, shooting occurred as the crowds entered Sandy Row. This archetypal political funeral, which was attended not 'merely by people in McConnell's own rank in life, but largely, if not mainly by persons whose position was such that any supposed sympathy on their part with any section of the rioters, was likely to prove the surest stimulant to further violence', was later described as a 'peculiarly menacing demonstration'. Surprise was expressed that none of those carrying firearms at it was arrested. This highly organized and successful demonstration, however frightening in its implications, since several people who had been sworn in as special constables took part and openly carried their batons, rang down the curtain on the riots, which, apart from one isolated shooting incident, petered out the following day.[11]

Prolonged urban conflict on such a large scale and in an expanding industrial city was then unprecedented in the United Kingdom and naturally the cessation of violence was immediately followed by demands for an immediate and thorough inquiry. At a meeting in the Catholic Institute a memorial was drawn up for submission to the Lord-Lieutenant calling for the appointment of a royal commission with full powers to investigate all matters directly or indirectly connected with the origin and progress of the riots. This petition which bore 5,000 signatures, including Dorrian's, and was presented by a deputation of prominent Catholics on 21 September 1864, complained in particular of the unsuitability and partiality of the local police, and pointed out that the 'memorialists attribute this and other grave abuses to the conditions of the municipality — whose constitution and practices have been and are the subjects of grave dissatisfaction to the community'.[12] The government, to the disappointment of the Catholic appellants, did not grant anything as extensive as was sought and merely appointed a commission under two barristers to investigate the peace-keeping arrangements in the town, the efficiency of the police force, the response of the magistrates and local authorities to the civil strife, and empowered them, if necessary, to make recommendations in these areas. During the twenty one days of sittings it examined 127 witnesses, including the mayor and three ex-mayors of the town, the magistrates who had been involved, several aldermen and town councillors including the chairman of the police committee and some of his predecessors, many of the wealthiest mill-owners, manufacturers and traders of Belfast, and clergy of various denominations. The commissioners later voted that the differences of opinion among the witnesses were comparatively slight and claimed

11 *Report of the commissioners of inquiry*, 15.
12 U.Ob., 24 Sept. 1864.

that their recommendations were derived from the general consensus of the information they received.

Dorrian gave evidence before the commission on the fourth day of its hearings and answered questions about the size and proportion of the Catholic population, its composition, the law-enforcing arrangements for the borough and his own intervention with the magistrates to save the Bankmore penitentiary. Like many witnesses, he indicated strong dissatisfaction with the local police and complete lack of confidence in the impartiality and effectiveness of the force. And he remarked that his house would not have been smashed a year previously, if the local police had interfered.[13] Law and order were then enforced in Belfast by about 65 members of the Irish constabulary and 160 local police. In their report on the riots of 1857 the commissioners had expressed concern at the composition of this force — there were then only seven Catholics in it — at the way it was recruited and at the known Orange sympathies of some of its members. Since then the number of Catholics had decreased by two though the Catholic population had continued to increase. The commissioners duly recommended that the town be policed by a uniformed force of some 450 well trained and disciplined men drawn from the constabulary, and remarked that 'considering the peculiar circumstances of Belfast, the violent religious and party animosities that have so long prevailed there, and no less the spirit of suspicion necessarily generated by such an unfortunate state of things, any force of a strictly local character would inevitably give dissatisfaction'.[14]

Dorrian was also questioned about the magistracy and the role of the town council in appointing or controlling paid magistrates. He firmly supported the suggestion that two paid magistrates should be appointed by the government, and not by the town council, to administer law and order, and expressed his distrust of the local body, whose members were strongly Conservative[15] and Protestant, in the rather circuitous statement that appointments by it 'as at present constituted of the officers could not be said exactly to give satisfaction to the general community'.[16] He made it clear that he was not

13 He pointed out that of the 40,700 Catholics in Belfast the majority of the workers were employed in mills and that a large number were artisans. The labouring class, he thought, was divided equally on a religious basis but 'a great deal more wealth' was to be found among the Protestants and Presbyterians. *Report of the commissioners of inquiry*, 75-76.
14 Ibid., 20.
15 The commissioners explained that throughout their report they used the terms Conservative and Liberal in the sense in which they had been used by witnesses; 'the term "Conservative" being applied to those Protestants regarded as unfriendly to Roman Catholics, and the term "Liberal" being used to include the latter and such Protestants as are considered favourable to them'. Ibid., 5.
16 Ibid., 73.

suggesting that magistrates should be appointed on a denominational head count as long as they were fairminded and energetic men. Observing that there were a great many Protestants in whom he had as much confidence as he had in Catholics, he declared that he would like to see 'persons of energy,[17] vigour and knowledge' appointed and 'if that was realized, I would not care whether they were Protestants or Catholics; but in a mixed community it is reasonable that there should be a share from all sections of the community'. Asked if he thought there was a sufficient number of Catholics qualified to act, he responded calmly to the condescending and contemptuous innuendo in the query by answering that there were 'several, both among the liberal Protestants and among the Catholics, very well qualified to fulfill the duties of magistrates'. He reminded the commissioners that the Catholic clergy co-operated fully in maintaining peace by inducing their people to stay indoors and by refusing to attend funerals, if they were accompanied by large crowds; he referred to one priest, Geoffrey Brennan, who refused to go to a funeral if it was accompanied by more than a few persons, though he left it to Brennan himself to relate how he and another priest were fired on as they were leaving St Malachy's Church to try to calm their excited parishioners on 15 August.[18]

In their report the commissioners accepted the general criticism of the local police force which had been voiced by both Catholics and Protestants, and not only did they observe that the composition of the force created suspicion among Catholics that 'unbiassed assertion of authority and impartial vindication of the law' did not exist in Belfast but went on to point out that the method of selection operated to the exclusion of Catholic recruits. They considered the small Catholic representation in the force — only five members out of 160 — as 'somewhat remarkable'. Furthermore, the subjection of the force to the town council, a body composed not merely of Protestants, but of Protestants who were regarded as adverse, both by the Roman Catholics, and by the 'Liberal' section of the Protestant community, would alone deprive it of the trust of the Catholic community. This distrust was heightened by the suspicion of the existence 'to a considerable extent' of Orangeism among the members, and the denial of such a connection was not easy to believe given that Orangemen were not prohibited from entry to the force and that Orangeism was numerically strongest among that class, the yeomen, artisans and labourers, from which the local police were drawn. The organization, drill and general regulations of the force

17 Other Catholic witnesses were more specific when accusing the magistrates of inefficiency, hesitancy and tardiness in taking action.
18 Ibid., 75-6.

were defective, the men bore 'the appearance rather of street beadles or street keepers rather than of members of a well organized police force' and their residence in districts likely to be 'the theatre of factious disturbance' was objectionable. The commissioners recommended the abolition of the local police and their replacement by a larger number of regular constables under the control of a commissioner appointed by the government who would enjoy magisterial authority but would not discharge judicial functions.

The magistrates, despite the severe censure cast on them by some witnesses, were exempted from responsibility for not preventing the riots because the local police displayed a very curious ignorance about the preparations for burning the effigy, and the mock funeral; and the rioters had invariably withdrawn by the time they could collect a force sufficient enough to disperse them. Moreover, these men were not trained to cope with violent disorder on such a vast scale, and, though two or three of them committed serious errors, they were not chargeable with neglect of duty.[19] The commissioners refused to recommend the abolition of honorary, unpaid magistrates, but considered themselves obliged with a 'sense of humiliation' to recommend the expediency of ensuring that, of the two resident, stipendiary magistrates in Belfast, one should be a Protestant and the other a Catholic.[20]

Commenting on the inevitability of Orange festivities leading to disorder, the commissioners felt bound to ask why any party should obstinately adhere to such celebrations:

> In other countries good feeling and good sense have buried in generous oblivion the memory of civil strife such as they commemorate, nay, even that of angry conflict with external enemies. Why is it otherwise in Ireland? Can neither the discouragement of the powerful and influential, nor the adverse opinion of the wise and good induce those who indulge in such vain and mischievous displays to remember the claims of citizenship, of charity, or of civilization? Till they shall, we greatly

---

19 The reluctance of the magistrates to take prompt and decisive action was strongly criticized by Catholic leaders during the riots. On 13 Aug. the *Ulster Observer* editorialized: 'if we were to judge by appearances we would be inclined to believe that they regard with indifference, if not with secret satisfaction, the tumult and strife which are daily bringing disgrace upon us'. A deputation of leading Catholics went to Dublin to urge the Privy Council to suppress the magistracy and appoint two commissioners to take charge of Belfast. Neutral papers also attacked the magistrates' handling of the riots. The *Times* remarked: 'the riots of Belfast are a dishonour to the good government of the kingdom, and upon those magistrates who had the authority to keep the peace and forebore to use it rests the discredit of putting us to shame before the world'. (quoted in B.M.N., 29 Aug. 1864).

20 *Report of the commissioners*, 19.

fear that Belfast will continue subject, in some degree to a recurrence of such evils as have heretofore afflicted it . . .

Convinced from the information placed before them that 'the elements of contention were never more rife' in Belfast, they also regretted being obliged to predict that as the Catholics grew stronger trials of strength between the two parties would become more likely and the ensuing collisions would become more fierce and bloody.[21] And, reflecting on the suffering and loss sustained by the innocent and those least able to bear it, they quoted with singular aptness the eloquent and sympathetic description of a violent scene by Isaac Nelson, a Presbyterian minister, to illustrate the plight of victims, irrespective of sect or party:

> For these four — or shall I say three — melancholy nights my Protestant neighbours remained up, wandering around the houses, playing 'The Protestant Boys' and 'The Boyne Water' and using phraseology which I believe will in future be foreign to our towns. Having taken possession of the highway, they maltreated, in spite of all remonstrances, every passer-by who would not use certain language. I am speaking of a number of persons with whom I had been to a certain extent acquainted for years, and can state to be most well-conducted and quiet persons. I saw that crowd come up to the houses of four poor members of the Latin Church. I did not then know myself exactly their religious denomination. I saw the furniture broken to pieces on the floor, and I saw the houses as you express it, gutted . . . I hold as responsible for these three or four nights melancholy proceedings all who heard of and did not oppose them . . . The mobs in my neighbourhood not only hunted poor Roman Catholic neighbours out of their houses, but I had to go and beseech them to grant so many hours to these poor people to take their furniture out of the place . . . I could have sat down and wept when a poor little girl came with a pet canary bird in a cage, when the poor people had been driven from their houses, the children in one direction and the father and mother in another.[22]

II

It was to prevent a recurrence of scenes such as this, indeed to counteract the attraction of political violence at every level, that

21 Ibid., 17.
22 Ibid., 16.

Dorrian played an active part in the National Association, a pressure group of clergy and laity whose aim was to influence politicians with a view to obtaining remedial legislation on the three main issues that in varying degrees concerned Catholics: land, education and the established church.

The origin of this movement is not fully clear. Suggestions for some such body may have arisen among the group who organized the erection of the O'Connell monument. At any rate some members of that committee were actively involved in the Association and it has been suggested that Peter Paul McSwiney, the lord mayor of Dublin, and James Kavanagh, the former inspector of national schools who had strenuously criticized the national board for anti-Catholic bias, were the most likely members to have persuaded Archbishop Cullen to become more politically involved.[23] Among the other prominent Catholic politicians to declare support were John Blake Dillon, W. J. O'Neill Daunt, the old O'Connellite, Sir John Gray, the owner of the *Freeman's Journal*, Myles O'Reilly, who had led the Irish brigade to the defence of the papal states, and Richard Devitt, a Dublin city councillor.

The Independent party, which had attracted widespread clerical and lay support for its policy of opposition to all governments that would not make concessions to tenants a part of their policy, had collapsed in the mid-1850s amidst intense bitterness. Cullen had become the target of fierce abuse because he did not publicly censure Sadlier and Keogh, the two prominent members of parliament who broke their pledges and accepted office in Lord Aberdeen's administration. Since then there was no party or movement of any significance committed to the removal of serious grievances at a national level. John Martin's pursuit of O'Connell's repeal programme enjoyed little support and the Whig members of parliament, who sought or obtained the help of Catholic clergy, did so at a personal and local level and made no concerted effort to present a broad popular policy. The Fenians had moved in to fill the vacuum in Irish political life. And Fenianism possessed what Martin and the Whigs lacked — a clear, simple policy with a powerful emotional appeal. The Fenians could project themselves as the rigidly honest, unsullied exponents of genuine nationalism — a nationalism uncontaminated by political compromises or parliamentary deals and independent of the influences of British political parties. The heady emotional appeal of Fenianism spelt serious danger to clergy and constitutionally-minded politicians. They believed that the policy of violence was both morally wrong and doomed to failure, and feared

23 P.J. Corish. 'Archbishop Cullen and the National Association of Ireland' in *Repertorium Novum*, iii, no.1 (1962), 21.

that it would not only delay much-needed reforms but would also bring suffering and damage to those whom it was supposed to benefit.

Archbishop Cullen tangled sharply with the Fenians when he forbade church services for the burial of Terence Bellew McManus in 1861. In the following year condemnations of secret societies were included in some of the bishops' pastorals, and at their official meeting in May resolutions were passed warning Catholics against all secret associations, whether oath-bound or not, though acknowledging that they suffered many injustices. In 1864 Propaganda informed Cullen that a condemnation by Pius IX of all societies that plotted against church or state applied to the Fenians.

Among many clergy and politically-minded laity there was a realization that a condemnation of a physical force movement was not sufficient without some reference to and guidance on the problems requiring redress, and indeed there was a broad consensus about the kind of reforms that were needed, though not necessarily about their order of importance. The bishops wanted the removal of those restrictions in the national system of education which prevented schools with only Catholic pupils from teaching religion at any time of the day and from displaying religious symbols; in short, they wanted a fully denominational system. They also wanted a charter and some form of endowment for the Catholic University. They wanted an end to the privileged position enjoyed by the established church; this church, to which tithes were paid from adherents of all or no religions, was shown by the census of 1861 to contain less than one seventh of the population of the country. The right of tenants to be protected from unjust eviction and to obtain compensation for improvements they had made to their holdings was also widely recognized. If justice were to be offered to the Irish Catholic people, these were the areas where it would have to come.

A general meeting to launch the Association was held in Dublin on 29 December 1864, and, though the Fenians in their paper, the *Irish People*, wrote bitterly scathing articles about the new movement, they did not try to disrupt it. Among the episcopal names summoning it were those of Denvir and Dorrian. The most notable absentee from the list of bishops' signatures was John MacHale, who doubted the capacity of the new body to achieve the worthwhile ends it had set itself and who feared it would be afflicted by the same kind of betrayals which destroyed its like-minded predecessor, the Independent party.[24] All but ten of the bishops of Ireland signed the requisition and, though one might have expected the northern

---

24 E.R. Norman, *The Catholic church in Ireland in the age of rebellion* (London, 1965), p.141.

bishops to sign en masse to summon up an alternative to the violence that had been the lot of Belfast, in fact five of them did not do so. But the two men with responsibility in the key see did sign and, though Denvir did not pursue the matter with much enthusiasm, Dorrian, his more politically-minded and determined coadjutor, certainly did.[25] Seven bishops were present at the inaugural meeting – the archbishops of Dublin and Cashel, and the bishops of Ardagh, Ross, Cloyne, Elphin and the coadjutor of Meath (Thomas Nulty).

The meeting resolved that the National Association would work for a bill to provide compensation to tenants for improvements carried out by them, the disendowment of the Church of Ireland, and equality of rights in education for all denominations. The Association was to be a pressure group, not a party, which would seek to convince people of the fairness and reasonableness of its aims, would help to positions of influence those who honestly accepted these aims and would support only that party and those candidates for office who would pledge themselves to establish by law the tenants' right to compensation, and the disendowment of the established church. A committee was appointed to act on behalf of the Association, and one of its main purposes was to diffuse the ideals and policies which had been agreed on. In effect this meant that the Association would look to the Liberals for the realization of its goals and would offer support to those Liberals who were prepared to back its views.

Dorrian had long been convinced of the need for legislation in all three fields, and of the wisdom of campaigning vigorously at national level to secure it. But he had never placed much faith in the liberal professions of the Whigs or in their sincerity in working for a genuine amelioration of the grievances felt by the majority of the Irish people. O'Connell remained his ideal political leader, and repeal of the union, enabling an Irish parliament to deal with Irish problems and to use, protect and exploit Irish resources, his national vision. In fact he did not attend the procession in Dublin in connection with the laying of the foundation stone of the O'Connell memorial because he believed the Whigs had succeeded in hijacking O'Connell's name and fame. He explained to Tobias Kirby:

> I did not go because I believed there was too much *Whiggery* with some of the leaders, and I look upon Whiggery as the evil

---

[25] Denvir tried to enlist the support of MacHale. But MacHale refused to join and argued that 'instead of sincerely and earnestly labouring for the attainment' of the 'laudable objects' of the association, some would make use of them 'to forward their own selfish purposes'. (B. O'Reilly, *Life of John MacHale* (New York and Cincinnati, 1890), ii, 536.)

genius of Ireland — a few offices for traitors and starvation and oppression for the rest of the Catholic people.[26]

And, just as the priests had played a highly significant role in the O'Connell campaign helping to direct and channel national aspirations into a moderate constitutional movement, so he foresaw the priests again using their restraining influence to curb the excesses of their people and ensure that politics remained peaceful and nonviolent. In fact he attributed the development of Fenianism to the withdrawal of this steadying and moderating influence, presumably referring either to the synodal legislation introduced under Archbishop Cullen's influence in 1853-4 (which in fact limited but did not prevent clerical participation in politics) or to the collapse of clerical support for the Independent party after the repudiation of their pledges by Sadlier and Keogh. Remarking that it was unfortunate that the priests were for a term withdrawn from politics, he drew the inference that ordinary people with no one else to follow but Whig power-seekers naturally turned to the men who could promise them what they wanted by violent means. He predicted that the Association would have a long struggle to establish its credibility:

> For people were then driven in despair to combine illegally, when they saw that nothing was to be done but sell them for sops to place hunters. The National Association is sound at heart, but the country will be long in coming to *believe that*, after having been so often betrayed. However I hope it will work its way and do good in time.[27]

And, indeed, internal wrangling and sharp disputes about its aims soon helped to realize this forecast. Thomas Nulty, the recently appointed coadjutor of Meath, took a life-long interest in the land question and defence of tenant rights against landlord power. He was an impulsive, headstrong man, who had little patience with those who sought compromise and consensus, once he was convinced of the merits of his own views. The Meath clergy had been active in the Tenant League, and the appointment as coadjutor bishop in 1864 of one who felt deeply about tenant right acted as spur to those who wanted more urgent action on the land question. Nulty's pastoral in Lent 1865 pulled no punches about the subservience of the Irish MPs to the Whigs and several of his priests began to grow more restless within the Association. A meeting was called on 29 April to deal with the anxieties and criticisms of the Meath clergy. Nulty and repre-

26 Dorrian to Kirby, 10 Aug. 1864, A.I.C.R.
27 Ibid., 16 Feb. 1865.

sentatives of his clergy, the committee of the National Association and five bishops, including Cullen and Dorrian, hammered out an agreement which tightened the rules governing the conditions that permitted the Association to support candidates, with a view to ensuring that a more vigorous policy of independent opposition would result. A resolution was passed that the Association would pledge itself to the policy of parliamentary independence, would not support any candidate who in a vote of confidence on a ministry, would not bind himself to vote against any government not committed to legislation in favour of compensation for all improvements made by the tenant, and would recommend Irish constituencies to oblige their representatives to accept no office from any government not prepared to legislate for such compensation. Members elected by the aid of the Association would be bound to abide by the majority decision of the party in parliament which held the same principles.

Dorrian was jubilant at the result of the decision to strengthen the conditions for obtaining the support of the Association. On the one hand it avoided the policy of complete independent opposition which some critics in the 1850s had regarded as futile, and on the other hand it eliminated support for uncommitted Whigs who might be tempted to use the Association to achieve office at the price of a promise which they had no intention of keeping. He reported contentedly to Kirby:

> I am happy to say the result is most satisfying. It is a perfect amalgamation. The Independent Policy is fully recognized, but not factious opposition. Opposition however to any government which will not make the land a cabinet measure — no seeking of favours — and as far as the policy of the Association can go, the minority of MPs to be bound by the majority. This will make us all right, please God.[28]

Dorrian's satisfaction was not shared by all supporters of the Association, either clerical or lay. Cullen thought the terms of agreement too rigid and while he approved of binding the MPs to vote against a government not prepared to legislate for compensation for tenants only in cases of votes of confidence, thus leaving them free to vote according to conscience on other issues, he thought complete insistence on unanimity in the party was too extreme. And the absence of any reference to the disendowment of the established church led to the accusation in the press that this plank had been dropped from the platform.

John Blake Dillon, one of the founders of the *Nation* and a leader

28 Ibid., 2 May 1865.

of the physical force wing of Young Ireland in 1848, who was perhaps the most influential and prestigious figure active in the Association, tried to clear up misunderstandings and difficulties by circulating to all present at the previous meeting a more compact formula of commitment to be made by those whom the Association would support in future. While this emphasized the obligation of parliamentary candidates to commit themselves to independent opposition and to promise to work for the aims of the Association, and in a vote of confidence to vote against any government not prepared to compensate tenants for their improvements, it did not refer directly to the other demands for majority decision and promises not to seek office.[29]

Hostile reaction to this development resulted in requests for a meeting to clarify the situation. This eventually took place on 19 June and, though the Association could report that it had been active in petitioning parliament and educating public opinion, the ill-feeling created by the charges of altering the rules was only calmed by an agreement to observe the original resolutions of 29 April, subject to whatever alterations a committee to be appointed for that purpose might make. Dorrian's description of this contretemps 'there was some hitch with the Meath priests, some other gentlemen and the committee of the National Association . . . all about words' certainly understated the strength of feeling involved, but perhaps he was trying to play down his own central role in resolving the difficulty. For it seems to have been he who took the initiative in making peace, and as he was then the most junior member of the episcopal bench, having succeeded to the see only six weeks previously, this activity betokened a deep commitment to getting the church to work for the redress of the grievances which the Association had highlighted. As he reported to Rome, he, MacHale, Derry (Clonfert), Keane (Cloyne) and Nulty (Meath) discussed the problem privately during their general meeting at Maynooth and arranged to contact Dillon the following morning (22 June) at Coffey's Hotel in Dublin. Late at night on 21 June Dillon and Dorrian went to see Cullen and persuaded him to join them. The bishops of Ardagh and Elphin, who had been active members from the beginning, also joined. A compromise was hammered out. According to the terms then agreed, electors were only urged to bind their representatives to vote for the objects of the Association and oppose any government not in favour of compensation for tenants, and were advised to oblige them not to accept office from a government not so committed. And the electors and their representatives were also encouraged to take counsel together in order to secure general uniformity of policy.

[29] Corish, loc. cit., pp 28-33.

These terms were certainly more flexible and allowed more freedom to those whom the Association might back, and permitted the Association to be less rigid in its conditions for offering its support. Dorrian was delighted with the atmosphere and described the 'cordiality' as 'refreshing'. But in his enthusiasm he may have read too much into the attitudes of some of the participants. At any rate he reported that MacHale declared he would join the Association, if it consisted only of those present, but would watch if it followed the policy then agreed on and then act accordingly. To Dorrian's suggestion that he make known publicly his support for the policy as decided at that meeting he responded affirmatively and promised to reveal his hand at a suitable time.[30]

Dorrian's desire to win MacHale's public backing for the Association was very understandable, for the archbishop of Tuam enjoyed a considerable measure of national popularity. As a result of his determined support for O'Connell, his energetic opposition to British legislation that was widely perceived to be inimical to the interests of Irish Catholics, and his denunciations of official policy during the famine, he had won a reputation for uncompromising patriotism. His powerful advocacy of the aims of the Association would at once invest them with an emotional appeal and a sentimental force that would attract attention, interest and sympathy. He might even confer the halo of nationalism on the movement and transform it into a national crusade. But MacHale was incapable of playing second fiddle to anyone, least of all to Cullen, who enjoyed a far superior power and influence at Rome and who was coming to dominate the hierarchy in a way MacHale had once aspired and attempted to do. Rather than co-operate in any movement in which his was not the most prominent ecclesiastical voice, MacHale was prepared to stand back and even snipe at it from the sidelines. Only a couple of days after Dorrian thought he had conscripted him for the Association, MacHale blasted it in a public letter read out at a tribute to Gavan Duffy, one of the disillusioned exponents of the independent opposition in the 1850s. MacHale declared in favour of the old policy in all its 'plenitude and vigour', pronouncing independent opposition to be 'the highest grade of patriotism to which our best men have ventured to aspire as a test of parliamentary candidates'.[31] The archbishop of Tuam was not going to exchange the role of national ecclesiastical prophet for the prosaic one of membership of a political pressure group which had been forced to make compromises by the necessities of practical politics.

The election of July 1865 did not produce any strong, cohesive

30 Dorrian to Kirby, 27 June 1865, A.I.C.R.
31 Corish, loc. cit., p.36.

body of National Association-backed MPs, though Dillon and Gray were elected. Whigs of varying shades of commitment received support, and the Association could boast that 'nearly all the new members have declared for some part of our programme'.[32] But, in fact, it could not claim to have made any significant alteration to the complexion of those representatives who owed their seats to the Catholic vote. In Ulster only two Liberals were elected. Lord John Hay, a Scots-born Liberal, stood in Belfast but came in a poor third. He had interviewed Dorrian and obtained his support, but that was not of major significance in a constituency where Catholic voters were very much a minority. In November 1865 Nulty and the Meath clergy withdrew and founded their own tenant right group.

Meanwhile, Dorrian was losing faith in the effectiveness of the Association. Bewailing the lack of union in the episcopal body — 'I wish our Synods were such as, after submission of our Resolutions to the Holy See all guerilla malcontents should have to lay down their arms and be allowed no longer to play into the hands of the enemy' — he went on to assure Kirby in Rome that the support given by some of his colleagues to Whiggery was very foolish:

> If a bishop supports at an election a man who has supported the Ecclesiastical Titles Bill or one who has contributed to Garibaldi's Fund, what must be the consequence? Our National Association has failed to touch the *heart* of the country from its too great and too evident leanings towards the great liberal party instead of being *truly independent*.[33]

Dorrian here put his finger on the central weakness of the Association. Unlike the repeal movement it was not led by a charismatic figure of great eloquence and ability and it lacked the simple rallying cries, the emotional slogans, the appeal to basic patriotic fervour that gave O'Connell's campaigns an intense power of attraction. The issues which it sought to attack were also too diffuse. And the fear that the Association was being used by Liberal opportunists to advance their own careers militated against it in some clerical quarters. Dorrian represented this attitude most strongly when he commented adversely on the credulousness of some of his episcopal colleagues:

> I still think some of us have more faith in the friendship of the Whigs than this class of politicians are worthy of. Indeed, I have more hope from the Conservative party and would have nothing

---

32 Norman, op. cit., p.171.
33 Dorrian to Kirby, 28 Sept. 1865, A.I.C.R.

to do with those liberal Catholics, who make the confidence of Bishops the way to advance themselves. I fear some of us are simple as doves without the cunning of serpents.[34]

But other factors were coming together to favour the execution of at least a land and church policy for Ireland. Pressure for disestablishment of the Church of Ireland was building up in England where voluntaryism, or the principle that each denomination should be responsible for its own finance, was gaining ground. The Association made contact with the Liberation Society, a pressure group campaigning for the disestablishment of all churches and equality for all denominations, and fed it with valuable statistics and other information about the Irish ecclesiastical scene. The departure of Palmerston and Russell and the accession of Gladstone to the leadership of a Liberal party in which the influence of the Whigs was constantly diminishing gave a boost to the hopes of those who placed their faith in remedial legislation. The Association continued its work of propaganda and contributed to the awareness of the problems concerning the land and the established church which helped impel Gladstone to introduce his reforming legislation. And with the granting of disestablishment in 1869 and the Land Act of 1870 education alone remained, but here the Liberals and Radicals were as committed to the non-denominational principle as the Whigs. With the defeat of Gladstone's university bill and the replacement of his government by the Tories the Association was wound up, but some of its leading members, including Dorrian, had long ceased to make use of it or expect it to make any significant contribution to the removal of the disabilities under which Catholics suffered.

III

The National Association had owed its origin in large part to the challenge posed by Fenianism to the church and consitutional politics. Founded in 1858 by James Stephens in Ireland and by John O'Mahony in the United States, this movement derived its name from the legendary Celtic warriors, the *Fianna*, and aimed at restoring Ireland to its rightful place in the polity of nations as a sovereign, independent republic. Both Stephens and O'Mahony had taken part in the 1848 rising and they and their associates preached the necessity of revolution as the only effective means of achieving true national freedom. Preparations for the violent overthrow of British rule were made in secret, and units or 'circles' of oath-bound

34 Ibid., 16 Nov. 1865.

members were formed to advance the conspiracy. To prevent penetration of the movement and preserve maximum secrecy, each circle was kept in ignorance of the existence and activities of the next, but the official organ of the conspirators, the *Irish People*, preached revolution openly for two years before being suppressed by the authorities.

The Fenians fell foul of the church authorities on two scores: they advocated violence and their society was secret and oath-bound. For O'Connell's philosophy of peaceful constitutional agitation, which for the clergy had remained the ideal method of achieving political change, the Fenians had nothing but contempt. The *Irish People* boasted of ridiculing and condemning the 'absurdities . . . the baseness — of the O'Connellite doctrine of moral force'[35] and poured scorn on the right or claims of priests to interfere or give guidance on political matters. The youth of Ireland was invited to prepare to meet 'the foe in an ordered phalanx' and assured that Ireland would with 'one sweep of her unfettered arm hurl the invader into the sea'.[36] 'To impute the sorrows of our land solely to the will of God' was a 'blasphemy' as 'England was the head, foundation and centre of them all'.[37] An Irish revolution was depicted 'as one of the grandest events in history'[38] because it would involve the overthrow of an imperial system greater than any the world had seen since the fall of Napoleon. The true models of Irish patriotism were those who had engaged in armed strife and Irishmen were bidden to reject the pernicious view that their struggle could only be carried out with the help of a foreign power.

Before these views were so openly and daringly expressed in print, the Fenians had clashed with the church. Secret or occult societies had long been the subject of ecclesiastical condemnation by the papacy, which regarded their existence as destructive of the rights of church and state, and their use of oaths as improper and unjustified, and suspected that those engaged in them were or could become anti-clerical or anti-religious. Secret societies with revolutionary goals had been, particularly in Italy, extremely anti-clerical and anti-religious and dismissed the church as a mere bulwark of reactionary regimes. In Ireland secret agrarian societies, which had obliged their members to take action against landlords or fellow-tenants, either of the same religion or not, had been condemned by the bishops for a century, but some pursued a sporadic existence under a variety of names depending on local circumstances and grievances.

35 I.P., 30 Jan. 1864.
36 I.P., 23 Jan. 1864.
37 I.P., 16 Apr. 1864
38 I.P., 13 Feb. 1864.

In the north, the Ribbonmen, who were partly an agrarian and partly a defensive society for Catholics against Orangemen, were thought to be widespread and powerful. Both Bishop Denvir and Archbishop Cullen were worried about their extent and influence in Down and Connor, and Dromore in the 1850s but few cases came before the courts.[39] In 1859 fifteen men were charged in Belfast with membership of the 'Knights of St Patrick Thrasher Society' which was alleged to be an alternative name for the Ribbon society but all were released on bail.[40]

The Fenians, however, were a much more serious challenge. They were organized on a national rather than on a haphazard, local basis, they had a single and distinct aim with a powerful emotional appeal — the expulsion of English authority from Ireland — and their propagandists put their message across with great effect. Their hostility to the archbishop of Dublin, who became the principal scapegoat for their anger against the church, descended to a bitter personal level, and the general tone of hostility to clerical involvement in politics introduced a new element into the relationship between priests and laity. The exaggerated figures given for the membership of the Fenian society by political enemies as well as friends frightened some bishops into believing that the movement was far more powerful and deep-rooted than was in fact the case.

Specific incidents fanned the flames of general hostility. In 1861 Archbishop Cullen forbade a lying-in-state and Requiem Mass for Terence Bellew McManus, one of the leaders of 1848, whose body had been exhumed and brought from America. Patrick Lavelle, a turbulent and pugnacious priest of the archdiocese of Tuam, who had provoked serious disorder and insubordination among the staff of the Irish College, Paris, took up the Fenians' case as a convenient stick with which to beat the majority of the hierarchy. MacHale, to whose diocese Lavelle belonged, resolutely refused to discipline his contumacious subject, partly because he may have had a sneaking sympathy for Lavelle's bellicose Anglophobia and partly to discommode and spite the archbishop of Dublin who repeatedly demanded that Lavelle be disciplined. For almost a decade MacHale and Lavelle fobbed off Roman orders for Lavelle's punishment by a series of diversionary tactics. This embarrassed the bishops and weakened their united and effective response to the movement. But Cullen kept insisting that Fenianism was included in the general

---

39 In his report to Rome in 1855 Denvir referred to a pernicious society widely scattered in Ireland, to whose members the bishops refused the sacraments. But he claimed that about four years previously, as a result of persuasion from himself and his clergy, it had begun to decrease and had almost disappeared. (Denvir to Propaganda, 19 Nov.1855, A.P.F. S.C.(Irlanda), 32, ff 579r-582r).

40 B.M.N., 17 Jan. 1859.

condemnation of secret societies long issued by the church, though Lavelle insisted vehemently that this was not so.

The groups which proved most susceptible to Fenian propaganda were artisans, tradesmen and shopkeepers. The Irish regiments in the British army were infiltrated, and many Irishmen who fought in the American civil war also swore allegiance to the 'republic' and promised to fight for it when released from their service. Membership of the movement was far from uniform throughout the country; Munster and Leinster were much more heavily represented than Ulster and Connaught. The Fenians were never strong in Antrim and Down. It has been claimed that 'fraternisation in a recreational setting was at the heart of fenianism in the early and middle 1860s';[41] the movement provided opportunities for social contacts, and drilling, its only serious military activity, was a form of pastime.

This would help to explain the attractions of Fenianism to Catholic workers in Belfast, some of whom may have joined in search of the congenial social contacts and companionship which, because of sectarian attitudes, they could not find at a wider level. Little serious evidence of military activities or preparedness ever emerged. Between February and May 1866 three Fenian suspects were arrested in Belfast and in January 1867 nine men were arrested and charged with Fenianism, and a quantity of lead, bullets and bullet moulds were seized. Twenty rifles were found in the Pound and a number of men were detained. But the police discovered no real proof for the scare stories published in the Tory press and Fenianism was never a serious threat in the north of Ireland. Few opportunities for infiltrating bodies of any significance were open to the Belfast Fenians.

Dorrian feared, however, that the Catholic Institute, the social and cultural club for Belfast's Catholics, was being used as a base for Fenian propaganda, and this added to his dislike of the Institute and his anxiety about its potential for causing mischief. When, shortly after succeeding to the bishopric, he organized the special devotions for the jubilee which Pius IX had proclaimed, he was naturally concerned about the reaction of the Fenians. Elsewhere some of them had deliberately stayed away from the sacraments rather than confess to membership of the society and be asked to withdraw from it. But Dorrian was delighted with the outcome in Belfast. He reported happily to Rome: 'the Fenians have to a man submitted'.[42] After the government clamp-down on the *Irish People* and the arrest of the leaders, Dorrian, like many other bishops and civic leaders, assumed that the movement was at an end, and expressed his

41 R.V. Comerford, *The Fenians in context* (Dublin,1985), p.111.
42 Dorrian to Kirby, 27 June 1865, A.I.C.R.

pleasure at the termination of this damaging and destructive political distraction. 'The Fenians were valueless but to do harm', he told Tobias Kirby.[43]

Fenianism, however, was far from moribund and in fact gave proof over the next half century of a remarkable tenacity and will to survive. The bivouacking of forces and brief skirmishes in February and March 1867 posed no serious threat to the police, and the death of Fenianism was again predicted. In a stern and bitter condemnation of the rashness and recklessness of the rising of 1867, the *Ulster Observer* pointed out that there was no need to offer advice to the farmers and peasantry of Ulster, for they had followed the counsels of their clergy and had never yielded to influences which in other parts of the country had led to ruin.[44]

In his Lenten pastoral of 1 March Dorrian attributed the revolutionary mania that was to be found both at home and abroad to a system of education from which the religious and civilizing influence had been excluded and which, by making men atheists, had deprived them of the power of distinguishing between right and wrong. Exhorting his people to shun all illegal bodies, he reminded them of St Paul's injunction to Christians to be subject to higher powers and went on to ask: 'Is it not then the blindest folly to listen to the arguments of the selfish and sordid apostles of a false and odious liberty, who would seduce by private intrigue and lying pretexts our simple, and, in most instances, well-disposed countrymen from an allegiance which is of divine obligation'? Expressing the hope that they would not be duped by wicked men, he encouraged them to try to amend what was bad by honourable, public and legitimate means; if they used such means, they would succeed because God would bless their efforts but, if they used dishonourable and unlawful means, they would not meet with permanent success, and temporary success, if brought about in such a way, would ultimately bring ruin and misery.[45]

Sympathy and emotional support for the Fenians, especially for those who had been given harsh prison sentences, built up after the execution of three of their members, Allen, Larkin and O'Brien, who had accidentally killed a policeman in attempting to rescue a colleague from a prison van. Protest meetings were held widely throughout Ireland and Requiem Masses were celebrated in many churches for them. The Amnesty Association staged public meetings calling for the release of the imprisoned and generated much sympathy for them. Cullen and some of the bishops were afraid that this

43 Ibid., 28 Sept. 1865.
44 U.Ob., 7 Mar. 1867.
45 U.Ob., 5 Mar. 1867.

sympathy would be exploited for future violence and the strong-arm tactics used by Fenians to break up constitutionally-organized meetings in defence of the Land Act lent force to this anxiety. The continued defence of Fenianism by Lavelle, who insisted that it was not covered by the condemnations of the freemasons or continental secret societies, and the electoral victory of the Fenian, O'Donovan Rossa, who was then serving a jail sentence for felony, led to Archbishop Cullen's seeking a final, definitive statement from Rome. On 12 January 1870 a solemn and formal decree declared that the American or Irish society known as the Fenians was included among those condemned and forbidden by the papacy and was numbered among those bodies to the membership of which was attached the penalty of excommunication. This was the decisive answer to those who had argued that membership was compatible with loyal devotion to the church.

In his Lenten pastoral of 1870 Dorrian gave explicit guidance on this persistent and troublesome issue. Defining patriotism as the promotion of the interests of one's native country 'by redressing wrongs, removing grievances, alleviating misery, ameliorating its material condition, and, as good citizens, by justice, industry, and honour, wreathing for it a crown of glory radiant with virtues in the chivalry and holiness of its children', he declared that there were many wrongs to be set right in Ireland. But afer centuries of misgovernment and oppression a Joseph had appeared in Egypt who would provide corn for their people, and a reign of justice and toleration had commenced among them. He asked rhetorically whether the stubborn refusal or prevention of further boons could be called patriotism, and then went on to contrast the unhappy consequences of the activities of secret societies with what should flow from Gladstone's policies.

> Must it not be admitted that the efforts to ameliorate the condition of Ireland by the action of 'secret socities' and the other sins which accompany them are undoubtedly immoral? What waste of time and money, what desolation to families, what habits of idleness and neglect of industry, what stagnation to trade, what spirit of hatred and revenge, and what nightly revellings, with their other indescribable consequences follow in the train of what many unthinking and generous men call and believe to be love of their and our native land? Is that worthy of the name of patriotism which degenerates into what is so ignoble and leads to so many wretched and untimely deaths? Let those who think otherwise examine their own hearts and see whether they are not out of place in taking upon themselves self-imposed responsibility by encouraging plans and schemes which God

does not approve and will not bless. This is not patriotism. It is not courage, but fatuity.

Having quoted the papal decree, he pointed out that excommunication was applicable not only to those who joined the movement but also to those who gave encouragement to others to join it, to those who provided houses as meeting places for members of the society, to those who contributed funds to it, and to those who do 'not apprise the spiritual authorities of what could lead to the conversion of their chiefs'.[46]

Acceptance of this decree and repudiation of violence as a means for effecting political changes did not preclude sympathy for those who were languishing in jail as a result of their involvement in revolutionary activities. The Catholics of Belfast were as supportive of the prisoners' claims for release as their co-religionists elsewhere. When William Harbinson, one of the leaders of Fenianism in Ulster, died in Belfast jail in September 1867, a huge crowd of between 30,000 and 40,000 took part in his funeral.[47] Thereafter, both at public rallies and in the press that catered for the Catholic community, demands for the freedom of the imprisoned were frequent and enthusiastic. The *Ulster Observer*, which had attacked the rebels and the whole ideology of violence most passionately, also contemptuously repudiated the demands of the Tory press for severe sentences on all who were arrested for treasonable conspiracy. The revelations of the infiltration of the Fenian movement by spies and the suspicion of their having acted as *agents provocateurs* brought forth a damning indictment of government policy in this regard: 'she (England) has been ungenerous to the highest degree of injustice, and obstinate to the last extremity of perversity'.[48] And reports of the cruel maltreatment of prisoners in English jails provoked impassioned criticisms both of the system of punishment and of its wholly disproportionate severity.[49]

The *Ulster Examiner* (another organ of Catholic opinion which was founded in 1868) was equally, if not more, outspoken in this regard. Gladstone, who found himself propelled along the road of reform by the very excesses of the Fenians, decided that part of his response to Irish grievances should be the release of some of the prisoners. In February 1869 he set free forty nine of the eighty one prisoners; nine of those serving sentences in Australia and twenty three in England were still detained. The *Examiner* described his refusal not to let out

46 B.M.N., 25 Feb. 1870.
47 R.V. Comerford, op. cit. p.147.
48 U.Ob., 30 Apr. 1867.
49 'The discipline of Pentonville and Portland is an elaborate machinery of ingenious torture.' U.Ob., 23 Mar. 1867.

all the detained as 'ungenerous and unjust'.[50] It later remarked that the prisoners had served sentences that were long enough, and it summed up a widespread view by claiming that they had acted 'from the purest of misguided motives'.[51]

Meetings to demand the release of the remaining prisoners continued to be held and to draw support in Belfast. In October 1869 the Amnesty Association organized a great meeting at Hannahstown, at which between 8,000 and 10,000 were present.[52] Dorrian aligned himself with this campaign in his pastoral of 1870 when he expressed regret that this great boon had not been fully conceded. And it was this support for the prisoners as much as their alleged participation in the movement that led Protestants to identify Catholics as 'Fenians' and ultimately to win for that word the pejorative connotation that it still enjoys when applied to Catholics in the north of Ireland.

IV

After 1864 Belfast escaped any further outbreak of serious sectarian conflict for the remainder of the decade. Orange parades and the psychological build-up to them accounted for minor acts of violence from time to time in various parts of Ulster. In July 1869 Orangemen fired several rounds of shots at the church and parochial house at Aghagallon, but no one was injured. In Belfast Catholic girls were attacked as they left one of the large mills.[53] And rumours of an attack on the recently opened church at Ardoyne caused Catholic men from the Pound to march to its defence and two days of rioting ensued. Papers representing Catholic interests were highly critical of the response of magistrates to some of these incidents and complained loudly that those of Orange sympathies were unduly lenient to Orangemen accused of intimidating behaviour to Catholics or of vandalizing Catholic-owned property. But as the majority of magistrates and grand juries were Tory in politics, these complaints were ineffective.

Catholics should have found their natural political home with the Liberals. That predominantly Presbyterian party shared some of the same principal concerns, especially on the land question, but religious and political suspicions prevented any kind of serious or lasting union. The newspapers which championed the respective views of Presbyterians and Catholics sowed distrust among their readers

50 U.Ex., 25 Feb. 1869.
51 U.Ex., 25 Apr. 1869.
52 B.M.N., 4 Oct. 1869.
53 U.Ex., 15 July 1869.

with widely different and hostile attitudes on Italian unification, ultramontanism, the missionary activity of Presbyterian clergy in Connaught and occasionally on doctrinal questions. In political terms Catholics felt they were courted for support only at elections and ignored at other times. And being very much the junior partner they were unable to do much to rectify this situation. But this inattention to Catholics was also due to the inefficiency, poor organization and carelessness about the registration of voters which characterized the Liberal party at the time.

When Lord John Hay called with Dorrian in 1865 to solicit his support, the *Ulster Observer* reported the visit favourably and encouraged Catholics to vote for him. In 1868 Thomas McClure, a wealthy Belfast merchant, carried the Liberal banner. Long prominent in Liberal circles, McClure was an elder in the Presbyterian church, who had wanted the Liberals to ignore Catholic issues and voters in favour of a distinctively Protestant campaign in a previous election, and who had helped raise funds for the Connaught mission. But with the prospect of Gladstone winning the election and carrying significant reforms and faced with the danger of William Johnston, the populist Orange leader and hero of resistance to the government, winning a seat, Catholic support went extensively to McClure. And though Catholic voters in Belfast accounted for less than twenty per cent,[54] their contribution to McClure's victory was highly important.

The campaign for the disestablishment and disendowment of the established church, which was sponsored by the National Association, had been gathering momentum since the publication of the returns of the census of 1861. These revealed that the Church of Ireland represented only an eighth of the total population of the country. With strong pressure also coming from non-conformist bodies it was evident that the Liberal party, when returned to power, would tackle the problem.

The Church of Ireland was divided in its response to this threat, but in the north Protestants of other denominations rallied to its support. The disendowment of the church was presented as a violation of the terms of the Act of Union, a betrayal of trust and an attack on property. Tory landlords who feared that they could be the next victims of Liberal reforming legislation took up the defence of the church. At a meeting of 10,000 Protestants, presided over by the leading aristocrats, gentry and MPs, the redoubtable Presbyterian leader, Henry Cooke, recalled his very powerful contribution to the alliance of Presbyterians and Episcopalians in 1834: 'it is now more

---

54 Brian Walker in *Ulster parliamentary politics 1868-86: the formative years*, an unpublished thesis presented to Trinity College, Dublin, estimates the Catholic percentage at between 15 and 19.

that thirty years since I attended here in this field and proclaimed the banns of holy marriage, intellectually and spiritually, between the Established and Presbyterian churches, I am glad after thirty years to see such a glorious progeny here today'. He described the Church of Ireland as the noble branch of that noble tree planted in the sixteenth century by the reformers.[55] A Protestant Defence Association was formed to resist disestablishment. At its public meetings Gladstone's proposals were denounced as a sop to Fenianism, a victory for ultramontanism, and a betrayal of the Presbyterians, who would lose their *Regium Donum*.

Cooke himself died in December 1868, shortly after Gladstone came to power. His funeral arrangements created an embarrassment for Dorrian. He had attended Denvir's funeral two years previously and Dorrian presumably intended to reciprocate the gesture of goodwill, but a committee was formed to organize the funeral and decided to turn it into a tribute to his public life. Dorrian wrote to the secretary explaining that this decision practically prevented all who were not prepared to pay 'deference to the life and labours' and to offer 'a mark of respect to his public character and worth' from attending. This, in Dorrian's view, was tantamount to asking those who were present to endorse all Cooke's public acts and labours, and he regretted that he could not do so.[56]

The Catholic bishops had long regarded the privileged position of the Church of Ireland and its compulsory financial support by adherents of other religions as intolerable. They had made clear their opposition to any form of concurrent endowment or any levelling up in terms of state grants. Consequently, they lost the annual grant to Maynooth as the Presbyterians lost the *Regium Donum*, but they regarded this as a price well worth paying for the termination of a long standing grievance. Once Gladstone had solved the church question it was inevitable that he would turn his attention to the land question.

For decades Irish tenants had complained of insecurity of tenure and the evictions which took place because of the clearances of their estates by some landlords after the famine had led to the tenant league of the 1850s. The 'Ulster custom' allowed tenants in the north to remain in their holdings as long as they paid their rents and to sell the goodwill of their tenancy on vacating it to anyone whom the landlord was prepared to accept. But this custom did not have the force of law and an attempt to give it that authority had failed in 1847. The legalization of the custom was the minimum expectation of those who looked to Gladstone for redress in this field.

55 B.M.N., 1 Nov. 1867.
56 U.Ex., 17 Dec. 1868.

A meeting of all the clergy of Down and Connor was organized in St Malachy's College on 5 November 1869 to discuss acceptable terms of land reform. Resolutions were passed unanimously declaring that the relations between landlord and tenant were abnormal and unsatisfactory because the rights of the landlord were legally secure, while the tenant's rights were without legal protection. Consequently, the priests called on the government to remedy this state of things by a measure of legislation founded on just rents and security of tenure, and declared their belief that 'only on these principles can legislation satisfy the Irish people, remove the cause of that alienation of feeling unhappily existing between landlord and tenant in many parts of the country and lay the surest foundation of lasting peace and permanent prosperity'[57] The Ulster landlords reacted by playing the Orange card, arranging big Protestant demonstrations and depicting the forthcoming legislation as another phase in the unjust spoliation of property owners carried out at the behest of ultramontane bigots and communistic agitators.[58]

In the event the Ulster custom was given the force of law wherever it existed. Elsewhere the tenant was granted security by being assured of compensation for any improvements which he carried out on his holding, but of much greater significance was the enactment that obliged the landlord to compensate the tenant whom he displaced for any reason other than non-payment of rent. Tenants who wished to purchase their farms were also enabled to borrow two thirds of the cost and repay the state over a period of thirty five years. Gladstone's Land Act proved a disappointment precisely because it did not legislate for one of the conditions which the Down and Connor clergy had pinpointed as essential to creating good relations between landlords and tenants: just rents. There was no provision made for determining fair rents; as a result landlords were free to raise the rents as they chose and tenants had no redress if they were evicted for non-payment.

Gladstone's legislation angered the Conservatives who were outraged by the disestablishment of the church and by what they regarded as his indefensible attacks on property, and disappointed some Liberals who considered his Land Act too timid and anaemic. It was from among those who were alienated by these measures that Isaac Butt drew support for his Home Government Association.

Butt was a Donegal-born Protestant, a graduate of Trinity College, Dublin and a lawyer who had sat in parliament for many years as a Conservative. He had shot to prominence with his defence of Fenian prisoners and his work for the Amnesty Association. He

57 B.M.N., 8 Nov. 1869.
58 B.M.N., 10 Dec. 1869.

had long been interested in ameliorating the condition of the poorer tenants and it was from reflecting on this need for co-operation between the propertied and the Catholic poor to avoid the dangers of revolution that he came up with his idea of a federal relationship between Britain and Ireland. He envisaged the restoration of an Irish parliament of Lords and Commons with an Irish executive having control of internal affairs, but with Westminster retaining control of foreign affairs, defence, war and major taxation. When Butt summoned a meeting in Dublin in May 1870 to form a committee to carry his ideas into effect, the majority who attended were Protestant, including disappointed Conservatives and Liberals as well as constitutional nationalists. Those who expressed an interest in a native government in Dublin would have envisaged the continuance of a Protestant majority among the Irish MPs.

Butt's proposals, however, did not attract any significant support from the landowning or influential Protestants or from the general body of Protestants in Ulster. They regarded the union as the guarantee of their status and security, however much they might regret the temporary aberrations to which a Gladstone could succumb. On the other hand Catholic sentimental attachment to repeal had never disappeared though opportunities for realizing it had been wanting; the *Ulster Examiner* had expressed this enduring view in June 1868, when it editorialized that a native legislature was the only remedy for their grievances, since the union was a fertile source of evil to Ireland.[59] When an opportunity arose to channel this aspiration into a coherent political policy, as it did with Butt's incipient demand for Home Rule, the nationally-minded Catholics of Belfast responded positively.

59 U.Ex., 6 June 1868.

7

The struggle for a Catholic press

I

During the 1840s and 1850s the Belfast and Ulster, or perhaps it would be more accurate to say the North East Ulster, Catholic community had been served by the *Vindicator* and the *Ulsterman*. Edited by Catholic nationalists, these papers broadly reflected the political views of their readers and highlighted the social, educational and economic grievances of Catholics. In 1859 Denis Holland transferred his paper, the *Ulsterman* recently renamed the *Irishman*, to Dublin and the Catholics of Belfast were left without an organ of their own. The *Whig*, as its name indicated, represented Northern Liberals and had a mainly Presbyterian readership; the *News-Letter* represented the Tory, Orange and Church of Ireland party; and the *Belfast Morning News*, founded in 1855 and owned by the Read brothers, who were Catholics, disclaimed political attachments but tended to support the Liberal line and tried to draw readers from all sections of society.

However, the more vocal and active leaders of the emerging Catholic middle class regarded the political and religious views of the *Belfast Morning News* as too grey and wishy-washy and decided to found an organ of their own. A group of prominent business and professional men including Bernard Hughes, D.R. Brannigan, Matthew McMullan, Patrick McCourt, Terence O'Brien, Alexander O'Rorke — virtually the same people who three years previously had established the Catholic Institute as a study and recreational centre for the Catholics of the town — came together and through McCourt, an acquaintance of Archbishop Dixon's, obtained the approval of the bishops of the Armagh province to found a paper that would cater mainly for the Catholic community. McCourt asked the coadjutor bishop of Down and Connor to help in the search for a suitable editor and sub-editor, and Dorrian, who had tremendous faith in the apostolate of the press, contacted Bartholomew Woodlock, the rector of the Catholic University in Dublin. The job description he gave Woodlock placed heavy emphasis on the religious character of the journal and he certainly expected the editor to be an able, willing and circumspect apologist of Catholicism:

> Its most leading feature must be its Catholicity; & this of that argumentative, truthful, Christian, scholarlike, yet moderate & temperate sort of thing, which will make it a means of great usefulness, circulating through this materialistic community & doing away with prejudices, without giving offence . . . Do you know or can you know of any man of ability & true Catholic heart, whose prudence & discretion would be up to the mark & whom you would be inclined to think would suit? I say nothing of his politics, because if he be truly Catholic, he should be left to his own independent mind & the course of future events to form for his paper any very decided course in that way.[1]

Evidently Woodlock recommended Andrew Joseph McKenna, a young journalist attached to the *Dublin Evening Post*, for Dorrian wrote back expressing satisfaction with McKenna's suitability, and characteristically indicating impatience with McCourt's casual approach to the serious difficulties involved.[2] McKenna, a native of Cavan, who was then aged twenty eight, had studied for the priesthood at Maynooth but had changed course and taken up journalism. Able, intelligent, widely-read and endowed with a fluent pen, he was destined to play a highly important, if at times very controversial, role among Belfast Catholics until his death ten years later.

The first edition of the *Ulster Observer* rolled off the presses on 1 July 1862, boldly proclaiming its policy in an editorial 'prospectus'. Bemoaning the absence of a Catholic journal in Ulster as an anomaly and a grievance, given the numbers, wealth and intelligence of the Catholic body and their state as 'an enslaved people', resulting from remote causes which 'still injudiciously affect their dearest interests as citizens and debar them from privileges which it is the right of every free man in every free country to enjoy', McKenna explained that they were entitled to their own journal to expose their views and vindicate their rights. The main object of the *Observer* was to publicize the injustices — the non-representation or wholly inadequate representation of Catholics in parliament, on the magisterial bench, in the grand jury room and jury box, in municipal bodies and Boards of Guardians — and by firm advocacy help to rectify them. But as the paper owed its origin to no narrow sectarian spirit, it also set itself the 'proud mission' of pleading for those national measures in which the common rights of every sect were involved, and it

1 Dorrian to Woodlock, 8 Nov. 1861, D.D.A.
2 Ibid., 22 Dec. 1861.

singled out for special emphasis tenant right and the need for the tenant to feel secure in his home; it also pledged itself 'to advocate the principles upon which education depends for its freedom and utility'. And, while committing itself to the defence of human and civil rights, it promised to engage wholeheartedly the 'unjust ascendancy' which 'still pursues and persecutes our co-religionists of the North', and which they were forced to confront in 'the Law and its administration — in society and its conventionalisms — in every department of public life and in many of the relations of private intercourse'. It also undertook to engage the intolerance and bigotry which confronted the Catholic church in Ulster.[3]

The paper was published by the Ulster Catholic Publishing Company, a limited liability company with a capital of £5,000 in 5,000 shares of £1 each. Its board of directors consisted of thirty one members, under the chairmanship of Terence O'Brien of Belfast. Ten of the directors, of whom one was a priest, came from the town, and included the leading Catholic businessmen, Daniel Brannigan and Bernard Hughes; of the other twenty one ten were priests and between them represented every county in Ulster apart from Cavan and Donegal; Tyrone, Derry and Armagh had also lay representatives. At its inauguration the *Observer* also boasted that it enjoyed the approval of every bishop in Ulster, four of whom had become shareholders, and that among its other shareholders it numbered 75 priests and upwards of 150 laymen. The addresses of the directors, however, indicate that the balance of the paper's interests lay in Belfast and North East Ulster.

The policy which it set itself was calculated to appeal to the vast majority of Catholics, and their initial response was wholly favourable. At a function in the Catholic Institute to raise funds for parochial Sunday schools, Patrick Clarke, one of the curates of the town, in proposing a toast to the *Observer*, declared that his co-religionists were proud of the paper and 'prouder still of the gifted young editor who conducted it'.[4] Published thrice weekly, its sales soon increased to five thousand (a respectable figure in Ireland at that time) and at the meeting of shareholders in April 1863 the directors declared a handsome dividend. Its coverage of local politics and ecclesiastical affairs was quite extensive. Most of its British and world news was taken from the British press and general agencies. Though hewing to a Catholic line and tackling what it regarded as injustices and inequalities, it was not unnecessarily offensive or sectarian.

McKenna himself took an active part in the cultural life of the Catholic community of the town and soon won recognition as an able

---
3 U.Ob., 1 July 1862.
4 U.Ob., 23 Aug. 1862.

lecturer on subjects of Irish literary and historical interest. His work gave general satisfaction to those associated with or interested in the progress of the paper, for on 12 January 1865, a mere two and a half years after its inauguration, a deputation led by Hughes, Brannigan and McMullan waited on him at his offices and presented him with three hundred guineas, a salver and an address of congratulations and good wishes. Hailing him as a most distinguished journalist, who had justified the commendations with which he had been introduced to them, they praised his enthusiastic commitment to every political struggle for the good of his fellow men and acknowledged the influential niche which he had carved out for the paper.[5] The directors would have probably known that the coadjutor bishop had by then lost confidence in the paper and their gesture in making this generous presentation may have been something of a public repudiation of his challenge as well as a confirmation of their confidence in the editor.

Dorrian had been initially pleased with the *Observer*. In response to a query from Archbishop Dixon, who was obviously alarmed at the revolutionary implications of a speech made by the editor, Dorrian admitted that McKenna had referred to Wolfe Tone but denied that he hinted at a rising in 1868; and possibly to counter misinterpretations he had followed up the speech with a moderate, judicious and anti-revolutionary article on politics and politicians. Though conceding that the journal was capable of very decided improvement, Dorrian concluded on a favourable note: 'I think the *Observer* is doing good service and may be recommended. For *should* the Editor fail in his duty, there are the means of displacing him and substituting another. I have not approved of *every*thing but we can get nothing *perfect*'.[6] At a personal level Dorrian and McKenna must have been on very good terms, for the bishop had officiated at the editor's wedding in February 1863.

However, a year later, the scene had changed dramatically. In June 1864, while he was still coadjutor, he wrote to the board of directors to let them know that the bishops and clergy of the province wished to have an organ which was Catholic and orthodox but unfortunately the *Observer* was not such. Instancing its recent omission to acquaint its readers with a parliamentary division on the Irish education question, which had appeared in the *Whig*, he accused it of being so inconsistent and unorthodox that any bishop would feel constrained to sound the alarm. He subsequently explained that he had objected both to the political and literary departments; the former he found inconsistent and the latter he felt was neglected:

5 U.Ob., 14 Jan. 1865.
6 Dorrian to Dixon, 13 Apr. 1863, A.D.A.

I consider its tone was very inconsistent blowing in one direction this day and in another direction tomorrow, and that there was no uniformity of opinion or feeling carried out by the conductor of it. I pointed out what I considered were gross errors in not giving news in a paper in which we took pride. I believe that the article that I called the rhapsody was written without deliberation or reflection, and in a way that no student would have written it. I wrote the letter because as I was living in Belfast the other Bishops of the province expected that I should give advice in reference to the paper . . . I was anxious that he [the editor] should be removed, not merely on account of his deficient way of conducting the paper, but because I believe his stamp of character was not such as to constitute him a proper editor for a Catholic journal.[7]

Dorrian's specific objections are not clear. The *Observer* reported Catholic events and reviewed the writings of Catholic authors — though presumably not as extensively as Dorrian would have liked. Personal reservations about the editor may well have been the major factor in contributing to this episcopal censure. McKenna had become perhaps the most prominent literary figure associated with the Catholic Institute and his activities there helped raise his profile in the Catholic community. And by 1864 Dorrian had grown suspicious of the Institute which he regarded as representing at least a dangerous challenge to, if not a downright rejection of, legitimate episcopal authority.

The editor's silence throughout Dorrian's bruising encounter with the Institute confirmed the bishop's worst suspicions of him. Dorrian regarded it as tantamount to a stab in the back; when he most needed the support of a local Catholic paper to explain and justify his actions against the hostile criticisms and bitter charges of ecclesiastical obscurantism lavished on him by the local and English press, he did not get it, and to rub salt in the wounds the *News-Letter* taunted the *Observer* with its refusal to comment on this divisive issue. Shortly after the crisis over the Institute broke, he had written to Kirby in Rome to enlist his aid in preventing McKenna from receiving a papal honour.[8] And on the same day he wrote to the archbishop of Dublin pointing out that 'McKenna has been for a considerable time giving the utmost dissatisfaction here by his overweening desire to be leader in our ecclesiastical and political affairs'. He went on to explain that 'Dr Denvir is thought to be easily managed, but every attempt is made to ignore me, and with *some* success'; but since the bishop's

7 B.M.N., 21, 24 Feb. 1868.
8 Dorrian to Kirby, 2 May 1865, A.I.C.R.

approval was required for this honour Dorrian was determined to counterbalance Bishop Denvir's 'softness' and block this development at source. He also explained to Cullen that he could never have any confidence in the editor's 'moral principle and honesty' and indicated that two of Cullen's priests as well as Nicholas Conaty, the bishop of McKenna's native diocese, could justify his reservations. But apart from a reference to the editor's role in the dispute over the Catholic Institute and to his inviting a heckler at a recent election meeting, who had charged him with being drunk, to settle their differences outside, Dorrian did not specify what McKenna's faults were.[9]

Those who took the bishop's side in the dispute over the Institute were aware of McKenna's views and consequently their confidence in him diminished. But the editor had other opponents apart from the bishop's friends. Isaac Butt, who later defended him in a court case, admitted that by 1864 some of the shareholders were dissatisfied with his management of the paper, probably because they thought his political views were too liberal. And Butt was obviously concerned to put the most favourable interpretation on his client's behalf. However, matters did not come to a head for nearly two years. At the meeting of directors on 6 August 1867 a resolution was passed dismissing him from his post as editor, when he had served three months' notice. The chief instigator of this move was apparently Owen Kerr,[10] a newsagent and publisher, who was a close friend of the bishop and who had published Dorrian's controversy with the Anglican rector, William McIlwaine, in 1865.

Two days before the expiry of the notice a committee was appointed to take charge of the paper, pending the appointment of a new editor; its chairman was John Cunningham, parish priest of Carrickfergus, and among its five members were Patrick Clarke, the administrator of St Mary's Church, and Owen Kerr. When they accosted McKenna in his offices to present him with his notice of dismissal, he reacted angrily, refused to accept their injunction and attempted to keep control of the paper. McKenna's friends rallied to his defence. His supporters among the shareholders convened a meeting on 5 November, when they had failed to persuade the board of directors to do so, and succeeded in rescinding the previous resolution which called for the editor's dismissal. Three prominent directors, Bernard Hughes, James Kavanagh and William Ross, backed McKenna but the secretary of the company challenged the

9 Dorrian to Cullen, 2 May 1865, D.D.A.
10 In *Belfast newspapers, past and present* (Belfast,1921), A.A. Campbell singles out Kerr as the most determined of McKenna's enemies. Kerr was later quoted in a libel action as having said that McKenna, when he was a student in Maynooth, was given twenty four hours to leave the college. (B.M.N., 24 Mar. 1869)

legality of this meeting,[11] and the board of directors later confirmed their original decision. McKenna was compelled to submit. In a signed valedictory on 31 December he claimed he had been loyal to the terms of the prospectus on which the paper was founded, insisted that no charge had been brought against him or blame attached to him, and maintained that he had given confidence and hope to the Catholics of Ulster. But because of financial and unforeseen and exceptional exigencies the company to which the *Observer* belonged had to be wound up.

The liquidators appointed by the shareholders put up the copyright of the paper and the entire plant and equipment for sale in January 1868. McKenna announced that he would publish the *Weekly Observer* and a tri-weekly, the *Belfast Observer*. But the Ulster Catholic Publishing Company, which was then being compulsorily wound up, brought an injunction in the Vice-Chancellor's court in Dublin against his use of the title *Weekly Observer* lest people might think a paper so named was an offshoot of their paper, the *Ulster Observer*. Though the Vice-Chancellor found the appellation *Weekly Observer* unobjectionable, he decided that the title *Belfast Observer* was objectionable.[12] Accordingly McKenna christened his new paper the *Northern Star* and launched it on 6 February 1868.

From an ecclesiastical point of view the paper could scarcely have been wound up on a more unhappy note. When presented with his notice of dismissal on 6 November, McKenna vented his anger on Patrick Clarke, one of the members of the deputation, whom he proceeded to accuse of very serious breaches of priestly duty. When Clarke denied the charge of having traduced him for the previous three years, the excited editor claimed that he had a letter from the pope thanking him for his services and offering him the knighthood of the Holy Roman Empire; and he knew who prevented him from obtaining the honour. He went on to arraign Clarke with having drunk his wine, eaten his beef, defamed him and then, his charges

11 John Cunningham, parish priest of Carrickfergus, who had been chairman of the meeting on 6 Aug. 1867 which gave McKenna three months notice, took the chair at the extraordinary meeting of shareholders on 5 Nov. which McKenna was instrumental in calling with a view to overturning the previous decision. McKenna's opponents objected that the meeting was illegal because it was not properly convoked. McKenna proposed that Cunningham be removed from the chair. John Rea, who was present as a shareholder and as Cunningham's legal adviser, later applied for a summons against McKenna, Edward McHugh (McKenna's father-in-law) and William Ross in the Belfast police court for verbal abuse of Cunningham. Rea remarked in court that language which would not have crossed the lips of an Orangeman was used to priests on that occasion and added that D.R. Brannigan and other laymen were similarly treated. (B.M.N., 2 Dec. 1867).

12 B.M.N., 12 Feb. 1868. On 4 June 1870 McKenna brought back the title *Ulster Observer* and his paper became the *Northern Star and Ulster Observer*.

rising to a crescendo, declared: 'You prostituted the confessional in my regard'. To Clarke's bewildered exclamation of disbelief, McKenna expressed his willingness to repeat the charge in writing and to call a witness to testify to the truth of it. On the following day McKenna wrote to Clarke telling him that he had given his solicitor instructions to take immediate proceedings for slander on the grounds that Clarke, 'in a most respectable house and in the presence of a distinguished clergyman' had stated that he had been forced to give up McKenna's spiritual direction since his conduct was so gross. But Clarke, believing that he bad been the victim of untrue and unjust accusations, instituted legal proceedings.

Dorrian was concerned about the painful embarrassment and scandal to which the case could give rise, and he unburdened himself to Cardinal Cullen. He explained that the matter had been put into the hands of a solicitor before he had heard of it, but that everyone knew the charge was 'false and unprovable' and that since 'the other priests in town feel very acutely that one of their body should be charged as the most abandoned priest has never been charged before', he did not intend to interfere. In fact he took some solace from the reflection that the exposure of this calumny might do good by undeceiving people about McKenna's character and principles. For McKenna, whose companions were 'Queen's College people and Freemasons', only two or three of whom attended the sacraments, had formed the nucleus of an anti-clerical party in Belfast.[13]

Cullen apparently replied by counselling a gentle approach in the hope that McKenna would retract his accusation without subjecting the church to the unfavourable publicity an action in a court of law would bring. But Dorrian was convinced of the futility of such tactics and answered by asserting that he had tried to use 'softer influences' over the past two years, but to no effect. McKenna 'by plausibility and pretence' had been gaining ground with the clergy and had not stopped 'at any misrepresentation to effect his object'. He had deceived some priests, especially those from other dioceses, who were unaware of the real nature of his behaviour; and the favour and friendship with which these clergy indulged him were responsible for the support afforded him by Bernard Hughes and others.[14] Had

13 Dorrian to Cullen, 21 Nov. 1867, D.D.A.
14 Monsignor Nardi, a judge of the Roman Rota, had recently visited Belfast and had undertaken to obtain a papal honour for Bernard Hughes. Dorrian was very critical of Nardi's interference, and refused to sign a formal request to Rome for Hughes, whom he blamed for giving important support to his opponents in the dispute about the Catholic Institute and for backing McKenna who was 'doing incalculable injury to religion over the whole province'. (Dorrian to Nardi, 12 Nov. 1867. A.I.C.R.) Dorrian also singled out William Ross, a wealthy mill owner, as a supporter of McKenna's.

he never come to Belfast, its Catholic community would be the most united in the world, but since he came 'the harm done is beyond conception'. Principles were being sown which would produce bad fruits and all the priests of the town believed that his sojourn among them would cause further harm. The honour of the diocesan priesthood was involved in the slander of one of their number, and they insisted on being vindicated.[15]

Not surprisingly McKenna was much less willing to let the case proceed. He too wrote to Cardinal Cullen but put a very different gloss on the attitudes of the clergy: he maintained that the universal opinion of Catholics in Belfast, both lay and clerical, was that the action should not go ahead. He had done everything possible to effect a settlement and 'as a last resource to avoid scandal and to conform to the request of so many good and disinterested men' he appealed to the cardinal to judge the matter either in person or through a delegate, declaring himself ready to submit to the verdict.[16] However the cardinal did not choose to intervene and the case was tried before the court of the Exchequer in Dublin in February 1868.

As Clarke's counsel pointed out and Dorrian's testimony confirmed, the violation of the secrecy of the confessional involved permanent suspension from sacerdotal duties for any priest guilty of such an outrageous betrayal of spiritual trust. Clarke strongly denied any such breach of obligation, claimed that he was in McKenna's house only two or three times, but admitted hearing the witness to whom McKenna had referred say that he (Clarke) had given the editor 'a very bad character'. As this witness had died before the case came up, no further explanation of this was offered other than Clarke's; and according to this, after McKenna's arrival in Belfast, Clarke had given him good moral advice. Dorrian in his cross-examination confessed that some of the directors had consulted him unofficially about McKenna's dismissal, and that he had given his approval. Confronted with the evidence that three prominent directors — Bernard Hughes, James Kavanagh and William Ross — objected to McKenna's deposition, Dorrian conceded that his reply would be very unpleasant: despite their apparent support for the editor some of them had told him, privately, that, if McKenna were in their employment, they would not keep him for twenty four hours.

The case terminated with McKenna's surrender. He wrote to Clarke denying that he had ever intended 'either by language or thought to cast upon you the imputation you have attributed to my words'. He further explained that his remarks were uttered in the heat of the moment and that he wished to withdraw every imputation

15 Dorrian to Cullen, 25 Nov. 1867, D.D.A.
16 McKenna to Cullen, 13 Feb. 1868, Ibid.

which his words might have conveyed; moreover, he expressed his willingness to pay all the costs of the trial.[17]

A more bitter and tragic end to the high hopes with which the *Ulster Observer* had been launched six years earlier could scarcely have been imagined. The paper which had been called into existence primarily to advocate the interests of the Belfast Catholic community died amidst a welter of unfavourable publicity, with the general public eavesdropping on the tensions and divisions within that community. Neither side in the dispute, however, was prepared to give up in despair and withdraw from the field of journalism. Within the first three months of 1868 the Catholics of Belfast and Ulster had two journals — the *Northern Star* managed and edited by McKenna and the *Ulster Examiner* under the control of his opponents — competing for their allegiance and support.

II

The *Examiner* rolled off the presses for the first time on 14 March 1868. Under the motto '*pro aris et focis*' (for altars and hearths, or God and our native land), it introduced itself as the rightful heir to the principles on which the *Observer* had been founded but which it asserted, with a polemical touch that was often to mar its style, had unhappily not been fully or consistently carried out. Unashamedly Catholic, it defined itself as the recognized organ of Catholic opinion in Belfast and Ulster and promised Catholics that it would command the approval and inspire the confidence of their spiritual rulers. Dedicating itself to advancing the physical, social and political cause of the Irish people in a constitutional manner, and to supporting anyone, irrespective of party, who worked for these goals, it bewailed the gloomy condition of the country and singled out for special mention 'the cankerworms that prey upon the vitals of the nation': emigration,[18] a vicious land code and clearance system, neglect of the rights of the majority on educational issues, the existence of a church establishment. It also set itself the heroic task of calming the sectarian animosities that kept the people of Ulster divided and looked forward to the end of party displays that stained the fame of Belfast, 'this great and flourishing seat of industry, this emporium of commerce, this Athens of Ireland'. Recalling the malign influence of immoral literature on France, it promised to

17 B.M.N., 21, 24 Feb. 1868.

18 The criticism of the forced emigration of the Irishman from his rich native soil was garnished with a quotation in the original from that 'Homer of Italian poets' about the bitterness and pain of exile. This was a *terzina* from Dante (*Paradiso*, xvii, 58-60), a somewhat precious and esoteric reference for readers of the *Examiner*.

devote a column to literary criticism and thereby to alert its Catholic readers to unorthodox opinions and evil principles. In return the editor claimed the support of every Belfast and Ulster Catholic who was proud of his faith; of 'the bishops and priests whom we cherish and love as the guardians of our religion, and whose characters we will defend from misrepresentation'; of liberal men of other persuasions who respected knowledge, consistency and truth; and of lovers of literature of every class.

Side by side with this editorial statement of policy, the new journal made bold to publish with 'mingled feelings of pride and pleasure' a warm letter of encouragement from the bishop of Down and Connor. Stating that an honest and independent journal that would teach the Catholic people to be truly patriotic, foster industry, avoid extravagance, use their money wisely and understand the evil of intemperance was greatly needed, Dorrian foresaw the *Examiner* making a valuable contribution to its readers, if it handled these subjects prudently. Though realizing that a newspaper was far from being a prayer-book or a manual of controversy, he felt sure that much good or harm would result from the way it dealt with politico-religious questions; and especially at a time when the leaven of unorthodoxy was, without their seeing it, corrupting some among them who regarded themselves as staunch upholders of the truth, a journal representing Catholic views should be fully orthodox. In giving his approval to the policies of the paper, Dorrian went on to quote a papal exhortation to Catholic laymen to defend their religion under the guidance of their bishops, and knowing the publishers of this new journal, he expressed his confidence that they would make this 'the only accredited organ of the diocese' both good and useful. He concluded in the best homiletic tradition with a prediction-cum-exhortation: their politics would be Catholic, they would be liberal as far as was consistent with charity and justice, they would be conservative in upholding legitimate rights, they would be as independent as honesty and purity of principle allowed, and they would be uniform and consistent.[19]

This letter was addressed to Owen Kerr and T.E. Fitzpatrick, whose names appeared on the *Examiner* as its publishers. The ownership of the paper is more difficult to determine. Michael Cahill, a curate at St Patrick's Church, subsequently revealed that he took it over in 1870 or, perhaps, late in 1869, as sole proprietor and editor[20] and elsewhere the bishop was credited with buying it from Kerr and Fitzpatrick. It seems likely that Dorrian invested substan-

---

19 U.Ex., 14 Mar. 1868.
20 Cahill, writing in Jan. 1877, remarked that he had had charge of it for the past seven years.

tial sums of money in it from the beginning.[21] His letter of recommendation and the pledge of submission to spiritual rulers contained in the opening leader suggest that he was more than an interested and sympathetic supporter. Indeed the style of the editorial with its quotations in Latin and Italian strongly resembles Cahill's, when he was later generally acknowledged to have editorial responsibility. In the absence of hard evidence it is not possible to know what degree of ownership and authority the bishop exercised during the first two years of the paper's existence, but it is a reasonable assumption that it was extensive. He certainly regarded a Catholic press as a valuable pastoral aid, an important instrument for creating a Catholic atmosphere among his people, for educating them about current developments within the church, about ecclesiastical history and doctrinal orthodoxy, and for helping to form in the local church a sense of unity, loyalty and pride. Consequently he was prepared to invest heavily in it. Cahill's proprietorship was merely nominal: Dorrian was the real owner for at least seven years.

From the beginning the *Examiner* devoted much more space to religious material than the *Observer* had done. While the latter had reported quite widely on events of Catholic interest — the establishment of new churches or religious institutions, charity sermons and subjects of special political interest and significance for Catholics — the *Examiner* devoted proportionally a large amount of space to articles on Catholic belief and to lengthy pieces on topics of Irish ecclesiastical interest. This was very much in keeping with Dorrian's concept of a Catholic paper: one that not only would keep its readers abreast both of general and church news but that would also lead them to a wider and deeper knowledge of their faith and, by acquainting them with the spiritual achievements and cultural influence of their church in the past, enhance their commitment to it in the present. As a nationalist and O'Connellite, Dorrian assumed that the politics of any newspaper loyal to the church would run along constitutional and national lines. The *Examiner* did not disappoint him in this general respect but the controversial and aggressive tone which its leaders often adopted in asserting Catholic rights and challenging both the British government and the local political establishment tended at times to create unnecessary antagonism. Despite the opposition of the *Northern Star* competing for virtually the same readership, the *Examiner* got off to a good start; on 1 January 1869 it could congratulate itself on having achieved success

---

21 In writing to Kirby in Rome shortly after it was launched, Dorrian remarked, 'I have got a new Catholic paper here', and later he sent him a copy 'of a new Catholic paper we have started here and from which I expect much good'. (Dorrian to Kirby. 24 Mar., 15 May 1868, A.I.C.R.)

far beyond the most sanguine expectations of its founders, and with characteristic pugnacity challenged its enemies to point to a single line not dictated by the purest of motives.[22]

However, the purity of its motives was shortly to be challenged in court. When the *Belfast News-Letter* taunted it about McKenna's being chosen to speak on behalf of the press at a dinner for the Belfast Liberal MP, Thomas McClure, the *Examiner* remarked that this comment was 'evidently written by someone not too familiar with the style of our diurnal friend, although sufficiently so to make us recognize a writer who, more than once, has found the *News-Letter* a safe medium for the outpouring of abuse on a Catholic bishop, a Catholic people, and Catholicity in general, which he dared not publish elsewhere'.[23] It was no secret that McKenna was charged by his critics with passing information to the bishop's opponents during the controversy over the Catholic Institute, when the *Observer* remained silent, and McKenna, now detecting this accusation behind the gloss of the *Examiner*, sued for libel.

The presence of Isaac Butt as his counsel ensured even more publicity for the case than it might otherwise have had, and in the course of his defence Butt dredged up again the controversy over McKenna's handling of the *Observer*, the part he played in the dispute over the Catholic Institute and the attitudes adopted by the bishop on these bitterly contentious issues. Dorrian was stung by the references to his role in the affair and wrote to the *Examiner* to point out that the principle for which he had contended in the crisis over the Institute had been decided by the highest authority of the church (evidently referring to the encyclical and Syllabus of 1864). As he was misrepresented, he had felt obliged to remain silent while a storm of abuse, the dying echoes of which had been heard in Butt's submission, raged for weeks. But he was 'so perfectly right in that whole matter that no proper authority, from that day to this, did or could say that [he] had not acted prudently or rightly'. He then went on to refer in an oblique and laboured fashion to McKenna's significant silence during the controversy: some parties without his knowledge did take steps to find out why no explanation was forthcoming in a quarter where silence was connivance with wrong. But he had already decided to have no truck with McKenna: 'long antecedently to this, however, general circumstances had contributed to form a conscientious and unalterable conviction in me to be guided in certain personal associations by a prudent and necessary

22 U.Ex., 1 Jan. 1869.
23 U.Ex., 23 Mar. 1869. The dinner for the press at which McKenna spoke was held on 9 Feb. 1869. The *Belfast News-Letter* referred to the absence of any speaker from the *Examiner* in its comments on the dinner on 12 Feb. and the *Examiner* replied on 13 Feb. 1869.

reserve'.[24] However, McKenna won this round; the *Examiner* was found guilty, fined £250 and costs which were thought likely to equal the size of the fine.

On 1 November 1870 the *Examiner*, which had been published thrice weekly, became a daily. In announcing this development the editorial pointed out that the Protestant population of Ulster, which was smaller than the Catholic, was served by two dailies and thirty other journals which appeared once, twice or three times weekly. The Catholics required a daily organ to protect and promote their political, social and religious interests and to expose the wrongs under which they suffered. Before this change had taken place, however, another one of greater moment had occurred: Michael Henry Cahill had taken over managerial and editorial responsibility for the paper. Though a formal announcement to this effect was not made, Cahill's close association with the paper gradually became known, and Cahill later admitted the extent of his connection in a farewell editorial on 6 January 1877.

Cahill had come to Belfast in 1868 and joined the staff at St Patrick's. Born in Kilkenny in 1844, he entered the order of Oblates of Mary Immaculate in 1858 and pursued his studies for the priesthood at Autun in France and at Sicklinghall in Yorkshire before returning to Inchicore in Dublin where he was ordained in 1867. He was then put in charge of a school in Dublin but left the order in the following year and transferred to the diocese of Down and Connor. A scholarly man with a flair for literature and an extensive knowledge of Latin, French and Italian, Cahill wrote easily, fluently and at generous length. The editorship of a newspaper gave him scope for the use of his undoubted literary talents, and in assigning him to this work Dorrian almost certainly chose the most suitable priest, who was free and available. Being resident in St Patrick's he was convenient to the offices of the paper, which were also in Donegall St., and he was able to combine both his pastoral and literary work without difficulty. His role seems to have been that of a managing editor, who dictated policy, laid down the religious and political lines which the paper was to follow and wrote many of the more important leaders. The day to day tasks of supervising reports and organizing the layout seems to have devolved on Edward Byrne and Daniel MacAleese, who were often described as the editors. Cahill's style, earnest, robust, combative, with its long flowing periods and occasional quotations from the classical or romance languages, was impressive, and the role he played, though little acknowledged in public at the beginning of his career, was certainly known in Belfast newspaper circles. But some Catholics, including some of his clerical

24 U.Ex., 25 Mar. 1869.

colleagues, were unhappy with his attitudes and approach. They regarded him as unnecessarily abrasive and polemical, volatile and intemperate, and were annoyed and hurt by the vigour and acerbity of his tone on political and ecclesiastical issues. Though his advocacy of constitutional nationalism corresponded to the general aspirations of the majority of his readers, his bitter hostility to what he derisively dismissed as Whiggery proved at times a needless and painful embarrassment.

For some time Dorrian must have been pleased with the vigorous defence of Catholic views which the *Examiner* put forward. It championed Catholic claims to financial support for denominational education at all levels with passion and consistency; it defended Catholic doctrinal beliefs with clarity, determination and skill, but when its enthusiasm passed over into sharp polemic and embroiled Catholics in hurtful political controversy, he must on occasion have questioned the prudence, moderation and balance of his journalistic advocate.

A.J. McKenna, shortly after the demise of the *Ulster Observer*, started the *Northern Star*, which continued to pursue the same political and religious approach as the *Observer* had done. Like the *Examiner* it was an enthusiastic supporter of Isaac Butt and Home Rule, and it fought sternly against abuses, such as those of the grand jury system, which militated most harshly against Catholics. McKenna himself retained the friendship of some at least of the Catholic clergy, for on 12 August 1870 he was attacked in Coleraine by Apprentice Boys returning from their celebrations in Derry, and made his way to the home of the parish priest of Portrush.[25] His nationalism, unlike that of the *Examiner*, strayed over the edge of constitutionalism. He took the view that Home Rule meant complete separation from England, and insisted that it could not be achieved by peaceful means: 'the truth is that the gentlemen who advocate and promise us Home Rule, as O'Connell so often and so vainly promised repeal, must go further than they have yet gone, or retreat ignominiously . . . Home Rule means separation; and for that separation we must be prepared to draw the sword'.[26]

McKenna also, no doubt with tongue in cheek, defended Dorrian on one occasion. In the course of a trial before the magistrates at Banbridge, reference had been made to the bishop's ownership of the *Examiner* and, rebuking the magistrates for their ungracious behaviour in listening to what amounted to an unprovoked attack upon the bishop, McKenna, in a signed editorial which commented on the suggestion that Dorrian controlled the *Examiner*, remarked with an

25 N.S., 25 Mar. 1871.
26 N.S., 3 Oct. 1871.

apparent show of concern and a real depth of sarcasm that it was a well-known fact that the means of the Catholic bishop were more than exhausted by the religious claims upon his resources.[27]

The competition between the two papers was brief. McKenna died suddenly on 4 April 1872 at the early age of thirty eight, and his death drew forth generous tributes from other Belfast papers to his ability and dedication as a journalist. Leading politicians, including the mayor of Belfast, and clergy of different denominations were among the large attendance at the funeral and the bishop read the prayers at the graveside.[28] Many of the most prominent Catholics of the town, including Daniel MacAleese of the *Examiner*, formed a committee and collected money to erect a monument to his memory in Friar's Bush cemetery. Edward McHugh, the father-in-in-law of the deceased, who had invested heavily in the *Northern Star*, sold it six months later to Michael Cahill, and in its editorial entitled 'valedictory' the paper declared that the merger had perhaps come about in the best interests of Ulster and Ireland as Catholic opinion could obtain expression better through one organ.[29]

The *Ulster Examiner*, which had changed its name to the *Daily Examiner* in 1870 but became the *Ulster Examiner and Northern Star* in 1873, consistently supported the cause of Home Rule until its demise. Among those who attended the inaugural meeting to establish a branch of the Home Rule Association in Belfast was Michael Cahill, and both in the columns of the paper and at public meetings he remained a powerful and determined advocate of self-government. The local leaders of the movement, J.G. Biggar, John Duddy and Isaac Nelson, were quick to appreciate his support and to accord him a prominent place on their platforms. Though Dorrian did not commit himself in public on this issue for some years, Cahill would have known where his sympathies lay and how disillusioned he was with the Liberal party. When Christopher Palles, a Catholic and a Liberal, stood for Londonderry City in November 1872, Cullen wrote to Dorrian seeking the support of the *Examiner* for him. Dorrian's reply revealed his attitude to the Liberals much more clearly and convincingly than his relationship to the *Examiner*:

> I have no more right to interfere with the *Examiner* than Your Eminence to control the *Nation* or Dr Delany [the bishop of Cork] the *Cork Examiner*. I am very wrongly charged with everything wrong or foolish that may appear in it, whereas I have *never controlled a single line in it* and could not without a

27 N.S., 14 Oct. 1871.
28 N.S., 6,9 Apr. 1872.
29 N.S., 30 Nov. 1872.

stretch of authority which would be arbitrary and thus do great harm. As long as it is an *open question* it would not be too safe to act with too high a hand. I have the greatest respect for Mr Palles, but there is a very angry feeling against him for coming in to break up the party after Mr Biggar had got 500 votes promised . . . I only know that the party who have invited Mr Palles are our worst enemies. Still I should be glad to see him on the Bench. But I have no power to interfere further than I have done to disapprove of the tone and phrases applied to him personally . . . The division is sad but it is the work of Presbyterian Liberals: and the Catholics seem tired of playing second fiddle to them. I am no great advocate of Mr Biggar but that is a question for the Electors and it would be tyranny on my part to attempt further interference than by expressing my opinion which I have already done.[30]

That he had not controlled a single line in the sense of checking the material which appeared in the paper was undoubtedly true. But as long as the ecclesiastical, and to a lesser extent, political policy of the paper corresponded to his wishes, he did not have to do so. In this case he realized the difficulty and embarrassment that might be involved in the paper changing its course to support the Liberals, and as he, unlike Cullen, placed little or no faith in that party, he saw no reason for interfering in a tricky and difficult situation. He preferred to let Cahill get on with the daily running of the paper, though he was obviously aware of the *bêtises* which his hot-headed curate was capable of committing. The analogy, however, which he drew between the relationship of Cardinal Cullen and Bishop Delany to the *Nation* and the *Cork Examiner* was false: neither of these bishops had invested money in these papers and so neither of them had the proprietor's right to exercise influence on them.

The election in Derry took place in the midst of uproar, excitement and some fisticuffs. Palles, who had the support of the archbishop of Dublin and the bishop of Derry, Francis Kelly, came second in the poll with 522 votes, easily defeating Biggar who obtained only 86 votes but being well beaten by the Conservative candidate.

Thomas Macknight, an Englishman, who edited the *Whig* for many years, subsequently quoted Lord O'Hagan, the Belfast-born Catholic whom Gladstone had appointed Lord Chancellor of Ireland, as saying that Dorrian could 'shut up his curate at any time'.[31] Macknight, a distinguished journalist and dedicated Liberal, who

30 Dorrian to Cullen, 11 Nov. 1872. D.D.A.
31 Thomas Macknight, *Ulster as it is* (London, 1896), ii, 269.

had little sympathy for Irish nationalists, referred in his memoirs to the local Catholic paper 'started under Dr Dorrian's personal influence and at the time edited by one of his curates' and claimed that when the paper changed hands it appeared in evidence that Dorrian had advanced £2,000 for its support and was therefore its virtual proprietor at the time of the Derry election.[32] But Macknight also admitted that Dorrian said after the defeat of Sharman Crawford, the Liberal landlord, in Co. Down that 'in the contest his people had made so many sacrifices he would never again call upon them to incur similar hardships'.[33]

But the ownership and indeed editorial responsibility were not admitted at the time. On 27 December 1872 Cahill repudiated in the *Examiner* the assertion made by Macknight that its leaders were written by the Catholic clergy.[34] And Daniel MacAleese, who was variously described as proprietor, sub-editor and publisher, was fined and sentenced to four months imprisonment for contempt of court when he called in question the impartiality of a judge, who inflicted different sentences on Catholics and Protestants who had been involved in riots.[35] Cahill later revealed that he had written one of the two offending articles and was prepared to face the judge but was prevailed upon not to do so.[36]

Dorrian himself was named in a case which was brought for a claim of £20 for printing work done for the paper. The defending counsel offered to meet the case on its merits if MacAleese's name were substituted for the bishop's, and added that Dorrian had no more to do with the paper than the accusing lawyer. But this lawyer, the colourful and eccentric John Rea, insisted that Dorrian had spent £3,000 or £4,000 on establishing the printing office and denied that any other investors were involved.[37] And when Robert Chamney, the manager of the *Irish Teachers' Journal* complained to Dorrian of the criticism made of his journal for its comments on a proposal then

---

32 Ibid., pp 236, 269. Macknight was unsympathetic to Dorrian whom he rightly diagnosed as having little regard for the Protestant Liberals and whom he believed was one of the strongest nationalists on the episcopal bench. He claimed that on one occasion Dorrian 'with the utmost gravity and apparent consciousness of infallible authority' declared that sooner or later Home Rule would be granted and that 'Ireland will then be able to govern herself. We shall have colonies too!' According to Macknight the *Examiner* then averred that Ireland had a right to the Atlantic seaboard where the New England colonies had been established. There is no other evidence for such unlikely imperial ambitions.
33 Ibid., p.55.
34 D.Ex., 27 Dec. 1872.
35 B.M.N., 6 Aug. 1873. A presentation to cover his costs was made to MacAleese on 5 Aug. 1873. Among those present were M.H. Cahill and J.G. Biggar.
36 U.Ex., 6 Jan. 1877.
37 D.Ex., 17 June 1872.

being mooted to increase teachers' pay and establish boards of management to run the schools, Dorrian replied at length and both letters were published. Denying Chamney's allegation that the *Examiner* represented his views 'on public topics', Dorrian insisted that 'the conductors of that journal have neither been influenced nor inspired by me in any article or subject from first to last'. Suggesting that they were more competent judges of their work than he would presume to be, he argued that it would be little short of impertinence for him to interfere on any subject other than one relating to faith and morals, where he would be bound to signify his disapproval, if necessary, since the paper claimed to be a Catholic one; and his attention had never in fact been called to anything against faith or morals. He went on to protect himself from being identified with its views:

> But you have just as much to do with its articles and correspondence as I had or have ever exercised; *nor am I called upon to approve of all it may publish as I am not responsible.*

The *Examiner* itself weighed in with characteristic gusto by declaring that the musty slanders so often repeated respecting the inspiring of articles in it by Dr Dorrian had received at last a death-blow from the letter of his lordship. The editors and proprietor alone, it affirmed, without naming them, were responsible for the conduct of the journal.[38]

Doubtless Dorrian was technically correct in his reply to Chamney. Even had he wished, he would not have had the time to interfere in the day-to-day running of the paper and as long as the broad outlines of its policy satisfied him he may have felt that he could not do much more than call occasionally for greater restraint by the editor in his use of language. Having assigned Cahill to this work he probably thought that it would be insensitive and hurtful to pry too closely into the minutiae of his reportage or try to moderate his severity of tone. And in an age when newspapers representing different political views, groups and interests did not hesitate at times to savage each other, the *Examiner* was never dilatory in adding its contribution to this journalistic warfare. In an editorial on the increasing use by the clergy of the Church of Ireland of Roman collars, it declared that 'so contemptible, however, and so childish is this apeing [sic] the dress of Irish priests on the part of the ministers of a Church that grew fat on the spoils of the people, that it is with difficulty that we can at all speak seriously on the subject' and went

38 U.Ex., 14 Nov. 1874. Chamney's letter was dated 5 Nov. and Dorrian's reply 6 Nov.

on to make the brutal observation that 'appear in what clothing it may the wolf is no less a wolf'.[39] And commenting on the hostility of the *Northern Whig* to Home Rule, it observed that if the editor should write on political topics affecting Ireland, it was but proper that it be clearly understood that he was alien to her in blood, in sentiment and in religion.[40] And though the *Belfast Morning News* was owned by Catholics, the *Examiner* stigmatized it as a 'Presbyterian organ' and referred sarcastically to its comic editor Barney Maglone (in fact, one of its colourful columnists) principally because the *Belfast Morning News* supported the Liberals and tried to appeal to a readership drawn from all denominations.[41]

Admittedly the *Belfast News-Letter* was highly polemical and gave free range to the bitterly anti-Catholic diatribes of rabblerousing clergy like Hanna and McIlwaine. And when the *Whig* commented favourably on the progress of the Presbyterian mission in the west of Ireland or denounced the ultramontane despotism of the Catholic church, the *Examiner* was quickly moved to anger. However, it found plenty of legitimate targets when it attacked the anti-Catholic proclivities of the Orange Order and the grand juries, or when it exposed the petty bigotry of Boards of Guardians or the sectarian shenanigans of some of the Belfast public or semi-public bodies. And in dealing with the mis-representations and calumnies heaped on the Catholic church by the religious zealots of the time, it often replied in kind to their vehement invective. When Cahill, under his own name, engaged Professor Porter of the Assembly's College in a controversy over the relative incidence of crime in the Catholic and Protestant parts of Ireland, he set out to rebut Porter's argument that the Protestant areas were much less crime-ridden in a rational manner by appealing to the statistics of crime in England and Scotland, and by explaining the agrarian background to much Irish crime.[42]

The conflict of the *Examiner* with McKenna was not fully terminated with his death. For his widow and father-in-law brought an action against it more than a year after it had acquired the *Northern Star*. The terms of the sale in November 1872 had specified that Michael Cahill was to pay £4,725 for the copyright, plant and equipment but the paper had debts of £1,365. Disputes over the collecting and payment of the debts and the delay in paying the last instalment led to the court case. The claims of McKenna's representatives were substantially upheld as the judge awarded them more than ninety per cent of what they sought or £906 out of the £946.[43]

39 U.Ex., 28 Feb. 1872.
40 U.Ex., 19 Feb. 1872.
41 U.Ex., 27 Apr. 1875.
42 D.Ex., 14 Mar. 1872.
43 U.Ex., 12 Mar. 1874.

At a political level the *Examiner* gave increasing support to Home Rule. It espoused the most vigorous expression of that cause and never flinched from backing the more aggressive parliamentary tactics of Parnell and his friends, when other supporters of the movement considered parliamentary obstruction as embarrassing, improper and counter-productive. It quickly grew impatient with Butt's gentlemanly restraint in advocating self-government for Ireland and excessive regard for the traditional proprieties of the House of Commons, and became and remained a faithful advocate of Parnell's more combative style. Though it had on occasion grudgingly given support to the Whigs *faute de mieux*, the gathering strength of the Home Rule movement absolved it from any obligations to that party.

In 1873 when a Catholic standing as a Liberal in a Belfast municipal election had been defeated in Smithfield ward, the *Examiner* claimed that he owed his defeat to the refusal of Presbyterians to vote for him, even though the Catholics had voted for the other Liberal candidate, who was a Presbyterian. Pointing out that there were 220 Catholic voters in the ward and that the Catholic Liberal obtained 231 votes, it concluded that there were only 11 Presbyterians liberal enough to vote for a Catholic. The influence of Presbyterian Liberals, it predicted, would be insignificant until they were prepared to act in concert with their Catholic friends.[44] In 1874 it campaigned vigorously for the election to parliament of Thomas McClure, a Presbyterian and Liberal, informing the Catholic electors that they were bound to support him 'warmly, earnestly, enthusiastically'.[45] But the honeymoon with the Liberals did not last long. By 1876 Cahill was writing about the 'good, conscientious, upright men' in the Tory party who could settle the land question much better than the 'craving Whigs'.[46] A few days later, he explained that he was neither a Whig nor a Tory but insisted that the land question was more likely to be settled by fair-minded Tories rather than by 'those grinding Whigs who, while receiving the last penny from the poor tenant farmers, prate of tenant-right and independence'.[47]

Undeterred by the angry reaction to his views in Liberal circles, Cahill returned to the fray to lambaste the Catholic members of the Whig party. Asserting that the most notorious landjobbers and rackrenters were Whigs, he declared that he had no hesitation in claiming that Catholic Whig landowners were the worst of this bad

44 U.Ex., 26 Nov. 1873.
45 U.Ex., 3 Feb. 1874.
46 U.Ex., 25 Jan. 1876.
47 U.Ex., 29 Jan. 1876.

lot. Since 1870 Whigs had contested the just rights of tenants and had compelled them to contract out of the benefits of the Land Act. Turning to their organ in Belfast he was equally scathing: the *Whig* had called him a 'reverend Catholic caluminator' but, if it were a calumny to expose the hollowness of Whig trickery, he pleaded guilty. Then, reaching back into the past, he reminded his readers how this English organ styled the priests of Spain 'cut-throats and murderers' and insulted the priests of Ireland by describing them as 'uneducated boors'. He then proceeded to bash the *Belfast Morning News*, which he pointed out was owned by a Catholic but conducted for merely commercial ends, and to its recent accusation that the *Examiner* had not been distinguished for its advocacy of the cause of the tenant farmers, he retorted that the *Examiner* was the unflinching champion of the tenants when the *Morning News* was a mere budget. The Whigs, he insisted, were the worst enemies of everything Catholic, constitutional and religious; when the Tories were willing to grant a measure of Catholic university education to Ireland, their plans were frustrated by 'infidel Whigs' who were trying to make the children of the country grow up as atheists and deists through the agency of godless education.[48]

Within a year Cahill had severed his connection with the *Examiner*. In a signed letter in the editorial column on 6 January 1877 he announced that he had sold the paper to Charles J. Dempsey. Reviewing his seven year association with it, he made bold to claim, that it had helped produce a marked improvement in Ulster public opinion, and he remarked that 'when national autonomy was but whispered in secret places, this journal inscribed Home Rule upon its banner, and was the first in Ireland to uphold a cause which is now the very pulsation of the national yearning'. Similarly, it had fearlessly espoused the rights of the tenants to fair rents, free sale and fixity of tenure with a determination to see the peasant firmly rooted in the soil. It had also advocated the right of Ulster Catholics to education, especially at university level, where they had been badly treated. Apologizing to anyone whose 'acutest sensitiveness' he might have wounded, he explained that honesty and independence had always been given priority in the paper over commercial prosperity; had he acted otherwise he would then be unquestionably richer. A Catholic journal, he concluded, was a necessity, if Catholic wants were to be advocated, and, as the one man who had sacrificed most

---

48 U.Ex., 1 Feb. 1876. The *Belfast Morning News* replied to some of Cahill's strictures on the Whigs by calling in question Cahill's knowledge, judgement and prudence. Remarking that he was a young man and admitting that some young men had achieved political distinction, it added: 'There are young men and young men. When extreme indiscretion, vanity and ignorance are added to youth, the case is somewhat altered'. (B.M.N., 6 Feb. 1877)

for the Catholic people of Ulster, he urged them to look steadily to their interests, if they meant to have any influence in Belfast and throughout the province.[49]

This farewell explicitly admitted Cahill's role in the *Examiner* during the 1870s, and thereby left him open to any shafts that its opponents might aim at it; no longer was its clerical connection concealed, either partly or fully, as it passed entirely into lay control. But Cahill did not give any explanation of the financial position of the paper, let alone comment on the losses which it had undoubtedly suffered, and he neither referred to the source from which his control had come nor to the price paid for it by Dempsey. The precise amount of Dorrian's investment in the press was never disclosed. But if the plant and equipment of the *Northern Star* was valued at £4,725 in 1872, it is safe to assume that the launching of the *Examiner* cost something in the same region. Dempsey's purchase of the paper salvaged some of the investment, but when incidental expenses are taken into account, the total loss could scarcely have been less than £6,000.

The new proprietor, who belonged to a prosperous publican family, reverted to the original practice of three weekly issues instead of six, but otherwise there was little change. In the leader of 9 January the paper committed itself to maintaining the policies it had previously followed, and promised to be as Catholic and national as ever. It faithfully carried out this promise until its demise in 1882. With the polarization of politics between Home Rule and Unionism, the Liberal party was being gradually squeezed out and there was little or no room left for two newspapers of a Liberal hue. Consequently the *Belfast Morning News* swung in behind Home Rule and from the early 1880s its views were very similar to those of the *Examiner*. When Dempsey took over the *Morning News* he dropped the title of the *Examiner* from its front page but kept it as a secondary title above the editorial.

Cahill, however, retained some contact with the *Examiner* until his death. In 1878 Dempsey explained that the paper had a sub-editor but not an editor as such; he engaged three or four leader writers, of whom Cahill was one.

Cahill's connection with it ensured that the church would be blamed for any extreme opinions which it might express. And when the *Examiner* praised Lord Beaconsfield for releasing Fenian prisoners and favourably contrasted this policy with that of the Liberals, the *Whig*, adverting to the violation of their oaths by Fenian soldiers, wrote scathingly about the seditious ravings of an organ 'on all questions of faith and morals understood to be under the

49 U.Ex., 6 Jan. 1877.

most careful supervision of the Most Rev. Dr Dorrian'.[50] Dorrian replied the following day:

> I have so much work on hands, I have no time for 'supervision', much less for 'careful supervision' of any such articles. In truth, I have never inspired, or supervised or been in any way conscious of any publication in that or any other paper except under my own name. Often even I do not approve of what I read; but that depends on whether the arguments of the writer be more solid than my own way of viewing the question. *In dubiis libertas.*

He then went on to say that he condemned Fenianism just as he condemned Freemasonry and all secret associations injurious to church or state. However, this explanation did not satisfy the *Whig* which interpreted his words as meaning that he condemned 'charity equally with sedition', and further correspondence followed on the attitude of the church to Freemasonry.[51]

When in June 1878 a Belfast confraternity was attacked on its return from an outing to the countryside and riots broke out, the *Examiner* in angry frustration commented that, if their opponents would not have peace, they would accept the challenge, and predicted that, if the police would keep clear of the streets for one week, rioting and party feuds in Belfast would cease forever. Condemning this language as an incentive to violence, the *Belfast Morning News* expressed regret that a newspaper subject to high religious influences and edited by a Catholic clergyman should pander to the worst passions of the ignorant and bigoted multitude.[52] And it was because of the hostility shown to Cahill by the *Belfast Morning News* in the wake of the victory of Lord Castlereagh in Co. Down over the Liberal, William Drennan Andrews, in 1878 that Cahill subsequently took an action for libel against Daniel Read, the proprietor of the *Morning News*. The editor of the *Morning News*, Hans McMordie, had been one of the Liberal's agents, and angered by the *Examiner's* role in the election, its comments on Cahill grew more and more acerbic. Finally, in reference to a rumour that Cahill was anxious to become an assistant commissioner of Intermediate Education, it taunted him with allowing his venality to overcome his patriotism: 'The fiery ecclesiastic who is wont to make the walls of St Mary's Hall ring with denunciations of England's tyranny and lamentations over Ireland's wrongs was quite prepared recently to exchange the trade

50 N.W., 9 Jan. 1878.
51 N.W., 15 Jan. 1878.
52 B.M.N., 5 June 1878.

of a patriot for £1,000 a year to be paid by the British Government'. Cahill, who called Dorrian as a witness to his character, duly won the case, but his victory was purely nominal: he was awarded damages of one farthing.[53]

The *Examiner* continued to excoriate Whig landlords and to praise their Conservative counterparts as just and generous, and since Cahill held these views strongly, it seems likely that he wrote or inspired leading articles along these lines. By 1878 he was claiming that it was the duty of every Catholic, 'of every man not imbued with Communistic notions to oppose them'.[54] He did admit however that not all his co-religionists would agree with his views. But priests were loth to engage him in public debate. However, when Hugh McCann, parish priest of Rasharkin, allowed his name to be attached to an advertisement for the Conservative candidate, Edward McNaughten, in which he spelt out Cahill's arguments about the generosity of Tory landlords in giving sites for churches, schools and presbyteries,[55] John Lennon, parish priest of Loughguile, and Edward Watterson, parish priest of Dunloy, firmly rejected McCann's claims, estimated that only a very small minority of the eighty priests of Antrim would support him, and declared themselves in favour of the Liberal cause.[56]

Cahill died suddenly in 1881 at the age of thirty seven. The *Ulster Examiner* in its obituary described him as a most reckless opponent of sham and humbug, liberalism that coerced and 'patriotism' that fought for place.[57] The *Whig* paid tribute to his vigour and earnestness as a journalist but regretted that he often showed little discretion and judgement; 'as a public journalist' it remarked 'he had had no self-restraint, no regard for the ordinary courtesies of the profession'.[58] However, he had no monopoly of these deficiencies: Belfast journalism was a highly robust profession and self-restraint was not one of the more obvious qualities of its practitioners.

With Cahill's death, Dorrian's last link with journalism was severed. The *Morning News* continued to report Catholic affairs generously and in its enthusiastic support for Home Rule expressed the political feelings of the vast majority of its Catholic readers. Writing ten years after Dorrian's death, James O'Laverty, the diocesan historian, who served in the diocese throughout his episcopate, singled out the *Ulster Examiner* as perhaps the bishop's only failure. The *Examiner*, he explained, had been founded because

53 U.Ex., 24 Dec. 1878.
54 U.Ex., 14 May 1878.
55 U.Ex., 25 Mar. 1880.
56 U.Ex., 26 Mar. 1880.
57 U.Ex., 15 Dec. 1881.
58 N.W., 16 Dec. 1881.

of Dorrian's regret that the Catholics of Belfast did not have a newspaper 'to advocate their legitimate national aspirations, defend and explain their religious principles, and to combat sectarian bigotry and ascendancy'. O'Laverty believed that this incursion into journalism proved costly both in terms of finance and of personal relations, and he concluded:

> He [Dorrian] was, however, unfortunate in some of the persons to whom he confided it; they acted imprudently and in their hands it became a two-edged sword, dangerous not only to foes but even to friends, and frequently in its wrathful zeal it lashed with serpents the Catholics who happened to step aside from the political line that it had chalked out. Fortunately, however, the Bishop seeing that it was compromising himself, sacrificed the thousands which he had lost and ceased connection with it.[59]

O'Laverty's views were very probably shared by a large number of his clerical colleagues, and, as a verdict on Dorrian's involvement in the apostolate of the press, cannot be challenged.

---

59 O'Laverty, *Down and Connor*, v, 620.

8

Home Rule gathers momentum

I

Gladstone's attempts at pacifying Ireland annoyed and angered those whose interests and privileges were adversely affected by them. Conservative landowners were antagonized by the Land Act; and both they and the clergy of the Church of Ireland regarded disestablishment as the violation of the solemn guarantees given by the British government in 1800. At the other extreme, various tenant societies representing Catholic tenants expressed great disappointment with the Land Act, which they considered too timid and niggardly. Gladstone's concessions to the Amnesty movement disappointed the 'advanced' nationalists and Fenian sympathizers who hoped for the release of all the prisoners. The only common denominator in these elements was disappointment with Gladstone and yet out of these disparate and conflicting forces Isaac Butt welded together the Home Government Association, the first body to advocate Home Rule. This was not a new party, it did not set up branches throughout the country and in fact saw itself as little more than a pressure group, a force for educating public opinion. No precise arrangements were formulated for translating these plans into practice, though Butt encouraged the establishment of local Home Rule associations.[1]

The base of the new movement, however, was still very narrow and insubstantial. The Catholic hierarchy was waiting for Gladstone's intervention in university education. Satisfied with disestablishment and the Land Act, the bishops had high hopes that Gladstone would attempt what none of his predecessors had had the interest or courage to attempt, namely, to grant a charter and financial help to the Catholic University or make third level education for Catholics available on terms which the hierarchy could accept. Bishops and clergy, who were very anxious to settle this thorny problem, did not feel that there was any justification for

1 D. Thornley, *Isaac Butt and Home Rule* (London, 1964), p.95.

abandoning the Liberals (who were delivering the goods) for a policy that might not be realized for a long time, if ever. In the first two years the bishops held aloof and even those known to be sympathetic to repeal were unwilling to abandon a party that seemed committed to instituting genuine reforms. But the initial sympathy felt for self-rule among disparate groups began to disintegrate as the Protestant gentry, fearing their power would be swamped by the secrecy of voting by ballot, which became law in 1872, soon began to withdraw. The movement in consequence widened at the other end, where Home Rulers began to take on Catholic Liberals at by-elections. In 1871 Butt himself won a seat in Limerick despite the opposition of the bishop and William Monsell, the prominent Liberal, and a few months later a young Protestant Home Ruler triumphed over the combined efforts of Bishop Moriarty and the clergy of Kerry to return a Catholic Whig.

Moriarty, who tended to be rather hasty and blunt in his political judgements, chose to refer to Home Rule in a letter to the electors as 'one of the most mischievous movements to which you have ever been urged or excited' and appealed to them to be patient and wait for a few more good measures from the imperial parliament before parting with it.[2] Two days later, the Belfast paper, the *Daily Examiner*, took the bishop of Kerry severely to task. Remarking that it had been sceptical of a policy which had attracted the support of Tories and Orangemen, nevertheless, it roundly condemned Moriarty's manifesto which it described as 'impolitic, ungenerous and unnatural', for backing 'an alliance with men who have been unrelenting persecutors of our race', and insisted that the bishop of Kerry was wrong in saying that the Irish episcopate and priesthood did not desire Home Rule.[3] Whatever latitude Michael Cahill, the priest who edited the paper enjoyed, it certainly did not extend to attacking bishops unless he had good reason to believe that his criticisms struck a favourable chord in his own master. He obviously assumed that Dorrian would not be opposed to a criticism of a fellow bishop for attachment to Whiggery, and may have either sensed or been given direct evidence that his own bishop's sympathies were swinging towards Home Rule. Liberalism held fewer attractions for Cahill's readers than for many of their co-religionists elsewhere in Ireland and, in fact, the quasi-permanent political homelessness of the East Ulster, and especially the Belfast, Catholics exposed them early to the attractions of Home Rule.

And indeed Belfast was one of the first towns in Ireland to set up a Home Rule branch. A well-attended meeting chaired by Joseph

2 Ibid., p.127.
3 D.Ex., 13 Jan. 1872.

Biggar, the Belfast Protestant Fenian, was held in the premises of a Catholic club in Donegall St. on 16 April 1872. Biggar claimed that Belfast Catholics were unanimously in favour of Home Rule and that their sympathies were shared by a large number of Protestants. John Duddy, a longtime political activist of 'advanced' views, declared that their object should be to raise up 'a bleeding and downtrodden country to being a free, federal and independent state' but explained that federalism not separation was their aim. Revd Isaac Nelson, a Belfast Presbyterian minister, who expressed his pleasure at finding himself associated with men from what he rather quaintly, if engagingly, called the Latin Church,[4] actually proposed the resolution that a Home Rule Association be founded. Michael Cahill was also present. The Protestants, Biggar and Nelson, were far from representative of their co-religionists in Belfast, the vast majority of whom held coldly aloof from the movement only to oppose it passionately when it gathered momentum and became a serious political force.

A few months later Home Rule became, by accident, the beneficiary of further clerical sympathy. J.P. Nolan, a Home Ruler, defeated a Conservative at a by-election in Galway County in February 1872, but the loser challenged the result on the grounds of improper clerical behaviour in support of Nolan. Judge Keogh not only found in favour of the petitioner but took advantage of the occasion to give vent to extremely offensive observations about the clergy in general, their educational background and manners, and about the likelihood of their abusing the confessional to intimidate voters when the secret ballot was introduced. A howl of protest was raised by both priests and Catholic people all over Ireland against Keogh's outrageous criticism. The bishop and clergy of Down and Connor met on 24 June in St Malachy's College and passed resolutions against the 'groundless slander' and 'wicked misrepresentation of Catholic doctrine' made by Keogh regarding the possible use of the confessional and against his attempt 'to prejudice the mind of England against our just demands for Denominational Education by holding up to public esteem the godless Queen's Colleges'. They also called on the government to repeal a statute which practically vested the representation of the people in the hands of one irresponsible judge. And a substantial collection was taken up to defray the expenses of the petition of the bishop and clergy of the Galway constituency against Keogh's verdict.[5] A large open-air meeting was held in Belfast in July to protest further against Keogh's judgement and to collect funds for a reversal of his

4 B.M.N., 17 Apr. 1872.
5 B.M.N., 26 June 1872.

decision.[6] And when Isaac Butt paid a visit to Belfast he was very enthusiastically received, both by nationalists and by those who were working for the release of the Fenians.[7]

The riots of August 1872 were a further factor in propelling Catholic opinion towards the safer haven of constitutional nationalism. In 1871 the Party Processions Act, which had forbidden parades likely to lead to a breach of the peace, was repealed. As a result the Orangemen resumed their marches in July 1872. Nationalists were tempted to imitate their opponents and a procession was organized for 15 August, the feast day of the Assumption, by Joseph Biggar and some of his Home Rule and Amnesty associates. The purpose of the march according to the organizers was to call the government's attention to the widespread demand for the release of the remaining Fenian prisoners and to encourage Gladstone to pursue a policy making for equality among all the citizens of Ireland. When their plans became known, Catholic magistrates begged some Belfast priests to use their influence to have it stopped, but the pleas of the clergy went unheeded. The leaders were determined to claim the same rights as the Orangemen, whose marches had passed off peacefully, and proposed to set off for Hannahstown from Carlisle Circus, the starting point used by the Orangemen. This assembly point immediately offered opportunities for conflict. The militant Presbyterian minister, Hugh Hanna, announced that hordes of papish rebels were gathering to wreck his church and thereby instantly inflamed Protestant opinion. A crowd estimated at between 5,000 and 10,000 assembled to block the processionists. Much to the indignation of the *Daily Examiner* the marchers were then prevented from assembling at Carlisle Circus and the magistrates did not take vigorous action to prevent them from being attacked and stoned by their opponents as they made their way up the Falls Road. In the evening hostile crowds gathered on the streets and Hugh Hanna drove up the Shankill Road and, to vociferous cheers, thanked his supporters for ensuring that the marchers did not assemble at Carlisle Circus. Catholic-owned taverns on the Shankill Road were attacked, and elsewhere violent scenes occurred and unleashed riots that lasted for almost a week, with the familiar pattern of strife between the mainly Catholic and Protestant districts and the intimidation and expulsion of residents whose religion differed from that of the majority of the particular area. A Methodist chapel and a Catholic school were wrecked. The final toll amounted to 4 deaths, 40 serious injuries and four times as many other casualties, 73 injuries among the police, the expulsion of 837 families from their homes and the

6 D.Ex., 24 July 1872.
7 D.Ex., 7 Aug. 1872.

total destruction of 247 dwelling houses.[8] The *Whig* placed the responsibility for the riots and bloodshed on 'the most ignorant, reckless and worthless section of the Orange party'.[9]

In this trial of strength the Catholic working class, being much smaller in numbers than its Protestant counterpart, understandably came off much the worse.[10] And when the disturbances ended, the Catholic press repeated the familiar charges against the incompetency, carelessness or partiality of the magistracy and demanded a commission of inquiry, but this request was refused. A leading article in the *Whig* charging the Catholic clergy with apathy during the riots drew a prompt and vigorous denial from James Hamill, the administrator of St Joseph's parish. Hamill insisted that the truth was the exact opposite of this accusation:

> The Catholic clergy of the town were most energetic during the riots in restraining the indignation of their people, justly roused by the barbarous and bloodthirsty deeds of the Shankill Road rioters. Were it not for their wise counsels, a fearful retaliation might have been taken for the plunder of their co-religionists by a band of Orange marauders.

He claimed that the police would testify that by day and night the clergy went among their people trying to calm them down; otherwise the reactions would have been much worse.[11] On the following day the *Daily Examiner* reported that it had received several communications from the Royal Irish Constabulary in support of Hamill's statement and thanked the police for confirming its view that the influence of the clergy had never been more beneficially used. In the wake of the riots, numerous and forceful calls were made for the establishment of a Catholic Defence Association, and when Orangemen attacked a convent in Lisburn where a bazaar was being held,[12] sectarian feelings were further exacerbated.

In such an atmosphere constitutional nationalism provided a welcome safety valve for angry and embittered Catholic feeling. And

8 A. Boyd, *Holy war in Belfast* (Tralee,1969), p.116. D.Ex., 13-23 Aug. 1872. N.W., 16-23 Aug. 1872

9 N.W., 19 Aug. 1872

10 According to the census of 1871 Catholics represented 31.9 per cent of the population of the town.

11 N.W., 26 Aug. 1872.

12 D.Ex., 10 Oct. 1872. The experiences of the French nuns in Lisburn at the hands of the Orangemen were described by the historian of the founder of their order: 'cris sauvages, insultes grossières, jets de pierres, bris volets et de fenêtres, toute arme paraissait bonne à ces forcenés'. (F. Leray, *Au service des Ames. Un apôtre Le Père Jean Gailhac Fondateur des Religieuses du Sacré-Coeur de Marie* (Paris, 1939) p.137).

when the *Daily Examiner* defended Home Rule, maintaining that it went *pari passu* with the education question and claiming that Ireland could not be happy and prosperous until she was free and her children were educated according to the dictates of parental conscience, it was rallying confused and insecure Catholics to the one banner that seemed to offer hope, protection and security.[13]

Dorrian, however, was anxious to prevent purely Catholic bodies from being so identified with one political view that those who did not subscribe to it would feel isolated or unwelcome. When P.J. Hamill, a Belfast curate, in proposing a vote of thanks to a lecturer, who had spoken to the Belfast Catholic Young Men's Society on international trade, went on to speak of what Ireland could achieve, if blessed with Home Rule, Dorrian duly emphasized that politics should not be discussed at that society. Significantly, however, there was applause when he added that no political subject had been introduced from which he differed or to which he was opposed. The applause increased greatly when he added that he 'was free at the same time, to observe that there is scarcely one amongst us as a lover of his country would not be inclined to adopt, to the fullest extent, those sentiments which have been given expression to'.[14]

And expression was vociferously given to these sentiments at a big Home Rule demonstration in the Ulster Hall a few weeks later. A dozen priests joined the crowd to hear Biggar, Duddy, and M. H. Cahill make stirring speeches in favour of Home Rule, deny that it threatened the break-up of the empire and invite the support of all denominations for the movement.[15] The *Examiner* felt obliged to rebut the taunts of the *Whig* and *News-Letter* that prominent Catholics, such as justices of the peace, had not turned up. It replied that an apology had been received from Bernard Hughes, and asked, rhetorically, who among the thousand present cared whether the JPs were there or not.[16] When Dorrian refused to ask the *Examiner* to endorse Palles, the Liberal candidate who was standing against a Conservative and a Home Ruler in a by-election in Londonderry City, he was probably giving rein not only to his own feelings but also recognizing that the tide among his people was flowing strongly in the direction of Home Rule.[17] And, in fact, the *Examiner* gave strong editorial support to Biggar.[18]

Gladstone's attempts to solve the Irish university question not only lost him the goodwill of the bishops and the support of Irish

13 D.Ex., 17 Oct. 1872.
14 D.Ex., 8 Oct. 1872.
15 D.Ex., 30 Oct. 1872.
16 D.Ex., 1 Nov. 1872.
17 Dorrian to Cullen, 11 Nov. 1872, D.D.A.
18 D.Ex., 21 Nov. 1872.

Catholic Liberals in 1873 but also, incidentally, gave a great fillip to Home Rule. A year previously O'Neill Daunt, the old O'Connellite, had failed to attract any bishops to the cause, but, once they felt let down by Gladstone, their obligations to the Liberals ceased and they were free to consider the merits of other candidates. In September the bishop and clergy of Cloyne announced their backing for the Home Government Association, and in anticipation of a general election Butt decided to issue a general circular under the names of three MPs and Daunt calling for support. He was particularly anxious to secure the help of the bishops, and he and his colleagues wrote asking them to sign the requisition. Archbishop MacHale and Bishop O'Hea agreed to do so in September and of the other ten bishops to whom the request was made only Donnelly of Clogher, Duggan of Clonfert and Dorrian declined. Dorrian explained that his refusal was dictated by prudence rather than by lack of sympathy. The political circumstances obtaining in the north of Ireland demanded that he remain silent:

> My adhesion in any public way would I believe, irritate rather than soothe the opponents of Home Rule in this part. What is most desirable would be to conciliate and weld together the different classes and to try and make the movement by far more *protestant* especially in the North. These faction or party fights through the country for 'Home Rule' or 'no Home Rule' are a source of much mischief. And it is, I think, essential to show that if 'Home Rule' were obtained, Protestants and Catholics would cease these broils and live at peace. For without this a Home Government would be impossible.

Dorrian went on to remark that the only suggestion he need make for ways of promoting a national and brotherly spirit was that 'Catholics sometimes would do well to forbear even when in the right and that they ought to be taught to do so'. He concluded by urging Butt to direct his political and national apostolate as effectively as possible to Protestants and assured him that Catholics would not be unresponsive: 'make progress with the Orange and Protestant party and the Catholics will see then how to assist'.[19]

The political sagacity manifested by Dorrian, both in his refusal to commit himself publicly to Home Rule at that time and in his advice to Butt to cultivate Protestant support, was beyond question. Thirty two years previously he had seen O'Connell's repeal mission to Belfast represented as a sectarian attack on Protestants, and mayhem threatened on the streets of the town. Though Butt enjoyed the

19 Dorrian to Butt, 8 Oct. 1873, N.L.I. MS 8695 (31).

advantage over O'Connell of being a Protestant and so less easily accused of merely masquerading as a nationalist to lead an anti-Protestant movement aimed at establishing a Catholic Ascendancy in Ireland, still the adoption of a high profile by a bishop at such an early stage would have aroused or inceased suspicions of hidden religious motivation.

Dorrian was always careful not to let his nationalism transgress the boundaries of strict constitutional propriety; he always treated the crown and its representatives with proper respect and deference, and was anxious as a spiritual leader to demonstrate the loyalty of Catholics to the institutions of state by his presence at public functions or participation in public occasions where the monarchy or government was involved.

In May 1872, along with his Anglican and Presbyterian colleagues, he joined a committee composed of the leading aristocrats and public figures of Counties Antrim and Down which was set up to organize a public banquet for Lord Dufferin (a Whig landlord and distinguished diplomat at whose home Dorrian had occasionally dined), who had been appointed the governor general of Canada.[20] Earlier in the year he had associated himself with landlords, members of parliament and public representatives in Co. Down in the presentation of an address to the queen on the recovery of the Prince of Wales. Unable to attend the meeting at which the address was to be drawn up, he wrote to Col. Forde, one of the organizers, begging that his name be attached to the requisition of the meeting, and remarking that the restoration of the prince to full health had been hailed by all classes with most profound gratitude to God.[21]

Understandably, he regarded his contribution to the preservation of peace as his primary civic duty. After the riots of August 1872 the clergy were desperately anxious to ensure that a repetition of such unnecessary violence was avoided. An Ulster Catholic Association was set up with their active support to encourage Catholics to refrain from giving any provocation to others and to show patience and restraint, if they themselves were provoked. In an address to the Catholic people of Belfast and Ulster on the eve of the annual Orange parades in the following year, the Association commended them for their 'attention to the admonitions of your pastors who have ever inculcated patience and forbearance' and begged them to carry on with their normal work during the Orange celebrations, to stay away from the route taken by processions and to give every co-operation to those entrusted with the preservation of peace. Furthermore, it suggested that Catholics stay inside their own homes in the evenings

20 N.S., 14 May 1872.
21 B.M.N., 5 Feb. 1872.

during the celebrations and that they avoid using any expression or performing any act which might remotely lead to trouble of any kind. The Association expressed the commendable, if chimerical, hope that 'by the carrying out of these suggestions the ill-feeling hitherto so easily engendered, and so much fostered by interested parties differing from us in religion, may be eradicated from our midst' and concluded with the impeccable aspiration that emulation in the sphere of social advancement, the promotion of Christian charity and the prosperity of the country might permeate all sections of the community.[22]

As a result of clerical advice and pressure, no public demonstrations by Catholics took place on St Patrick's Day or on 15 August 1873. And when election time came around in 1874 Dorrian again appealed strongly to his people for the avoidance of all offence during it. While encouraging all who enjoyed the franchise to use it as a trust for those who did not have it, he stressed that each one should decide how to vote according to his conscience.[23] The *Ulster Examiner* showed no such reluctance to guide Catholic voters. Though by then committed firmly to Home Rule, and anxious to see the return of Butt with 80 followers it declared that it was 'reluctantly compelled' to give its enthusiastic and undivided support to the Presbyterian Liberal, Thomas McClure; the Ulster Catholic Association duly endorsed him. The celebrated Johnston of Ballykilbeg, the Orange populist or 'miscreant' as the *Examiner* called him, had as his Conservative colleague a Presbyterian, J.P. Corry, and with the Presbyterian vote split, McClure lost.

Though deprived of a chance to vote for Home Rule in the elections, the sentiment in favour of it continued to grow among the Catholics of Belfast. And, when at a St Patrick's Day dinner a short time later Dorrian referred to the issue, his audience showed how popular support for the movement was. In proposing the toast to the queen on that occasion, the bishop rejected the accusation that Catholics were disloyal to the state by appealing to their desire to be guided by Christ's teaching that tribute be paid to Caesar. Claiming that they were fortunate to have a sovereign who so engaged their affections, he extolled the queen as a model of domestic virtue and one so deeply concerned about the well-being of her subjects that, had it been in her power, she would have already remedied all their grievances. The toast to his native land afforded him the opportunity of declaring that love for Ireland could not be genuine if it did not contain a wish to see Ireland happy and free, and governed not by strangers but by those who were natives of it. But, though he did not

22 U.Ex., 2 July 1873.
23 U.Ex., 2 Feb. 1874.

conceal his sympathies, he took pains to indicate that union among Irishmen was an essential pre-condition: 'He was not one', the *Belfast Morning News* reported, 'who wished to see Ireland govern herself while her people remained divided. If he thought that a home parliament would lead to divisions and religious bitternesses and altercations, or to the decay of trade or agriculture of the country, he would scorn to be its advocate (applause). But if the people would go together and acknowledge from motives of patriotism, love for common country and that they would forbear with each other and be tolerant in everything civil and religious, then he believed that a Home Government would be a blessing to Ireland (applause)'.[24]

This coveted harmony, however, was proving ever more elusive; in fact sectarian feeling was growing ever more acute. A few months after Dorrian's plea, Belfast papers reported two court cases concerning incidents where Catholic priests were insulted publicly on the streets and an occasion when nuns were jeered by a mob.[25] Underrepresentation of Catholics, then constituting a third of the population of the town, among the Poor Law Guardians became a source of grievance, especially when disputes involving the religion of orphans arose, and the *Ulster Examiner* was not, in practice, guilty of much exaggeration when it charged that 'the fact of being a Catholic excludes a man, as if by necessity, from the Town Council, the Water Board, the Guardianship of the Poor, the Jail, the Lunatic Asylum, the Harbour Board, the General Hospital — the one motto which they have in common is "no Catholic need apply"'.[26] The decision by the town council to erect a public monument to Henry Cooke further exacerbated politico-religious differences. Cooke, the friend and confidant of Tory and Orange landlords, was remembered by Catholics for his opposition to O'Connell and his resistance to political reform which could prove beneficial to them. A civic commemoration of a religious leader whose life and work was regarded by perhaps a third of the citizens as divisive and politically partisan was bound to provoke further mistrust. The *Ulster Examiner*, which articulated the political opposition to the move by citing Cooke's efforts to 'prevent the faithful being called to prayer in St Malachy's by the toll of the bell' as an example of his illiberality, replied to the claim of the *News-Letter* that Dorrian had attended Cooke's funeral by quoting the letter he wrote at the time giving his reasons for being unable to attend. Dorrian had then explained that if he had been allowed to take part without compromise of principles in order to pay 'a tribute of respect to the social kindness and consistency of

24 B.M.N., 18 Mar. 1874.
25 U.Ex., 15 Oct. 1874.
26 U.Ex., 23 Oct. 1874.

character that were to be admired in him [Cooke]', he would have done so.[27] Cooke, however, received the final municipal accolade: the statue of the earl of Belfast, a member of the Donegall family, was removed and Cooke's erected on the site. And as Johnston, the Belfast MP, threatened to lead his Orange supporters in procession to the unveiling, nationalist marches at Glenavy, Lurgan and Poyntzpass were attacked, because their banners and mottoes were said to provoke loyal Protestants.[28]

Though Dorrian had been careful not to commit himself publicly to Home Rule in 1873 or 1874, his response to the national appeal on behalf of Isaac Butt, its improvident and spendthrift leader, in 1875 was tantamount to commitment. Since its formation in 1872 the Belfast Home Rule Association had grown annually in strength and numbered many prominent Catholic laymen on its committee. The Presbyterian minister, Isaac Nelson, an early and active recruit, remained a lifelong enthusiast, but extremely few co-religionists followed his example; they had decided that their security and position were best guaranteed by the union, and claimed that Home Rule was a Catholic, if not a rebellious movement. When forwarding his subscription of £10 to the Butt Testimonial Committee, Dorrian refrained from commenting on Butt's politics, though he pointed out that he considered it 'simple justice not to suffer one who so exclusively devotes his time and talents to the service of his country — and at such sacrifice — to remain uncared for by those for whom he labours'. And he expressed a hope that there would be a generous response to requite Butt for the services he had so long rendered 'to the important questions he has so heartily espoused'.[29]

Though growing in strength, Home Rule did not monopolize all nationalist feeling in Belfast, and friction occurred among constitutional nationalists as they prepared to mark the centenary of O'Connell's birth. More serious conflict, however, had arisen in Dublin about the nature of the celebration and the role to be played by the competing claimants to O'Connell's heritage. The lord mayor had decided to emphasise the achievement of Catholic Emancipation to the virtual exclusion of O'Connell's other political aims and aspirations, and a Liberal rather than a Home Ruler had been chosen to deliver the solemn address of commemoration. A meeting was called in Belfast to choose representatives to attend the Dublin ceremony, and Dorrian was elected chairman. Sensing opposition among some who were present to the occasion taking on too much of a Catholic character, Dorrian pointed out that such a demonstration

27 U.Ex., 10 Aug. 1874, quoting Dorrian's letter of 17 Dec. 1868.
28 B.M.N., 19 Aug. 1875.
29 U.Ex., 12 July 1875.

must be Catholic because the majority of Irishmen were Catholic. But he predicted that genuinely liberal Protestants would take part because they realized that O'Connell, far from being a bigot, laboured as much for the dissenter or Presbyterian as for the Catholic. Since Catholics were ground down under the burden of penal laws, their grievances had been greater, and consequently O'Connell devoted his efforts primarily to their relief. Confident that the centenary celebrations would rally the Catholic heart and mind to him who liberated them, Dorrian anticipated that it 'would make them thoroughly understand their strength . . . [and] embolden them to go forward and look for the redress of the other grievances under which they still labour'.[30] To help the organization of the occasion in Dublin, collections were taken up in the Catholic churches of Belfast, and £250 was raised.

When a further meeting was called by this committee, which represented mainly middle-class Catholics, a few of the more 'advanced' nationalists attended, to object to its assumption of the role they had already adopted. Pointing out that they had made arrangements about tickets, they complained that their committee of 'working men was working up to the eleventh hour when the matter was taken out of their hands'. This led to sharp exchanges about arousing class feelings and divisions and to the insinuation that the 'nationalist' committee was a front for the Foresters. Michael Cahill argued that there could be no division between Catholics and Home Rulers since he supposed the Home Rule Association of Belfast did not contain more than twenty four members of other religious denominations.[31] A breach was avoided by agreeing that the committee appointed at the meeting which Dorrian had attended should be widened to include representatives of the other one. The tensions among O'Connell's Belfast admirers were of little significance compared to the divisions that emerged in Dublin and which led to the exchange of blows at the speeches in O'Connell St. and to the disruption of the banquet in the Mansion House in the presence of distinguished foreign guests. When Dorrian was later mistakenly accused of wanting the publication of a centenary record, he wrote to the *Freeman's Journal* to explain that he would much prefer to see a prize of £100 offered for the best essay on 'the present and future of Ireland, socially, politically and religiously'.[32]

And the disputes in Belfast did not damage enthusiasm for Home Rule or lead to any splits among the leading activists. 1876 began

30 B.M.N., 30 July 1875.
31 B.M.N., 2 Aug. 1875. The Foresters were a Catholic philanthropic society whose members generally represented a conservative form of nationalism.
32 F.J., 25 Nov. 1875.

with a huge rally in favour of self-government. J. G. Biggar, the Belfast pork butcher, who as MP for Cavan had become notorious in Westminster for obstructing the business of the House of Commons in an effort to draw attention to Irish grievances, was the principal speaker. Joining him on the platform were ten priests of the diocese of Down and Connor, the parish priest of Moira and the leading members of the Belfast Home Rule committee — John Duddy, Andrew McErlean, Isaac Nelson and the sub-editor of the *Ulster Examiner*, Edward Byrne. Biggar spoke dismissively of the tenant right societies — meetings had recently been held in Ballymena and Crossgar — which stood aloof from the Home Rulers' land campaign and which, with the aid of the Liberals, were fighting for the extension of the 'Ulster custom'. The Orangemen, he claimed, were being used as tools of the Tories and landlords. Michael Cahill, whose eloquence at times carried him beyond the bounds of prudence and fairness, questioned the sincerity of the Whigs' commitment to land reform, charged their two MPs, who sat for Londonderry County, with being place-seekers, and wondered why Sharman Crawford and his brother did not apply their principles to their own tenants. He affirmed that Home Rulers stood for fair rent, free sale and fixity of tenure, and Isaac Nelson, though admitting that neither of them could distinguish a Swedish from an Aberdeen turnip, stressed the need for a solution to the agrarian problem. Edward Byrne declared that the movement supported denominational education.[33]

Dorrian did not attend the Butt Testimonial, no references were made to him, but few of the principal participants could, by then, have had any doubt about his views. The presence alone of ten priests on the platform, apart from the contribution to the Butt Testimonial, was sufficient evidence of his benign acceptance, if not public promotion, of the Home Rule cause. A short time before the meeting he explained privately to Butt why he was unwilling to preside on such an occasion. His reluctance stemmed from his fear that Catholics might suffer retaliation as a result:

> One great reason I have for not taking the chair at a Home Rule meeting — but I have others — is that it would expose many of my people to secret persecution and injury in their employment. You may wonder at this, but not a doubt of it. We must hope that the question will make more way and that prejudices will grow less.[34]

---

33 B.M.N., and U.Ex., 25 Jan. 1876. Cahill remarked that Professor Smith's agitation would subside if he had the tenant right of the Queen's College, alleged that Law, the former Attorney-General, wanted a tenant-right judgeship, and William Drennan Andrews, later a candidate for the Down County constituency, wanted a tenant right of the Queen's Bench, Common Pleas or a Bankruptcy judgeship.
34 Dorrian to Butt, 16 Dec. 1875, N.L.I. MS 8697 (35).

Dorrian's circumspection and sensitivity in this respect were in stark contrast to the belligerent approach of the *Ulster Examiner*, which regarded itself as the mouthpiece of the Catholics of Ulster. On the day following the report of the Home Rule meeting, its leader severely rebuked and, indeed, scarcely stopped short of trying to intimidate those Catholics who had held aloof from Home Rule. Chastising them for their selfishness in refusing to show political solidarity with the majority of their co-religionists, it accused them of meanness and snobbery, and of a desire to hob-nob 'with a shoddy local aristocracy' at the expense of 'the human ladder that raised them up'. Admitting that the movement had not 'an elevated position in the social scale', embracing as it did priests, publicans, traders, Catholic artisans, and the 'Catholic great unwashed', but few of the 'Upper Ten', the *Examiner* accused the prominent absentees of denying the movement that very respectability, the absence of which, they maintained, was holding them back.[35]

Without making a public stand on Home Rule, however, Dorrian shortly made a highly important symbolic gesture in that direction. In April 1876, he invited Isaac Butt to give a lecture in St Mary's Hall, very shortly after its opening. The hall had been built as a recreational and educational centre for the Catholics of Belfast and the invitation to Butt to deliver the first public lecture in it was tantamount to official diocesan approval of the man and his policies. No one who did not enjoy the episcopal favour would have been given such an honour and Dorrian's attendance at the lecture was as explicit a form of public approval of Home Rule as he could have given without making a direct statement in its favour. He used the occasion, however, to appeal to his people to show tolerance towards Protestants. Insisting that he himself was tolerant and liberal while sticking firmly to his principles, he claimed that nothing could be gained by intolerance and bigotry. And although he regretted that both these evils flourished too abundantly in Belfast and its neighbourhood, he made it clear that he would be very pleased to think that his friends would always manifest a liberal approach towards those who differed from them in class or creed.

The *Ulster Examiner* had declared in advance that the cause of Home Rule was so identified with its chief that, when Butt would appear among them, the cheers would not be for the lawyer or lecturer but for the arch Home Ruler. This prediction was amply realized for Butt, who spoke on John Philpott Curran, was most enthusiastically received by a capacity audience. J.G. Biggar, in thanking the bishop, paid tribute to his 'earnestness, industry and

---

35 U.Ex., 26 Jan. 1876.

perseverance'.[36] Dorrian did not attend the banquet given in Butt's honour, which was hosted by leading Home Rulers. But the invitation to the Home Rule leader to lecture in the new centre, of which the Belfast Catholic community was so proud, had given him a boost and status that no other prominent Catholic in the north of Ireland could have conferred.

The gathering strength of the movement, especially if manifested publicly by a parade, carried with it the inherent danger of occasioning strife. After the riots of 1872 political processions of all hues had been banned within the town boundaries. Dorrian and his clergy had constantly stressed the value of non-provocation under any circumstances. But in 1876 the Orangemen again marched, and the more advanced nationalists of the town, who were growing more assertive and impatient, decided that they would not be outdone. When Dorrian heard that preparations had been made for a parade, he wrote a pastoral letter against it and appealed, in St Peter's Church, to the organizers to cancel it. He pointed out that the Protestant procession had done them no harm and suggested that Catholics should display more wisdom, good sense and forbearance than to demonstrate simply because Protestants had done so. He reminded them of St Paul's injunction to exhibit themselves in much patience in tribulation, and emphasized that 15 August was not a national day but a religious holy-day. He would have heartily approved of excursions of confraternities for social and recreational purposes, but a political demonstration was not the way to proclaim the strength of Catholics; that would best be shown by industry, sobriety, the practice of their religion and forbearance.[37] The *Ulster Examiner* weighed in by advising Catholics not to imitate the Orangemen and thereby afford them an opportunity for laughter, and by arguing that the bishop deserved the gratitude of the community for his advice.[38]

But the pleas were in vain; the determined activists of the Home Rule circle insisted on going ahead. Contingents from Glenavy, Antrim, Lisburn and Portaferry joined in the march to Hannahstown. John Duddy, who presided, proclaimed their duty to hold such monster meetings until their demands were met and called for a more aggressive and more vigorous policy of obstruction in parliament. Though Duddy expressed confidence in Butt while mistrusting his more lukewarm followers, John Ferguson, one of the leaders of the British section of the movement, called for the election of more men of the stamp of Parnell and Biggar. And so in the struggle

36 B.M.N., 20 Apr. 1876.
37 B.M.N., 31 July 1876.
38 U.Ex., 31 July 1876.

shaping up between Butt, with his insistence on a gentlemanly and respectful approach to the traditions of the House of Commons, and his rising lieutenants, Parnell and Biggar, who sought notoriety by flouting those very traditions in the most provocative and contemptuous manner, this Belfast meeting aligned itself with the more eager and impatient camp. On their return journey the marchers encountered some sporadic stone-throwing, and ultimately about twenty civilians and three policemen were treated for bruises and scalp wounds.[39]

A year later Dorrian again failed to get a similar march cancelled. When he heard that a plan had been proposed by a group of nationalists — not the Home Rule leaders — to stage a march in honour of O'Connell's birth, he beseeched them to call it off, reminding them that if his advice been followed in 1876 much evil and social and domestic sorrow would have been avoided:

> I again beg of you, for the sake of peace, to forego all such silly and foolish purposes. O'Connell's motto was peace — moral, not physical force or bravado — and our principles ought to be conciliate not to widen the breach with our neighbours.
>
> There are many things which, like you, I have to complain of also; but the way to victory is peace, conciliation and abstention from empty displays, which the sensible men of your own party refuse to join . . . To live in peace and charity is not to ignore patriotism.[40]

Again he went unheeded, though his and his clergy's appeals stripped the parade of significant support. Orange opponents of the march intervened as predicted; sectarian tension mounted in consequence. Parades and demonstrations near Belfast came to be regarded as a necessary public expression of Home Rule sympathies.

National feelings, however, found more peaceful and less dangerous outlets when Parnell and Biggar visited Belfast in September. Some three thousand gathered to hear them in St Mary's Hall and to commit the Home Rule support of Belfast to the obstructionist wing of the parliamentary party, though Michael Cahill, the chairman who introduced Parnell, the young landlord who had been returned to parliament in the previous year, delicately described their purpose as an endorsement of the policy of 'meddlesome energy'. The cool reaction of the meeting to Butt's name and its rapturous welcome for Parnell and Biggar left little doubt about its loyalty in the struggle for leadership. Cahill, who was almost certainly responsible for the

---

39 U.Ex., 16 Aug. 1876.
40 U.Ex., 2 Aug. 1877.

advice given by the *Examiner* to Butt that he should bow to the determined wishes of the country or else relinquish the fight, also chaired the public banquet given to Parnell in the Linenhall Hotel, and to vigorous applause defended Parnell's policy of independent and strenuous opposition.[41] Dorrian personally did not take sides in the battle for power. A conference of the Home Rule associations of Ulster was held in Belfast two months later to ensure that the principles of the movement were advocated in all constituencies in the province and that the establishment of a peasant proprietary was canvassed as the solution to the land question. The three most active Belfast clergy in the movement — Cahill, J.P. Greene and James Hamill — took part.[42]

As Home Rule progressed in Belfast, the political separation of Protestant and Catholic increased proportionately. As early as 1871 William Johnston of Ballykilbeg, the vigilant and committed opponent of popery, had declared that Home Rule was Rome rule, and this view found a ready response in Protestants of both the Tory and Liberal variety. The Liberal party was the chief victim of this division. Where it could once count on Catholic support without bothering about a *quid pro quo*, Catholics now found in Home Rule a more reliable vehicle for their social as well as their national aspirations. Always suspicious of the emphasis placed by local Liberals on mixed education, which they viewed as an obstacle to their demands for a more denominational system rather than a firm adherence to educational principles, they turned increasingly to the Conservatives for backing for their educational policy. Local antipathy between the *Whig* and *Examiner* contributed to this process.

When the *Whig* criticized the *Examiner* for praising Beaconsfield's release of Fenian prisoners, the *Examiner* replied with a ferocious denunciation of the editor of the *Whig*, whom it described as a 'pompous scatterbrain Cockney' who seemed to have only a capacity for insulting and reviling the Catholic church, Catholic dogma, the Catholic priesthood and every Irish national aspiration. It went on to claim that there was no more pliable tool of the Ulster Tory party, and accused him of destroying the Liberal party by severing the Catholic and Liberal elements in the province.[43] Michael Cahill followed up this broadside by advising Catholic electors to vote for the Conservative candidate, Lord Castlereagh, against the Liberal in a by-election for Down County, once the Conservative had indicated a more favourable attitude on the education issue. And, with breathtaking hyperbole, a leader in the *Examiner* described Castlereagh's

41 B.M.N., 27,28 Sept. 1877.
42 B.M.N., 26 Nov. 1877.
43 U.Ex., 10 Jan. 1878.

success as 'the most glorious victory since the Clare election'.[44] This hostility to the Liberals on education was matched by serious criticisms of their sincerity in the support they gave to tenant right societies. The *Examiner* challenged the Route tenant right association to try to elect members of parliament on the land question if it really sought tenant right.[45] And Cahill was very scornful of Liberal members of parliament who did not support Butt's land bills, and at a Home Rule meeting remarked that Sharman Crawford, the Liberal member for Down, should be sent back to teach Sunday school.[46] By 1879 the *Examiner* was declaring that the professing Whig was most illiberal and anti-Catholic, 'the Veriest enemy of everything we hold dear'.

And as Butt's popularity declined and Parnell's rose, Belfast Home Rulers looked more and more to the rising star. Parnell was enthusiastically cheered in St Mary's Hall on 10 February 1879, when he insisted that the only way to make an impression in England was to pursue their demands energetically and stop at nothing within the constitution.[47] The *Examiner* hailed Parnell as the most 'thoroughly honest, practical and hard working man' amongst the energetic wing of the Irish party.[48] And it gave Butt an ultimatum: either relinquish the leadership or set himself sternly at the head of the party.[49]

II

The last years of the 1870s witnessed destitution among small farmers reminiscent of the famine years. A combination of extremely wet seasons, a general economic depression in Britain and increased competition in foodstuffs from the United States, led to a catastrophic decline both in the yield of crops and in their value. The total value of agricultural output fell from £43.7 millions in 1876 to £40 in 1877, to £39.4 in 1878 and to £35.5 in 1879. Livestock and livestock products underwent a similar decline, and the tonnage of potatoes fell from 4.2 millions in 1876 to 1.8 in 1877, 2.5 in 1878 and 1.1 in 1879. The decline in value of the potato crop, and it was on this crop that thousands of small farmers and labourers depended for subsistence and survival, was equally calamitous: from £14.7 millions in 1876 to £6.77 in 1879.[50]

44 U.Ex., 14 May 1878.
45 U.Ex., 21 May 1878.
46 U.Ex., 12 Sept. 1878.
47 B.M.N., 11 Feb. 1879.
48 U.Ex., 11 Feb. 1879.
49 U.Ex., 15 Feb. 1879.
50 Moody, *Davitt*, pp 328-9.

Dorrian had always been concerned with the plight of small farmers. As pastor of the exclusively rural parish of Loughinisland, he had had first-hand experience of their struggles to earn their livings, and this agrarian crisis stirred his sympathies deeply. In his pastoral letter for Lent 1879, when he had explained the jubilee indulgence proclaimed by Leo XIII, he referred sadly to the circumstances then prevailing, when 'most are in sorrow and many starving'. An immediate local anxiety was pressing on his mind: the threat of yet another procession. Though he pleaded for 'peace, sobriety, patience and tolerance' and begged his Catholic people not to hold an outdoor demonstration,[51] the political activists among them again manifested their stubborn resistance to clerical interference, and two thousand marchers set off from Smithfield to Hannahstown. Despite very bad weather conditions some four hundred Protestants turned out to block the route at the borough cemetery, but rioting was kept to a minimum. Painful though these disputes and disturbances might be, they paled into insignificance when compared with the desperation of those whom starvation stared in the face.

For, with the deterioration of the agrarian situation in 1879, the condition of thousands of families in the west of Ireland became critical; many simply could not pay their rent and so were put out of their holdings. The total number of tenants evicted for non-payment of rent during 1877 was 406, but in the following year evictions rose to 834 and during 1879 the figure increased further to 1098.[52] A protest against unjust rents in the small village of Irishtown in Co. Mayo on 20 April drew a crowd variously estimated at from 4,000 to 13,000, and sparked off a protest movement that was destined to have far-reaching consequences. Michael Davitt, the son of parents evicted from their home in Co. Mayo, who had spent seven years in prison under the most brutal conditions for his part in the Fenian movement, was largely instrumental in organizing this protest and, though he himself was not present at it, he proceeded to apply all his energies and compassion to the crisis facing the small farmers of Mayo and to highlight their sufferings at public meetings. He demanded that the system of land ownership be changed to one of peasant proprietorship and he threw himself into the work of organizing huge protests against evictions and unjust rents. Aware that Parnell alone enjoyed the authority and status and possessed the political qualities necessary to lead this land movement, he invited Parnell to assume the leadership, and Parnell, apart from any personal sympathy he might have had for the suffering tenants, realized that he could not afford to pass over an offer which opene

51 U.Ex., 1 Mar. 1879.
52 Moody, *Davitt*, p.290.

up large vistas of political power and influence. Davitt and John Devoy, (one of the most influential of the American Fenians), pledged the support of numerous Fenians in Ireland and America, provided the Fenian ideal of national independence to be achieved through physical force was not abandoned, the demand for land reform was nothing short of a peasant proprietary and that the self-government aspired to was one with real power over national interests involving an executive subordinate to a national parliament.[53] Parnell, however, without committing himself formally to these conditions, agreed to speak at a protest meeting in Westport on 8 June, and in due course assumed the leadership of the land movement.

To the consternation and anger of the organizers, the redoubtable archbishop of Tuam, John MacHale, fired a shot across their bows. The mounting agrarian distress had been accompanied by increased violence and attacks on landlords and their agents, maiming of cattle, and destruction of property became more frequent and menacing. MacHale, zooming in on this aspect of the crisis, and doubtless also aggrieved that he had not been consulted about the proposed demonstration, issued a broadside against the meeting in the *Freeman's Journal* of 7 June. Referring to the threats and crimes recently committed in Mayo and assuring the people of that county of the sympathy of their clergy for the victims of oppression and rack rents, he counselled them against attending the meeting which had been 'convened in a mysterious and disorderly manner' and 'organised by a few designing men'.[54] Though he enjoyed the reputation of being an unflinching nationalist and a fearless critic of the misgovernment of Ireland, his advice was ignored, and Parnell and Davitt both turned up to address a crowd of four thousand at Westport. And when, a month later, he returned to the fray and with characteristic outspokenness warned his flock of the danger of 'finding themselves at the tail of a few unknown strolling men, who, with affected grief, deploring the condition of the tenantry, seek only to mount to place and preferment on the shoulders of the people',[55] Davitt again rejected the charge and the meeting went ahead.

MacHale's attitude in fact was representative of the views and fears of those bishops and clergy who focussed particularly on the crimes accompanying the agricultural depression and evictions, and who believed that Davitt and his friends were agitators taking advantage of suffering and deprivation to stir up strife and conflict. Mindful of the dark passions which disputes about land could kindle

53 Ibid., pp 296-300.
54 Ibid., p.303.
55 Ibid., p.308.

in Irish breasts, and of the terrible deeds to which they had given rise over many years, they were frightened of a recrudescence of bitter agrarian crime. While agreeing that injustices could and should be remedied, they distrusted the methods which Davitt and Parnell were adopting and suspected that those leaders were using peasant discontent for more dangerous, if not nefarious, ends. They regarded the pursuit of such tactics, with the accompanying explosion of anger, revenge, hatred and, perhaps, unattainable expectation as likely to lead not only to the spread of communistic and atheistical views but, much more ominously, to a serious outburst of violence which could only end in defeat, repression and worse suffering.

Other churchmen, of whom Thomas Croke, archbishop of Cashel, quickly came to be the acknowledged leader, viewed the crisis from a very different angle. While admitting and deploring the acts of violence which besmirched the land movement, they considered these as but a symptom of a basically unjust system of land ownership and tenancy, which required to be remedied. The abuses associated with the agitation did not invalidate the grounds for the agitation itself, which were eminently reasonable and, indeed, pressing. The church, they held, could not stand idly by and turn a blind eye to the presence of manifest and cruel evils, or a deaf ear to the cries of the weak, the oppressed and the marginalized. To ignore the painful condition of its people would be a grave omission of duty, a repudiation of the obligations of religion, and would, ultimately, provide an excuse or justification for people to abandon their religious practice.

Though some bishops and clergy were to distrust Parnell and Davitt, the majority came to trust and support them. There was certainly no conflict of view between the bishop of Down and Connor and his clergy on the issue. Caution and circumspection may have prevented Dorrian from attending the highly successful meeting held in St Mary's Hall on 15 October 1879, but more than twenty of his clergy joined Parnell, Biggar and Isaac Nelson, on the platform. Support was vigorously and vociferously offered to Parnell and Biggar for their campaigns in favour of peasant proprietary and Home Rule. The *Whig* wondered what the bishop could think of the language used on the occasion, which, it argued, would not be easily reconciled with 'the inculcations of the Catholic Church in favour of law, order and respect for the rights of property'.[56]

Less than a week after this meeting Davitt gathered together a committee of supporters, including a few priests, and founded the Irish National Land League in Dublin under Parnell's presidency. Its aims were to bring about a reduction of rents and to turn the

56 N.W., 16 Oct. 1879.

occupiers of the soil into its rightful owners. Joseph Biggar became one of the treasurers, and Davitt one of the secretaries, and with this further 'new departure' heavy emphasis was placed on the achievement of an equitable solution to the land crisis. And to this end the Fenians and the advocates of physical force were prepared to throw their weight behind Parnell. With the establishment of the Land League public meetings protesting at the terrible conditions being endured by many small tenant farmers grew more frequent, and a more desperate tone crept into the speeches, as evictions for non-payment of rent stared more and more people in the face. Funds were raised to support those who had been evicted and pressure was brought to bear on farmers not to rent land from which their neighbours had been expelled.

When Davitt and a couple of colleagues advised the tenants at Sligo to look to their own needs first before giving their landlords what they could spare, all three were charged with sedition. And when Parnell went to protest at the threatened eviction of a small farmer near Balla, some eight thousand escorted him to the cabin of the threatened victim. Though Thomas Brennan, one of the secretaries of the Land League, made a speech for which he was later charged with sedition, Parnell contented himself with giving impeccably correct advice by counselling them to keep a firm grip on their homesteads and refuse to pay an unjust rent.[57]

Dorrian was certainly not perturbed by the accusations (made by those sympathetic to the landlords' interests) that the movement was communistic or revolutionary. Though he never aspired to the kind of flamboyant public leadership which Croke enjoyed, and, had he so wished, could never have won the kind of public acclaim which Croke, by virtue of being an archbishop and having charge of a diocese in which very few Protestants resided, acquired, he was and remained as firmly committed to both the social and political goals of Parnell as Croke himself. Two days after the heated protest meeting at Balla, which could so easily have erupted into violence, he forwarded to Rome a calm, reasoned judgement on Parnell's advocacy of the tenant's case and revealed a warm sympathy for the victims of the depression:

> My view is in favour of Mr Parnell, who is misrepresented by the English and Irish Press, by the landlord party, and and even by such men as Sir G. Bowyer and Whig catholics. Parnell is bringing to the surface the misgovernment of Ireland, the misery of the people and the wrongs of Ireland. People howl at him; but he is cool, confident and constitutional. He is not the

---

57. Lyons, *Parnell*, pp 97-102.

enemy of religion. His policy could have obtained for us the O'Connor [sic] Don's Bill; nor does he encourage Fenianism. The exasperation of our people at the neglect of the government and want of sympathy of those who ought to be their friends, alienates many and drives our people to Fenianism. If the people see Bishop and Priests going against them in their misery, and showing no sympathy for them religion suffers.

The Bishops & clergy are on the side of law and order — there may be indiscretions — but let the Government strengthen their hands, and they will have an influence over their people to keep them from despair and attach them to religion. This is the right policy . . . we must sympathize with the suffering and save our people. The more as Government will do as little as possible . . . The misery of the poor would be without a word but for Parnell. We have a crisis to go through and the reception of the Bishops by the Lord Lieutenant was not promising.

But priests and people must keep *united* and I hope nothing shall induce the Holy Father to interfere against the friends of the distressed and famishing poor.

Enclosing a defence of Parnell, to prove that his principles were not irreligious, he pointed out in conclusion that the protest at Balla had 'saved the fever stricken family from death by the roadside'.[58]

And indeed this explanation of Parnell's activities proved very helpful to the correspondent to whom it was sent. For Tobias Kirby, a short time later, was summoned to the Secretariat of State at the Vatican and asked to comment on complaints that had been received there about the use of violent language at public meetings by bishops and clergy and their support for 'the policy of Mr Parnell which is represented to the Holy See as one of extreme political views and tending towards Socialism'. Kirby pointed out that, though some ecclesiastics might on occasion use expressions of a reprehensible nature, the Irish bishops and priests were on the side of order, and that it would be very dangerous for the clergy in the present crisis to stand aloof from their flocks. The Under Secretary of State agreed that it would not be prudent for the Holy See to take any action in the matter. Kirby, duly informing the archbishop of Dublin of this discussion, remarked that he himself was not well informed about the situation in Ireland, but then went on to quote favourably from a letter of a northern bishop which, apparently, had convinced him of the innocuousness of Parnell's behaviour and thereby contributed to

58. Dorrian to Kirby, 24 Nov. 1879. A.I.C.R. The Ol'Coinor Don's bill was designed to provide a system of university education acceptable to Catholics.

the defence he had made of the churchmen associated with the Land League.[59]

Until his death Dorrian never budged from the line chalked out in this letter. The social dimension of religion implied, of necessity, support for the weak and suffering. Christian charity compelled bishops and priests to interfere to remedy harsh and unjust systems of land tenure. Any neglect of this obligation could only detach from religious practice the people who felt abandoned by their clergy. And he never allowed the excesses committed in support of the Land League or the extreme language of which a few of its defenders, both clerical and lay, were guilty to detract from the need to strive for a just solution to the land question. As opposition to the League mounted among influential landlords in Ireland and their friends in England, who forwarded denunciations of intemperate speeches to Rome, he held firmly to the justice of the tenants' cause and always insisted on the distinction between the legitimacy of that cause and the unlawfulness of the crimes that sullied it.

---

[59] Kirby to McCabe, undated, but before 7 Dec. 1879, D.D.A., also Kirby to John Pius Leahy, undated, Dr.D.A.

9

Primary and secondary education

I

By 1860, when Dorrian became coadjutor bishop, Ireland was covered with a network of primary schools, the large majority of which were in effect denominational. The bishops would have much preferred a *de iure* to a *de facto* denominational system, and they felt aggrieved at the government's reluctance to permit this transformation. They resented the regulations and restrictions which prevented three quarters of the population from enjoying a fully Catholic form of education, and symbolic rather than significant grievances, such as the disproportionate representation of the main religious groupings on the board of commissioners, fed this discontent.

The national system of education had been founded in 1831 to make state funds available for the combined education of children of all denominations. The charter of the system, the letter of the Chief Secretary, Lord Stanley, to the duke of Leinster, who had been appointed chairman of the board of commissioners which was empowered to put the new scheme into effect, referred to the preference which would be given to applications for aid bearing the signatures of both Protestant and Catholic representatives, and laid down that the schools were to be open for separate religious instruction on one or two days weekly, the remainder of the time being devoted to combined moral and literary instruction. Time could also be set aside for teaching religion either before or after ordinary school hours, and clergy or representatives of each denomination were entitled to conduct classes for children of their own faith. The commissioners were permitted to make grants for the erection and equipment of schools and for the salaries of teachers, if the local applicants could provide one third of the costs. Schools which were built with financial aid from the board were vested in three trustees and were bound for ever to observe the rules of the system. The non-vested received only grants for books and teachers' salaries, and were only obliged to observe the commissioners' rules when in receipt of such grants. The appointment and dismissal of teachers were left in the hands of the patron or manager. Of the first seven members of the board three belonged to the Church of Ireland, two were Catholics, one a Presbyterian and one a Unitarian.

While Stanley's letter was still in draft and consultations were being carried on with potential commissioners, the Chief Secretary was forced by pressure from Protestants to add a clause declaring that it was not intended 'to exclude from the list of books portions of sacred history or religious or moral teaching as may be approved by the board'. This opened the way for the compilation of four volumes of extracts from scripture and a book by Richard Whately, the Anglican archbishop of Dublin, entitled *Introductory Lessons on Christian Evidences* (later re-named *Lessons on the Truth of Christianity*) which, like all other publications of the board, were made available to schools at cost price for use during the hours of combined teaching; managers remained at liberty to use any books they chose, but those provided cheaply by the board obviously enjoyed powerful advantages. Though at the parliamentary commission which preceded the establishment of the system (the recommendations of which were substantially followed in 1831), Daniel Murray, the Catholic archbishop of Dublin, had agreed to the publication of such scripture extracts, he did so not out of any enthusiasm for such a development but rather because he believed Catholics could not succeed in persuading the government to give up its grants to the proselytizing religious societies (which were then extensively conducting schools) and establish a system free from the suspicion of proselytism, unless they made some kind of concession to the Protestant insistence on biblical study being given a place even in the general instruction.[1]

The system encountered determined opposition from both the established and Presbyterian churches. Church of Ireland opponents claimed that they alone, as the official church of the country, should have the entire care of the education of all youth, and they objected to the implication that the religious equality which the system sought to favour prevented them from fulfilling their obligation of converting Catholics. They also objected strongly to the limitations placed on the use of the bible in the schools (though they were of course free to use the bible as much as they wished during the time set aside for separate religious instruction). The Presbyterians expressed their hostility with even more vigour and variety — in some instances even to the point of attacking and destroying national schools. They insisted that no limitation should be placed on the use of the bible for educational purposes, and scornfully rejected the right of Catholic

---

[1] Murray to Cullen, 24 Dec. 1838, A.I.C.R.

priests to visit the schools to give religious instruction to their children. They rejected the principle of restricting religious instruction to fixed days, which they contemptuously dubbed 'popish holidays', or even to hours before or after combined instruction. After a series of negotiations with government ministers in London and with the commissioners in Dublin, they eventually won a major concession. The board agreed to re-define in effect a non-vested school as one to the erection and equipment of which it had not contributed, and to allow the manager of such a school to arrange for religious instruction at any time during ordinary school hours. Moreover, such schools would only be bound by the regulations of the system, while they were receiving grants from the board in the form of teachers' salaries and books at cost price, and the rule, which had previously been interpreted as placing the onus on the manager or teacher of ensuring that no child was present at the religious instruction of a denomination to which he did not belong, was re-interpreted to mean that in a non-vested school a child could not be compelled to attend the religious classes to which his parents objected; the onus of absenting itself from the religious instruction given by Presbyterian teachers now devolved on the child or its parents.[2]

The Catholic reaction, on the other hand, was fairly favourable. Before 1831 the state had allocated money to religious societies which the Catholic church had accused of overt or covert proselytism, and the institution of an alternative which eliminated common study of the scriptures and other religious matter in response to their strongly expressed anxieties at the commissions set up by the government in the 1820s, met with their approval. So while the other denominations, or especially their clergy, held back the Catholics pressed ahead with applications either for aid for existing schools or for assistance in the erection of new ones. The first application from Co. Antrim[3] came from Bernard McAuley, the parish priest of Ballymena, and the first from Co. Down[4] from Thomas Kelly, the bishop of Dromore. The third application from Co. Antrim bore the signature of William Crolly, bishop of Down and Connor, and, as in the other cases, a number of Catholic and Protestant laymen also signed.[5] This sought grants for the first school officially sponsored by the Catholic community of Belfast which had been opened in 1829 beside St Patrick's Church in Donegall St. With episcopal example and encouragement, applications for aid from the diocese of Down and Connor increased consistently over the next few years.

2 D.H. Akenson, *The Irish education experiment* (London,1970), pp 185-7.
3 P.R.O.N.I. ED6/1/1/1.
4 Ibid., ED6/1/3/1.
5 Ibid., ED1/1/3.

However, under the influence of John MacHale, archbishop of Tuam, some Catholic bishops challenged the claim of the national system to provide education free from all taint of proselytism, and delated it to Rome as dangerous to the faith of their children. The Holy See eventually decided, in 1841, to allow each bishop to make up his own mind about it, but warned that no books containing material damaging to the scriptures or doctrines of the church should be tolerated in the schools and that only literary instruction should be given in common.[6]

This decision ensured that the majority of the bishops who accepted the system were free to make use of it by observing these safeguards. Bishop Denvir followed his predecessor's policy, supported Crolly and Murray in their rebuttal of MacHale's complaints in Rome, and encouraged his priests to seek aid from the board for their schools. But two developments caused anxiety to the less committed supporters of the system in the 1840s: legislation affecting bequests to charities, and the establishment of the Queen's Colleges, and a decision of the commissioners in 1846 requiring that all schools subsequently receiving aid from them be vested in the board. After an examination of the evidence submitted to it on the Queen's Colleges, Rome decided that grave danger to the faith might arise from them, counselled the bishops to take no part in them and advised them to set up their own Catholic university. Though the institution of the colleges and Rome's adverse reaction did not impinge directly on the primary school question, the reluctance of the government to make any significant concessions to the bishops' requests tended to diminish their gratitude for the national system, to harden episcopal attitudes on educational matters in general, and, ultimately, to make the bishops less tolerant of what they regarded as the defects of the national schools.

By 1846 the managers of schools where the majority of children were Catholic were almost invariably the local parish priests, and they feared that this directive from the board about vesting schools in it was but a prelude to a demand for more obnoxious forms of control. And another decision taken by the commissioners in the following year, which removed the onus from teachers in vested schools of withdrawing children from the religious instruction of a denomination other than their own, added to this suspicion. The foundation of model schools, which were designed to exhibit the most improved methods of literary and scientific instruction, and to train young persons for the office of teacher, further antagonized

---

6 A.P.F., *Acta*, 203, ff 412r-413r. The congregation of Propaganda in 1839 forbade Catholics to participate in the national system but the pope did not ratify this decision.

both bishops and priests. Thirty two were planned — one for each county, to be sited in the principal towns — and the first was opened in 1849. It was hoped that they would attract the keenest students and that future teachers would emerge from them through the system of paid monitorships with which they were endowed. The models were built and conducted exclusively by the board, which retained control over the appointment of teachers and the provision of books, two powers to which the bishops took strong exception. They also objected vehemently to the absence of adequate moral supervision of pupils attending the models and to the establishment of boarding houses where they could lodge.

Dorrian, who had been stationed in Belfast from 1837 to 1847, when these issues were being hotly debated, subsequently testified that, if he had lived in his predecessors' days, and had had their experience, he would have entertained their views, and, in fact, did partially entertain their views. What later made him differ from them was his experience of the restrictions which prevented Catholic-managed schools from being more overtly Catholic, and that bugbear of many Irish bishops, which did not exist in Crolly's time — the model schools. As a curate in Belfast he was never called on to apply for aid to the board, but on his transfer to Loughinisland as parish priest, this responsibility did devolve on him. By the late 1840s some thirty schools in Co. Antrim under the management of parish priests had been connected with the board, and perhaps half that number were sponsored by a genuinely mixed committee of Protestants and Catholics. But the hostility of several Protestant clergy and landlords ensured that some priests were virtually compelled to provide for Catholic children alone, and the difficulty of procuring sites from those who were opposed to the system delayed requests for aid in some places. In supporting the application of Bernard Dorrian, Patrick's older brother, who was parish priest of Lisburn, Bishop Denvir wrote to A.R. Blake, one of the Catholic commissioners:

> May I take the liberty of submitting to your consideration the very harassing situation in which several of the clergy of the Diocese of Down and Connor are placed, respecting sites for schools, by the bigotry of antieducational Landlords who refuse to give such sites for National Schools. In consequence the pastors have no other resource than the taking of ground from independent and well disposed tenants who cannot do otherwise than charge rent for the same. Unless this plan be resorted to thousands of children must remain, as for instance in Lisburn, without education. The pastors and members of their flocks are willing to become sureties to the Board of Commissioners for the payment of such rent and deeply interested as I am in this

matter I earnestly implore that such guarantee may be accepted seeing that otherwise many populous districts will be debarred the benefits which your System is conferring on more fortunate portions of the County.[7]

In the part of Co. Down which fell under the jurisdiction of the bishop of Down and Connor there were proportionally more joint applications for aid in the earlier years. But these diminished as each religious group found the system could be easily turned into a more denominational one.

A serious complaint arose in Belfast in the 1850s, and Bishop Denvir was forced to appeal to the board of national education. He charged that the Catholic children in the Lancasterian Girls School in Frederick St. were compelled 'to attend to scripture reading, singing of Protestant hymns, explanation of Scripture given by a Protestant mistress every morning before the hours appointed for secular instruction'. As a result of an investigation carried out by their inspectors, the commissioners concluded that the complaints were justified and ordered the school authorities to ensure that Catholic children were neither compelled nor induced to attend such instruction.[8] This incident caused Denvir particular embarrassment, for a short time before, in 1853, he had consented to fill the seat on the board left vacant by the death of Archbishop Murray. His decision to accept this appointment provoked a cool, admonitory letter from Rome,[9] and as a consequence of unfavourable impressions reaching Propaganda, his service was destined to be short. Though the

---

[7] P.R.O.N.I. ED1/2/167. Denvir to A.R. Blake, 24 Oct.1844, enclosed in Dorrian's application for aid. Dorrian informed the commissioners that the Protestant clergy of the town, apart from Dean Stannus, were in favour of his application. But Dean Stannus was not only the local rector but also the agent of the landlord, the marquis of Hertford. Two other priests, Daniel Curoe and John Lynch, whose parishes covered Antrim, Randalstown, Ahoghill and Portglenone, referred in their communications with the board to the hostility of local clergy and of Lord O'Neill to the national system.(P.R.O.N.I. ED1/8/18 and ED1/1/58.) When Francis Turnley, the landlord of Cushendall, appealed to the commissioners to re-connect to the board the school under his patronage which catered mainly for Catholic children, Marcus Faloon, the rector of Layde, protested: 'I cannot see why the Board should be solicited to grant aid to the Cushendall School, merely to save the pocket of a wealthy landlord — I am sure there are many parts of Ireland overrun with Popery, superstition and idolatry, where the money sought to be granted to the Cushendall School might be more advantageously expended than in this Parish, which is so well supplied with schools'.(ED1/2/146.)

[8] *Copies of all correspondence between the commissioners of national education in Ireland and the committee of the Lancasterian industrial national school, Belfast, relative to the charges made by the Reverend Dr Denvir against the system and management of that school* . . . H.C. 1856 (88), liii, 447-500.

[9] Propaganda to Denvir, 31 Mar. 1853. A.P.F. *Lett.*,343, f.211rv.

departure of Archbishop Whately from the board in the wake of a row caused by the refusal of his colleagues to compel Clonmel model school to use his book, *Lessons on the Truth of Christianity* (which Cullen had denounced in a pastoral after it was condemned for doctrinal errors in Rome), was interpreted as beneficial to Catholic interests,[10] the decision of the board in 1855 to establish minor model schools was regarded as provocative and unfriendly by the Catholic authorities. And this policy, which arose from a recommendation of a commission of the House of Lords that the board should establish schools in areas where poverty prevented local representatives from making any contribution, raised the hackles of the bishops who feared the foundation of a further chain of schools outside clerical influence or control. Denvir's membership of the board was one of the first victims of this decision: he was advised by Rome to withdraw as soon as possible, a counsel to which reports of his less than satisfactory conduct of his own diocesan affairs may well have contributed.[11]

At the same time the commissioners introduced a rule that was designed to allay some Catholic anxiety. A teacher was obliged, on the first occasion on which a child of a different denomination attended his or her class in religious instruction, to forward a certificate to that effect to the parents or guardians of the child. This still fell short of the original understanding of the rules, which placed the onus on the teacher of excluding children from the religious instruction of a denomination to which they did not belong. The combination of these irritants continued to feed the impatience of the bishops, and the new episcopal leadership of the second half of the century was much less tolerant and compliant than had been that of three or four decades earlier. An episcopate that was conscious of having little influence with the government, and that had been grateful for Catholic Emancipation and an end to state funding for proselytizing societies had given way to one that was much more conscious of its rights, less mindful of the removal of civil restrictions on the social and political activity of its people and more determined to put the British boast about favouring democratic freedoms and fair play to the test.

10 Cullen described Whately as a very subtle and cunning enemy, and remarked that this was was a very favourable development. (Cullen to Fransoni, 24 Aug. 1853. A.P.F. S.C.(Irlanda), 31, ff 548r-551r.) Though Whately believed that mass education would diminish the superstition behind Catholicism and that his *Scripture Lessons* contributed to that end, he has been exonerated of the charge levelled against him since the publication of his daughter's biography of a complete and deliberate machiavellian use of the national system for the purposes of proselytism. (D.H. Akenson, *A Protestant in purgatory* (Hamden, 1981), pp 171-2.)

11 Propaganda to Denvir, 21 Feb. 1857, A.P.F. *Lett.*, 348, f.99rv.

Accordingly, on 5 August 1859 the bishops submitted a joint memorial[12] to the Lord-Lieutenant, conveying to the government 'the growing anxiety which naturally fills their minds on finding their authority so completely disowned in the various schemes for educating the Irish people, which have been put in operation for several years'. They argued that their authority, both legal and constitutional, was ignored in the nomination of members of the board, in the framing and rescinding of its rules, in the appointment of inspectors, in the selection of books and especially in ensuring that an adequate share of pure Catholic teaching was given to the Catholic pupils. Referring to the anomaly of the leaders of a vast Catholic population having no officially acknowledged control over the education of their children, they asked indignantly if such an abnormal situation would be tolerated in any other country, were the roles reversed and Protestants constituted the majority. They deprecated any wish to deny the rights of the state to see that public funds applied to education were rightfully expended, and maintained that a confusion of claims and erroneous obligations deriving from that right had led 'to a most unwarrantable and annoying interference with the religious and spiritual functions of the Catholic episcopacy'. Consequently, they concluded that the faith of Catholic children could not be safe under any mixed system of education, and so, respectfully but earnestly, requested 'such a participation in educational grants for the separate instruction of Catholic children as the numbers and fidelity of the Catholic people, as well as their contributions to sustain the burdens of the State, amply entitle them'.

Curiously this petition was based on abstract rights rather than on concrete evidence of the damage done by the system. The absence of statistics pointing to abuses or to numbers of injured Catholic children indicate that the bishops were more aggrieved by the needless exclusion of a more positive and beneficial form of education, which could and would contribute more effectively to their spiritual mission, than by losses sustained in the schools. What galled them in particular was the discrepancy between the methods used for disbursing public money for education in England and Ireland: in England the Treasury made direct grants to denominational schools while in Ireland support for denominationalism was officially regarded as taboo.[13]

12 *Copy of the memorial of the Roman Catholic prelates relative to national education in Ireland, and of the reply thereto of the chief secretary* . . . H.C. 1860 (26), liii, 659-62.

13 The Privy Council began grant-aiding the schools of the Catholic Poor School Committee in 1847. The amount allocated was in direct proportion to what the committee raised so that the funds provided by the Privy Council rarely exceeded one third of the entire costs. In 1856 a Catholic training college at Hammersmith, originally established for Christian Brothers, was opened to laymen, and in the same

But, if the bishops chose to argue from principle, so too did the government. Combined education had been introduced by the Whigs and the Whig government, then in office, adhered firmly to the principle which had motivated the party for three decades. On behalf of the government, Edward Cardwell, the Chief Secretary, acknowledged the paramount importance of religious training but reminded the prelates of the other province of education, which was common to all denominations. Recalling that the report of the previous year, 1858, revealed that eighty four per cent of the pupils and eighty per cent of the teachers in the national schools were Catholics, and that eighty per cent of the salaries paid to teachers went to Catholics, he noted that the system had then been in operation for nearly thirty years and had conferred the greatest benefits on the population of Ireland. If the bishops' demands were conceded, he insisted, the 'National system would be overthrown, and a system of sectarian education substituted for it, calculated to revive social divisions in Ireland and to stimulate feelings which it is the object of every just and liberal government to allay'. He assured them in conclusion that, if any grounds of complaint about impropriety in the operation of the system existed, their grievances would be carefully considered.

In a lengthy and exhaustive rejoinder[14] the bishops put forward both abstract and practical reasons for their request. Expressing their willingness to promote every branch of science and literature, they repudiated any system in which education was restricted to temporal and material concerns, to the exclusion of the all-important interests of immortal souls, of religion, of eternity. Arguing that religious instruction should be given separately, they denied that 'secular education can be properly imparted without the sanction of religion, and without blending it with the lessons and practices of religion'.

Descending to details, they claimed that in many schools belonging to Presbyterians in the north Catholic children were not allowed to receive any Catholic education; that in schools vested in the board all instruction in history, philosophy and even morality, in so far as such things were taught, was withdrawn from all religious influences; and that the symbols and images of religion were forbidden in all schools. They traced the development of the rule about childrens' participation in the separate teaching of the denomination to which they did not belong, and maintained that originally Catholic children were not allowed to attend Protestant instruction unless their parents gave positive orders to that effect and vice versa,

year training colleges for women were established in Liverpool and Hastings. They received 75 per cent grants.

14 *Copy of further correspondence relative to national education in Ireland.* H.C. 1860 (206), liii, 665-87.

whereas the rule had been altered to one which simply forbade the compulsory attendance of a child at instruction to which its parents objected, with the result that 'poor Catholic children, not as yet acquainted with the value of their faith, may be induced, by the promise of food or clothing, or by the influence of a landlord or employer to attend Protestant religious instruction, nay may be infected with error before they themselves understood the danger, or their parents become aware of it'. They then quoted the apposite comments of the head inspector of the board: 'in all the schools which I visited in Belfast that were taught by Presbyterian teachers, the practice prevailed of giving *common* religious instruction to all, none of them retiring. Indeed it is pretty general throughout the counties of Antrim and Londonderry, but I never observed it to prevail in any other part of the country'. And they charged that the board had concealed this testimony and that thousands were being so instructed. The recent change announced by the board which ordered a teacher to give notice to its parents when a child attended the religious classes of another denomination was but a mockery and a delusion, for it afforded no protection against proselytizing patrons and threw the burden of deciding whether the instruction was suitable or not 'on persons generally poor and uninstructed, perhaps unable to read the notice sent to them'.

The bishops also complained about the use of books which purported to teach common Christianity, a vague and undefined religion, from which all mention of mysteries, of the Trinity, the Incarnation, the Divinity of Christ and other leading principles of Christianity were omitted. To these works, the *Scripture Lessons* and the *Evidences of Christianity (Lessons on the Truth of Christianity)*, prepared by Revd James Carlile and Archbishop Whately, they added others, compiled by other Protestants, which gave 'an anti-Catholic colouring to their pages, omitting matters considered necessary by us and insinuating or teaching dangerous errors'. And, though the use of such books was not technically compulsory, schools were in fact obliged to use them, since they were made available at a very low cost and free stocks were presented to each school. If Cardwell did really mean that the bishops enjoyed rights recognized by the government, they wanted to know what those rights were. Had they been consulted about the appointment of Catholic commissioners or on the selection of books? Had the *Scripture Lessons*, which had been repeatedly condemned, been removed from the model schools? Had they been given any control over the training of the future teachers?

The bishops also singled out the agricultural and district model schools for special condemnation, contrasting the arrangements for female students very unfavourably with their English equivalents, which were under the direction of nuns. The central training institute in Dublin, they charged, was staffed for the most part by Protestants of every denomination. Rejecting Cardwell's claim that separate education stimulated sectarian feeling, they maintained that the contrary was the case and referred to an incident in which Presbyterian boys in the Belfast Model School had caricatured the sacrament of penance. And they quoted the favourable judgement of inspectors on convent and Christian Brothers' schools. The limitations recently placed on nuns which allowed them to have only one school connected with a convent, and those which forbade Christian Brothers to have schools connected with the board, were retrograde.

Far from accepting Cardwell's point that the overwhelming number of children and teachers in the national system were Catholic, the bishops used this admission to bolster their own demand for separate grants, and summed up most of their case with the contention that 'by a legal fiction' innumerable schools built by Catholics under Catholic patronage, that had never been attended by a Protestant, and, in districts where no poor Protestant resided, 'have been declared to be mixed schools, and are treated as if it were necessary to protect imaginary Protestants against Catholic instruction '.

The bishops had decided that the government's rigid adherence to the principle of mixed education had led to the foolish, awkward and exasperating practical situation where fully Catholic schools were bound by a tiresome set of rules designed for a genuinely mixed system. And, what was worse, this involved a conflict with their spiritual obligations to ensure, if possible, that their flocks had a purely Catholic education. Common sense, they believed, was being sacrificed on the altar of a principle, one which did not apply in most of Ireland, where little mixing took place, and one which denied the higher spiritual advantages that would have accrued from converting a *de facto* denominational system into a *de iure* one.

At the same time, nineteen Catholic members of the House of Commons also wrote to Cardwell,[15] repeating many of the strictures contained in the bishops' letter. They reminded him that the changes made in the system had affected it 'in its *fundamental* principles and its *essential* characteristics', and noted that various Protestant clergymen had declared publicly that 'but for the changes in question they could not conscientiously have joined that system, but that owing to them they *now enjoy opportunities of inculcating on children in their schools, not of their own faith, those religious doctrines*, which they hold specially precious'. Observing that Cardwell, in his reply to the bishops, had made no mention of the non-vested schools under

---

15 *Copy of a letter on the subject of national education in Ireland* . . . H.C. 1861 (212), xlviii, 683-6.

Protestant patrons, many of whom would not allow a Catholic priest within the walls of their schools, they suggested that he was doubtless well aware that in very many schools Catholic children possessed, under the changed rules, no religious teaching whatever except what was imparted to them, with a judicious assurance that their faith was not to be tampered with, by persons accustomed, both in private society and at public meetings, to stigmatize as a mass of superstition, imbecility and idolatry, the religion of their parents. They recalled, in question form, many of the bishops' complaints. The pleas of both parties, however, were ineffective.

The correspondence led to one change, though it was not one much calculated to impress or appease the hierarchy. A supplemental charter was granted by the government to the board of commissioners raising their number to twenty, one half of whom were to be Protestant and the other half Catholic. Appointments were made to bring these changes into effect and announced in June 1861. Otherwise the system carried on as usual, though, by a further change in 1866, schools towards the construction of which a grant had been made no longer had to be vested in the board; the pre-1846 arrangement whereby they could be vested in three trustees was restored.

By the time this exchange took place the system had, as Cardwell claimed, been in existence for nearly three decades. As the commissioners pointed out in their report for 1859[16] the number of national schools then in operation was 5,496. The total number of those whose names appeared at some time on the rolls for that year was 806,510, but the average number enrolled was 519,175 and the average daily attendance of children was 269,203. From the publication of the first report for the year 1833, which showed that 789 schools were connected with the board and 107,042 pupils were on the rolls, the system had indeed made spectacular progress.[17] The denominational percentages represented among the pupils for 1859 were: Roman Catholics 83.9, Church of Ireland 5.1, Presbyterians 10.5, other dissenters 0.44, and 0.04 were not accounted for in the returns, but according to incomplete returns which had been furnished to the commissioners on 31 March 1858, 267 schools in Co. Antrim out of 338 were mixed (a further 37 were not accounted for), and of these 266 were under Protestant management, 56 were under Catholic management and 16 under the board. In Co. Down 231 of 276 schools were mixed (a further 22 were not accounted for), and of

---

16 *Twenty sixth report of the commissioners of national education in Ireland . . . for the year 1859.* [2706] H.C. 1860, xxvi, 5-15,29-37,377-93,414-25.

17 The fastest rate of growth had taken place in the 1840s. At the end of 1839 there were 1,581 schools with 192,971 children on their rolls connected with the national board; a decade later those numbers had risen to 4,321 and 480,623.

these 194 were under Protestant management, 80 under Catholic management and 2 under official management. In Ulster about eighty four per cent of the schools were attended by pupils of various denominations; but, since the presence of one pupil of a different denomination from the rest constituted a mixed school, this statistic is of little value.

Of the 257 teachers trained during the year, 206 were Catholics, 17 Church of Ireland and 34 Presbyterian. Fourteen model schools were then in operation and eight were being built. At the largest of these, the Belfast Model, about a quarter of the pupils or 315 out of 1,231 were Catholic; in Ballymena 28 Catholics and in Coleraine 43 were in attendance out of totals of 199 in each school.

The commissioners in their report referred indirectly to the charge that had been raised by the bishops, of great numbers — they said 70,000 — of Catholic children attending scripture classes in schools under Protestant patronage. They stated that, in 1,351 national schools, of which Protestants were patrons, there were 50,184 Catholic children enrolled and of this number 1.816 joined in the scripture classes under Protestant teachers. In addition, 409 Catholic children joined in reading the *Scripture Lessons* and the book of *Sacred Poetry* with Protestant teachers during the time set aside for religious instruction and a further three, at the instance of mothers and guardians, who were Protestant, received instruction in the Protestant catechism.

The report contained tables showing the religious complexion of all the pupils whose names were on the rolls for the quarter ending 31 December 1859. From these it emerged that in Co. Antrim there were 12,359 Catholic pupils out of a total of 43,118, and in Co. Down 11,206 out of 31,158. In Co. Antrim 2,606 students were attending mixed schools staffed by Protestant teachers, and in Co. Down the corresponding figure was 2,352. In Co. Antrim 4,864 were enrolled in mixed schools staffed only by Catholic teachers; in Co. Down the corresponding figure was 5,062. The remainder were in schools with teachers of different denominations.[18] In 1859 there

---

18 James Heald MP, who interested himself in the operation of the national system during a visit to Ireland in 1851, observed in 1854 that he had found a mixed education prevailing to a considerable extent in Belfast and vicinity. 'In the town of Belfast for instance, where the schools were under Protestant patronage, there was a very considerable attendance of Roman Catholic children as well as children of other Christian bodies . . . but as regards the schools under Roman Catholic patronage, I found, I think without an exception, that the children attending the schools were Roman Catholic children'. He also remarked that he found throughout Ireland a far greater disposition on the part of Roman Catholic parents to send their children to Protestant schools than there was on the part of Protestant parents to send their children to Roman Catholic schools. (*Report from the select committee of the House of Lords appointed to inquire into the practical working of the system of national education in Ireland.* H.C. 1854 (525), xv, pt i, 430-31.)

were fifteen schools in Belfast under Catholic patronage, but this figure included the separate male and female schools in Donegall St. and in Chapel Lane, a male and infants' school in Alexander St. West, a boys' school in May St. and two girls' schools in Crumlin Road and Hamilton St.[19] The Donegall St. and Bridge End schools were under clerical patronage, and the others were managed by the St Vincent de Paul Society. In these Belfast schools the full enrolment was 9,984, and the average attendance was 5443. In the rest of Co. Antrim two schools — at Glenariffe and Glenshesk — were under Catholic lay patronage and 43 were under clerical management. This group included male and female schools in Antrim, Lisburn, Randalstown, Cushendall, Knocknacarry, Ballymacricket (Glenavy), Harryville (Ballymena) and Loughguile. In the Down part of the diocese there were 34 schools under Catholic clerical patrons, one under a Catholic lay patron and a convent school in Downpatrick. In seven parishes — Kilcoo, Kilkeel, Killough, Castlewellan, Grange (Kilkeel), Ballydock (Dunsford), Ballyphilip (Portaferry) and Ballykinlar — there were male and female schools. The other eighteen were mixed. Their total enrolment was 4,456 and their average attendance was 2,902. The schools in Coleraine had 149 pupils on the rolls and an average attendance of 112. These schools with a total of some 3,900 pupils probably contained at least 3,500 Catholics.

As these statistics show, the national system had become recognized as the normal vehicle for establishing Catholic parochial schools in each parish. But though the parochial network, by 1860, was impressive there were still large gaps. The parishes of Larne, Kircubbin and Saintfield[20] and those places which shortly achieved parochial status — Bangor, Holywood, Ballyclare, Ballintoy, Armoy, Carnlough, Whitehouse — did not have schools under Catholic management. There was no parochial school for boys in Downpatrick. In many other parishes the number and location of the schools did not at all satisfy local requirements. Catholic children were quite well represented, in proportion to the general population, in the whole of Counties Antrim and Down, but many of them were in mixed schools.

By 1860 Dorrian was well acquainted with the general development and practical working of the system. He had no substantial complaint about the schools, of which the parish priests were patrons, though he certainly would have preferred denominational

19 The others were located in Millfield, Union St., Cullingtree Road and Wolfhill (Ligoniel).
20 Schools under Catholic management in Saintfield had received grants from the board before 1859 but by that year their connection with it had been severed.

education. The schools at Loughinisland were typical of hundreds, indeed thousands, throughout the country: non-vested schools, which were built by the parish and to which the board gave aid in the form of books and teachers' salaries and which were under the management of the parish priest. The clergy had come to regard the foundation of such schools as part of their pastoral responsibilities and viewed them as an invaluable aid in producing a more religiously-informed people.[21]

Within the diocese of Down and Connor the model schools encountered the same clerical antipathy as elsewhere. At first some of the priests had been well disposed to them; William McCreedy the head inspector regarded John Lynch, the parish priest of Ballymena, as a 'cordial' supporter of the schools that opened there in 1849. But Lynch's enthusiasm soon turned to distrust and hostility. In February 1850 he lodged an objection to the celebrated doggerel contained in the children's books, 'I thank the goodness and the grace, that on my birth have smiled, and made me, in these Christian days, a happy English child', not because of its pathetic xenophobia, but because the lines 'and taught to pray a useless prayer, to blocks of wood and stone' could be maliciously misinterpreted to refer to

21 As the commissioners faithfully maintained the fiction of encouraging combined education an inspector was detailed, on receipt of an application for aid, to consult the local clergy of all denominations. By the 1850s the *de facto* denominational situation was accepted by the vast majority of clergy but some few did raise objections. Among these was Robert Hill, the vicar of Aghalee, who opposed the application of Cornelius Magee, the parish priest of Aghagallon, for aid for the Derrynaseer school. He charged that Magee, since coming to the parish, had 'on all occasions manifested the bitterest hostility against the Established Church, both publicly and privately. And I have good reason to fear that, as in all probability members of my Church will be sent to Derrynaseer School, Mr Magee would not scruple to tamper with their religious options. I have, during a long period, lived on good terms with my Roman Catholic parishioners, but this seems to give offence to Mr Magee'. (P.R.O.N.I. ED1/4/99, 28 Oct. 1857)

When John Lynch applied for aid for the Harryville schools, Revd J.H. Smyth approved but Revd M.Moore claimed that Lynch already had schools and that his policy was to detach Catholic children from the Model. Revd John Crozier feared the decline of Guy's School, which was managed by Revd J.M. Dill, and also the future decline of the Model in favour of 'an avowedly and *thoroughly Sectarian School*'. Though the inspector reported in a similar vein, the commissioners overruled him. (Ibid., ED1/5/1)

When Hugh McCann, parish priest of Rasharkin, applied for aid for a school at Killens, Finvoy, he met some tough local opposition and the suggestion was made that the local landlord should be the patron. McCann insisted that 'no committee could be formed capable of understanding or teaching me my duties to my flock'. Andrew Todd, the Presbyterian minister of Finvoy, pointed out that Protestants outnumbered Catholics in Finvoy by four to one and claimed that 'the great majority of the parents at Killens cannot have confidence in the liberality of the Revd Hugh McCann's views on the subject of education, as he does not permit the children of his people to attend the Crushenbracken N.S.'. (Ibid., ED1/6/136, 27 Jan. 1866)

Catholics' use of images. In July 1850 Lynch entered an objection in the visitors' book to 'the bad taste, not to say the extreme injustice of selecting descriptions of characters from such writers as Gibbon, Hume and Robertson for a mixed school professing neutrality'. In the following year he went further and protested against a fundamental principle of the board being set aside — the right of forbidding books — and here he was anticipating the confusion that led to the brouhaha over Whately's resignation. The inspector assumed that he had in mind the *Lessons on the Truth of Christianity* and Sullivan's *Literary Class Book*, though in fact he singled out a reference in the *Girls' Reading Book* to the belief of Catholics in 'the saving power of consecrated ground', which he not unjustifiably described as 'an imposition upon Protestant credulity as well as a calumny on Catholic faith'. The inspector was sensitive to the issues raised by Lynch, whom he described as 'a most able and intelligent man', and sought the help of the Lords' Committee in conciliating the Catholic church and attaching it more firmly to the system, by the removal, if necessary, of any passages which could fairly be described as objectionable from the books.[22]

The indelicate incident at the Belfast Model, in which Protestant children burlesqued the confessional, gave great offence to the local Catholic clergy and was interpreted by the Catholic chaplain as the final proof that the models were not conducted with proper control, adequate discipline and vigilant protection for the rights of religious minorities.

In May 1862 the hierarchy struck a heavy blow against the models. It passed resolutions directing priests, from the beginning of the following term, to desist from sending any person to be trained as a teacher either at the model schools or at the central training college in Dublin, and from that date to cease employing in schools under their management teachers who had received training in those institutions. Moreover, as a mark of disapproval, all clergy and nuns were forbidden to visit model schools, even for the purpose of giving religious instruction. In response to the demands of Myles O'Reilly, MP for Longford, some light was thrown on the vexed question of the scope offered by the national system for interference with the faith of children by teachers of a different denomination. Information was sought from all schools connected with the board about the number of pupils to whose parents notification had been sent of their attending religious instruction given by a teacher of a different creed during the year 1862. Further questions revealed the number of Catholics who read the scriptures from the authorized version. It

---

22 *Report from the select committee of the House of Lords . . . into . . . national education in Ireland.* H.C. 1854 (525), xv, pt i, 455-60, 508-9.

transpired that, in Co. Antrim, parents of over 1,100 Catholic pupils had received notification of their children's attendance at religious instruction given by Protestant teachers, and that some 400 Catholic pupils were reading the authorized version along with their Protestant classmates. In some schools the number of certificates issued was small. But in others it was suspiciously large: in Skerry 33, in Glenarm (female) 38, in Glenarm (male) 56, in Cairncastle 24, and in a few others more than 10 were issued. There was no indication of the number of times those to whose parents a certificate had been sent had actually been instructed by a Protestant teacher. In some cases it was made clear that a Protestant parent had requested instruction by a Protestant teacher for a Catholic child, and in others the instruction may have consisted of explanations of the *Scripture Lessons* or of the *Sacred Poetry*. Nonetheless, the number of certificates to which the subsequent report referred created anxieties in the minds of the Catholic clergy about the risks of pressure being brought to bear on frightened children or confused parents by Protestant teachers, especially in districts where Catholics constituted a small minority.[23]

A few months after Dorrian succeeded to the see of Down and Connor, the bishops of Ireland again submitted proposals to the government for adjustments to the national system.[24] Their hardening of attitudes was indicated at the outset when they made clear that their request for changes did not reflect any form of approval of the principle of mixed education. Dividing the national schools into ordinary and model, they asked that in all ordinary schools, whether vested or non-vested, in which only children of one denomination were enrolled, permission should be given for 'the fulness of distinctive religious teaching . . . in the course of daily secular education, with full liberty for the performance of religious exercises and the use of religious emblems'. Characterizing many existing national schools as already denominational, they sought an end to the 'pure fiction' by which they were treated as mixed, and practices of piety and symbols of religion were excluded from them. This would put an end to the 'godless' character of the whole system, and in the exclusively Catholic schools the teachers would be Catholic, the books treating of religious, moral or historical matters would be Catholic, the inspectors would be Catholic and 'if objectionable, subject to the veto of the Catholic bishop of the diocese in which their duties lie', and the managers, subject to the veto of the commissioners, would be at liberty to choose suitable books for secular instruction. Nuns' and Brothers' schools, which were not in receipt of grants, could be

---

23 *Returns . . . of all the schools . . . days and hours set apart for all religious instructions given in the school and nature of same . . .* H.C. 1864 (481), xlvii, pt i, 4-67.
24 *Powis Commission*, pp 185-7, pt i, vol.i.

connected with the board. And the same denominational principle which applied in England should be recognized for both Catholic and Protestant children in Ireland.

In mixed schools security was to be provided for the religious minority. They pointed to the 1,600 certificates issued by Catholic parents in Ulster in 1862 to permit their children to attend religious instruction given by Protestants as evidence that the faith of that number had been 'interfered with'. Consequently they required more stringent protection for the faith of religious minorities. With regard to the model schools they declared that they would be satisfied with nothing less than their abolition. Indeed, their condemnation of the models was unreserved and unrestrained — they charged that the teachers and other officials of the board made every effort 'to incite Catholic pupils and the parents of Catholic pupils to schismatical acts of insubordination against Catholic priests and Catholic bishops'. They suggested that the buildings which housed those obnoxious schools should be converted into training schools of a denominational character or reformatories or put to some other useful purpose.

Sir George Grey, the Home Secretary, to whom this petition was presented, passed it on to the commissioners in Dublin. And the commissioners conveniently, and legitimately, took refuge behind their non-political status; they replied that they were an administrative body and would continue to carry out their duties 'to the utmost of their power, with impartiality and efficiency'. The main consequence of this exchange was a further tightening of the rule about the presence of children at religious instruction in the schools: no pupil registered by its parents or guardians as a Protestant was permitted to attend religious instruction given by a Catholic teacher, and vice versa, and no pupil was allowed to be present at any religious instruction to which its parents or guardians objected. Three Protestant commissioners protested against this change, and a proviso was added, enabling a parent to enrol his child in the religious class by declaring his wishes, in writing, in a book specially kept for that purpose. Chichester Fortescue, the Chief Secretary, suggested to the commissioners of education in June 1866 that model schools for the training of teachers might be established on the same principle as ordinary national schools. But, though the commissioners expressed approval, they took no action on this matter.

In fact vehement Protestant support for mixed education made the government's task more difficult. As the Catholics came to demand change in the direction of denominationalism, Protestants, and especially Presbyterians, who had previously been unenthusiastic about the national system, became its most outspoken advocates. They forwarded memorials to the Lord-Lieutenant, protesting against the possible establishment of voluntary training colleges and the extension of aid to convent schools. The Ulster National Education Association, which was founded in 1859 and represented both Presbyterian and Church of Ireland views, clothed its hostility to Catholic educational progress by denouncing the concessions to sectarianism that would be involved in tampering with the models or instituting church-related training colleges.[25]

Dorrian was not surprised at the government's reaction, and considered it an ill wind which would blow some good among the credulous and naive supporters of the Whigs in Ireland. He distrusted their claim to be the party that worked for rightful freedoms and believed that their advocacy of the mixed principle in education proved how seriously their practice digressed from their precepts. He gave vigorous expression to these views in a carefully prepared reply to Archbishop Cullen's enclosure of the letters of Sir George Grey and Lord Wodehouse, the Lord-Lieutenant:

> For I never expected that the Whig government would, in the face of their European practice in church affairs, admit episcopal control over education or give up a System in favour of which they have lost no opportunity of parading everywhere their predilection, unless under a compulsion which has not only been applied but instead of which has been substituted an obsequious confidence of a most unaccountable description . . .
>
> Yet I am not disheartened. For the time shall come I hope (perhaps is now at hand) when Catholics must awaken to the utter folly of setting Landlords and their tenants in bitter antagonism by sending to Parliament, to prop up this System of false hopes from a false party, men who, at home, worthless and selfish place distributors, create about them an unhealthy Catholic atmosphere in which is produced a spawn of parasites unsound in faith and disloyal to the Church, who sneer at opinions, yea even at the laws of their Bishops, who accept positions in Queen's Colleges and in Model Schools, whilst their patrons on whom they depend and by whom they receive such training are *directly* and *without any necessity*, engaged in obtaining these appointments and promoting these institutions condemned by the authority these men affect so much to revere. I think we woefully betray our cause by bandying compliments and by fraternizing with this class of men as if we sympathized with the attitude of hostility and spirit of disobedience they continue to exhibit.

25 *Copy of revised rules . . . dissents from or protests against the adoption of any of the above rules* . . . H.C. 1864 (157),xlvi, 367-71.

Dorrian himself went on to exhibit a mood of tough defiance. Interpreting the commissioners' reply as a contemptuous rebuff, he suggested that the bishops were obliged to give it an authoritative (by which he meant a fighting) answer. Such a response was necessary, both to reassure the simple people who would have been scandalized by its 'atrocious insolence', and to prevent the church being put back to the hedge schools and penal laws. He then took up a point that he was to develop on many occasions:

> I am absolutely appalled at the notions on religious matters and the disregard for authority I find growing again amongst those Catholics who can point to the example of those laymen with whom Bishops are known to visit, to travel, and to be in daily intercourse. For my part I am not able to reconcile it with consistency.

In fact his prescription for Catholics who abetted, in any way, forms of education condemned, in whole or part, by the leaders of their church was a firm smack of ecclesiastical censure.[26] This had worked with his own troublemakers in the dispute over the Catholic Institute in Belfast, and he proceeded to recommend, though not to define, a 'sharp remedy' in this situation. By a bold stand against his own opponents he had got more than he expected. In responding to the commissioners he therefore proposed that the bishops should 'lay down the law for them, for teachers, and for all at this most important crisis'.[27]

This was indeed a belligerent approach and, however understandable, coming from a young bishop who had flexed his muscles so successfully on the home front, was not calculated to impress or cow the commissioners of national education. Half that body owed no spiritual allegiance to the hierarchy, and even the Catholic members were independent-minded men who knew that no penalties of a religious nature could be imposed on them. Moreover, they had a government at their back that was not likely to be put to flight by the noise of ecclesiastical artillery. The weakness of the attack on the Whigs lay in the absence of a credible alternative. A decade later

---

[26] The Catholic commissioners at the time were Thomas O'Hagan (a distinguished barrister and future Lord Chancellor), the earl of Dunraven, D.R. Pigot (Chief Baron of the Exchequer), Henry Monahan (Chief Justice of the Common Pleas), John O'Hagan (a barrister and professor in the Catholic University), Laurence Waldron MP, John Lentaigne (Inspector General of prisons), Thomas Preston (a magistrate) and J.D. Fitzgerald (a judge of the court of Queen's Bench). Some of these men, especially the O'Hagans and Dunraven, had prominent clerical friends.

[27] Dorrian to Cullen, 8 May 1866, D.D.A.

Catholics could cheerfully support Home Rule, but in the 1860s voting for the Tories was not practical politics.

II

The Conservative party, from whom Dorrian hoped for some concessions on the national system, came to power in 1866. It duly entered into negotiations with representatives of the bishops on the university question but neatly shelved the problem of primary education by appointing a royal commission, under the chairmanship of Lord Powis, to investigate all aspects of that thorny problem. This commission conducted a most thorough and searching examination of Irish primary education, and eight large volumes, containing a report, the evidence of a wide variety of witnesses and detailed statistical information about various kinds of schools and their enrolments were subsequently published. Dorrian appeared before the commission on 9 June 1868 and gave lengthy evidence about his experiences of and views on primary education.[28]

While admitting that there was 'a great deal of what is laudable, and what is beneficial and advantageous' in the national schools, and that they had done and were doing a great deal of good, he argued that, as they were in effect denominational, they would do still more good if the books were of the proper standard, and if the religious element were not excluded. Lord Stanley's scheme he characterized as 'a system of education based on the atheistical principle, if carried out, but practically the Atheistical principle turned out denominational'. There were Presbyterian and Protestant schools which Catholics never entered, and Catholic schools under the board which no Protestant ever entered. It had therefore become 'nearly denominational', but he wanted all limitations on its movement in that direction removed. He did not believe that religious and secular education should be separated: 'education in order to be proper education, must take in not merely the physical man, but the spiritual man, the moral man, and by excluding any of them you are not giving the proper education in giving instruction to the intellect merely, but are forming a very dangerous element, indeed; for if the intellect becomes well informed, and there is not virtue to balance it, there must arise danger to society'. Since information was imparted by the senses as well as the intellect, children should be exposed to religious symbols and the religious and secular integrated: 'a great portion of a child's education is to be found in what we call the

---

28 *Powis Commission*, pp 341-70, pt iii, vol.iii. The other bishops who gave evidence were Cardinal Cullen and William Keane of Cloyne.

surroundings — its teachings are in the air, and the tone of the place, and the way in which the various acts are performed'. This principle was most noticeably exemplified by the methods employed by the Christian Brothers, who stressed the conscientious obligation of children, before God, to study earnestly. Teachers, therefore, contributed substantially to these 'surroundings' by their deportment, tone and habits. His own experience had taught him that children were 'much deteriorated in their morals and manners', when religion was separated from ordinary instruction. And he referred, enviously, to the arrangements made by the colonial government in Victoria, Australia; the bishop of Melbourne received £10,000 yearly and for every £100 he collected he was permitted to allocate a further £200 from that fund for the erection of schools and churches in his diocese.

Dorrian's most scathing criticisms were reserved for the model schools. They were irreformable and should therefore be abolished and replaced by denominational training colleges for candidates aspiring to become teachers. He instanced a couple of abuses that had occurred in the Belfast Model, in which children of mixed marriages, who were being brought up as Catholics, had been forced by teachers to receive Protestant instruction. Presented with an extract from an inspector's report about 'the harmonizing influence of non-sectarian education' with particular reference to the absence of dissension among the pupils of different religious backgrounds at the Belfast Model, he replied that during recent disturbances the Model pupils had been out on the streets like the other rioters. The principal reason for his hostility to the models lay in their total exclusion of religion[29] and the defective kind of deportment resulting from that omission. He had personal experience of the improper and objectionable tone which children acquired at the model schools and he went on to enlarge on it: 'they to some extent become imbued with airs and notions that are unsuited to children; there is a degree of stubbornness, of indocility, of conceit about them so much so that the children, whether boys or girls, when they come from a model school either to the Christian Brothers' schools or to convent schools, are at once known, and until they are trained and brought into the tone of these schools they are considered a great drawback'. Furthermore, he found a similarly unpleasant tone about the teachers in the models: 'there is not a spirit of union or kindliness amongst them, but of bickering and criticism of each other'. He did not approve of

---

29 Provision was made for separate religious teaching in the models and at one time Revd Richard Marner and some of the Sisters of Mercy taught in the Belfast Model. Marner withdrew when he felt that the school was not being fairly or properly conducted.

clergy entering the models to teach religion, for their presence in those schools would suggest a form of approval of a defective system. He also objected to the cost of the models and to their attracting the children of parents who could afford to pay school fees rather than the children of the poor. By calculating the cost of running them, by dividing the teachers' incomes by the number of pupils, it transpired that for each child £4 per year was being spent, in contrast to the schools run by the Christian Brothers or nuns where the corresponding figure was nine and ten shillings.

The bishop also made clear his unease, both at the virtual control of the commissioners over the selection of books for ordinary schools and also at some passages contained in the general text books. While admitting that patrons were free to select the books for their schools, he insisted that in effect they were forced to choose those produced by the board, which were made available at half-price. The board only gave that facility to its own books, but, if the Christian Brothers' books were included in its catalogue, he would take them in preference. The choice of suitable and harmless reading matter in their schools was ultimately part of a bishop's responsibility to his flock. He also singled out a few passages from the fourth reading book, which he deemed unsuited to children.[30] And he explained that a book could weaken the faith of a Catholic child not only by what it contained but also by what it omitted; by treating of religious issues and ignoring central doctrinal matters, it could present a very distorted and even false view of Catholicism. If the board published books of which the heads of the different churches approved, it would then be guaranteed their acceptance in the schools, and greater satisfaction would result.

Not surprisingly, Dorrian lavished much praise on the schools

30 These included the 'Character of an educated Gentleman' which he thought would be a very objectionable character for a child to follow. And he felt the piece did not do justice to the author 'who rather brings him to a different *finale* from what it would be expected the purport of this character would lead to'. This was in fact the famous definition of a gentleman given in Newman's eighth discourse on 'knowledge viewed in relation to religion' in the *Idea of a University*, and the author did not intend to reflect on his gentleman in religious terms at all. Presumably it was the possible indifference of the gentleman to religion that Dorrian considered blameworthy. Other passages which he regarded as unsuitable were taken from *The Tempest*, and poems entitled *The Braes of Yarrow* (Logan) and *Mariana* (Tennyson). He thought the last stanza of *Mariana* led to suicide and the other extracts partook too much of love tales.(*Fourth Reading Book*, (Dublin, 1867), pp 84-5, 143-5, 359-64.)

The gentleman's possible indifference to religion also annoyed the Elementary Education Committee of the General Assembly of the Presbyterian Church, which complained as well about a stanza of *Mariana* and about unscriptural practices which were referred to in the book. (*Minutes of the proceedings of the General Assembly of the Presbyterian Church in Ireland*, 1861-70, iii, 991.)

conducted by the nuns and the Christian Brothers. And he regretted the regulations which restricted the nuns from receiving the full financial help from the board to which they were entitled. And when it was put to him that the capitation grant to convents was introduced because nuns were not classified as teachers in the ordinary way, he replied that he would be happy to have the nuns' qualifications tested by their pupils' results. In particular, he complained of the failure to grant aid towards the payment of assistant teachers in convent evening schools. Those schools (which he had warmly encouraged since his succession as bishop) afforded opportunities for girls who were forced by necessity to earn their livings in factories and mills to acquire some education after finishing their daily work. He spoke feelingly of the grim working conditions and appallingly long hours to which the 500 girls who attended the evening classes at the Convent of Mercy were subject. On leaving the factories and mills, those workers, aged between eleven and twenty, went to class for two hours each evening during the winter and were taught reading, writing, religion and deportment. Were it not for the beneficial influence of the nuns, the girls would have been exposed to grave moral dangers, yet the board refused to pay salaries to assistant teachers or monitresses for them.

He also placed heavy emphasis on the role of the teacher in transmitting the faith both by word and example. His own experience had taught him that 'a teacher whose demeanour is religious and whose deportment is proper will have more influence in forming the manners of children than the literature used in the schools'. Consequently, the appointment of teachers was of crucial importance to the maintenance of the right spiritual ethos in the school. The preservation by the clerical managers, and ultimately by the bishops, of the control of appointments was a 'function the prelates of the Church cannot abdicate'. The church should likewise be allowed to run training colleges for teachers with the financial assistance of the state. And though he did not absolutely insist on having Catholic inspectors for Catholic schools, he did draw attention to the bishops' request that that should be the normal pattern.

Since the educational concern of the bishops was so intense and the national system affected so many Catholic children, Dorrian also suggested that the commissioners should in the main be acceptable to, and trusted by, the hierarchy: 'the prelates . . . should feel satisfied that the persons appointed . . . were free from bigotry and prejudice, and were persons who would fairly and conscientiously carry out the system, without using it in the slightest way as an engine of proselytism'. He indicated that the bishops would be willing to suggest the names of men in whom they had confidence, but he had no objection to the board being representative of other religions. He felt that it should consist of voluntary members and should be independent of all political parties.

Pressed as to how provision was to be made for small religious minorities — he was given the example of sixty two Catholic children scattered in small minority groups in schools managed by Protestants in the parishes of Ballymena and Ahoghill — he admitted that in such cases guarantees of non-intervention with the religious allegiance of those children was all that could be sought; the Catholic population was too small in such areas to establish a school under Catholic management. He mentioned two instances, in Cairncastle and nearby, where the Catholic minority was not offered the protection to which the board's rules entitled it: in Cairncastle religious instruction was given to the Catholic children on the *Scripture Lessons* and *Sacred Poetry* during the time for separate instruction on a Saturday, and in the other school an Anglican taught religion to the Catholic children. In the first instance the inspector took notice of the infringement but took no action. Dorrian was critical of the reactions of the board to complaints about such matters; he felt it was very reluctant to correct such abuses. Pressed further as to whether he knew of any case where a child had been induced to change its religion, he answered that he had known of one case in Belfast, but admitted that such cases were not numerous.

Powis and his colleagues were certainly left in no doubt about Dorrian's commitment to the Catholic philosophy of education. The views they heard on the spiritual values of denominational schools were those that had been taking shape over the previous two or three decades throughout the British Empire and the United States, and in those countries of continental Europe where state schools were neutral in terms of religion. The belief that religion is 'caught' by the attitudes and atmosphere prevailing in a church-related school as well as in the actual teaching of religion and in exercises of piety underlies the whole concept of Catholic education. When Dorrian spoke about the influence of 'the surroundings' of the school and of the deportment of the teacher, he was articulating the basic arguments for denominational education. In Loughinisland he had come to appreciate the opportunities offered by the national system, and, with his customary energy and determination, had ensured that his children were given the best available facilities. His reply to Powis that 'looking after an elementary school is one of the most important duties of a parish priest' expressed his own deep commitment and concern, and his subsequent remark that a bishop possessed abundant means for enforcing this responsibility represented official policy in Down and Connor throughout his episcopate.

That Dorrian's accession had given an additional fillip to the provision of schools by his clergy did not pass unobserved. D.C.

Richmond, an assistant commissioner of the national board, whose wide experience endowed his observations with significance, told the Powis Commission[31] that he believed the clergy of Down and Connor were 'nearly unanimous in reflecting the determined championship of a denominational system of education advocated by their Bishop'. He went on to contrast the more 'stringent' policy and approach obtaining in the diocese with that of the archdiocese of Armagh and indicated that he might have heard some variety of sentiment on mixed education from the Armagh clergy. He concluded that a 'less uncompromising spirit' fired the Armagh priests and thought that some of them even looked on the national system with a friendly eye. But when Richmond went on to deplore the establishment of a school under Catholic management in Conway St., Belfast, close by one under Presbyterian management as a sacrifice 'of all regard for judicious distribution to the appetite for sectarian display', he was donning the mantle of King Canute; his own board had given up the fight for genuinely mixed schools.[32] Significantly, he paid a warm and generous tribute to the success of the Christian Brothers and explained that their religious enthusiasm, backed by the preferential support of the clergy, achieved for them what 'no machinery of perfection can produce elsewhere'. He did not, however, admire the docility and submissiveness which he believed that the Brothers' system of relying on 'the sentiment of personal attachment' produced, and contrasted it unfavourably with the 'robustness and independence of character which a method of greater freedom tends to promote'.

Though the Powis commission did not call for a radical restructuring of the national system, many of its recommendations gave satisfaction to the bishops. It suggested that the board of commissioners should give aid to training schools or colleges which were conducted by voluntary societies or religious bodies and which submitted their pupils to examinations; the grant should not exceed three times the sum provided by the patron or manager. In addition, the provincial model schools should be gradually discontinued and leased as voluntary training schools. It also recommended that any books to which the board did not object could be used in the schools and that the commissioners should not extend any privilege or preference to a particular series of books. It proposed that the distinction between convent and ordinary schools should cease.

31 *Powis Commission*, pp 173, 179, 239, pt ii, vol. ii
32 Richmond gave examples of the attendance of Catholics at a few national schools where the teachers were Protestant: at Whiteabbey there were 52 Catholic children out of a total of 391, at Kircubbin 34 out of 156, at Aldoo near Carrickfergus 70 out of 133, at Ballyeasborough near Kircubbin 45 out of 210 and at Hunter's Lane, Donaghadee 26 out of 113.(Ibid., 188)

Arrangements should be made for testing nuns belonging to enclosed orders within their convents; those not classified should be paid on the basis of their pupils' results. Where two schools under different denominational management had been in existence in an area for three years with an average attendance of twenty five pupils, they should be allowed to become denominational as long as no Protestant child was permitted to attend Catholic religious instruction and vice versa. Many other proposals were made about the classification and appointment of teachers, payment by results, and about practical and financial details of administering the system. The bishops had no reason to object to any of the commission's proposals, but by the time they were published the Liberals had returned to power. Partly because of their involvement in other Irish reforms and partly because of their commitment to maintaining mixed education intact, they took no action.

III

Opponents of the national system continued to air their grievances and seek redress. One of its most trenchant and outspoken critics, James W. Kavanagh, a former head inspector, visited several schools in Ulster in 1868 to check on possible abuses. Prone to exaggeration and hypersensitive to covert forms of proselytism, his strictures cannot always be taken at face value, but, when on a visit to Belfast in 1868, he reported on the changes he observed there since his last sojourn in the town eleven years previously, there is little reason to disbelieve him. The mixed system, he averred, had disappeared in the town and colleges, churches and schools were springing up on every side.

Kavanagh visited many schools in Belfast and the immediate neighbourhood and collected information on the number of Catholic children attending them. In a school at Donaghadee, managed by a Presbyterian minister, where there were 5 Catholics and 76 Presbyterians on the roll, he claimed that the teacher had forged the parents' names on the certificate book authorizing their children to receive religious instruction. At Killinchey he found two certificates, one of which had been signed by the child's mother and was recognized by the inspector as illegal, but, when he inquired if that child was excluded from the religious class, he was told that the teacher would never prevent a pupil from hearing God's word. In Ballymacarrett he called at a school with 6 Catholics and 237 Presbyterians, was told that the inspector never inquired about the rule and that the teacher allowed the children who could not read to remain for the religious instruction. Other teachers told him they put out their Catholic pupils when Protestant children were being taught religion, but he was furiously attacked by the headmaster of the Sullivan schools in Holywood and not allowed to see the certificate book. In the Academy St. school, managed by the fiery divine, Hugh Hanna, he noted that there were 18 Catholic and 64 Presbyterian children; the headmistress explained that between one third and one half of the children were illegitimate and difficult to manage. Kavanagh did not underestimate the depressing situation in that school, for he also claimed that the assistant was a prostitute.

His conclusion about the treatment of these small Catholic minorities, if accurate, was certainly an indictment of the mixed system. He maintained that in Ballymena, Lurgan and Portadown, as well as in the Belfast area, parents were persuaded by some subterfuge or other to sign the certificates authorizing their children to receive religious instruction from Protestant teachers. They were asked if they wanted their children to have all the advantages available in the school and then told to sign. Not one in six of those who signed could write and consequently did not realize what they were doing. Kavanagh claimed that Dorrian was horrified when this information was brought to his attention.[33] However, he was not renowned for scrupulous accuracy and, for an opponent of the national system, these were the most explosive charges that could be made. Dorrian himself, who had his ear close enough to the ground to detect such abuses, significantly only complained of two schools where Catholic children were forced to attend religious classes of another denomination. But while mixed schooling lasted, accusations, however vague or flimsy, of proselytism were bound to be made.

Dorrian knew that the best antidote to charges of the kind made by Kavanagh was to ensure that the diocese was covered with an extensive network of schools under Catholic management. Not all Catholic children could be guaranteed the opportunity of attending such schools, as there were large tracts of Antrim and North Down where the Catholic population was too thin and scattered to enable a parish priest to make provision for very small minorities. But he strongly encouraged his clergy to keep opening more schools, not only in the centres of their parishes but also in the peripheral districts. He was most assiduous in delivering or presiding at charity sermons and attending functions which were organized to raise money for building or repairing schools. He always took advantage of those occasions to stress the value and importance of a form of education in which religion was safely and satisfactorily taught, and this theme often recurred in his Lenten pastorals. He kept insisting that no parent could sanction the dangerous system of mixed education

[33] Kavanagh to Cullen, 27 Sept. and ? Oct. 1868, D.D.A.

'unless under the pressure of necessity; and this necessity must be real, for if there was any other place to which he could send his children and where a proper education could be received by them, then no such necessity existed'.[34] It was his ambition and goal to see that necessity constantly diminishing.

IV

The deteriorating relations between Protestants and Catholics after the riots of 1864 in Belfast helped to make the schools more denominational. Reports of Catholic clergy being insulted when visiting mixed schools also increased this religious solidarity. The *Ulster Examiner* occasionally reported instances of illiterate parents being cajoled or coerced into allowing their children to be present during religious instruction given by Protestants. The foundation of the National Education League of Ireland to promote non-denominational education, which was supported by some prominent Protestants who were recognized as militantly anti-Catholic, helped accelerate the opposite process. In response Dorrian exhorted his people more strongly to support schools under Catholic management. In his pastoral of 1872 he recalled the evidence which had emerged in parliament about hundreds of Catholics being instructed in catechism and scripture out of Presbyterian books by Presbyterian teachers.[35] And he recalled that his two predecessors, Crolly and Denvir ('a man of unsuspecting candour') had accepted the guarantees that the national system would be free from the suspicion of proselytism; had they lived later they would not have believed that every suspicion had been removed.[36]

With such sensitivity to the least aberration in the administration of the system, Dorrian, not surprisingly, was quick to pounce on any directives that could be interpreted as diminishing rightful clerical control of the faith and morals of Catholic children. When the board announced the terms of a new contract that was to be made between managers and teachers as part of a deal giving the teachers an increase in salary, he immediately wrote a public letter pointing out that

---

34 B.M.N., 20 Dec. 1867.

35 In 1872 the returns of all schools for which certificates were used permitting children to attend religious instruction in a denomination other then their own were published. These revealed that in Antrim (including most of Belfast) 81 Catholic children were receiving religious instruction from Protestant teachers. In the Down part of the diocese the figure was 8. (*Copy of all minutes and proceedings from 1st day of May 1866 to the present time, relating to changes of rules or of practice as to religious instruction* . . . H.C. 1872,(416), xlvi, 744-5.)

36 D.Ex., 10 Feb. 1872.

under the agreement, which neither managers nor teachers could break within three months, the commissioners alone could dismiss a teacher and, if a Catholic manager tried to dismiss a teacher on a serious charge such as heresy, the teacher could appeal to the commissioners. He termed this new rule 'mischievous' and observed that it was too high a price to pay for the legitimate claims of teachers to higher incomes.[37]

A year later he grew more apocalyptic as he reviewed the consequences for Catholic education of the revolutionary spirit that had swept across Europe and, in particular, attitudes that had recently been revealed in government circles which 'would go far to shake the belief that the Government had the disposition to give equal and evenhanded justice in the matter of education of the Catholics of Ireland'. The views of these influential people (presumably he was referring to the Liberals' scheme for university education) demolished the sense of security, hitherto enjoyed by the church, that no breath of proselytism should touch the education of Catholic youth. Referring awesomely to the mighty struggle to diminish the rightful role of the church in education, he went on to declare:

> a great want had been supplied when the National System had been ushered into existence, but if the National System was to be corrupted, poisoned in its source; if it was to be made work upon a bad and unsound basis, and if it was to be made the means of propagating among the Catholics of Ireland feelings of disrespect for the Church of God as established, then he thought that there would be only one feeling with regard to it . . . It would be better for them to go back to the hedge schools, or to remain in ignorance, and to know nothing of scientific knowledge . . . to lose all those advantages — and that would be a great sacrifice and a great loss — yet it would be better for them, he thought, were they to consider their spiritual interests, and the words of their Blessed Lord 'What does it profit a man if he gain the whole world and lose his own soul'.[38]

However, there were no dark designs being drawn up in Whitehall to make the national system less amenable to Catholic management and direction. Though many of the recommendations of the Powis commission may have been put into effect very slowly, the whole tide of opinion was moving towards greater denominationalism. Dorrian, in fact, realized that he had far more reason to be grateful for the opportunities the system offered than to be aggrieved at its

37 D.Ex., 18 Nov. 1872.
38 B.M.N., 22 July 1873.

defects. Consequently, he strove to ensure that every Catholic community in the diocese was conveniently served by a national school under clerical patronage. When he became bishop of Down and Connor in 1865, there were 116 schools under Catholic management (three were managed by laymen) with a total enrolment of 17,855 and an average daily attendance of 10,781. At the end of 1884 Bangor and Ballyclare did not have schools under Catholic patronage, but all other parishes had at least one such. During his episcopate some schools were enlarged and divided to form separate male and female schools; some fifty others, including single sex schools, were opened. The only school remaining under lay Catholic patronage in 1884 was Killyleagh. The report which was issued by the ecclesiastical inspector of the diocese in January 1885 showed that at the end of 1884 (the last full year of Dorrian's life) there were 179 schools under Catholic management (only one of these was lay controlled) with 19,363 pupils on the rolls, an average attendance of 12,853, and an attendance of 14,019 for the examination in religious knowledge.[39]

According to the census of 1861 the percentages of Catholics over the age of five who could neither read nor write for Counties Antrim and Down and Belfast were 34.1, 38.3 and 30.2[40]; twenty years later these figures had dropped to 24.0, 26.5 and 20.8; by 1891 they had decreased further to 18.1, 21.6 and 14.4.

It was appropriate, therefore, that the Catholic teachers of Belfast should have played a special part in the celebrations to mark the silver jubilee of the bishop's episcopal ordination. In their tribute to him they claimed that the school districts embracing Belfast and vicinity had attained a rank in national education second to none and, in the case of the Catholic schools, attributed this in no small degree to his generous patronage. The quality of the school accommodation had been vastly improved and the excellent system of school inspection had done much for the spread of religious knowledge. In reply Dorrian recalled that, on his arrival in Belfast as bishop, their schools were 'scanty and rare'. The situation had been immensely improved, and splendid schools had arisen. Acknowledging the exalted nature of their vocation, he congratulated the teachers on their conscientious devotion to their work, and to enthusiastic cheers declared himself in favour of compulsory education, especially in

---

39 *Report of the religious examination for the Catholic schools in Down and Connor for 1884* (Belfast, 1885), p.1. There were also 1,200 pupils, who were not Catholics, enrolled in these schools.

40 The corresponding figures in 1861 for the Church of Ireland were 20.7, 19.2 and 14.9; for the Presbyterians 11.2, 10.2 and 8.2. By 1891 the Church of Ireland percentages had decreased to 11.3, 10.6 and 9.3; the Presbyterian equivalents were 5.7, 5.6 and 4.9. (*Census Ire.*, 1891, ii, 475-6.)

towns, if it did not force the starving poor to expose themselves to great want.[41]

The teachers' compliment on the growth of the national system under clerical patronage both in quantity and quality in Belfast was certainly deserved. Twenty years earlier the number of schools managed by Catholics was woefully inadequate for the children seeking admission to them. The standard of school buildings, the equipment and general facilities for the children were low. Some country parishes suffered similar handicaps. Dorrian, on assuming the reins of office, set about remedying this neglect, and he made the provision of suitable and well-furnished national schools an integral part of his pastoral plan for the town and the diocese. Down and Connor was the first diocese in Ireland in which a priest was assigned full-time to the task of inspecting religious education in the schools, and of submitting a report,[42] which contained the marks awarded in, and the comments made on, each school, to the bishop and parish clergy. Dorrian invested heavily in the apostolate of primary education and left the diocese with a generally satisfactory system of national schools under clerical management.

V

One of the strongest complaints which the hierarchy persistently levelled against the national system of education was the monopoly of teacher training enjoyed by the board through its model schools and national training college in Dublin. The Powis report, which was published in 1870, made satisfactory recommendations in this respect: the models should be phased out and financial support given to denominational training colleges. In 1871 the bishops resolved to ask Cardinal Cullen to take immediate steps to establish a central training school, and sixteen of their number proved their earnestness in this respect by subscribing £100 each. Gladstone's government, however, chose to devote its final attempt at conciliating Irish Catholics to a solution of the university problem. When it fell on this issue no initiatives had been taken in primary education. In 1873 as university reform had loomed closer, Cardinal Cullen and Bartholomew Woodlock, the rector of the Catholic University, made plans to extend it so that it would embrace a number of colleges, including a training college, and, as a result, draw wider benefits from the anticipated changes. They proposed to locate the training college near the University and place it under the care of the Vincentians.

41 M.N., 20 Aug. 1885.
42 The first report covered the year 1879.

Some bishops hoped for bigger educational concessions from the new Conservative government, and, when the Chief Secretary for Ireland, Sir Michael Hicks-Beach, promised to meet the demands of an Irish MP for higher salaries for teachers and for institutions to provide them with better professional training, they felt their hopes would not be disappointed. Accordingly Cullen and Woodlock decided to open a centre in Dublin which could take advantage of financial help as soon as it was offered. In November 1874 Hicks-Beach requested the board of national education to consider extending support to new training colleges, and received a favourable answer.[43] But Protestant, and especially Presbyterian, hostility to the proposal forced him to back-track, and in March 1875 he announced that the government had abandoned all plans for intervention in this contentious area.[44] In response to his investigations the commissioners supplied Hicks-Beach with statistics detailing the number of trained and untrained teachers in the national schools. These showed that 3,842 were trained and 6,118 untrained; of the trained 2,640 and of the untrained 5,007, or about five sixths, were Catholics.[45] Clearly, with or without state funds, the Catholic church would have to make some kind of training available, if it intended to maintain its ban on Catholics attending the commissioners' training college in Marlborough St.

Consequently, the bishops addressed this problem at the national synod of Maynooth in 1875 and appointed a committee from their body to manage a proposed college. The four members selected for this task were Dorrian, who became chairman, Conroy (Ardagh), Moran (Ossory) and Lynch (Kildare). Lynch had been a Vincentian, and it was hoped that he could liaise easily with his former colleagues; Conroy and Moran had taught in Clonliffe College and been former secretaries to Cardinal Cullen. Dorrian was the senior by age and episcopal appointment, and his nomination to this position was an acknowledgement by his colleagues of his concern about education and of his determination to tailor the national system to Catholic needs. The committee held its first meeting on the day of its appointment (17 September) and arranged that the recently purchased house at 2 Drumcondra Road — to be known as St Patrick's

---

43 *St Patrick's College, Centenary Booklet, 1875-1975* (Dublin,1975), pp 6-10.

44 Shortly after these proposals were announced the moderator of the General Assembly of the Presbyterian Church waited on the Lord-Lieutenant to remonstrate against the establishment of denominational training colleges. Memorials from the National Education League of Ireland and from the education committee of the General Assembly against changes in the national system and especially against non-vested training colleges were presented to the Lord-Lieutenant. (H.C. 1875 (201), lix, 569-74)

45 D.H. Akenson, *The Irish education experiment*, p.354.

Training College — was to be open for the reception of students six weeks later, on 31 October. The bishops had already agreed that the Vincentians would have charge of the general discipline and moral and religious formation of the students, and that the superior, with the approval of the episcopal committee, would appoint and, if necessary, remove staff. They had also decided that the college would be funded by diocesan contributions at the rate of £2 per parish, and the committee made arrangements to circularize all the bishops and parish priests in Ireland about the fund-raising methods that had been chosen.[46]

Dorrian sent a letter to each bishop, dated 7 October, announcing the opening of the college and leaving it to his discretion to decide whether the sum of £2 should be an offering from the priests, as the synod had recommended, or should be collected from the laity. The bishops were earnestly requested to send promising subjects to the college, and the hope was expressed that, with the cordial and generous co-operation of the hierarchy and clergy, the project would be successful and soon be recognized by the state.[47]

The co-operation which the episcopal committee duly received may have been cordial, but it was certainly not generous. Two years later it submitted a report to the assembled bishops, reminded them of their own rule about subscriptions and enclosed a statement which showed that only £1,901 had been received from the sum of £4,382 that was due. Three dioceses — Waterford, Down and Connor, and Elphin — had contributed more than their share, and four had contributed nothing. In the Armagh province Kilmore had paid nothing, Meath had paid £3 out of £268 due, Ardagh £30 out of £164, Derry £72 out of £148, Raphoe £81 out of £104, Dromore £61 out of £72, Armagh £42 out of £220, Clogher had paid the exact amount and Down and Connor had given £15 extra. In its early years about two thirds of the bishops made personal contributions — mostly £100 — and Dorrian was among the faithful number who subscribed annually. In accordance with a decision taken in 1876, one half of the sum subscribed by each diocese was set aside to pay for students whom the bishop had recommended; at the end of the second academic year Down and Connor had eight students — the largest number from any diocese — receiving grants from the diocesan fund, and seven teachers who had been trained in the college — again the largest number — had been appointed to schools. The report and accompanying facts, both financial and

---

46 Minutes of the committee of St Patrick's Training College, Dublin. A.S.P.T.C.D.
47 Ibid.

educational, left no doubt about the earnestness of Dorrian's commitment to Catholic teacher training.[48]

However, despite the slow response from many of the dioceses the committee extended its premises and opened a boys' school to give the trainees practical experience. Consequently, the president of St. Patrick's was forced to appeal to clergy and laity for funds to cover capital as well as running costs. By October 1878 the debt had reached £1,172 and the committee resolved to ask each bishop for £20 for the building fund. In view of the development and costs involved, the committee was aggrieved that, despite the decrees of the synod, 42 Catholic men were being trained in Marlborough St. and only 31 in their institution, though 59 had received training there during the whole year. The archbishop of Dublin bailed out the committee with a loan, and, despite further prodding, the president was again forced in 1880 to send out a list of arrears to all the bishops. This showed that Down and Connor, Dublin and Elphin were the only dioceses which owed nothing; seven dioceses still owed more than £150 each and the total arrears came to £2,346.[49]

Dorrian was not present at the committee meeting in 1880 which took the decision to ask the archbishop of Dublin to communicate with the Chief Secretary and press urgently on the government the claims of Catholics for a system of training which they could conscientiously use. It is unlikely that he would have put much trust in the goodwill of the new Liberal administration — but financial pressures were propelling the bishops to seek help. The training college did not have the resources necessary for proper development, was in fact bedevilled by debts to the end and ran the risk of not passing the inspection that was likely to be carried out by the commissioners of education, if grants materialized. The hierarchy called again for aid for denominational training colleges in 1881, and their case was strengthened by the financial difficulties which plagued the Church of Ireland college in Kildare Place. In 1883 the Liberals were ready to make a gesture of conciliation, and the Chief Secretary suggested to the commissioners that grants should be made available to colleges under local patronage on the English model. The management of such colleges was to be left in private hands, the board of education was to determine the courses and examine the students, and grants of £50 for men and £35 for women were to be offered, depending on the success of the college in examinations and in teaching over a two year period, provided the total sum did not exceed three quarters of the approved expenditure.

The episcopal committee met in May to review their plans in the light of this development. They inspected their buildings on Drum-

[48] Cullen papers, D.D.A.
[49] Ibid.

condra Road, and, as Bishop Moran subsequently explained, they were all 'quite unprepared to find the dormitories & other departments in such a state of filth & dirt'.[50] They realized that they would have to find some more suitable building and, despite an initial anxiety about expense, purchased Belvedere House, Drumcondra from the Christian Brothers. They also planned to submit the Baggot St. convent training school, which the Sisters of Mercy had been operating for the approval of the board of national education. The new arrangements did not specify how many colleges could be set up, so that finance became the crucial factor governing their establishment. Bishop Gillooly of Elphin, who took as much interest in education as Dorrian, was very disappointed with the government's plan;[51] he could not foresee sufficient money being available to set up an adequate number of provincial colleges. Dorrian must also have toyed with the idea of opening a college for the north. Sir Patrick Keenan, the resident commissioner of national education, who worked closely and harmoniously with the bishops in launching the new scheme, reported to Cardinal McCabe (Cullen's successor in Dublin) in June that Dorrian's proposed college might be initiated during the year.[52] But Dorrian quickly decided that this was not immediately possible. Moran informed McCabe, a week after Keenan wrote, that the project of four provincial colleges was not feasible;[53] the most that could be attempted was one in Cork and a national one in Dublin, and he went on to say that several of the bishops of the west and north would patronize the national college in Dublin, and that Dorrian would not think of establishing one at present, being 'entirely in favour of having one large National one well carried on in Dublin'.

The old training college ceased to exist and four bishops, including Dorrian, were deputed to sell it and clear off all its debts. Belvedere House was placed under the charge of Cardinal McCabe, who entrusted it to the Vincentians, was accepted by the commissioners of national education as suitable for 100 students and opened its doors to 74 in September 1883. The archbishop of Dublin provided the necessary funds until a loan was made a few years later by the Board of Works. In the second academic year the number of students increased to 137, the results of the examinations were very satisfactory and the new St Patrick's soon achieved the success that had eluded its predecessor. Two years later seven of its students originated from Down and Connor.[54]

50 Moran to McCabe, 14 June 1883, D.D.A.
51 Gillooly to McCabe, 23 Aug., 9 Sept. 1883, D.D.A.
52 Keenan to McCabe, 10 June 1883, D.D.A.
53 Moran to McCabe, 17 June 1883, D.D.A.
54 *Report of St Patrick's Training College, Drumcondra for the session 1885-6* (Dublin,1886), p.2.

Dorrian, however, did not abandon his intention of founding a training college at some future date. Significantly, it was he who seconded the resolution proposed by Gillooly of Elphin in October 1884 that the bishops deemed it an indispensable condition for the extension of the new training college system and for the adequate training of teachers that the grants from the Treasury should cover the whole authorized expenditure of the colleges, and that grants and loans should be given for the erection of suitable buildings outside Dublin; without those amendments, primary education and, indeed the good order of society, would suffer. Dorrian, however, did not live long enough to pursue whatever ideas he may have had about provincial colleges. Much of his remaining time was spent preparing for the meeting of the bishops with the officials of Propaganda in Rome and then an illness supervened. A college for women students was established in Belfast fifteen years after his death.

Dorrian's contribution to the establishment of St Patrick's Training College was a convincing proof of his real commitment to denominational primary education; when other bishops, who joined in passing the same resolutions about the rights of their people to have schools reflecting their faith and ethos, neglected to organize collections and allowed their training college to drift into virtual bankruptcy, Dorrian put his money where his mouth was, and both by his financial and personal efforts did his utmost to ensure that properly trained Catholic teachers, without whom the kind of education they aspired to could not be had, would be available in increasing, if still inadequate, numbers.

VI

If Dorrian regarded the provision of national schools under Catholic management as a primary pastoral responsibility, his interest in secondary and tertiary education was no less keen, even though both these branches were the preserve of that small section of people that could afford to pay for them and consequently touched but a tiny proportion of the entire population. By 1860 the bishops had come to realize that without government support they could do little in tertiary education, but in the secondary field they felt an obligation to maintain diocesan colleges not only to feed the major seminaries but also to afford opportunities for those boys who might wish to proceed to professional or commercial careers. And they relied on the expanding orders of nuns to provide a similar kind of education for girls.

When Dorrian was approached in 1861 about affiliating the diocesan college to the Catholic University, he replied enthusiastically to the rector's invitation. He had hopes that this policy would have beneficial results both in the secondary and tertiary sectors of education, and would improve the academic standing of St Malachy's:

> Now in this town there is a great cry for a respectable Catholic school, & many not having confidence in our Seminary, have their boys at Protestant Schools. The Bishop wonders at this, but some parents think young Priests not good teachers, however good preachers they be, & prefer sending their children elsewhere.[55]

St Malachy's was duly affiliated, and this meant that a university examiner visited it annually to conduct the matriculation and scholarship examinations. A student who was successful could pursue his studies for the faculty of Philosophy and Letters for two years in the College before proceeding to the University, where he completed the course for the baccalaureate.

On succeeding to the see Dorrian moved quickly to enlarge St Malachy's and to bring the academic and residential departments together on the same campus. Boarding accommodation was provided for 100 boys, and the chapel and refectory were designed to seat 200 and 150, respectively. But by 1867, when he made a formal report on his diocese to Rome, all these places had not been taken up; there were then 30 boarders and 80 day pupils. To correspond with this expansion the College was given enhanced status: a president was appointed and the staff was increased to five, of whom three were priests and two laymen.[56]

In 1870 another secondary school known as Down Classical Academy was established at Downpatrick under a diocesan priest, Charles Church. Provision was made for boarders to lodge in the town but the numbers attending remained small, and the Academy had a very short life. Two secondary schools for girls also opened in 1870: the Dominican nuns established a boarding and day school in Belfast and a French order, the Sisters of the Sacred Heart of Mary, established one in Lisburn. The Mercy Sisters in Downpatrick also extended their school to include boarding facilities for girls wishing to obtain secondary education and their order in Belfast established a secondary department.

St Malachy's College, however, engaged Dorrian's solicitude and sympathies much more than the others. It was a direct diocesan responsibility, and the bishop not only personally appointed its

55 Dorrian to Woodlock, 21 Jan. 1862, D.D.A.
56 Dorrian to Propaganda, A.P.F. S.C.(Irlanda), 35, ff 1087r-1092r.

clerical staff but also concerned himself intimately in its development, expansion and progress. After 1871 the number of free places at Maynooth was drastically reduced, and as a consequence the bishop found it cheaper to detain aspirants to the priesthood longer in St Malachy's and have them read some or all of the courses in humanity, rhetoric, logic or natural philosophy which were taken in Maynooth before the study of theology. In 1872-3 six of the ten students who entered Maynooth for the diocese passed directly into the theology course. The staff was increased not only to deal with these seminarians but also to cope with the increase in secondary pupils.

Since there were no official state examinations for secondary schools, St Malachy's held public examinations of its pupils once or twice annually, to allow parents to monitor their childrens' progress and to advertise its merits to others who might be encouraged to send their sons to it. Often as many as twenty clergy attended and Dorrian usually used the occasion to defend the principle of Catholic education and encourage support for Catholic schools. He once remarked that some Protestants had studied in St Malachy's and retained happy memories of their student days, and promised Protestant parents that, if their children enrolled in it, they would there be assured of a sound secular education, a good moral tone and no interference with their religious convictions.[57] It seems unlikely, however, that more than a handful of Protestants ever attended it; they had sufficient opportunity for studying in an environment more in keeping with their own traditions.

Dorrian, like many of his episcopal colleagues, chafed at the absence of state support or endowments for secondary education and proclaimed his willingness to accept a system of payment according to the results of examinations.[58] When this was eventually conceded in 1878, he welcomed it warmly, described it as the fairest measure ever given to the Catholics of Ireland and looked forward to St Malachy's carrying off a fair share of the prizes at the first Intermediate examinations.[59] He encouraged the further

57 U.Ex., 22 July 1873.
58 At the examinations held in the Christian Brothers' School in Oxford St. in 1878, Dorrian declared: 'We say to the Government: give us a system of education, elementary, intermediate, or university on the principle of payment by results and we will be perfectly satisfied. We can never be satisfied with a system that endows some establishments and excludes others on denominational grounds'. (U.Ex., 12 Feb. 1878.)
59 He had, however, one reservation: he did not think this legislation should apply in the same way to girls. He explained that far from wishing to limit in any way the intellectual attainments of ladies, he favoured the passing of an act of parliament which would provide an education suited to their sex, wants and position in society so that they would make better wives and be better prepared to discharge in society those duties for which they were especially equipped. But he could not approve of 'an attempt to subvert society and to establish a blue stocking in every family by the

expansion of the College in 1881-82, personally contributing £1,500 to the costs which exceeded £14,000. In that year he reported to Rome that the staff consisted of six priests and six laymen, and the students numbered 70 boarders and 150 day pupils — an increase of over fifty per cent since 1867.[60] The academic achievements of the pupils in the first years of the Intermediate examinations handsomely repaid the trouble and toil of developing the College. In 1883 Dorrian wrote cheerfully and enthusiastically: 'Our college stands third in all Ireland and first, considering proportion in numbers'.[61] With the establishment of the Royal University the distinction between secondary and tertiary education was blurred, as students from all colleges were free to sit the university examinations. Dorrian consequently aspired to develop third level studies in St Malachy's, and with its expansion envisaged it as a university or arts college for the Catholics of Ulster. Fittingly St Malachy's was chosen to play a special part in the celebrations that marked the golden jubilee of his episcopal ordination. And though the president over-indulged in the grandiloquent language customary on such occasions, when, in an address, he saluted the bishop's contribution to the development of St Malachy's, nonetheless the achievement in view of the financial demands being made for so many other diocesan institutions was impressive:

> As the zeal of your great predecessor, St Malachy, restored and imparted lustre to the schools of Bangor, so under your fostering care the old Seminary of Vicinage has been ennobled, enlarged and developed into the present college, with its spacious halls and stately proportions. St Malachy's College is a standing monument to Your Lordship's solicitude and zeal in the cause of Catholic education.[62]

By the end of Dorrian's episcopate the Catholic community in the Belfast area was well supplied with secondary schools for both boys and girls, and Downpatrick had a secondary school for girls. The rest of the diocese was less favoured but boarding places in Belfast were available for those who could afford to pay for such accommodation. St Malachy's had undoubtedly achieved distinction, but part of the price paid for this had involved a wearing and damaging struggle with the Christian Brothers.

introduction of a system of education which would not be in keeping with the position of females'. (B.M.N., 20 July 1878.)
60 Dorrian to Propaganda, A.P.F., S.C.(Irlanda), 39, ff 658r-665r.
61 Dorrian to Kirby, 22 Nov. 1883, A.I.C.R.
62 M.N. 20 Aug. 1855.

VIII

Dorrian's invitation to the Christian Brothers to staff a school in Belfast was one of his first pastoral and educational initiatives. It was a move that was warmly and spontaneously welcomed especially by the better informed and more articulate members of his flock, who were conscious of the handicaps facing the children of their working class co-religionists through limited opportunities for education and who felt that keen and dedicated educators, as the Brothers were reputed to be, could so raise the standards that all could avail of them. The bishop at first proposed to ask the teachers in the Donegall St. schools to transfer to the new school he had erected in Barrack St. and bring the Brothers to Donegall St. But to avoid inconvenience he changed his plans and offered them the new school. The emissary whom they sent in 1866 to investigate the situation took an unfavourable view of the facilities on offer in Barrack St., which he claimed were 'too small for the *Eclat* which should surround their first beginning in Belfast.' However, the promise of the Donegall St. schools seemed to satisfy him, and Dorrian agreed to improve their furnishings and equipment and to have them available by Christmas. But to his great chagrin the emissary, on his return to Dublin, reported that the Donegall St. schools were totally 'unsuited', even though the teachers in them had by then agreed to move, and, to make matters worse, the Brothers who had been earmarked for Belfast had been posted elsewhere.[63] Dorrian persisted and immediately after the departure of Cardinal Cullen, who had come to Belfast for the dedication of St Peter's Church, renewed his offer to the superior general of either school, or both, as soon as he had completed another for which the plans had been approved by the town council. He also offered a guaranteed income of £30 per year for each Brother or £100 for every three.[64]

Despite misgivings the Brothers decided to accept the offer, and on receipt of Dorrian's letter, James A. Hoare, the superior general, replied that they would leave for Belfast on a symbolic date, the feast day of St Malachy (3 November), and commence work within the octave. Taking up Dorrian's suggestion that it would be easier for the Brothers themselves to supervise the provision of adequate and proper equipment in the schools, he arranged that the superior of the little group would co-ordinate this work with the bishop.[65] On 12 November the four Brothers began work in Barrack St. and admitted

---

[63] Dorrian to Br R.A. Maxwell, 23 Sept. 1866 in Foundations and their resources, MS, A.C.B.G.R.
[64] Ibid., 17 Oct. 1866.
[65] Ibid., Hoare to Dorrian, 23 Oct. 1866.

300 boys to their classes. Their arrival was enthusiastically greeted by the Catholics of Belfast.

In November 1867 they were given charge of the St Patrick's schools in Donegall St. in addition to their schools in Barrack St. In April 1874 St Malachy's School in Oxford St., funded for the most part by a bequest of £2,000, opened to receive 160 boys; two Brothers were appointed to staff it, and with three in Barrack St. and six in Donegall St. their number, including the superior, increased to twelve inside eight years.

The schools likewise prospered and increased. When D.C. Richmond, the area inspector of the national board, visited Donegall St. and Barrack St. for the Powis Commission, he found enrolments of 566 and 388 with attendances of 513 and 339, respectively; few schools could boast of such a high percentage of their enrolled pupils being present on any given day. Richmond remarked that every national school might envy that attendance record and added that the Brothers' position was so strong that they could afford to expel irregular boys. Though he questioned the result of the disciplinary methods employed, which he feared was opposed 'to the formation of that robustness and independence of character which a greater freedom tends to promote', even if 'true and earnest adherents of the Church' were thereby formed, he was nonetheless immensely impressed by the strict order he found in the schools and admitted that he had seen 'many National Schools which are models of good order, but in none have I witnessed such a soldier-like precision of discipline as is attained in the schools of the Christian Brothers in Belfast'. He was greatly struck by the popularity of the Brothers which he attributed to the expressed predilections of the priests, and in the case of poor parents to the 'professedly gratuitous character of instruction', and observed that, if any further motive were required to explain this preference, it was to be found 'in the attraction presented by lives of devotion and self-sacrifice, and from the spirit of enthusiasm which the Brothers throw into their work'. They were more cultivated men than the average national schoolteacher.

However, Richmond put his finger unerringly on one of the issues that contributed to the controversy between the bishop and the Brothers: the background of the pupils who frequented their schools. He noted that the order no longer adhered strictly to the condition of poverty which their rules prescribed in the choice of pupils, that in fact they tried to attract the sons of the Catholic bourgeoisie and that as a result their schools showed less signs of poverty than any others which he had visited. The 'ragged schools', which were also located in Barrack St., contained a large minority of Catholic boys who should have had first claim on the Brothers, but these 'ragged Arabs' were free to attend an exclusively Protestant school with no guarantee for their religious liberty beyond the good sense of the ladies who managed it and the teachers whom they employed. The parents who could afford to send their sons to the Model School had withdrawn them at the exhortation of their clergy and filled the Brothers' schools to the exclusion of others; in the higher class in Barrack St., seventeen out of the thirty five boys, whom he had examined, had transferred from the Model. Consequently, the Christian Brothers in Belfast had become 'a sort of lower-middle-class school corporation' and, to the intense annoyance of the teachers of the Catholic national schools, had attracted their best and most remunerative pupils, and from that social class which could supply the most suitable students they rejected the incorrigibles and retained 'the crème de la crème'.[66]

Dorrian was probably so glad to see the Catholic children leaving the Model for the Brothers' school that this social question did not initially disturb him. In 1871 he invited the Brothers to staff a boys' Industrial School, which had been established in temporary premises two years earlier, and which he hoped to re-locate in the country, leaving behind only the boys who were apprenticed to trades.[67] But the superior general replied that he had already promised to send staff to schools in six other towns, apart from having to increase the staff at the Artane Industrial School in Dublin.[68] A disappointed Dorrian appealed again to Hoare, reminding him of the needs of a locality 'where opposition is so rife' and pointing out that the application for Belfast had preceded that for Artane,[69] but to no effect. Three years later the superior general did send additional Brothers for the new St Malachy's schools but by then tension between his colleagues and the bishop had surfaced.

For some years after their arrival in Belfast the Brothers found their financial situation rather difficult. The bishop paid them a modest stipend for their personal upkeep, but they volunteered to equip the schools with blackboards, books, maps, writing materials, and other requirements. The average weekly receipts from 400 boys in Barrack St. from November 1866 to May 1867 was £1.13s.4d. and, because of the initial outlay, the school was more than £99 in

66 *Powis Commission*, pp 236-9. pt ii, vol.ii.
67 Dorrian to Hoare, 7 Jan. 1871. Copy in Foundations and resources MS, A.C.B.G.R. The industrial school for boys was first established in Donegall St. in 1869. Two years later it moved to Milltown House and obtained a government grant with permission to maintain 65 boys, who were taught various trades. It was enlarged and reconstructed in 1873 at a cost of £770. A similar school for girls was conducted by the Sisters of Mercy on the Crumlin Road. By 1874 the girls' school contained 16 voluntary pupils and 50 who were detained by court order. Both schools were under the patronage of St Patrick.
68 Hoare to Dorrian, 14 Jan. 1871, Ibid.
69 Dorrian to Hoare, 23 Jan. 1871, Ibid.

debt. Two years later, when enrolments had been doubled, and the fees received from the pupils amounted to £144.6s.8d for the year, the Brothers' debt on school expenses was reduced to £36 but their expenditure on their private residence still exceeded their income by more than £14.[70] Gradually, by judicious use of their meagre resources, and by the spartan deployment of educational facilities in the classroom, the debts were brought under control.

As the budget was tight, the Brothers were concerned when the annual collection for their personal maintenance was not announced in St Patrick's Church in March 1872. The local superior, Lewis Caton, not only drew the bishop's attention to the omission, but also detailed some of their expenditure, which made it difficult for them to live within their incomes. Dorrian took advantage of this opening to unburden himself of some of the reservations he had been forming about the community.

He pointed out that the poverty of the offerings was the consequence of the great dissatisfaction of many people at their teaching children who ought to be in other schools, 'whilst you refuse the poorer ones on the plea of "no room" '. He reminded Caton that it had always been his intention that the Brothers, on coming to Belfast, 'would afford the poor — *not the rich* — the opportunity of a good christian education' but that both clergy and people had now got 'a contrary impression' and 'satisfaction is not the result'. He then raised other complaints: the Brothers' schools were more expensive than the national schools and boys were not allowed to absent themselves from class to serve Mass. Referring to a request that had been made for further equipment for the Brothers' residence — the replacement of blankets and sheets — he wondered why, had proper care been taken, such a request should have been necessary after such a short time, suggested that the people could not be burdened as a result of extravagance and pointed out that, if the Brothers kept their part of the bargain, he would keep his. Expressing his regrets that the clergy and the Brothers were not co-operating more harmoniously, he concluded by referring to the practice of making public collections to bring the pupils on excursions and expressed his disapproval of this practice 'as it gives a handle to objections' (though he did not specify if these were political or financial).[71]

Brother Caton replied to this barrage of charges as soon as he had assembled evidence to deny the accusation of not educating the poor. Explaining that some boys were refused admission to Barrack St. when it was first opened, because of shortage of space due to their taking 120 boys from the Model School, 'a class of boys the Brothers were most anxious to receive as well on account of the peculiar

---

70 Receipt and expenditure returns, MS, pp 338-40, A.C.B.G.R.
71 Dorrian to Caton, 20 Mar. 1872, A.C.B.G.R.

circumstances of their case as in compliance with your Lordship's own wishes in their regard', he insisted that even then 'the great majority of the children belonged to the humbler ranks of life, some of whom were of the destitute class' and maintained 'respectfully but emphatically' that, since the Brothers were given charge of the Donegall St. school, 'no poor child was ever refused permission . . . on the plea of "no room"'. Then, coming to a crucial issue which Dorrian had not raised but which lay behind the charge of educating the rich and which he and some of the priests had made orally, namely, that boys whose parents could afford the fees should be attending St Malachy's College, Caton pointed to the difficulty facing the Brothers on this score, when parents presented children for admission. He claimed that, by going out of his way to refuse admittance to boys of that class, he had only antagonized the parents, with the result that they refused to send their children to St Malachy's and instead sent them to other schools, including the Model.

To substantiate his defence Caton prepared and submitted to the bishop a list of the occupations of the parents of children then attending both schools[72] and left the bishop to draw his own conclusions. With reference to the charge that the Brothers' schools cost more than the national schools, he maintained that, if taxation were taken into account, the national schools were more expensive, and he explained that his confrères could not compete with the national schools in providing very cheap books, though the cost of theirs was as moderate as they could make them. Caton expressed his regret that relations with the clergy were not better, recalled that their plans for teaching catechism on Sundays had been overruled and promised co-operation in providing Mass servers in future. He denied that they had been extravagant; their income was small, being less than two shillings per day, and therefore less than half that of a labourer, and they had incurred heavy medical expenses extending over a long period due to illness, and the additional costs of replacements for the sick in the schools. He promised that the excursions, which had been first organized not by the Brothers but by 'externs in the town', would be discontinued, and suggested that any inconvenience or embarrassment associated with the collection would be removed, if the Brothers were themselves allowed to take up a collection during a fixed period of time each year and to support themselves from the proceeds.[73]

72 608 parents with the following occupations were listed: labourers, 209; tradesmen, 190; clerks, 13; small shopkeepers, 60; publicans, 5; orphans (whose fathers were dead), 60; butchers, 11; process servers, car drivers, pensioners, policemen, 48; pawnbroker, 1; solicitor, 1; inspector of national schools, 1; flax-buyers, 7; and builders, 2.
73 Caton to Dorrian, 29 Mar. 1872, Ibid. Caton also pointed out that he had stopped the collection for the boys' excursion when he heard about a bazaar being

Dorrian was not mollified. Informing Caton, in reply, that he had submitted the Brothers' defence to the clergy of Belfast, he objected to the implication that he had only 'allowed' them a small income and insisted that the sum fixed before their coming to Belfast was larger than the income which their superior told him was customary.[74] Strangely, the list of parents' occupations had failed to disprove the charge of the Brothers educating the children of the rich: 'those able to judge say that there will be found 100 of the children who ought not to occupy the places of the poorer ones who cannot pay and are the waifs in need of your charitable aid. It is not surprising that many should object to pay for the education of such well-to-do children as your lists present'. The clergy, he explained, were afraid that other religious communities would also request similar collections and charities would begin to compete with each other. The letter ended on a note of exasperation, as Dorrian reminded Caton that Barrack St. school was built by copper donations and Donegall St. by public and diocesan subscriptions, and asked querulously 'why should comfortable parents be allowed to exclude the poor for whom they were built?'[75]

But the inablilty of the Brothers to meet their expenses, which were further increased by sickness in the community, and their subsequent threat to pull out of one of the schools, forced the bishop to give some ground. When one of the assistants to the superior general presented these facts to him, he countered, firmly, that they themselves were to blame for the disappointing results from the collections, for they had refused to give wholehearted co-operation to the clergy in taking them up. The Brothers responded vigorously to these complaints by pointing out that the size of the collection was a matter of indifference to them, since they were limited to a fixed stipend, which he would not offer his butler or coachman, and assuring him that, if the practice that obtained in Dublin, Cork, Limerick or Derry were followed, whereby they were allowed to take up their own collection each year and have a charity sermon as well, much greater satisfaction would result. This concession was granted, and one bone of contention was accordingly removed.[76]

Whatever about clerical hostility, the Brothers continued to enjoy the favour of the Catholic public. Not only did they receive a generous bequest, which enabled them to open schools in Oxford St. in 1874 but in the following year a further bequest facilitated the

organized. This would indicate that the bishop objected to the excursions because they competed with other fund-raising activities.

74 In some towns in Ireland the Brothers received a stipend of £35 or £40 each per year. The collections from which this income was derived often exceeded these amounts.

75 Dorrian to Caton, 5 Apr. 1872. A.C.B.G.R.

76 J. Hearn 'Abstract of the establishments of the institute with their legal rights, their resources and liabilities', MS, p.542. A.C.B.G.R.

extension and renovation of the Barrack St. school. As there were no state examinations to test the success of pupils at that time, some schools had long since established the practice of holding their own examinations in the presence of parents and distinguished visitors. The Christian Brothers adopted this practice in 1877, and the bishop and fourteen clergy were present at an examination in Oxford St. in 1878. On that occasion Dorrian, looking forward to the introduction of the Intermediate Education Act, which promised to reward teachers in proportion to the academic success of their pupils in public examinations, expressed his confidence that children educated in their denominational schools would carry off their full share of the prizes.[77] In the event the introduction of this Act caused a further and deeper rift between the bishop and the Brothers, which was still unhealed when Dorrian died.

But even before this contretemps occurred in Belfast, tension had arisen at a wider level between the hierarchy and the Christian Brothers. At the national synod of Maynooth in 1875 the bishops passed legislation which the Brothers regarded as a diminution of the rights assigned to them by Pope Pius VII in 1820 in the brief ratifying their constitutions.

They objected to a decree which laid down that the bishops were to ensure that the constitutions which had been approved for the Institute were observed. They claimed that this endowed the bishops not only with spiritual oversight but also with the right to interfere in the temporal administration of their houses, to adjust their rules and ultimately change their whole system of government. The bishops replied that their purpose was merely to insist that the Brothers obey the regulations imposed by the appropriate ecclesiastical authorities. The Brothers also took exception to a decree which empowered a parish priest, his curate or an episcopal delegate to visit their schools to teach Christian doctrine and, in accordance with episcopal regulations, examine the children both in religious and secular subjects. They insisted that they had always made provision for the clergy to give religious instruction and examine their children in the catechism, but they feared that general examinations by those not acquainted with their special teaching methods could lead to misunderstandings, friction and unsatisfactory results. The bishops insisted that clergy enjoyed the right to examine the children in the national schools on secular subjects. The third area of dispute concerned the vesting of property in trustees and the right of the

---

77 U.Ex., 12 Feb. 1878. Presumably the Brothers felt that the pupils at their schools were included in this prediction. In thanking the bishop for presiding, Brother Slattery commented that during his twenty years experience as a director of a religious community he had not received from any patron as much uniform, kind and effective sympathy as Dorrian had shown him since coming to Belfast.

bishop or his delegate to check the accounts of the parochial schools of which the Brothers had charge. They maintained that the episcopal regulations about vesting parochial schools and the goods belonging to them in the bishop's name, and in those of trustees of whom he approved, involved the sequestration of their own property, which they had acquired by their own industry and from the patrimony of their members. The bishops argued that their legislation did not apply to the private possessions of the Brothers, nor to any donations or legacies they might have received; the decrees concerned only what belonged to parishes, and the regulations about checking the accounts of schools applied only to those which were parochial. There were of course many grey areas where ownership was not fully clear, especially where clergy had sponsored collections for the establishment of Brothers' schools with the general understanding that the Institute had special rights beyond those of national teachers.[78]

Both sides presented extensive cases at Rome, and a final verdict was given in 1880. This overruled the decree calling on bishops to ensure that the constitutions were observed, with the reservation that, if the bishops were aware of the non-observance of rules, they were to report the matter to the superior general, and, if he took no action, to the Holy See. The bishops or their delegates were authorized to conduct examinations on religious but not on secular subjects. Innovations in the methods of holding or administering property were excluded, with the result that the Brothers were entitled to act as trustees for property left to the schools, and to retain and acquire the rights of trusteeship.[79] This was a substantial victory for them and was strongly resented by many of the bishops.[80]

In 1879, when the first examinations under the Intermediate Education Act were held, this wider dispute was still unresolved. The misunderstanding and suspicion surrounding it were not conducive to harmonious relations between both parties at a local level. And though the Intermediate Act was designed to benefit secondary

[78] The disputed decrees were 303, 307, 308, 309 and 310. *Acta et decreta synodi plenariae episcoporum Hiberniae habitae apud Maynutiam* (Dublini, MDCC-CLXXVII)

[79] A.P.F., *Acta*, 248, f.77r.

[80] Some of the bishops wanted to reopen the case in the following year. Bishop Moran informed Tobias Kirby (5 Sept. 1881, A.I.C.R.) that Archbishop McCabe and Dorrian were anxious to have the decree *Romanos Pontifices*, which enhanced episcopal authority vis-a-vis religious orders in England, extended to Ireland. Adjustments were eventually made to this decision by Propaganda in 1885. The bishops were empowered to appoint a non-member of the Institute as one of the trustees of those parochial schools, of which all three trustees were Brothers. And an episcopal delegate was empowered to order a general examination, even in secular subjects, if after a written test he felt this was necessary.

schools, the distinction between primary and secondary was not drawn so finely as to exclude primary schools from preparing their senior classes for the examinations. The temptation to do so was obviously strong; success would bring financial rewards, prestige and the enhanced support of parents and benefactors. But Dorrian envisaged St Malachy's College as the exclusive centre of secondary education for Catholic boys in Belfast. He had already poured a lot of money into it, and in 1881-82 enlarged it further. His future plans for St Malachy's were threatened by the prospect of the Brothers developing successful secondary departments in their schools.

The bishop's coldness to the Brothers was shared by some, at least, of the Belfast clergy. In a long and angry letter reflecting a mood of frustration and disgust, James Slattery, the Belfast superior, explained the difficult and painful situation of the community to the superior general. 'For a considerable time', he began, 'we are in hot water with some of our local clergy', and then went on to charge these priests with trying to destroy their character as teachers by not allowing boys to go from the national schools to their schools and by encouraging their pupils to transfer to the seminary or the national schools. To achieve this result they downgraded the standards, both social and academic, obtaining in the Brothers' schools, pointed to the unsuitability of their past pupils for the civil service, and applied every kind of pressure to their fourteen successful candidates in the recent Intermediate examinations to induce them to transfer to St Malachy's. They further charged the Brothers with breaking their own rules by teaching chemistry, French and Latin, and accused them of not being competent to teach anything beyond the three Rs. Accordingly, a deputation of four Brothers went to complain to the bishop, 'thinking he would not tolerate such low, mean, shabby work on the part of his clergy' but, to their regret, found that he approved of the priests' action and emphasized that he wanted the Christian Brothers to confine themselves to the 3Rs, that it was his wish that any talented boys, rich or poor, would go to the diocesan seminary, and that 'with that establishment he would not allow anything to clash'. Furthermore, he pointed out that he intended to open Intermediate schools in connexion with the seminary and that he had given instructions to his priests and ecclesiastical examiner 'to select smart intelligent boys for that said place'.

Slattery went on to repeat the allegation made against them by the clergy of teaching the rich and not the poor, claiming that the clergy were not open to conviction on this score, and this despite the result of an inspection on this matter carried out by a priest on the bishop's orders, which revealed that their pupils, with very few exceptions, were indeed very poor and much poorer than those in the Eliza St. national school. When told by the bishop to discontinue teaching

Latin, they protested that their few monitors, who had begun the study of that subject, had already bought the appropriate books, and were then given permission to continue it until the end of the academic year. Slattery drew the obvious conclusion that their schools would sink in popular estimation under these restrictions, and predicted that they would be accused of failure. Exhorting his superior to defend their character from the unjust charges levelled against them, he pointed out that no dedicated teacher would tolerate such limitations on his work, and, then, allowing his exasperation to triumph over his equilibrium, expressed the wish that he and his community

> could step on board a ship at the Quay of Belfast and go to any part of the world where we could establish a home for ourself [sic] and be far removed from Irish soil, where we are subjected to galling tyranny of the most despotic type. You may take Dr Dorrian as the true exponent of Episcopal feeling in Ireland in our regard.[81]

Stunned by this fusillade, the superior general obviously inquired if Dorrian had actually declared that they should limit their teaching to the three Rs. Slattery insisted that he had explicitly given those directions, and, while admitting that he did not 'exactly say' that those who were successful in the Intermediate examinations should transfer to St Malachy's, maintained that 'he certainly meant as much'. Moreover, when Slattery explained that if they did not include in their curriculum the subjects which were taught in the national schools, some of their pupils would abandon them in favour of the national schools and the whole *raison d'être* of their Institute, 'the religious education of youth' would be completely frustrated, Dorrian had replied unsympathetically, 'well, let them go to the national schools'.[82]

Since not formally forbidden to enter pupils for the Intermediate examinations, the Brothers continued to do so. An uneasy truce existed for two or three years, but Dorrian contemplated submitting the dispute to the cardinal prefect of Propaganda. Perhaps realizing that it would be difficult for the congregation to give a ruling on an issue where there was little concrete evidence to rely on, he hesitated about doing so. But he entrusted one of his priests, who was visiting Rome, with the task of relaying his grievances to Tobias Kirby, the agent of the Irish bishops.[83] And relations between the clergy and the

81 Slattery to Hoare. The letter is dated October but from internal evidence and subsequent correspondence it seems certain that the year was 1879. A.C.B.G.R.
82 Ibid., 8 Dec. 1879.
83 Dorrian to Kirby, 24 Aug. 1881, A.I.C.R.

Brothers continued to deteriorate. Patrick Convery, the administrator of St Peter's Church, complained to Richard Maxwell, the superior general, of the non-cooperation of his colleagues in Barrack St. school: the national schools in the district had released boys for singing practice in his parish choir, but Brother Farrell[84] resolutely refused to give such permission, on the grounds that his pupils were preparing for the Intermediate examinations. Convery added that parents had complained that all the attention of the Brothers was devoted to those in the Intermediate classes, and reversing the charge that had been made against the clergy, accused the Brothers of trying to decoy the 'respectable children' from the national schools and of leaving the poor children behind, and thereby contradicting their original purpose in coming to Belfast.[85]

To Maxwell's reply, presumably to his query for evidence for the charge of decoying pupils from other schools, Convery instanced the case of two boys in a fatherless family who had been attending the Donegall St. school. He had arranged to pay the fees of the younger one at St Malachy's College, and, to his bewilderment, then heard that the Brothers had given orders to have the other one withdrawn from their school. To the repeated charge of teaching the rich Convery added the accusation that the Brothers were 'most exacting and unreasonable' in their annual house-to-house collections, and, for good measure, claimed that they had allowed the numbers enrolled in Donegall St. to drop almost by half and as a result there was 'a large number of children of the poor and ragged class roaming wild'. He concluded with a flourish or — from the point of view of the recipient — a very painful thrust: 'I think it is a strange thing to have the people of Belfast fleeced for the support of those Brothers and the poor neglected'.[86]

Convery, as he himself admitted, had been in touch with Dorrian about the substance of the first letter. Dorrian's patience was running out. He must have chided the superior general for the action of the Brothers in Belfast in allowing their pupils to attend some form of entertainment without supervision, and in his reply to Maxwell's explanation, pointed out that those pupils belonged to a class who should not be educated by collections taken up from people poorer than themselves. Then, apparently referring to that part of Maxwell's defence which had claimed that the Brothers had worked for him, he went on to issue an ultimatum:

---

84 This particular Brother was elsewhere singled out in the correspondence as being particularly uncooperative.
85 Convery to Maxwell, 11 July 1882, A.C.B.G.R.
86 Convery to Maxwell, 14 July 1882, Ibid.

At all events give up teaching the Classics; for, there is not room for two opposing institutions among Catholics in Belfast. In this they [the Brothers] have opposed my wishes for the last three years. In doing that they have not 'been working for me'.[87]

Since a knowledge of Latin was essential for any boy aspiring to the priesthood, this prohibition ensured that boys with that intention in mind would have to enroll in St Malachy's College. In insisting that aspirants to the priesthood should be educated in the local diocesan college, Dorrian was, of course, not exceptional; other Irish bishops enforced the same regulation. But in this case the restriction imposed on the Brothers had a much wider purpose than that of steering future priests to the local junior seminary. It was intended to ensure that that college was recognized as the sole secondary school for Catholic boys in Belfast, and that the Catholic community would have one strong, respected seat of learning able to compete with similar Protestant institutions, rather than have its resources dissipated among two or perhaps more institutions, all of which would in consequence be weak and academically undistinguished. The superior general, on receipt of this letter, immediately ordered his Belfast subordinate to discontinue the teaching of classics.[88] The prohibition against the teaching of Latin bore heavily on a few pupils who had already spent some time at that subject and wished to sit the examination in the following year. So the Brothers arranged that they would be coached outside school hours. But their choice of teacher, a student at the Queen's College, who was also teaching at Methodist College, only rubbed salt in the bishop's wounds. As Dorrian felt that his prohibition on Catholic students attending the Queen's College was somehow compromised by a student of that College being recognized by the Brothers as a suitable teacher for their pupils, he refused to approve. And he interpreted this arrangement as a devious circumvention of his orders and a wilful rejection of his authority, which he was not prepared to tolerate. As with the shareholders of the Catholic Institute and the Passionists, he insisted, firmly and brusquely, that episcopal authority could not be compromised:

> One thing I know, no one will be more friendly to the Brothers than I; but, if they set themselves in opposition to authority, I break with them and will not yield my trust.[89]

---

87 Dorrian to Maxwell, 11 Aug. 1882, Ibid.
88 Maxwell to Dorrian, 12 Aug. 1882 (copy in letterbook), Ibid.
89 Dorrian to Maxwell, 16 Oct. 1882, Ibid.

In his general report to Rome on the state of the diocese, which he forwarded in October 1882, the bishop referred to his grievances in general terms. Summarizing the history of his negotiations with the Brothers and the general and financial conditions on which agreement was reached, he accused them of being always discontented, especially with the financial arrangements, and promised to specify his complaints in a general statement which other bishops were making. Propaganda, in response to this, obviously called for an explanation from the superior general of the Brothers, and Maxwell submitted, among other documents, a copy of a recent reply to Dorrian about charges made by the bishop and some of the Belfast clergy.

Maxwell had visited Belfast in July to check on the vexed questions in dispute and to form his own judgement on the parental backgrounds of the students in the schools. He visited the classrooms, observed the dress and appearance of the pupils and submitted a full statement of the occupations of all the parents.[90] His observations convinced him that there was little affluence in the homes from which the children came. He pointed out that many were of the indigent class, and counted, in all, 260 children who were barefoot. In reply to Patrick Convery's comment that the numbers at St Patrick's schools had fallen drastically since their assuming charge of it, Maxwell quoted the official figures published by the board of national education for 1863 and 1864, which showed that the reverse had been the case. He rejected all accusations that the Brothers had enticed boys from other schools, but did admit that a Brother had been responsible for not sending boys forward to confession in the church, when asked to do so by the administrator.[91]

Dorrian passed on this letter to his clergy, and twenty six priests met in St Patrick's Presbytery, Belfast to consider it. In their analysis of its contents, which was forwarded to the bishop and subsequently to Rome, they devoted most space to commenting on the economic condition of the pupils' parents. They claimed that the poorest section of their people were the factory workers, and the small number of children of that class — 36 — who attended the Brothers' schools was a highly significant index of the status of the Brothers' students. They questioned the association of poverty with labourers, who, they maintained, earned good wages in Belfast and were, at that

---

90 The occupations of the parents of children at each school were listed separately and the totals were then given. The Brothers had in their schools children whose parents were: labourers, 234; clerks, 70; butchers, bakers, publicans, 139; and 36 whose fathers were dead.

91 Maxwell to Dorrian, 8 Sept. 1882. A.P.F. S.C.(Irlanda), 39, ff 715r-719r. Maxwell's figures for the enrolment at the Donegall St. schools were correct. The figures quoted by Convery and the Belfast clergy were wildly inaccurate.

time, on strike for twelve pence per hour. Artisans and sailors were also doing well and many of the latter were captains of vessels. The same could be said for the police, butchers, bakers and publicans. They concluded that over 500 children of well-off Catholics were attending the Brothers' schools. They repudiated the insinuation behind the figure for the barefoot children by pointing out that in the summer months, when Maxwell visited the schools, many children, who were not poor, chose to go that way to school. They repeated their complaint about the pupils not being sent forward when requested to confession, referred to particular cases of payment made for children to the Brothers, and contradicted the figure given by Maxwell for the enrolments in St Patrick's schools in 1864. Rejecting all suggestions of prejudice against the Brothers, they expressed their regret in the interests of charity and Catholicity at the role being played by the Brothers in Belfast. This letter, in Italian translation, was submitted to Propaganda, and whatever validity may have lain behind the priests' comments on the economic well-being of the parents involved — and few would be the cases in which an economist could detect anything approaching wealth — they were certainly lost on the Roman officials, who had no way of assessing the standards of living in a remote industrial town with an entirely different economic and monetary system from that to which they were accustomed.[92]

Maxwell, on receipt of the priests' interpretation of the financial standing of the Brothers' children, and conflicting evidence about particular points, must have written to Belfast for further explanations. Both the local superior and the community assured him in separate letters that the arguments against the poverty of the children were faulty, that many children paid nothing to their schools and that a great many paid no more than two or three pence each week. They challenged the priests' interpretation of labourers' incomes, argued that many of their children would not go to St Malachy's College because they could not pay the fees,[93] and claimed that their efforts to prepare their pupils for confession and Holy Communion had been made more difficult by the dates for these sacraments being changed by the clergy. Moreover, they regretted the spiritual consequences of the misunderstandings with the clergy; the priests of St Malachy's College, whose residence adjoined theirs, either did not celebrate Mass for them in the mornings or did so at unfixed and unsuitable times, with the result that they were forced

---

92 Belfast clergy to Dorrian, 11 Oct. 1882, Ibid., ff 744v-753r.
93 According to an advertisement in the B.M.N. of 2 Aug. 1882, day pupils at St Malachy's College in the higher grades paid £8 per year. Those in the middle, lower and preparatory grades paid £6, £4 and £2.10s.0d., respectively.

to go to a public Mass at a later, and inconvenient, hour in St Patrick's Church.[94]

Meanwhile the controversy had hit the press and the *Northern Whig*, always on the lookout for evidence of illiberal behaviour by Catholic churchmen, readily and gladly opened its correspondence columns to critics of Dorrian's policy. Sheltering behind *noms de plume* in the best Belfast tradition, these critics bewailed the painful consequences of 'the high handed action of the Roman Catholic Bishop', which deprived their children who had already obtained prizes of the opportunity of pursuing their education further. Having variously examined the reasons for the interdict on teaching classics, 'an interested parent' concluded that it was not the Brothers who would suffer 'by the arbitrary and uncharitable action of his Lordship' but the children of the working man, who were thereby condemned 'to a life of slavery and dependence', and prophesied ominously that, if the 'boycotting action' continued, it might have an important effect on more than one educational establishment and there might be 'an influx of scholars to the Queen's College'.[95]

The exchange took on a sharper note as another correspondent, who protested vigorously that he was a working man — perhaps too vigorously, in view of the style of his letter — reflected on the claim that the Brothers were introduced to Belfast to teach the poor and suggested that the bishop must have repented of his action, when he found 'the children of the artisans and labourers of the town outstripping money-grubbing farmers' uncouth and unclassical sons, who are destined, by aid of St Malachy's College, and after securing the cheap honours of Maynooth and of the Catholic University, to rank as clergymen, and in their two identities of lay and cleric combined to "ride upon the whirlwind and direct the storm of Irish political life"'. Pointing to the greater number of successes in 1881 and 1882 obtained by the Christian Brothers' boys as compared to St Malachy's, he explained that these results were, understandably, achieved by those whose entire lives were devoted to education:

> They do not adopt the profession of teaching as a stepping stone to a country curacy, or the next vacant comfortable parish, but live and die teachers of the poor. The pleasures of dining out at hospitable boards are denied to them in the world; outside there are no small tea-parties for them, or inviting-card parties; within there are no billiard tables, no "spoil-five", no convivial gossip, social or political, about the world without to

---

94 Slattery to Maxwell and the Belfast community to Maxwell, 21 Oct. 1882. A.C.B.G.R.
95 N.W., 4 Oct. 1882.

divert their leisure hours; but study and prayer, and prayer and study . . .[96]

These correspondents in fact damaged and weakened their case by their over-reaction and by extending their defence of the Brothers to an attack on St Malachy's College and the clergy of Belfast. Another 'working man', who was offended by this development, joined in the fray to air his suspicions about 'the studied silence of the Christian Brothers during this controversy', which, he suggested, was very 'strange and unaccountable' when the 'character and motives of the Bishop of the diocese are assailed and misrepresented, and obloquy . . . cast on the candidates of the priesthood and their parents'.[97]

Undoubtedly, both parties to the dispute had their suspicions about the identities of the eloquent working men. Patrick Convery, the administrator of St Peter's parish, informed the bishop that the attacks on him flowed, at the instigation of Brother Farrell, from the pen of the teacher from Methodist College, who was then engaged in giving extramural instruction in Latin to seven pupils of the Brothers' schools.[98] Dorrian was in Rome during October and November 1882. While there, he had handed in his report on the diocese and presumably in reply to a query for further information arising from his comments on the Brothers and on their replies, he submitted a further statement, together with the declarations made by the twenty six priests. Recapitulating the history of the Brothers' educational work in Belfast and of their partial neglect of the poor in favour of the rich, he summarized and characterized their behaviour as an attempt to create an *'imperium in imperio'* in defiance of his legitimate ecclesiastical authority. Recalling that they had continued to teach Latin and Greek for three years despite his instructions, he pointed out that their ultimate submission was even worse than their disobedience, for they had evaded the spirit of his orders by employing as a special tutor for Latin outside the normal class time, a nominal Catholic who was a graduate of the Queen's College, the attendance at which was prohibited under penalty of an ecclesiastical censure. Accordingly, he asked that his episcopal jurisdiction should be safeguarded in educational matters, that a recently issued constitution for religious orders in England which guaranteed episcopal authority over them should be extended to Ireland, and that the Brothers should not be allowed, without his authorization, to provide higher education and thereby put an end to the diocesan seminary.[99]

96 N.W., 11 Oct. 1882.
97 N.W., 20 Oct. 1882.
98 Convery to Dorrian, 2 Nov. 1882, A.P.F., S.C.(Irlanda), 39, ff 754r-755r
99 Dorrian to Cardinal Simeoni, 29 Nov. 1882, Ibid., ff 740r-743r.

A year later the Brothers' equivocal position was still bugging him. He remarked to Tobias Kirby that they were still holding aloof and asked plaintively: 'if the Brothers are to supersede the Bishop what use is a Bishop? Is this to go on?'[100]

It took the superior general a long time to respond to Dorrian's criticisms, and, perforce, he repeated many of his previous arguments. But he astutely drew the attention of the Roman authorities to a statement made by Dorrian in 1877, in which the bishop expressed his hope that with the passing of the Intermediate Education Act the Brothers' pupils would carry off their share of the prizes.[101] He argued that the prohibition on teaching Latin was unjust, as all the convent schools in Belfast and, of course, all Protestant schools, were free to teach it, pointed to the favourable reports given by the diocesan inspector who had examined their pupils on religious subjects, and asked if one college, where fees were charged, was sufficient in a city of 80,000 Catholics, eighty per cent of whom supported themselves 'by labour or industry'. Of the ten Brothers in Belfast, only three were involved in the Intermediate departments, teaching 70 of their total of 800 pupils, but accurate information could not be expected from the priests, who did not visit the schools and many of whom formed judgements about them based on hearsay evidence. Maxwell insisted that the general weekly charge per pupil was one penny, that a few paid two pence, a few three pence, about twenty sixpence, and eighty paid nothing, and, listing the occupations of the parents of the children, inquired resignedly if these groups did not constitute the poor, who were the poor? He explained the Brothers' side of the argument in individual cases that had been mentioned and, in conclusion, though promising to spare the cardinal a recital of particular instances of harsh treatment which the Brothers experienced from the clergy in Belfast, he repeated quite a litany of grievances and ended with the doleful observation that 'those whom we naturally expect should protect and encourage Religious engaged in the work of gratuitous education, a work in itself laborious and monotonous, are they who render the work more heavy by their bitter words and persistent opposition'.[102]

Propaganda passed no verdict on the dispute, and when Dorrian died in the following year the issues were still unsolved. In fact they were for the most part insoluble; there was no yardstick for determining when a few parents were sufficiently well off to be able to afford the fees at St Malachy's College, and judgements would

100 Dorrian to Kirby, 22 Nov. 1883, A.I.C.R.
101 This was probably a reference to the speech made by the bishop at the prize-giving in Oxford St. school in Feb. 1878.
102 Maxwell to Cardinal Simeoni, 28 Aug. 1884, A.P.F., S.C.(Irlanda), 39, ff 725r-739r.

have to remain highly personal and subjective. Propaganda could have done nothing other than encourage the Christian Brothers to dedicate themselves to the service of the poor, and this, they maintained, they were already doing. The only concrete issue in dispute was the teaching of Latin, and Dorrian's prohibition remained during his lifetime. His motives sprang neither from jealousy nor cussedness; he genuinely believed that St Malachy's College could cater for all the Catholic boys in Belfast who wished to pursue their studies to the Intermediate level, and that the Catholic community would be better served with one strong, successful secondary school, which could compete on equal terms with Protestant schools that enjoyed longer academic traditions and richer endowments, than by a number of schools sharing the available pupils among them and suffering in consequence from the weakness of small numbers and less specialized tuition.

Nonetheless, it was a policy which undoubtedly hampered some poorer boys whose parents aspired to the prizes of the Intermediate system and could not afford the annual fees of £6 or £8 at St Malachy's College. It also deprived the Brothers' schools of the opportunity of teaching the one subject to which at that time the greatest prestige was attached. In his dispute with the Brothers Dorrian was concerned with the prosperity and success of that diocesan institution in which he had invested much money, effort and thought, but his usual foresight in providing for the needs of an expanding population was missing. The dispute was as unnecessary as it was damaging, both in terms of educational development and of public relations.

10

The university question

By 1860 the Catholic University had been in existence for sixteen years. Called into being by the Synod of Thurles in response to a recommendation from Rome, the University had started off with high hopes under the rectorship of John Henry Newman. In 1851 £22,840 had been collected for its establishment in Ireland, and £4,735 and £3,100 in the United States and Britain.[1] In accordance with Cullen's views that it was better to start off modestly, the University was located in houses on or near St Stephen's Green, Dublin. But misunderstandings between the bishops and the rector over a wide variety of matters ranging from academic appointments to finance, a cooling-off in clerical enthusiasm for it and, above all, the absence of a charter, which alone could validate and make effective its degrees, bedevilled its progress. When Newman resigned in 1858, the annual collections had dropped to an average of between £6,000 and £7,000 and the student enrolment in the arts and science faculties to fifty. The only department that prospered was the faculty of medicine, which maintained about one hundred students; significantly, its degrees were recognized by the Royal College of Surgeons and consequently its graduates were assured of full professional acceptance.

The Queen's Colleges established by the government in 1845, which had been condemned by Rome as dangerous to the Catholic faith in 1847 and 1848, were duly opened in Belfast, Cork and Galway in 1849. To the rescripts of Propaganda the bishops in 1850 had added prohibitions restraining priests from any form of association with the Colleges, and strong exhortations to Catholic youth to avoid them. When Queen's College opened at Belfast, it numbered 5 Catholics out of a total of 195, and over the next thirty years a trickle of Catholics continued to frequent this mainly Presbyterian institution: in the decade 1849-59 the average was 13 or 7 per cent, increasing between 1859 and 1869 to 20 or 5 per cent but declining again between 1869 and 1879 to 16 or 4 per cent.[2] Two Catholics were among the first body

---

1 F. McGrath, *Newman's university: idea and reality* (Dublin, 1951), p.102.
2 Moody and Beckett, *Queen's, Belfast 1849-1949*, i, 143.

of professors: John O'Donovan, the distinguished Celtic scholar, who had no official students but continued to give a series of public lectures annually till his death in 1861, and Frederick McCoy, professor of mineralogy and geology, from 1849 to 1854. After 1861 the sole Catholic member of staff was James Cuming, one of the first students of the College, who became deputy professor of medicine in 1864, succeeded to the chair in 1865 and retained it until his death in 1899.[3] Once Rome and the Synod of Thurles had pronounced against the Colleges, neither Denvir nor Dorrian ever considered the Belfast College a suitable place for the education of Catholic youth. Dorrian's opposition to it was stronger than Denvir's; he regarded it quite simply as a symbol of injustice and argued that its income and endowments subsidized one religious denomination. He did not challenge the right of Protestants to receive state support for the educational institutions which they could conscientiously accept, but felt that Catholics had a similar right to support for institutions which they could attend; but no such institution or financial support had been made available to them. The Queen's College was a constant proof of educational inequality and, as the years passed without any solution to the problems of university education for Catholics, a more and more irritating one.

The bishops wanted a denominational university, fully supported by a government charter, to serve Irish Catholics, as Trinity College, Dublin served Irish Anglicans.[4] But two major obstacles stood in their way: the strength of anti-Catholic hostility in Britain, which prevented any government from risking a bold decision of this nature, and the commitment of the Liberals to the principle of mixed education. Though the Scottish universities satisfied Scottish majority religious aspirations, and Oxford and Cambridge satisfied the Church of England, English governments could not bring themselves to think of any scheme for Irish Catholics much different from the non-denominational character of London University.

Throughout his episcopate Dorrian took an active interest in all the proposals that were put forward to obtain government recognition and support for the Catholic University. The existence of the Queen's College in his diocese, which continued to attract Catholic students, however few in number, whetted this interest and made

3 Ibid., i, 116,128,175; ii, 581-2,606,609.
4 In 1856 the government chartered the 'Seminaire de Quebec' as Laval University. The rector of the seminary was always to be rector of the university, and he, the directors of the seminary, and the three senior professors of the faculties of divinity, law, medicine and arts were to constitute the council or governing body, which was empowered to appoint all professors, with the exception of those in the faculty of divinity. Their appointment was reserved to the archbishop of Quebec, the official visitor of the University.

him more concerned about this issue than many of his colleagues. Shortly after his succession the bishops and the government began to discuss the possibilities of granting some kind of official recognition to the Catholic University. Redress of Catholic grievances in the field of education was one of the principal demands of the National Association. In June 1865 The O'Donoghue, a Liberal MP, drew the attention of the House of Commons to the exclusion of Catholics from the advantages of higher education and suggested that this evil should be remedied by the grant of a charter to the Catholic University. Sir George Grey, the Home Secretary, admitted that reasonable complaints existed, and declared that the government intended to amend the charter of the Queen's University to enable it to grant degrees to students other than those of the Queen's Colleges.[5] Dorrian was pleased. He confided to Kirby in Rome that there was 'a prospect of obtaining an arrangement about the University that will not lower its status, leave education fully in the hands of the Bishops — chartering them for all property purposes as a corporation — and give the University a proper and safe representation on the Examining Senate'.[6] A little later he spelt this out more fully: 'If the Government will be honest and generous, giving us the *teaching uncontrolled*, and only ask a *reasonable* share in the Board of Examiners, I think we would be suicidal to refuse'.[7]

Grey proceeded to contact Lord Wodehouse, the Lord-Lieutenant, and influential Irish opinion. Informal discussions were held between two bishops, two Irish Catholic members of the government and other interested parties, and a plan was drawn up and submitted unofficially to the hierarchy at its meeting in August 1865. This envisaged the abolition of the Queen's University and the establishment of a Royal Irish University, controlled by a senate composed of an equal number of Catholic and Protestant members; of these three were to be Catholic bishops, two Anglican bishops and one a member of the Synod of Ulster. The Queen's Colleges and the Catholic college were, in the first instance, to affiliate to this new university (other colleges might later do so). There was to be one matriculation examination for the students of all the colleges, and the rewards of merit were to be available equally to all. The Catholic college was to be given a charter and the four archbishops were to become its visitors; they were to be empowered to appoint the rector, who with his governing body would name the professors, but the visitors could dismiss any professor for errors in faith,

5 E.R. Norman, *The Catholic church and Ireland in the age of rebellion*, pp 198-200.
6 Dorrian to Kirby, 27 June 1865, A.I.C.R.
7 Ibid., 16 Nov. 1865.

morals or conduct.[8] The majority of the bishops welcomed these proposals and Cullen sought an interview for representatives of their body with Sir George Grey. Though some Protestant opposition was raised to the plans, the meeting between Grey and the four archbishops took place in December. But they weakened their case by raising the whole subject of education and demanding the acceptance of the denominational principle both at primary and tertiary level. They suggested that the Queen's Colleges of Cork and Galway should become Catholic colleges and the Belfast College Presbyterian; Trinity College was to be reduced to equality of status in wealth with the others.

At its next meeting in Dublin the hierarchy decided to demand a charter and endowment for the Catholic University and they drew up proposals to that effect which gave the four archbishops and twelve bishops, as life governors, full authority in their college with the power to appoint and dismiss professors. A memorial signed by all the bishops, which acknowledged the value of the suggestions made by the government but which asked for an endowment of the Catholic University and a reconstruction of the Queen's Colleges on the denominational principle, was forwarded to Grey. Requesting a charter for their college within the new university, they also sought authority for it to affiliate schools and colleges, and asked that its examinations would not be hostile to Catholicism. A petition to the queen seeking a charter for the Catholic University was also despatched.[9]

Grey replied to Cullen on behalf of the government on 30 January 1866. Repudiating the bishops' charge that the Queen's Colleges had failed, he explained that the government had no intention of altering them or the principle on which they were based. But realizing that many could not take advantage of the education available in Trinity or the Queen's Colleges for conscientious reasons, the government proposed to alter the charter of the Queen's University to enable students of colleges other than the Queen's or Trinity to take degrees. While they were willing to recommend that a charter be granted to the Catholic college, they could not accept the draft submitted by the bishops; the archbishops might be constituted visitors to ensure the protection of the faith and morals of the students, but the governing body would have to contain a considerable proportion of laymen. It was not proposed to ask parliament to provide an endowment for the Catholic college, but, following the model of London University, to provide burses or scholarships open

8 Memorandum of George Butler, bishop of Limerick. 23 Aug. 1865, D.D.A.
9 *Copy of memorials . . . by the Roman Catholic prelates in Ireland on the subject of university and national education . . .* H.C. 1866,(84), lv, 248-52.

by competition to all students. The government also ruled out the right of the Catholic college to affiliate other colleges or schools, which it saw as belonging only to a university.[10] However, the likelihood of the cabinet making concessions to Catholics was diminished by protests from the Presbyterian and Methodist churches and from the graduates of the Queen's University against any plan to tamper with the Queen's Colleges or to affiliate a denominational and sectarian college to Queen's University.[11]

Dorrian was disappointed with the government's response. Writing to Cullen he observed that the opening discourtesy of Grey's letter (either his addressing Cullen as 'Most Reverend Sir' or, perhaps, the refusal to use the title 'Catholic University', which Dorrian thought the bishops could not surrender without insulting the Holy See) prepared him for the narrow policy it foreshadowed, for they were not being offered education that was free in essentials. On the contrary the bishops were being asked to sacrifice a fundamental principle which they were obliged in conscience to claim, for there could be no proper protection for faith and morals unless 'the guidance of the Church be supreme over the teaching and its machinery'. He proposed that the bishops should explain to the government that they could not accept some elements in the proposals that had been made and should point out that their system of church government was very different from the Protestant one; hence any plan which violated their liberties or rights did not really offer them equality. He argued that the government's willingness to provide education to all classes on equal terms would be judged by its readiness to reduce other universities and colleges to the same level as the Catholic University or to grant it the same privileges and power as the others. Unlike some of his colleagues, Dorrian never accepted the view that the Cork and Galway Colleges should be handed over to the Catholics and the Belfast one to the Presbyterians; consequently he told Cullen that he had no quarrel to find with this part of Grey's reply. Their policy was simply to avoid these colleges and 'all Catholics who voluntarily go to them and uphold them', and he suggested that the bishops should give instructions to confessors about imparting absolution to people who were carrying out principles which had been condemned by Pius IX in his Syllabus of Errors.

Dorrian then went on to develop this and another favourite theme: they should open their eyes to the 'hollowness of dependence or confidence in a class of politicians who are sacrificing us by their whispering diplomacy' (the Whigs) and there should be 'no future familiarity or coquetting with those who are daily betraying us by

10 Ibid.
11 Ibid., 261-6, 280-2.

coaxing disobedience of us from our people' (Catholic advocates of mixed education). His immediate practical suggestion was that they should form a registry association, and encourage their people to make use of the franchise to redress Catholic grievances, and soon they would have a power which both Whigs and Tories would feel.[12]

In this letter Dorrian gave expression to views on the university question that were to dominate his thinking for the rest of his life. He wanted a university fully controlled by the bishops which would enjoy the same advantages as Trinity or the Queen's Colleges. This was not to be achieved by cultivating Whig supporters of mixed education, Catholic or otherwise, but by firm and persistent advocacy. The suggestion that Catholics might choose members of parliament to represent their claims, however, seems remarkable in the wake of the virtual collapse of the National Association.

Drafts of the charter of the new university and of the Catholic college were passed on to the archbishop of Dublin by the Chief Secretary. Like Dorrian, Cullen objected to the bishops not being given full power in their own college; in a circular to his colleagues he explained that the rector and professors, as the body corporate, would appoint all professors and, though the archbishops, as visitors, could remove the rector and professors upon due inquiry, he noted that in the Queen's Colleges and Maynooth this power had to be exercised in open court. And, as no endowments were being offered to the Catholic University, the bishops would only lose their present rights without any compensating advantages. The proposal to alter the charter of the Queen's University to enable Catholic students to take degrees was welcome, but, since this could already be done at London University, he regarded it as a minor concession. He also objected to the proposals for the new senate, as all the members of the present senate would be retained and others added. Catholic bishops, as members of it, if they sanctioned awards and honours to students of the Queen's Colleges, would thereby be giving prestige to institutions which they had long condemned.[13]

Dorrian fully approved of Cullen's views. If a bishop, he replied, joined the senate of the new university, this 'would amount to an approval of the Infidel System in the Queen's Colleges'. The government was not trying earnestly to settle the problem. In fact the Whigs and their partisans made no secret of their hostility to clerical interference in education, whereas the Conservatives agreed that 'Religion should enter into all systems of Education' and were consequently more likely to concede 'a measure really more Catho-

12 Dorrian to Cullen, 4 Feb. 1866, D.D.A.
13 Circular to the bishops, 27 Feb. 1866, D.D.A.

lic than the Whigs ever can bring their hearts to consent to force on'.[14]

Cullen had come round to the view that it was better to postpone attempts to obtain a charter for the Catholic University, and to omit all mention of both it and the Queen's Colleges from the charter for the new university. The best they could obtain in the circumstances was a mere examining body.[15] The government acted on these lines. A supplemental charter for the Queen's University to enable it to examine students who were not enrolled in the Queen's Colleges was drawn up, and further legislation was envisaged to extend its scope, but before this could occur, the Whigs lost office and the Tories came back to power. The supplemental charter was challenged in the courts and an injunction was obtained which set it aside.

Dorrian continued to support the Catholic University and to encourage his people to contribute to it, though he was highly critical of its staff. He believed that the professors and teachers in the seminaries and diocesan colleges did three times as much work as the professors and deans of the University. He felt the bishops were getting a very poor return for the expenses involved in educating so few students. But he exempted the rector from condemnation and assured him that the University would have sunk hopelessly without his capacity, ability and untiring energy.[16] He also told Woodlock that he would join him in condemning the Conservatives, if they did not do more for the church than the Whigs.[17]

However, the Conservatives were destined to disappoint him. Contacts between the bishops and the new government, aided by the benevolent mediation of Archbishop Manning of Westminster, were initiated. But Manning reported ominously that while Disraeli, the prime minister, was prepared to concede a charter to the Catholic University, he excluded the possiblilty of endowment and also insisted that laymen would have to be admitted to the new governing body.[18] Negotiations, nonetheless, continued, and two bishops and Bartholomew Woodlock were deputed to present their case in London. In March 1868 Lord Mayo, the Chief Secretary, disclosed that the government was prepared to grant a charter to the Catholic

14 Dorrian to Cullen, 5 Mar. 1866, D.D.A.
15 Cullen to Bartholomew Woodlock, 26 Feb. 1866, D.D.A.
16 Dorrian to Woodlock, 2 Dec. 1866, D.D.A.
17 Ibid., 14 Nov. 1866.
18 Manning to Cullen, 10 Dec. 1867. Some of the Irish bishops were afraid that the government would appoint laymen who were 'Castle Catholics' or supporters of mixed education. This was a fear that John Henry Newman, the first rector of the Catholic University, found damaging. He told Woodlock that 'they won't further the University till they trust educated lay Catholics more'. (Newman to Woodlock, 4 Nov. 1874, D.D.A.)

University under a new governing body; its supreme authority would no longer be the bench of bishops but a senate consisting of a chancellor, vice-chancellor, four bishops, the president of Maynooth, six laymen, the heads of the affiliated colleges and one representative from each of its five faculities. The state would provide an endowment only by means of scholarships.[19] The bishops sought further clarification of these plans and were at first hopeful of achieving a settlement, provided they were given full authority to exclude morally harmful books and professors from the university, and some adjustments were made in the methods of appointing future chancellors and members of the senate.[20]

However, Lord Mayo's scheme fell victim to the vicissitudes of politics. Gladstone's resolutions on the disestablishment of the Church of Ireland were carried in parliament in May, and thereby precipitated a general election. The Conservatives, faced with the prospect of defending the Church of Ireland, could not afford to be accused of selling the pass to the Catholic church by giving it a denominational university. Consequently Mayo did not try to meet the bishops' requests in a conciliatory manner; he rejected their view that a prelate should be the chancellor of the new university and insisted that all appointments should be subject to the approval of the governing body. This put an end to the search for a solution with a Conservative government.[21] And before the year ended Gladstone and the Liberals returned to power.

The bishops were deeply disappointed. Had they got a charter and official validation of the degrees of the Catholic University on any kind of acceptable terms, they felt that they would have had a sure foundation on which to build their hopes for financial assistance. Their chances of obtaining recognition for a denominational university from the Liberals were slight, if not negligible. Dorrian could not resist taking a swipe at the distrusted Whigs when commenting on the outcome of their negotiations. He blamed the Irish members for not supporting the government on the charter issue 'instead of being so anxious for themselves' and, perhaps rather too hopefully, detected helpful sympathy on Disraeli's part: 'Gladstone is farther from the Catholic view than D'Israeli and will never yield to the Bishops' views as D'Israeli is inclined to do, but for the taunting and

---

[19] *Copy of correspondence relative to the proposed charter to a Roman Catholic university.* H.C. 1867-8,(288), liii, 779-88.

[20] Hansard, 28 May 1868, cxcii, 956.

[21] Cullen wanted Woodlock to secure from the government the right of bishops to exercise control over professors and books on matters of faith and morals. He also wanted the members of the senate to fill the vacancies in their own body rather than permit convocation to do so amidst agitation and dissension. (Cullen to Woodlock, 13,15,23,25 Mar. 1868, D.D.A.)

discordant conduct of the Irish MPs and the anti-Catholic Radicals'.[22]

With some apprehension the bishops awaited Gladstone's efforts to achieve a solution of the university problem. When he had tackled the land question and the disestablishment of the Church of Ireland, he turned his attention to it, but did not contact the hierarchy in advance of presenting his proposals. His solution was to enlarge the University of Dublin to make it the national university of Ireland and to add to its single constituent college, Trinity, the Queen's Colleges of Belfast and Cork, Magee College, Derry and any and every other college in Ireland which had a prescribed number of matriculated students. Queen's College, Galway was to close, and the new university was to have an annual endowment of £50,000, to which Trinity College was to make a contribution of £15,000. The Queen's Colleges in Cork and Belfast were to maintain their property but no other college was to be endowed in any way. This reconstituted university was both to be an examining body and to have a staff of professors. The proposal was a major disappointment to the bishops; they would receive no aid for the Catholic University, which would be merely one of many colleges affiliated to Dublin University, and they felt that insufficient provision was made for Catholic representation on its governing body. Catholic students would be attracted to the mixed colleges of the university and professors from Protestant colleges appointed to its staff. On the other hand, the students of the Catholic University would have been assured of professional qualifications and standing, if they successfully completed their examinations. Though some clergy were prepared to accept Gladstone's proposals as a significant step forward,[23] the bishops poured cold water on them, and called on the Catholic clergy and laity of Ireland to oppose them; when most Irish Catholic MPs did so, they helped bring down the government. Archbishop Manning's strictures on

---

22 Dorrian to Kirby, 15 May 1868, A.I.C.R. Dorrian was not the only bishop who disparaged the Whigs. John MacEvilly, the bishop of Galway, later wrote: 'The Whigs are near relations of the continental liberals — the moment they get into office you may as well bid adieu to any consideration of Catholic claims. I don't mean to be a great friend of Tory or Orange rule so far as Ireland is concerned but on educational subjects they are less bad. They have some lineaments, however extreme, of religious bearing, the others have none whatever'. (MacEvilly to Woodlock, 4 Feb. 1877, D.D.A.)

23 C.W. Russell, the president of Maynooth, was pleased with the safeguards and opportunities afforded by Gladstone's Bill. Describing the scheme as 'able and ingenious', he believed that it offered indirect opportunities for endowment but regretted its weak points, 'the fatal and I suppose unavoidable inequality in the positions of the rival colleges' and the ignoring of the ecclesiastical element in the council or senate of the University. (Russell to William Monsell, 15 Feb. 1873, N.L.I. MS 8318 (3).)

the Liberals would have been worthy of Dorrian: 'the tyrannous liberalism of this country can be cured by nothing short of a public disaster, which may God avert'.[24]

Gladstone was heavily defeated in the general election of 1874, and a phalanx of sixty Home Rulers replaced his broken Liberal party in Ireland. Isaac Butt, the Home Rule leader, who had helped the bishops formulate their case against Gladstone's proposals and who, though himself a Protestant, sympathized with many of their views on this tortuous question, drew up a university bill for presentation to parliament in 1876. As presented in the House of Commons the bill was designed to provide the Catholic University both with the finance and the degree of freedom of control in essential areas which had been missing in Gladstone's proposals. The Catholic University was to become, along with Trinity College, a constituent college of Dublin University and to be re-christened St Patrick's College. The bishops, as governors of the former university, were assigned control over all matters of faith and morals, and were empowered to appoint the rector, vice-rector and professors of divinity in St Patrick's; the college council was entrusted, subject to an episcopal veto, with the appointment of all other members of staff. The senate of the university was to consist of twelve members of the hierarchy and twelve laymen, and £30,000 was to be set aside for a site for St Patrick's College and £440,000 was to be taken from the church commissioners as a general endowment.[25] When the bill was submitted to the vote of the House of Commons in July 1877, it was heavily defeated.

Before the vote in the Commons was taken, Dorrian invited the Catholics of Belfast to a public meeting in his spacious new hall (St Mary's) to petition for a settlement of the university and intermediate education issues — highlighting incidentally both the greater assertiveness and increased assurance of the more extensive Catholic body in the town, as well as the advantage of having a large hall which could be readily used for such purposes. The *Ulster Examiner* explained in advance that the purpose of the gathering was to petition parliament for Butt's bill, and the editor, Edward Byrne, pointed out in a lengthy letter to the local organizers that he had good authority for stating that the primate, the archbishop of Cashel and two other prelates had met Butt and his colleagues, McCarthy and Mitchell Henry, and had agreed on the terms of the bill. Attention was called to twenty six years of failure in agitating for their rights in university education[26]

24 Manning to Cullen, 1 Mar. 1873, D.D.A.
25 D. Thornley, *Isaac Butt and Home Rule*, p.278.
26 Dr Alexander Harkin, who had been active in channelling support to Catholic schools from the St Vincent de Paul Society pointed out that the first donation, which amounted to £300, for the Catholic University had been sent from Belfast.

and to their willingness to support the rights of every denomination to the same educational privileges. The barrister who proposed the resolution in favour of Butt's bill thanked Dorrian for asking him to do so, and Dorrian, who had stage-managed the whole affair, read out a petition which asserted that, since the majority of the people of Ireland were not provided with a system of university or secondary education which they could in conscience accept, called for redress and for the terms laid down in Butt's bill or some similar and suitable system of university and secondary education.[27]

Though Butt's efforts failed, the Conservative party chose education as an Irish Catholic grievance which it could satisfy without too much political fall-out, provided support also came from the opposition benches. The general acceptance accorded in 1878 to the Intermediate Education Act, which provided indirect endowment for Catholic secondary schools through a system of prizes and payment by results, encouraged it to broach the university issue. News of the government's intention to legislate along these lines leaked out. William Delany, an Irish Jesuit educationalist with a sharp eye for the difficult underlying realities of the problem and a firm sense of the need to proceed at a judicious pace, persuaded The O'Conor Don, an Irish Catholic Liberal, and Arthur Kavanagh, a Tory, to anticipate the government and bring pressure on it to deal more generously with the question.[28] The O'Conor Don's bill proposed the creation of a third university in Ireland, to be known as St Patrick's, with power to affiliate colleges. It was to be an examining body and was to receive an initial endowment of £1,500,000, taken from the funds of the disestablished church, and the affiliated colleges would receive grants on the basis of their results in the university examinations. When the bill was being debated, the government announced that it was about to introduce its own bill. And with a general election in the offing it decided to tread cautiously through the religious minefield.

In imitation of The O'Conor Don's bill the government measure proposed to set up the Royal University, an examining body, which would award degrees to students irrespective of the college they attended, provided they achieved the requisite standards. The Queen's University was to be abolished, but the three Queen's Colleges were to remain and retain their property and endowments. In response to protests about the inadequacy of this solution, a clause was added empowering the senate of the new university to award prizes, exhibitions and scholarships. With this significant alteration casually announced in the course of the debate in parliament, the way

27 U.Ex., 7 Apr. 1877.
28 Thomas J. Morrissey, *Towards a national university* (Dublin,1983), pp 49-52.

was left open for indirect endowment of Catholic institutions on the model of the Intermediate Education Act. A few months later the charter of the university and the names of the senate were announced: of the thirty six members, eighteen were Protestant and eighteen Catholic.[29] A change of government occurred before the financial arrangements could be made, and Gladstone's government assigned the niggardly sum of £20,000 annually to the upkeep of the Royal University. A sub-committee of the senate, on which Monsignor Neville, the rector of the Catholic University, and Gerald Molloy, one of his professors, served, had hoped to establish forty eight fellowships worth £400 per year but was eventually forced to reduce the number to twenty six. William Delany worked hard to ensure an equal division of the fellowships, and in October 1881 the senate approved the arrangement whereby half the fellowships and offices were to be held by Catholics. It had already laid down that each fellow was obliged to teach in an institution of which it approved, and an 'understanding' was reached that the Catholic fellows would teach in the Catholic University.[30]

The reaction of the bishops to these developments was mixed, and they awaited the practical results of the senate's first deliberations without making a general pronouncement. Some, like Bartholomew Woodlock, the former rector of the Catholic University, who had been appointed to Ardagh in 1879, believed that the Royal gave them what they had long campaigned for — a *'jury d'examen'* without the obligation of submitting their youth to mixed teaching.[31] Others, like Dorrian, were disappointed. The bishop of Down and Connor had assumed and hoped that the Queen's Colleges would be disendowed;[32] endowment gave them an unfair advantage in the competition against the non-endowed colleges. He had committed the diocese to heavy expenditure on St Malachy's College in the wake of the Intermediate Education Act, and his ambition was to develop it as a centre of third level education. And when the bishops held a special meeting to discuss educational and particularly university problems on 10 January 1882, his plans were given a boost. They decided that the Catholic fellows should be attached to the Catholic University in Dublin, Maynooth and St Malachy's

---

29 The Lord-Lieutenant had consulted Archbishop McCabe and Bishop Woodlock about suitable Catholic nominees for the senate. McCabe in turn consulted his episcopal colleagues. Among those chosen were the archbishop himself, Woodlock, the former rector, Henry Neville, his successor, three other priests and twelve laymen. O'Hagan was appointed vice-chancellor.
30 Morrissey, op. cit. pp 53-60.
31 Woodlock to Cardinal Simeoni, 23 Feb. 1880, A.P.F. S.C.(Irlanda), 38, ff 537r-538r.
32 Dorrian to Kirby, 24 Sept. 1879, A.I.C.R.

College.[33] They claimed that, since the principal object of the Royal was to make higher education available to Catholics, not less that two thirds of the fellows should enjoy the confidence of the Catholic body. And they deliberately excluded Catholic officials of the Queen's Colleges from this corps of scholars whom they wished to represent Catholic interests. At a further meeting on 22 March they resolved that none of the money assigned for the fellowships of the Royal should be given to any of the present professors or officials of the Queen's Colleges, and, in the event of the senate acting otherwise, they suggested that Cardinal McCabe and Bishop Woodlock of Ardagh should consider resigning from it in protest. They also called on their representatives to support the bill for the disendowment of the Queen's Colleges and they named a delegation consisting of the archbishop of Armagh, and the bishops of Elphin, Down and Connor, and Ossory to confer with the Catholic members of the senate on the day before it met.[34]

A list of twenty six names from which it was hoped the Catholic fellows would be chosen was drawn up; of these ten were 'recommended in connection with' the Catholic University, eight 'in connection with' Maynooth and three 'in connection with' St Malachy's College. Five others were unattached. The candidates from St Malachy's were Henry Henry, the president, Henry Laverty and Henry O'Boyle, whom Dorrian described as professors of Classics, French and German and of Classics and Mathematics, respectively. He further claimed that their qualifications 'may be had in the results gained by their pupils in the Intermediate and other Competitive Examinations', and argued that it was very important that their candidates be successful; otherwise, as he told Bartholomew Woodlock, 'we cannot possibly compete with £12,000 a year to the Queen's College here in Belfast'.[35]

These resolutions were too hardline for the Vatican. Whether on his own initiative or whether prompted by George Errington, as this government agent at the Vatican subsequently claimed, Cardinal Jacobini, the Secretary of State, on behalf of the pope, requested the cardinal prefect of Propaganda to write to the archbishop of Armagh suggesting that the bishops seek more than half the fellowships but counselling them to be content with an equal share if they could not obtain a larger number; the hierarchy was further advised, in view of the complex circumstances with which it was dealing, that the

---

33 An Italian translation of the confidential resolutions passed at this meeting survives in A.P.F. *Acta*, 253, f. 517rv. The number of fellows to be assigned to each establishment was not given; Dorrian later claimed that St Malachy's was to be given three.
34 Ibid.
35 Dorrian to Woodlock, 2 Mar. 1882, D.D.A.

exclusion of all the professors of the Queen's Colleges from the office of fellow was not opportune.[36]

The senate of the university met on 18 April[37] and proceeded to name twenty one of the twenty four fellows whom it had decided to appoint at that time. Woodlock, the only bishop present, owing to McCabe's absence in Rome, carried out the Roman instructions by asking that more than half the fellows should be Catholic but, on being refused, contented himself with fifty per cent. In fact he found a strong majority of those present rather ill-disposed to Catholic education; nonetheless they selected nine Catholic fellows, eleven Protestants from the staffs of the Queen's Colleges and one Protestant from another college. Though Woodlock had asked that all appointments be delayed till McCabe's return, they did defer three of them with the 'understanding' that these would be assigned to Maynooth to enable its students to avail of the examinations at the Royal University.[38] The Catholic fellows chosen on this occasion were all connected with the Catholic University.

However, the majority of the bishops agreed with the majority report of a sub-committee of their body, which opposed the academic connection between Maynooth and the Royal. They feared the effect of such a connection on the discipline of the student body, its divisiveness among students who were capable of taking degrees and those who were not, and the possible damage academic qualifications might do to the spirit of humility, charity, piety and obedience among the students; they also feared that the professors might not be immune from the deleterious consequences that could arise from complete concentration on secular subjects, and foresaw possible conflicts of jurisdiction between the trustees of Maynooth and the senate of the University over the appointment of fellows to the Maynooth staff.[39] Though Cardinal McCabe scotched these fears and looked forward to graduates from Maynooth swamping those of other colleges in convocation and thereby electing more Catholics to the University senate,[40] the bishops, at their October meeting in 1882, reaffirmed the decision which they had taken four months previously. This meant that the three fellowships were available for distribution elsewhere.

Meanwhile the bishop of Ardagh had circulated his plan for the Catholic University. Until then that body consisted of the university

36 Simeoni to McGettigan, 10 Apr. 1882, A.P.F. *Acta*, 253, f 517v.
37 Only seven of the Catholic members of senate accepted an invitation to meet a delegation from the bishops, consisting of Dorrian, McGettigan (Armagh), Moran (Ossory) and Gillooly (Elphin) on 17 April.
38 Woodlock to Cardinal Simeoni, 7 May 1882, *Acta*, 253, ff 517v--518v.
39 Ibid., ff 520r-521v.
40 McCabe to Bernard Smith, 14 Aug. 1882, Ibid. 519rv.

building on St Stephen's Green, and the medical school in Cecilia Street. Few students attended lectures at St Stephen's Green, with the exception of those who took grinds from one or two professors for the examinations of London University.[41] The diocesan collections for it had ended, to the immense relief of most bishops, in 1881. Woodlock recommended that the Catholic University be reconstituted as a moral body and consist of the university college on St Stephen's Green, the medical school, Maynooth, a Jesuit hall, and halls attached to Blackrock and Castleknock Colleges. He suggested further that a hall at Terenure College might subsequently be included and that 'there might also be question later on whether St Malachy's College, Belfast, on fulfilling the required conditions, should not become a College of the Catholic University, and especially, if two of its Superiors be appointed Fellows of the Royal University, as, it is hoped, may be the case'. The bishops accepted this recommendation in principle but struck out St Malachy's and added Holy Cross College, Clonliffe, St Patrick's College, Carlow and St Kieran's College, Kilkenny. They also agreed that all the fellowships allotted to the Catholic University should be held in University College, and they entrusted that institution to the archbishop of Dublin. In October 1883, with the consent of the bishops, he handed it over to the care of the Jesuits.

Dorrian travelled to Rome to pay his *ad limina* visit in November 1882. Presumably he unburdened himself of his disappointment with, and anxiety about, the Royal in the course of his interview with Cardinal Simeoni at Propaganda, and, in response to the cardinal's suggestion, put his views on paper; at any rate his reservations, amounting to almost total disapproval of the new arrangements, survive in a letter written to Simeoni from Rome.

His grounds for complaint were threefold: the composition of the senate, the subject matter of the examinations especially in the field of philosophy, and the unfair distribution of the fellowships. But he prefaced his complaints with an explanation of his own particular interest in higher education and of the obstacles confronting his people in their search for it. Observing that the university question was of more concern to him than to the other bishops, he explained that Belfast was the centre of infidelity, Orangeism and hostility to things Catholic, with Protestants enjoying an almost total dominance in commerce, wealth and learning; the entire atmosphere was imbued with an anti-Catholic spirit.

---

41 J.W. Kavanagh, the professor of mathematics, reported to the rector that no students had turned up to his classes since term began and in consequence he had decided not to waste time by coming to give lectures. (Kavanagh to Woodlock, 19 Jan. 1876, D.D.A.)

The educational situation had been difficult. For twenty years he had fought to prevent Catholic students from frequenting the Queen's College. However, a few Catholics, the majority of whom came from outside his diocese, did attend this well-endowed institution which enjoyed an annual income of £10,000, and their number would have been greater, if he had not made such attendance a reserved sin. Had the Royal University operated on the same principle as the Intermediate Education Act, it would have given satisfaction, but it was in fact a continuation and confirmation of the system of education associated with the Queen's Colleges which had already been condemned; it was, in the words of a Catholic member of the senate, the 'quintessence of Queen's Collegism'.

The senate consisted of thirty six members, eighteen of whom were Catholics or, rather, so-called Catholics. Yet the bishops had suggested the names of eighteen people who were acceptable to them and had rejected the names of some of those whom Gladstone later appointed. Many of those selected favoured mixed education; not ten of them were orthodox and trustworthy. When, on the eve of the election of twenty four fellows, a delegation from the bench of bishops, of which he was a member, met, by appointment, the Catholic members of the senate, only seven of their number turned up; seven refused to attend.[42] From a senate so constituted nothing was to be hoped for; on the contrary, through a spirit of concession and fear more harm would be done to Catholic interests. The majority of the senate favoured mixed education and was therefore hostile to the church; many of its so-called Catholic members were timid and too ready to make concessions in the interests of peace. Eleven of the professors of the Queen's Colleges had been appointed fellows, and it was the spirit of those Colleges that prevailed in the Royal.

42 Those who came were the earl of Granard, Edmund Dease, Robert Lyons, Francis Cruise, Dean Neville, Revd James Kavanagh and Bartholomew Woodlock, the bishop of Ardagh. Neville was the rector of the Catholic University, Woodlock a former rector, and Kavanagh was a priest of the diocese of Kildare. Those whom Dorrian accused of refusing to attend were Lord O'Hagan, Lord Emly, Judge Morris, Judge Barry, Sir Robert Kane, Sir Thomas Redington and W.K. O'Sullivan. O'Hagan, a former Lord Chancellor, had long annoyed Dorrian by his support for mixed education; he was then a commissioner both of national and Intermediate education. Emly, a former member of Gladstone's cabinet, was suspect because of the Liberal commitment to the principle of mixed education. Kane was a former president and Sullivan was the current president of Queen's College, Cork. Redington, an under-secretary in Dublin Castle, was also a commissioner of national education. Most of these men would have been regarded by many bishops as 'Castle Catholics'. Archbishop McCabe and William J. Walsh, president of Maynooth, were also members of the senate. McCabe was in Rome when the meeting took place.

The course for the examinations supposed a full and familiar knowledge of recent Protestant authors in materialism and psychology, and this from students who were not equipped to deal with such material. In fact they could complete the course in psychology without ever hearing the word 'soul' mentioned.

He (and others) believed that, if the bishops were firmer in claiming their rights, the senate would be more disposed to treat them in a more equitable manner. The situation would be different, if all shared equally in endowments or if all had nothing. Justice was not satisfied by giving half the fellowships to Catholics; they were entitled to all the fellowships and, in yielding up this right, were bolstering up a system of education that had been condemned. How, he asked, could a diocesan college in Belfast be sustained from penury in competition with the Queen's College which enjoyed an income of £10,000 annually? The bishops had suggested that St Malachy's be allocated three fellows, but all the fellowships allocated to Catholics were to be given to one college in Dublin in support of the professors of the Catholic University, who, having spent £230,000, almost uselessly, had scarcely any students. The diocese of Down and Connor had contributed £400 annually for the past twenty years to the Catholic University when other dioceses had contributed nothing,[43] and yet St Malachy's College, despite its poverty, had produced better results. That University was an abstract entity consisting, supposedly, of colleges in or near Dublin, and it was difficult to see how students from colleges five or six miles distant could attend lectures in Dublin. If it were successful, only the rich would benefit, for the poor could not pay £100 each year to live in Dublin, and if in the Royal University scarcely any opportunity were given to the poor to obtain degrees, the convocation would consist of Protestants and the Queen's University would be resurrected. Centralization of the fellowships in Dublin was neither politic nor just, for the poor from the provinces could not avail of higher education there. If the income of the fellowships were halved or reduced, money would be available for teachers throughout the country, sound learning would be diffused and Ireland become again the island of saints and scholars. It would now be impossible, he concluded, to withdraw students from the condemned colleges,

43 In 1862 Bartholomew Woodlock, the rector of the University, drew up figures for contributions from each diocese on 'an assumed basis of their local circumstances, as to population and wealth' to enable him to collect an annual sum of £7,000. Down and Connor was assessed at £176 and was placed sixth in the Armagh province after Meath, Armagh, Ardagh, Kilmore and Clogher. In fact in 1862 it contributed £338, which was the second highest after Meath with £556 and came before Derry with £250. Fifteen years later Down and Connor was still second with £309 to Meath's £355, and Derry came third with £223.

where so many prizes were available, when bishops on the senate favoured the system. Yet the Holy See refused to allow the bishops to become commissioners of national education, even though that system was under the control of the clergy and much better in almost every way than the Royal University.[44]

To write in this mournful vein Dorrian must have been saddened and disillusioned with the outcome of many years agitation by Catholics for a suitable form of higher education. About the only positive conclusion one could draw from his review was that the Royal University might benefit the Catholics of Dublin or those who were fortunate enough to be able to pay for lodgings there. He was not alone in criticizing the examinations; other bishops had similar reservations, and to overcome their concern the senate later agreed to make alternative courses available in philosophy, so that Catholic students, who so wished, might opt for the one in scholastic philosophy. Doubtless, several bishops shared his lack of enthusiasm about the Catholic representatives on the senate,[45] but, if they still felt that less than justice had been done to them, most were prepared to give the scheme at least a grudging acceptance; the Vatican directive precluded total opposition. Dorrian, of course, had peculiar local problems, the full gravity of which might not have impinged on some of the others. The Queen's College in Belfast came under a stronger and more pervasive Protestant influence[46] than did its sisters in Cork and Galway, and Dorrian had striven against great odds not only to prevent Catholics from succumbing to the temptations of seeking its education and prizes, but also to provide a viable alternative. Three fellowships, or even one, would have added a princely revenue to the hard-pressed finances of St Malachy's College, and the prestige accruing from the presence of even one fellow on its staff would have encouraged some students at least to attend its classes while reading for a degree in arts or science. Without such aid and recognition he felt that St Malachy's was fated to plough a hard and lonely furrow in its struggle to compete with the Queen's College for the allegiance of

---

44 Dorrian to Simeoni, 29 Nov. 1882, A.P.F., S.C.(Irlanda), 39, ff 704r-712r.

45 Woodlock reported to Archbishop McCabe that the Lord-Lieutenant told him that the government could not avoid appointing to the senate those Catholics who were already associated with the Queen's University and went on to claim that the whole university plan, which the senate would work out, was more likely to be acceptable to parliament 'if framed by a Body not altogether "Ultramontane"'. (Woodlock to McCabe, 6 Dec. 1879. D.D.A.) Bishop Moran remarked, when the membership of the senate was made public, that 'some of the names are not everything that we could wish but on the whole I think they will be a working Senate'. (Moran to Michael Verdon, 25 Jan. 1880, D.D.A.)

46 In 1879 the Presbyterian divine, J.L. Porter, succeeded Revd P.S. Henry, who had been president of Queen's College since 1845. Porter was the son-in-law and biographer of Henry Cooke.

Catholic students and to maintain standards sufficiently high to enable them to compete successfully at the examinations of the Royal University. Whatever the Royal offered the Catholics of Dublin, those of Belfast were left with but a few crumbs of comfort; they could obtain university degrees, but, if they were compelled by financial reasons to prepare for them locally, they would have to do so under spartan conditions induced by shortage of money.

Dorrian did his best to strengthen the staff of St Malachy's, but, until his death, remained aggrieved by what he considered the maldistribution of the fellowships. In his prize day speech at the college in 1883 he referred to objectionable books which were prescribed for courses in the Royal University, and complained about the unfair advantages which those students enjoyed who were taught by those who set the examination papers. Reiterating his view that provincial colleges should have been developed within the University, he mentioned the advantages enjoyed by students at St Malachy's, where, in addition to excellent moral and religious supervision, they were often able to board with their families or relatives. The *Morning News*, in its editorial, upholding these views complained strongly about the system of education, which had been founded for Catholic students, being 'so manipulated and distorted' that only a small proportion of them shared in the benefits.[47] Dorrian returned to the attack a few days later in a pastoral letter appealing for funds for St Malachy's and his seminarians. Stating that it was most unfair to expend £4,000 'to the advantage of *one* school and leave others of greater merit in the Provinces unrecognized', he repeated his argument that twenty fellowships worth £200 each per year would supply the University with the best talent in the kingdom. He quoted in full a letter he had received which contained extracts from Sir Henry Summer Maine's treatise on ancient law that were unflattering to the Catholic Church, and asked rhetorically which of their Catholic senators would say he was not responsible for permitting such books to be prescribed?[48] Privately, he was much more scathing on the senate.[49]

In fact Dorrian's was far from being a lone voice bemoaning the monopoly of fellowships enjoyed by University College.[50] While the

---

47 M.N., 6 Nov. 1883.
48 The letter was dated 9 Nov. 1883, D.C.D.A.
49 Dorrian to Woodlock, 3 Dec. 1883, A.C.D.A.
50 The most persistent and influential opponent of the policy of granting all the Catholic fellowships to University College was William J. Walsh. He wanted the Catholic University to consist of two or three successful colleges among which the fellowships would be divided. George Butler, the bishop of Limerick, put the opposite case most forcefully when he argued that fellowships scattered throughout colleges 'will be frittered away & lost and the appointment of Fellows will degenerate into a series of jobs, by which individuals here & there, or Academics will benefit,

majority of the bishops had gone along with the view, so ably represented by William Delany of University College, that Catholic educational energies should not be dissipated (and thereby weakened) in many institutions, but that their intellectual power should be concentrated in one centre of excellence, which could achieve such distinction in the examinations of the Royal University as to make its demand for a more just and generous grant from the state irresistible, some ecclesiastics felt that the spread of the fellowships would have brought other and significant benefits to Catholics in higher education. Ironically Delany's was the very argument Dorrian used against the establishment of secondary departments by the Christian Brothers in their schools in Belfast; he claimed that the duplication of courses in several schools would lower the quality of Intermediate education available to Catholics, whereas the concentration of all their resources in St Malachy's College would produce higher standards and enable their youth to achieve greater distinction. But on the university question his thinking was dominated by local needs.

In May 1883 he forwarded to Woodlock the application which Henry Henry had made for a fellowship the previous year, when the bishops were disposed to recommend three fellowships for St Malachy's College.[51] But Woodlock, who accepted Delany's arguments, could do nothing for him. Two further fellowships for Catholics were due to be allocated by the senate of the Royal University on 30 January 1884. William Delany was not only keen to have two Jesuits appointed, as their incomes would help his struggling College, but he also had two distinguished scholars in mind: Robert Curtis and Gerard Manley Hopkins. However, Blackrock College was anxious to develop its tertiary sector and canvassed for one of the fellowships for a member of its staff, J.E. Reffé. William J. Walsh, the president of Maynooth, was present at the bishops' committee meeting which took place on the eve of the senate meeting, and won the bishops support for Reffé's candidature. However, the senate decided in favour of the two Jesuits, who were much better qualified academically. McCabe, though he did not regret the decision, nevertheless took advantage of the situation to resign from the senate. Walsh persevered in his support for Reffé and when the remaining fellowship, that had been left over for the Catholics, was being filled, tried again to have him elected, but the post went to a tutor at University College.[52] Walsh thereupon resigned from the senate. The battle for the diversification of the fellowships had been completely lost.

but by which Catholic Education will benefit little or nothing'. (Butler to McCabe, 10 Dec. 1881, D.D.A.)
   51 Dorrian to Woodlock, 13 May 1883, A.C.D.A.
   52 Morrissey, *Towards a national university*, pp 79-85.

Dorrian was depressed not only by University College monopolizing the fellowships but also by the transmogrification of the Catholic University. At heart he blamed some of his colleagues for their timid acceptance of a mere half-loaf. Writing to Kirby in Rome, he remarked: 'As to the University. It is gone. It is a mere Jesuit school. Rome listened to certain statements and tied up the hands of the Bishops about the Fellowships. We *could* have won our cause.'[53]

Moreover, his insistence on the claim of St Malachy's to some share of the funds made available by the Royal University annoyed some of his colleagues, who thought he was unnecessarily reopening issues that had been settled by October 1883. Bartholomew Woodlock passed on to Cardinal McCabe the report of the speech at the prizegiving in St Malachy's College in November 1883, with the comment that those remarks were very unfortunate.[54] He had already assured Dorrian that he accepted the fairness and justice of the case for a Catholic university college in Belfast and hoped that that concession could before long be wrung from their opponents; necessity and prudence, however, dictated the need for consolidating their strength at that time.[55] A year later Woodlock again forwarded to McCabe a 'very objectionable article' from the *Morning News*, which took up Dorrian's point about distributing fellowships around various centres, and expressed the hope that their enemies would not conclude from such comments that the bishops were divided and then begin 'to trade on our so-called dissensions'.[56]

However, Dorrian did not accept defeat passively. When, in response to continued Catholic criticism of the unfair and privileged position enjoyed by the Queen's Colleges, a royal commission was appointed to inquire into their effectiveness and to examine their finances, Henry Henry, the president of St Malachy's College, gave evidence. Henry presented the argument which Dorrian had often used that the Presbyterians enjoyed a virtual monopoly of endowments and scholarships in the province of Ulster. As he subsequently wrote in the *Morning News* in defence of his submission, he was not an opponent of higher education for the Presbyterians and Protestants of Ulster. But the Queen's College was sectarian and as such had rendered valuable service to the Presbyterian clergy and laity, whereas its usefulness to Catholics during the previous thirty years had been almost nil. Nineteen out of every twenty students during the past decade had been Presbyterian; the other twentieth included all other Protestants and Catholics, with the result that the College

53 Dorrian to Kirby, 27 Nov. 1883, A.I.C.R.
54 Woodlock to McCabe, 9 Nov. 1883, D.D.A.
55 Woodlock to Dorrian (copy), 28 Oct. 1883, A.C.D.A.
56 Woodlock to McCabe, 20 Nov. 1884, D.D.A.

was as Presbyterian in tone as St Malachy's was Catholic. Henry put his finger on one of the more tragic aspects of the problem when he asked how could Catholics be expected to frequent an institution whose students, in the presence of a royal commission, hissed him when he mentioned the name of the Catholic church?[57]

Henry's views on this issue, of course, corresponded closely with Dorrian's. And together they worked to realize the objective of making St Malachy's a university college for the Catholics of the north. And, in proportion to its numbers, it won in the 1880s an impressive number of prizes at intermediate level, and achieved considerable success at matriculation and the higher levels of the Royal University.[58] But Dorrian's dream of making it the 'Catholic University' of the north, to which he alluded on his last visit there on 19 August 1885, remained just that. Without state funding, which was an unrealistic expectation, this ambition could but remain a dream. A full and satisfactory solution to the problem of university education for Catholics was not to be achieved until 1908.

---

57 M.N., 10 June 1884.
58 William J. Walsh in transmitting the results of the first university examination of the Royal, which was compulsory for all students aspiring to a degree, noted that 6 students from Queen's College, Cork, 9 from Queen's College, Galway, 7 from Clonliffe College, 9 from Carlow College, 13 from Blackrock College and 12 from St Malachy's College had passed. He emphasised the significance of all these colleges beating Queen's College, Cork. (Walsh to McCabe, 6 Oct. 1883, D.D.A.)

11

Politico-religious issues and Roman reactions

I

The crisis provoked by the land struggle after 1879 had far-ranging repercussions, not least of which was its effect on the relations of the Catholic church in Ireland with the government and with the Holy See. This complex triangular relationship has rightly merited the interest of historians, but, apart from Dom Mark Tierney (who was permitted to research in Propaganda for his biography of Archbishop Croke, even though the papers for the pontificate of Leo XIII were not then available to scholars), no one has written about it, who has had access to the Vatican or Propaganda archives. The use of Irish diocesan archives and those of the Irish College, Rome, has gradually been yielding information on a period to which students of Irish church history have been attracted ever since the publication of the life of Archbishop Walsh in 1928. Though Dorrian did not play a leading role in shaping the principal responses of the bishops to the various stages of the land question or their justification of their positions at Rome — he could best be described as a constant and faithful supporter of Archbishop Croke's views — the subject is here treated more widely than his biography would otherwise deserve, because an examination of the Vatican and Propaganda archives has yielded material which throws fresh light on it.

II

As accusations against the part played by Irish churchmen in attacking the evils of landlordism began to pile up in Rome, the Holy See was faced with a delicate and difficult problem. On the one hand the evidence for the misery and hunger being experienced by many small farmers was incontrovertible, and on the other hand reports pointed to unjust and improper means being used to remedy the situation. The dreaded words, 'socialist' and 'communist', were used to describe the agitation associated with the Land League, and the charge was made that the obligation involved in the law of contracts was being repudiated. The bishops themselves were deeply divided on the morality of the League.[1]

The process of refining the social teaching of the church, to which the encyclical *Rerum Novarum* gave a powerful impetus, was moving at a slow and cautious pace in most Catholic countries in the early 1880s. The rights of ownership were scarcely questioned by many churchmen, and the sense of society's (as opposed to the private individual's) obligations to support the have-nots was still in a very rudimentary state of development. The defence of the Land League by the bishops who were favourable to it required skill and subtlety. They had to convince Rome that the policy of Parnell and Davitt was not one of encouraging people to shirk their lawful debts; on the contrary, they had to prove that the tenants enjoyed some share in the ownership of the land which they had made fertile by the sweat of their brows and, consequently, could not be expected to pay rents fixed by landlords, which were beyond their resources and were reducing them to destitution. The crimes which the crisis called forth, however sporadic and unwelcome to the organizers of the Land League, nonetheless, provided the kind of damning evidence which the enemies of the League could exploit in their efforts to prove to the Holy See that it was revolutionary, violent and irreligious. The struggle to convince Rome of the propriety of the aims and methods of the League and to ward off any hostile Roman intervention in Irish affairs that derived from the partial and self-interested evidence forwarded by the government, the landlords or their allies in Britain, lasted in one form or another to the end of Dorrian's life. Like Croke, the bishop of Down and Connor maintained that the real issue at stake was the defence of the innocent victims of an unjust system of land ownership, whose survival was often dictated by the caprices of landlords' debts, wet weather and bad harvests.

---

[1] Prof. E. Larkin in *The Roman Catholic church and the creation of the modern Irish state* (Philadelphia, 1975), p.24 maintains that five bishops — Croke, Dorrian, Nulty (Meath), MacCormack (Achonry) and Duggan (Clonfert) supported the Land League from the beginning and that the bishops of Limerick, Ross, Waterford, Kerry and Cloyne were favourable to it. Those who opposed it were Archbishops McCabe of Dublin, MacHale, MacEvilly (Coadjutor of Tuam), Moran (Ossory), Warren (Ferns), Walsh (Kildare), Delany (Cork), Gillooly (Elphin), Woodlock (Ardagh). Those who were neutral were McGettigan (Armagh), Donnelly (Clogher), Kelly (Derry), Leahy (Dromore), Conaty (Kilmore), Logue (Raphoe), Conway (Killala), Ryan (Coadjutor of Killaloe) and Lynch (Coadjutor of Kildare).

However, it was not difficult for the landlords and their sympathizers to forward catalogues of crimes to Rome and claim that these derived from an anarchic or communist movement which enjoyed clerical approval. So, faced with conflicting reports about what was really happening in Ireland, the congregation of Propaganda wrote in 1879 to Cardinal Manning, archbishop of Westminster (whose theological standing, as a result of his role at the Vatican Council, and whose reputation for political sagacity were high), for an explanation of the land crisis and the legitimacy of clerical involvement in it.

Manning's reply was characteristically thorough and judicious, and evinced that understanding and sympathy for the Irish poor which marked his episcopate. Explaining that for the previous three centuries the English government bore responsibility for the abnormal state of Ireland, he noted that the injustices suffered by the Irish in the past had left a very vivid memory. As an Englishman, he could not excuse their parliament for persistently neglecting the interests of the Irish people. Had that people not been profoundly Catholic and united to their clergy, they would have become revolutionaries like the Poles. The French clergy had remained in the sacristy and their people had obeyed the revolution; that danger existed in Ireland. Deftly quoting Gladstone's admission — the Fenians, not the English Government, gain whatever influence the clergy lose — Manning went on to emphasize the wisdom of tolerating a little excess from some priests rather than run the risk of weakening the only restraint which held back revolution. Strongly advising against a direct intervention of the Holy See 'on this most delicate matter' or the exclusion of the priests from political life, he suggested that a salutary admonition be given to the clergy and people to keep within the limits of the law and to abstain from all violence.[2] This sage and balanced advice, from one who was sufficiently removed from emotional involvement in this politico-religious issue to be considered dispassionate, and yet, by virtue of his political experience, contacts and understanding regarded as well-informed, rightly carried great and lasting weight in Vatican circles. Croke, Dorrian and their like-minded colleagues could scarcely have hoped for a more perspicacious defence and justification of their attitudes.

And as the situation deteriorated in the wake of the third bad harvest and reports spread of severe want and starvation among tenants in the west of Ireland, whose holdings barely afforded a subsistence livelihood in the best of circumstances, Dorrian took practical steps to alleviate some of the suffering. He sent a circular to

[2] Manning to Cardinal Simeoni, 23 Dec.1879, A.P.F. S.C.(Irlanda), 40, ff 864v-865v.

his priests asking that a special collection be taken up throughout the diocese 'for the suffering and depressed peasantry of the West of Ireland'. Lamenting the inactivity of the government in the face of near catastrophic problems, he expressed his surprise at its failure to provide employment rather than subject people to the demoralizing position of begging for alms. He himself made a personal appeal at St Patrick's Church and the response throughout the town was excellent: £539, a generous sum for the times, was subscribed.[3]

The distress was not confined to the western counties. In February 1880 Bernard McKenna, the parish priest of Kilcoo in Co Down, found it necessary to make a public appeal to relieve the misery prevailing in his parish. The *Ulster Examiner* reported that in many parts of Ulster people were in a most wretched condition.[4] Dorrian, who contributed £25, was annoyed at the official response of the government, which he characterized as a policy of doing nothing.[5] Anger at the paltry means taken by Dublin Castle to relieve the suffering — provision for help by Boards of Guardians to those who could not gain accommodation in workhouses — mounted in nationalist circles. When the *Examiner* remarked bitterly that men who could afford millions to butcher Afghans and Zulus could not see their way to giving a few thousands to avert famine in Ireland,[6] it was expressing a widespread feeling of growing impatience with the neglect of the government to take serious constructive measures to deal with the deteriorating conditions.

Dorrian devoted much of his Lenten pastoral letter to the crisis. Impatiently dismissing talk about workhouses being full or empty, and official statistics of distress, he insisted that the greatest inhumanity was committed by a government that allowed its industrious people to starve. Famine did not occur where wages could be earned, for foreign bread could always be bought. Referring disparagingly to the work of the relief committees, which had not yet distributed £30,000, when more than £1 million was sent to Bulgaria out of sympathy for the victims of Turkish atrocities, he observed tartly that, if they had worked as hard to obtain an act of parliament that would secure employment, they would have succeeded long since. The order of priorities should have been: the provision of employment for the able bodied before hunger could take its toll; the distribution of food and clothing to families where the parents were incapable of buying them. Insisting that the situation could not be met by almsgiving, which was merely a temporary solution, he

---

3 U.Ex., 20, 27 Jan.1880.
4 U.Ex., 17 Feb. 1880. In four months £439 was collected, of which £388 was disbursed for food, fuel and clothing.
5 Dorrian to Kirby, 21 Jan. 1880, A.I.C.R.
6 U.Ex., 10 Jan. 1880.

recalled the sad experience of 150 unemployed men in Co. Down, who had gone without their dinner on Christman Day.

Productive employment was the key to the solution, and one that lay within the powers of parliament, for, if it could spend millions on British interests in Egypt, it should have made similar efforts to create jobs for the starving poor. The first duty of a government was to feed its people; *regere est pascere* (to rule is to feed) was a divine axiom.

Having dealt with the obligations of the state on this central question of social justice (and, incidentally, gone well beyond the responsibilities of society as laid down by Leo XIII eleven years later in his encyclical, *Rerum Novarum*), Dorrian then turned to the problem of landlordism. He denied that this concept was evil, for scripture was not opposed to it, but he contended that it should be elastic, extending proprietary rights to the greatest number of owners in the widest possible way. If contracts were one-sided and unfair, they should be rectified not by violent social disruptions but by the supreme competent authority. Then, rebutting the argument of those who claimed that landlordism was evil because it was founded on unjust confiscation — an argument likely to lead to violence — he maintained that, however a man became the owner of land, whether by inheritance, industry, or confiscation in the past, the public good was best served by compensating a willing vendor rather than by any spirit of retaliation for past wrongs. Land tenure should be so regulated as to increase productiveness and give more employment to labourers. Exhorting his people to seek redress of their grievances only by constitutional means, he concluded by appealing for help for those in distress and by predicting that, ultimately, good would come out of the evil then afflicting them.[7]

The agrarian question figured prominently in the general election of March 1880. Parnell, who had gone to America on 2 January to rally support, both moral and financial, for the Land League among Irish emigrants, returned to spearhead the campaign of the Home Rule party. He decided to challenge the Liberal members who had stood aloof from the League and who counted on the support of the local bishops and clergy. He himself braved the opposition of the bishop of Cork to stand in Cork city, which he duly won, and two of his colleagues were only narrowly beaten in the county. In Wexford a prominent Catholic Liberal was annihilated by a Parnellite and everywhere, apart from the Conservative strongholds of Ulster, Parnell's candidates had great success. Sixty three nominal Home Rulers were returned, though many of them had made a very hasty conversion to safeguard their seats, and could not be relied upon to

7 B.M.N., 9 Feb. 1880.

give their committed and constant support to Parnell. Unlike some of his episcopal colleagues who had backed respectable Catholic Whigs, had incurred considerable opprobrium for their pains and been left bewildered by the narrow victories or defeats of their candidates after a bruising and bitter contest, Dorrian felt uplifted by the result. Elatedly he wrote to Rome:

> Ireland is erect and the drones and lukewarm MPs are set aside. Some Bishops and priests are shortsighted in opposing the active policy. The people see their way and must have themselves rooted in the land. They are right and will succeed. Don't believe the *Tablet* or Sir George Bowyer.[8] There is nothing against Religion in the agitation; but the poor, who are willing to work, have to starve and this must be put an end to. That's the whole case and the O'Connor [*sic*] Don, good as he was in many ways, has been set aside because of his want of sympathy with the tenants. Parnell has said nothing against equity and justice and time will tell. Hope is at last brightening.[9]

Parnell and Davitt could not have wished for a more favourable appreciation of their campaign or for a more withering analysis and contemptuous dismissal of their Whig opponents. Though Dorrian could do little for the Land League or Home Rule in his own diocese, his sympathies were fully behind those bishops who could and did use their influence in the Parnellite cause.

In the wake of this electoral success, the committee of the League decided to double its membership and to summon a conference on the land question in Dublin on 29 April. In default of attending it, Michael Cahill addressed an open letter to the secretaries. He suggested that the state should buy all land in Ireland and sell it to tenants at a reasonable price, that the state should vest all land belonging to public bodies or English, Scottish or other non-Irish owners, that waste lands should be reclaimed and given to tenants at a reasonable rent, that no farmer, without a special certificate from the land commission, should be allowed to farm more than fifty acres, and that sub-division should be ended. The conference contented itself with more limited objectives: it recommended that for holdings valued at £20 and under, the landlord's power of ejectment for non-payment of rent should be suspended for two years, and that for the same period a landlord should not be entitled to a rent higher

---

8 Sir George Bowyer, an English Catholic Whig, who had represented Wexford since 1874, was beaten in the election. The O'Conor Don, an influential Catholic landlord in Co. Roscommon, was also beaten; Davitt described his defeat as 'a great blow to Catholic whiggery and landlordism' (Moody, *Davitt*, p.372.)

9 Dorrian to Kirby, 14 Apr. 1880, A.I.C.R.

than the poor law valuation of a holding. It also suggested that a land commission should be established and empowered to transfer ownership of agricultural holdings from the landlords to the tenants, either by voluntary or compulsory purchase, with the state providing the capital and being repaid by annuities of five per cent of the purchase price over a period of thirty five years. If the sale were compulsory, the purchase price should be equivalent to twenty years' rent at the poor law valuation.[10]

Croke, never one to hesitate in publicly endorsing a policy he favoured, greatly heartened the Land Leaguers a month later by addressing an open letter to a meeting in his diocese. Referring to the suffering many Irishmen were then enduring and commending them for their patience and meekness in the face of it, he went on to repudiate most contemptuously the 'ugly names, and words of ominous signification borrowed from the vicious vocabulary of the Continent, . . . used to designate the efforts that are being made by well-meaning men throughout the country to prevent the Irish people from perishing at home or being drafted like cattle to climes beyond the sea'. Then, thinking of the catastrophic suffering caused by the bad weather, he proceeded to explain that it was 'cruel to punish a person for not paying a debt which nature has rendered it impossible for him to satisfy'.[11]

The very difficult circumstances obtaining in his diocese, where Catholics were very much a minority and where some landlords, especially those of a Tory and Orange complexion, vilified the land movement in their newspapers and diverted the sympathy of their tenants from it by beating the Orange drum, did not afford Dorrian opportunities for such spectacular leadership. But his sentiments were similar; in fact he was losing all patience with his episcopal colleagues who were so scared by the accusations laid at the door of the League that they were afraid to risk association with the movement in case the church would be in any way held responsible for the offences being committed against property. He found their prudence excessive. In June he confided to Tobias Kirby that 'the real enemies of the Church are those who have scant sympathy for the poor and they drive the people to despair. Prudence is necessary but the people sacrificed is hard to bear'.[12]

The bishops suffering from an excess of prudence must have been confirmed in their views by a letter from Cardinal Simeoni, the prefect of Propaganda, which was sent to the archbishop of Armagh but addressed to the whole Irish hierarchy. Simeoni had again

10 Moody, *Davitt*, pp 374-5.
11 F.J., 31 May 1880.
12 Dorrian to Kirby, 9 June 1880, A.I.C.R.

consulted Manning, and that shrewd ecclesiastical statesman had adverted to the difficulty that Propaganda would face in trying to intervene in political affairs in Ireland. Pointing out that a division between priests and people had occurred for the first time at the recent elections, when the majority of the people had submitted themselves to the direction of Protestants, unbelievers and nationalist Catholics, he argued that the loss of clerical influence was inevitable, if there was disunity among bishops and priests. He suggested that the Irish bishops could be invited to get agreement among themselves and formulate a programme of action.[13] Simeoni's letter, which was the first public Roman reaction to the conflicting reports reaching the Holy See about Ireland, closely followed Manning's proposals. Regretting the serious differences that had arisen and which had resulted in a majority of the people separating from the clergy and not hesitating 'to prefer the counsels of Protestants, of infidels, and of other wrong-minded persons', Propaganda now exhorted the bishops to apply an efficacious remedy to this evil. And this, it suggested, was to be found in a unity among the whole clerical body, which would keep the faithful within the bounds of union and charity. Consequently, they were invited to lay down a course of action which they themselves should observe and should impose on their clergy.[14] Though many of the bishops must have been taken aback by this analysis of the Irish religious scene, Manning had ensured that Rome did not tread on any delicate ground.

When the hierarchy held its customary meeting in June, the majority, to a greater or lesser extent, and especially prominent members like McCabe (Dublin), MacEvilly (Tuam), Moran (Ossory) and Gillooly (Elphin), still entertained reservations about Parnell and the Land League. But the series of resolutions which they issued were limited to an exposition of the rights and duties of both landlords and tenants and the moral obligation to avoid all 'unjust or illegal remedies' in trying to find a just and equitable solution to the land problem. To supporters of the Land League this counsel was mercifully uncontroversial, impeccable and bland, but to those who held that the rights of property were sacrosanct or who claimed that the Land League was either fomenting, providing a justification for, or at least not discouraging, agrarian crime, the episcopal generalities must have come as a great disappointment. Dorrian remarked to Tobias Kirby that they had not endorsed the 'not wise' pastorals of one or two of their number who had fallen foul of the Land League. In the circumstances the majority of the bishops had done all that was possible — eschew the use of violent means — and, doubtless, the

---

13 Manning to Simeoni, 3 May 1880, A.P.F., S.C.(Irlanda), 40, ff 860r-861r.
14 Simeoni to McGettigan, 1 June 1880, A.P.F., S.O.C.G., 1021, ff 58r-59r.

majority of those who were still suspicious of the motivation or behaviour of Parnell, Davitt and their allies did not feel that they could be any more specific in their guidance. Dorrian certainly felt that Simeoni's letter resulted from a misrepresentation at Rome of the real situation in Ireland and must have been pleased that the majority of his colleagues were not frightened into making any more detailed or hostile comment and limited themselves to repeating basic and unchallengeable principles of morality. His conviction of the opportuneness, value and moral necessity of the Land League had grown stronger:

> The latter [the Land League] speaks out plainly and but for it all distress would have been *absolutely ignored*. Parnell with all his mistakes has done good and is doing it. If any harm befal [sic] Religion, it will come not from him (for we can thwart him) but from those who eat and drink well and feel little or no sympathy with hunger and death. If the people take their own way it is only after they have been left to themselves and to merciless landlords, who are *indirectly* helped in the work of spoliation. I can only hint to some principles which I fear are not clearly understood at Rome. Otherwise that letter would not have been written to the Bishops. Some of us, very soft and easily made appear foolish, consider ourselves very wise to be sure.
> But let us not *drive away* the people or *blame* them for listening to their sympathizers . . . Things are represented falsely at Rome and it is well to be cautious about them.[15]

Dorrian's warning about the need for caution was not misplaced for misrepresentation at Rome was destined to last for several years and to grow more intense with the passage of time.

Events at home continued to contribute to the tragic circumstances which provoked these misrepresentations. In August the House of Lords rejected a government bill which would have entitled an evicted tenant to compensation if he could prove to a court that he was unable to pay his rent but that he was willing to pay a just rent which his landlord had refused. Thereupon, John Dillon, a dedicated supporter of the Land League, who had just been returned to parliament, declared in a most belligerent speech that farmers should prepare for a general strike against rent and promised that their leaders would see that every man who wanted a rifle would have one.[16]

The harvest of 1880, which matured early, proved much better

---

15 Dorrian to Kirby, 30 June 1880, A.I.C.R.
16 Lyons, *Parnell*, pp 132-3.

than that of 1879 — the output of the principal crops increased by a third — but the Land League was determined that the tenants would not be impoverished by being forced to pay back all arrears of rent to the landlords; the plan was that they should pay only what they could afford both in rent and arrears. And as evictions had increased in the second quarter of 1880, the reaction of the League became correspondingly more determined. On 7 September Parnell delivered at Ennis his celebrated advice, which sparked off the policy that became known as 'boycotting', from the name of its first well-known victim. Reiterating his oft-repeated counsel not to pay unjust rents, 'to keep a firm grip on your homesteads', he urged his audience to defeat the policy of eviction by a concerted effort to deny the landlord rent for land from which someone had been evicted; no one was to bid for that farm and, if anyone were to defy this policy, he was to be treated as the leper of old; he was to suffer total ostracism, 'in the fair and in the market place, and even in the house of worship'.[17]

This development, which had been foreshadowed earlier, was to place a weapon of immense power in the hands of the League, and a weapon against which there was ultimately no defence. And from this stage to a call for a total strike against rent was a small step.[18] The statistics of agrarian crime, which had dropped from 404 in the last quarter of 1879 to 294 in the first quarter of 1880, rose again to 355 for the third quarter of the year and reached the staggering figure of 1696 for the last quarter. The vast majority of these concerned intimidation, injury to animals and damage to property, and though the incidence of murders dropped from nine in 1879 to eight in 1880 and in fact the first victim of this phase of the land struggle had been a tenant shot dead by his landlord, the murder of Lord Mountmorres in September, in very brutal circumstances, aroused extremely strong criticism of the Land League, which was made to bear the brunt of the blame for it. The policy of the League was proving effective; evictions began to fall as landlords and their agents realized the strength and ruthlessness of the boycott weapon.[19] But the archbishop of Dublin felt compelled, in the wake of the Mountmorres murder, to issue a pastoral letter about the violence associated with the land struggle. Though he did not counsel passive acceptance of the tenants' condition, he blamed speakers at the Land League meetings for their provocative language against landlords and for not repudiating the extreme threats of hecklers. But what shocked and angered many of his readers was his claim that the government had given proof of its readiness and willingness to redress Irish wrongs,

17 Ibid., p.134.
18 Moody, *Davitt*, pp 420-21.
19 Ibid., p.421.

but had been thwarted by those who threatened to make Ireland ungovernable and who consequently played into the hands of those who refused to consider change.[20]

It was almost certainly this pastoral Dorrian had in mind when, in a letter to Kirby, he referred to one that was 'no doubt well intended but not necessary and not correct in its statements'. Remarking that such publications pleased officials but only irritated and provoked the people, he assured his Roman correspondent that there was 'nothing against the laws of God or man in this agitation — but the contrary'. He insisted that religion would be ruined if the priests in these circumstances refused their sympathy to their people, but he predicted that both bishops and priests would be 'true to principle and to duty and will not desert the church in her different wants'.[21]

On 2 November Parnell and a number of leading members of the Land League, including four MPs, were charged with conspiring to prevent the payment of rent and creating hostility between landlords and tenants. This unnecessary show of force in response to the agitation provoked instant and widespread indignation and protest. 3,000 people packed St Mary's Hall, Belfast on 17 November to register their anger and to establish a fund for the defence of the prisoners. Ten priests were present on the platform, Michael Cahill was called to the chair and, in the course of a vigorous speech against the charge that the prisoners had caused a disturbance between landlords and tenants, said he would like to know the man who would not cause a disturbance between landlords of the Irish variety and their tenants. He insisted that the object of the traversers — to sustain the Irish farmers in their holdings — was right and just, and J.P. Greene, the administrator of St Mary's parish, maintained that those who claimed that the Land League was revolutionary had been answered by Archbishop Croke and by the bishop of Cloyne, who had pointed out that they were tackling a great social problem and only wanted justice for both landlords and tenants. James O'Boyle, the parish priest of Saintfield, declared that there was no more holy task for a minister of religion than that of helping to save the lives of multitudes of people. And he confidently asserted that, had it not been for 'the obedience engendered in the Irish people by the teaching of the Catholic Church, all the might of England could never have stayed the power of Ireland'. He denounced the landlords for personal immorality and for destroying the morals of Irish girls who, he claimed, had once been 'as fair and pure as the snow on the mountain's brow', before they were corrupted by such contact. John Duddy, the veteran Belfast nationalist, complained that five million people were excluded from any interest in the soil and compelled to

20 F.J., 11 Oct. 1880.
21 Dorrian to Kirby, 1 Nov. 1880, A.I.C.R.

toil for the support and luxury of 10,000 idlers, who monopolized the land of the entire country.

Dorrian was not present but subscribed £5 for the defence fund and his letter enclosing this contribution was read out at the meeting. He pointed out that the 'traversers' were entitled to a fair trial and went on to argue that the government had an obligation to remove the causes of social injustice:

> They are engaged in what they say is a legal and constitutional effort, within the moral laws, to remedy a great social evil — to rescue from misery and starvation thousands of our people, and elevate our country from hunger, mockery and contempt to its proper rank in civilisation among the nations of the world. This is surely worthy of approval. The Government, therefore, might have done better to have begun by removing the cause of our wretchedness and discontent, and formulating a law to give every tiller of the soil a motive to improve and protect his holding.[22]

III

Croke and four of his suffragans from Munster were in Rome when Parnell was arrested. They were the first bishops to visit the Vatican since the agitation began. Pope Leo, at their audience, agreed that they should stay united with their people and assist them in their temporal needs, provided they avoided anything of a revolutionary tendency. Croke assured him that there was no such danger as 'the question lay not between the people & the govt. but between the people and their landlords, by whom they have been so long & so cruelly treated'.[23] The cardinal prefect of Propaganda also counselled them to sustain their flocks in their just demands, but advised them to exclude their clergy from political activity,[24] and seemingly felt the correct approach was to use pastoral letters to discourage violence and explain the rights and obligations of both parties. Croke put the most benign interpretation on all this advice and promptly sent off a contribution of £25 to the Parnell defence fund. The bishops of Limerick, Clonfert, Cloyne and Ross also subscribed. But the majority did not do so.[25]

22 B.M.N., 18 Nov. 1880.
23 Kirby to McCabe, 11 Nov. 1880, D.D.A.
24 Ma si adoperassero ad impedire la soverchia ingerenza degli ecclesiastici nei movimenti politici. (A.P.F. *Acta*, 250, ff 38r-40r.)
25 Typical of those still firmly opposed to Parnell — McCabe, Woodlock, Gillooly — was MacEvilly of Tuam. He explained that he was glad that some of the priests kept with the people thereby frustrating the 'godless agitators' and feared that, when a settlement was reached, a Fenian or revolutionary element would be left behind which would be hard to stop. (MacEvilly to McCabe, 19 Nov. 1880, D.D.A.)

Though Parnell and his fellow-accused had little to fear from an Irish jury (and, in fact, their cases were duly dismissed when the jury disagreed), an attack was being mounted in another quarter which might have had serious consequences for clerical participation in the Land League and ultimately for the whole relationship of priests and people in Ireland. In December 1880 George Errington, the MP for Longford (who had been elected as a Home Ruler of the Whiggish variety but later resigned from the party when Parnell became chairman), arrived in Rome to press his case against the immorality of the League and the impropriety of clerical involvement in it. Errington, a nephew of Cardinal Wiseman's ill-fated coadjutor, was a landlord of part English and part Irish Catholic descent. Educated at Oscott, he spoke and wrote French fluently, and his political and class contacts guaranteed him an entrée into the inner circles of the Liberal government.

But what impressed Granville, the Foreign Secretary, and Forster, the Irish Secretary, was that he undertook to offer them the assistance of a very powerful and influential ally in their campaign against the Land League — none other than the Vatican itself. They realized the immense potential of a Vatican condemnation of the League or even of significant elements of its policy and were keen to encourage the enlistment of such a formidable power. Though untrained in theology, Errington never doubted his knowledge of moral principles or understanding of moral questions, and from a 'holier-than-thou' attitude consistently dismissed in the next few years the moral views of the vast majority of bishops and priests as wrong and malicious. Self-righteous and self-important, Errington mistakenly believed that he was exercising far more influence than was in fact the case, and, ignoring or — more often — not detecting the subtleties and nuances of skilful Vatican diplomats, invariably thought that he had won some major concession, only to find that the papal intervention he so desired amounted to little more than general condemnations of violence and left the bishops ultimately free to decide how to apply accepted principles in their own particular situations.

Errington made contact in Rome with Bernard Smith, an Irish Benedictine, who was a consultor to the congregations of Propaganda and Oriental Rites.[26] Though Smith's personal knowledge of the

---

[26] A native of Cavan, Smith studied at the Irish College and was ordained for the diocese of Kilmore in 1839. In 1847 he was professed at Montecassino but forced to leave when the abbey was secularized during the revolution of the following year. He later became vice-rector of the Irish College and of the North American College before resuming the Benedictine habit. He spent most of his life in Rome, becoming in turn professor of theology and Hebrew in Propaganda College and rector of St Anselm's College. Pope Leo XIII ultimately appointed him titular abbot of Potirone. He died in 1892.

Irish scene in the 1880s was extremely limited, he had a very wide range of contacts, including some Irish bishops for whom he acted as agent, various Benedictine superiors in England and Australia, and many upper class English and Anglo-Irish Catholics whom he encountered on their visits to Rome. Errington relied on Smith to introduce him to officials at Propaganda and the Vatican and to pass on the contents of his letters to them. Smith remained sympathetic to Errington's views and critical of clerical involvement in the land campaign. But Errington found a more powerful ally in the person of Cardinal Edward Henry Howard. Howard, a cousin of the duke of Norfolk, who was widely regarded as the leading English Catholic, owed his rapid advancement to the red hat not to any personal merit but to his family name and position and to the desire of the Vatican to maintain its tradition of having British Catholics represented by a cardinal in the curia. Through his family background, education and military service, Howard was closely connected with the aristocracy and gentry, and naturally their cris du coeur about the injustices their colleagues were suffering in Ireland made a deep impression on him, particularly in the absence of any fair explanation or justification of the tenants' case.

A further factor favouring Errington's schemes was the emphasis being placed on ecclesiastical diplomacy during the pontificate of Leo XIII. Leo had spent a short time as papal nuncio in Belgium before his appointment as archbishop of Perugia and, perhaps, because of the very brevity of his service in Brussels (which his superiors at the time did not rate highly), was left with a rather inflated conviction of the value of diplomatic activity. Much of his time and energy as pope were to be devoted to solving problems with Germany, Spain, Portugal, Belgium, Switzerland, Austria and France by diplomatic initiatives.[27] And though his first and supreme priority was the restoration of the temporal power of the papacy and every diplomatic card that could be played was directed to that end, he was keen to link the Holy See as widely as possible with all powerful and influential governments. Unlike Pius IX, whose policies had led to church-state coolness, if not hostility, in many European countries, Leo was anxious to be a bridge-builder, and since the British government ruled several million Catholics throughout its vast empire, he, and consequently his officials, felt that the establishment of good relations with that government was very important. Britain might even be induced to exert pressure on Italy to come to terms with the Holy See.

---

27 Gambetta, the anti-clerical French leader, commented on Leo's election: 'They have elected a new Pope, the elegant and refined Cardinal Pecci . . . more diplomat than priest', cited in I.E. Ward 'Leo XIII: The Diplomat Pope', *Review of Politics*, xxviii (1966), 47.

Errington, in offering his services to Granville, the Foreign Secretary, explained that he hoped to assist the government by obtaining support in Rome for that section of the Irish clergy which believed that 'Religion at any cost should be on the side of order'.[28] And he further elaborated on this grotesque interpretation of religion as an arm of the police service by recounting to Smith his fear that 'the communistic and unchristian policy of Dr Croke has received some countenance in Rome'. If 'questions *really involving* . . . xtian doctrines as to society and property are ever left open', he argued, the position of the moderate clergy 'will become impossible, and the results will be actually very serious for the country, but what I think worst, *shameful for the church*'. In effect he sought a totally unambiguous condemnation of the Land League, which, he insisted, was directly responsible for 'the present astounding state of Social anarchy and for the numerous outrages & innumerable breaches of the law which are occurring'.[29]

Errington, complete with a dossier of Land League crimes, arrived in Rome and obtained an audience with the pope. He then called with Cardinal Jacobini, the Secretary of State, and at the congregation of Propaganda left a 'memoire', written in French, on the politico-moral questions disturbing Ireland. In this he argued that the agitation had taken on a character totally different from its original intention of seeking legitimate reforms, and he claimed that the leaders, with a remarkable cynicism, had excited an ignorant and enthusiastic people to the point of fanaticism. Those leaders even dared to say that no influence was more damaging to them than that of the Catholic church. Though the bishops in their assembly had passed a series of prudent resolutions, some of their number took the popular side, and they were quoted along with the most advanced authors in the socialist journals of the movement. Having painted this lurid picture of Ireland, Errington then chose his brighest colours to describe the favourable situation enjoyed by the church under British rule, referred to the concessions Catholics were obtaining, and observed that the interests of civilization and religion demanded that the *entente* of the two powers should be as cordial as possible. Nothing could bring this about more effectively than the re-establishment of diplomatic relations between England and the Holy See. Stressing that the time was providential, as anarchy was daily increasing, he pulled what he thought was a shrewd stroke by suggesting that Roman intervention before the reassembly of parliament on 6 January would have an influence and importance that it

---

28 Errington to Granville, cited in E. Larkin, *The Roman Catholic Church and the creation of the modern Irish state*, p.59
29 Errington to Smith, 21 Nov. 1880, A.S.P.B.R.

would not have later on.[30] Errington's case was carefully compiled and judiciously presented, designed to maximise the aspects that would appeal to Rome, but obviously Rome could not take action on the evidence of one party to the conflict.

So, faced with charges that had acquired a greater importance because of the interest the government had taken in pressing them (which Errington doubtless emphasized in his conversations) and the possibility, however remote, of moving at some future date towards diplomatic relations with Britain, the Vatican sought the opinions of other well-informed participants in or observers of the Irish question. The most forthright expression of opinions on the other side came from the irrepressible Croke, whose views arrived just in time for consideration by the Vatican before any action was taken. He too wrote in French, though he supplied an English version for the rector of the Irish College. Stating as incontrovertible facts that the Irish were the worst fed, clad and housed people in Europe and yet most devoted both to the practice of their faith and to the Holy See, he argued that it was preposterous to suppose that they could join in any movement opposed to faith or morals. Yet nine-tenths of the people at home and all of them abroad, all the junior clergy, and considerably more that half the senior clergy supported the Land League, and all bishops and priests believed the land laws were unjust. Fewer acts of violence had been committed in that year than at any corresponding time in the past twenty years; the leaders of the League, especially Parnell, Dillon and Davitt had consistently opposed violence and had not recommended the witholding of rents but only the non-payment of unjust rents. Defending Parnell as 'a man of high honour and unimpeachable character', Croke concluded with a stern warning about the dire consequences of a Roman intervention (obviously he meant in the form of condemnation) which he predicted 'would be attended with the most ruinous results'.[31]

Archbishop McCabe, however, submitted a very different interpretation of events; he was as despondent and melancholy as Croke was and self-assured. McCabe insisted that the doctrines of the Land League were subversive of the foundations of society since they gave each individual the right to modify or totally repudiate contracts which had been solemnly entered into. Accusing the League of intimidation on a massive scale, he charged that a reign of terror prevailed in a large part of the country and quoted Parnell's promise

30 A.P.F. S.C.(Irlanda), 40, ff 795r-802v.
31 Croke to Jacobini, 24 Dec.1880, A.S.V., S.S. 1880, Rub, 278, Prot. 49117, ff 214r-218r. This letter arrived too late for consideration by Jacobini and the other cardinals on 26 Dec. but was studied by the pope before he finalized his letter of 3 Jan. 1881.

to go much further, if his demands were not met. The conduct of some of the clergy was unjustifiable and damaging to religion, and their sermons in church were a source of grave scandal; good priests, who took part in meetings and tried to repudiate dangerous doctrines, were publicly insulted. The Holy See, McCabe explained, could intervene in some way to warn off those priests who were doing so much damage to religion.

The most potent obstacle, however, in the way of Errington and his friends was the towering figure of Cardinal Manning. Cardinal Simeoni had again sought Manning's advice and Manning's sympathies for the victims of injustice always transcended all narrow national allegiances. Manning began by putting the charges made against the whole body of the clergy into perspective: of twenty eight bishops, two or three had allowed their enthusiasm too much rein[32] and of three thousand priests perhaps one hundred had used excessive language. Consequently neither the episcopate nor priesthood was guilty of censure. The sympathies of both priests and bishops were in favour of the people, and he, Manning, though English and a believer in imperial unity, was cordially united with them in that respect. Warning of the danger of Ireland being sacrificed as Poland had been, he pinpointed the hazards she faced as originating in continental republicanism and in the implacable vendetta of Irish-Americans, many of whom had lost their faith. Then, with a finality that would have pleased the most determined Irish republican and must have stuck firmly in Roman memories for years, he declared that he would not conceal his view that the state of Ireland was intolerable and that the blame rested on England. Within the parameters of imperial unity (necessary both for Ireland and the religious salvation of England) and the right of owners to get just value for their property, he recommended that there should be a national restitution of the land by the English people to the Irish; just as England had once bought out owners of slaves, a similar remedy was required.

Out-'croking' Croke, Manning then declared that he himself would be regarded as a revolutionary by those who wanted papal intervention, and expressed his conviction that, if the English government did not succeed in contenting and governing Ireland within three years, the Irish-Americans would make her ungovernable. In that situation neither the pope nor the bishops could interfere, for a papal intervention would be denounced by both parties. But the pope could write a letter to the bishops praising the faith, patience and Christian virtue of the Irish people, and the bishops could deplore certain cruel outrages that had taken place as

---

32 Si sono esternati con una certa vivacità.

the work of the enemies of their country, and declare that in union with their people they would not cease to use all legal means to obtain for the tenants the guarantees and security which English and Scottish tenants enjoyed. Neither the pope nor the bishops could intervene without the risk of separating priests and people further, unless there was an explicit declaration of sympathy with the tenants.[33] Not for the first time, Manning's calm advice was accepted as impartial, and duly followed.

Cardinal Jacobini, the Secretary of State, who had won a reputation for skilful diplomacy as nuncio in Vienna, invited the cardinal prefect and secretary of Propaganda, and four other cardinals, to a meeting on 26 December, to discuss the possible contents of a papal letter on the Irish question.[34] On the following day Simeoni submitted a draft which, with a few changes by the pope, contained the basic ideas[35] used by Leo in his letter to the archbishop of Dublin, and which, as Errington had hoped, was timed to appear before the opening of parliament but was far too carefully nuanced to provide the succour that Errington's friends craved. Commending the Irish for their fidelity in the past, Leo encouraged them to show due obedience to their rulers, and recalling the advice given by Gregory XVI to act only with justice and moderation, he reminded the archbishop that he too had recently assured some Irish bishops who were visiting Rome of his anxiety for the welfare of Ireland and had reminded them that it was not permissible to disturb public order on account of it. The pope expressed his confidence in the justice and prudence of the civil authorities, observed that it would be safer for Ireland to avail of legal methods and avoid causing offence, and asked the archbishop and his colleagues to try to ensure that the Irish people did not exceed the limits of right and justice in these difficult matters.[36] Though Errington professed satisfaction and claimed that the government was very grateful, and some Irish bishops were embarrassed at the hint of a rebuke that could be read into it, the pope's letter did not make any significant difference to clerical support for and participation in the Land League.

Whatever Dorrian's private views about the papal intervention

33 Manning to Simeoni, 7 Dec. 1880, A.P.F. S.C.(Irlanda), 40, ff 831r-814v.
34 Jacobini to Simeoni, A.P.F., S.O.C.G., 1015, f.157rv.
35 Ibid., ff 159r-160r. Simeoni suggested to Jacobini that reference be made by Leo to the counsel he had given to the bishops whom he had met in Rome to distance their people from violence and rebellion against human and divine law, and to the reports that this advice had been forgotten in favour of the suggestions of Fenians and other revolutionaries, which had already been condemned. Simeoni also mentioned O'Connell's abhorrence of bloodshed. Leo's letter did not include references to the Fenians or O'Connell but did refer to the exhortations to peace of Gregory XVI in 1839 and 1844.
36 I.E.R., 3rd series ii, (Mar. 1881), 183-4.

were, it certainly did not alter his attitude to the Land League. And he made no effort to put the brakes on the increasing number of his priests who were attending the League meetings and who were inevitably given prominent positions at them. The very large and enthusiastic gathering that took place in St Mary's Hall, Belfast on 18 February to protest at the re-arrest of Michael Davitt could not have been held without his permission and implicit support. In his Lenten pastoral he repeated verbatim most of what he had written the previous year about the duty of a government to provide employment, the right order of priorities for the state in dealing with widespread distress, and the correct moral approach to the disputed issue of landlordism. He then went on to claim that the current agitation was not opposed in principle to an equitable settlement of the land question. And denouncing coercion as the weapon of the tyrant and not the right response to the problem of the hungering multitudes, he termed the latest dose of it 'unstatesmanlike, irritating and illogical'.[37]

The crisis absorbed Dorrian's interest, and he was always ready to make any contribution he could, at a national hierarchical level, to help deal with it. When the bishops met to draw up a letter to thank the pope for his intervention he was one of the fifty per cent who bothered to turn up. And when rumours of the establishment of diplomatic relations between England and the Holy See were bruited abroad, he indignantly rejected the idea.

During his visit to Rome in February, Patrick Moran, the bishop of Ossory, was startled to hear Cardinal Jacobini, the Secretary of State, raise the issue of diplomatic relations between England and the Vatican. As it transpired, Jacobini was really only sounding out Moran's reaction to the possibility of such diplomatic contact; no initiative had even been broached at the normal levels of communication between governments, though Moran suspected that prominent English Catholics in Rome, especially Lady Georgiana Fullerton,[38] were making unofficial approaches to the Vatican. Moran immediately took fright. As his mentor, Cardinal Cullen, had done in the 1840s, he viewed this suggestion with apprehension and

---

37 U.Ex., 26 Feb. 1881.

38 A couple of letters from A.G. Fullerton survive among the meagre correspondence of Cardinal Howard preserved in the archives of the Venerable English College, Rome. In one of them he bemoans 'the social, agrarian and political revolution' with which they have been faced for some time (20 April ?) and in another, dated 13 May, refers to the terrible news from Ireland which is afflicting Lady Georgiana (this almost certainly referred to the assassination of Cavendish and Burke on 6 May 1882). Lady Georgiana, who was a sister of Lord Granville, the Foreign Secretary, frequently sojourned in Rome. She had influential contacts both in the Vatican and in English government and diplomatic circles. The Fullertons bore the costs of erecting Ballintoy church.

horror, instinctively fearing the consequences of Irish ecclesiastical issues being filtered to Rome through the lens of an unsympathetic government, and he immediately conveyed his anxieties and fears to the archbishop of Dublin. McCabe, on receipt of this communication, passed on the news of this alarming prospect to all his colleagues and warned them of the importance of making their views known in Rome, if they believed this development were 'inexpedient'. All who answered — the vast majority — unanimously opposed such a development.

Dorrian's reaction was characteristically forthright: no price was too high to pay to oppose any machiavellian moves which could redound to the disadvantage of the church in Ireland: 'I would strain every nerve to resist an intermediate Nunciature in London between Ireland and the Apostolic See. I need not adduce reasons. Hunger and famine always welcome in preference to hostility and cunning. I have no faith in such Nuncio. It would be a death blow to our dearest religious interests.'[39] The bishops met in Dublin on 15 March and conveyed their views to Moran to be presented by him to the pope. They repudiated in the firmest terms any attempt to 'subject the affairs of the Irish Church to the care of a Nuncio resident in London', which, they averred, would 'destroy the filial confidence which has hitherto bound our people to the Holy See . . . and would create in the minds of the Irish race distrust for the decisions and appointments coming to them through his hands from the Holy See'. And they reminded the pope of the hard choice made by their predecessors who were prepared to forego the benefits of Emancipation rather than tolerate a government veto on episcopal appointments.[40] This formal response to an informal inquiry, though it left the Vatican authorities in no doubt about the strength of Irish episcopal feeling, transgressed the acknowledged Roman canons of consultation, and Herbert Vaughan, the bishop of Salford, was undoubtedly reflecting Vatican reaction accurately when he reported to McCabe that Moran's handling of the whole issue had been regarded as clumsy and indelicate.[41]

But the episcopal unity that was forged by the threat of English intervention in Irish ecclesiastical affairs did not extend to a proposal made on the same occasion that no bishop should make a public pronouncement on political questions on which they differed and that the minority should be bound by the majority. The suggestion was prompted by Archbishop McCabe's tactless denunciation of the Ladies Land League, which embarrassed some of his colleagues.

39 Dorrian to McCabe, 6 Mar. 1881, D.D.A.
40 Bishops to Moran, 15 Mar. 1881, A.S.V., S.S. 1881, Rub.278, ff 159r-161r.
41 Vaughan to McCabe, 28 Mar. 1881, D.D.A.

Riled by Parnell's consorting with the French communard, Henri Rochefort, and Victor Hugo, in Paris, whence he had gone after Gladstone's Coercion bill had passed into law, and appalled by the prospect of women taking to the public platform and conducting the Land League, with its attendant excesses, McCabe protested in his Lenten pastoral against 'this attempt at degrading the women of Ireland . . . from men who have drawn the country into her present terrible deplorable condition . . . men who have sent their agents to fawn on notorious infidels and revolutionists'.[42] Croke took advantage of a letter against this insinuation to congratulate its author publicly on challenging the 'monstrous imputations' cast upon the Ladies Land League by his brother of Dublin, and to predict that McCabe would not in future be allowed 'to use his lance so freely as he had hitherto done or to ventilate unquestioned the peculiar political theories which he is known to hold in opposition to the cherished convictions of a great and indeed overwhelming, majority of the Irish priests and people'.[43] This rebuff to the unpopular McCabe brought Croke a further wave of the popularity he dearly relished but caused embarrassment to his episcopal colleagues and immense damage to Croke's standing in Rome.[44] The breach was healed at Moran's suggestion by Croke apologizing to McCabe and, though the apology was less than half-hearted, since it referred to the canonical impropriety of the offence and did not withdraw the content of the offending letter, McCabe accepted it in a generous spirit. Dorrian, who was less volatile and more circumspect politically than Croke, doubtless shared in the general episcopal embarrassment at this contretemps, but as he later claimed that his own views resembled Croke's, there is every reason to believe that his annoyance with McCabe for the original faux pas would have been much greater than his displeasure at Croke's rejoinder.

42 F.J., 12 Mar. 1881.
43 F.J., 17 Mar. 1881.
44 Errington immediately alerted Smith about Croke's 'painful letter' in response to McCabe's *admirable* pastoral' on the Ladies Land League, and begged him to convey this information about the scandalous affair to Cardinals Jacobini and Howard and his friend Monsignor Masotti at Propaganda to ensure that the Holy See act to prevent the greatest dangers and scandals. (Smith to Errington, 18 Mar. 1881, A.S.P.B.R.) Lord Emly, the Limerick landlord and convert to Catholicism who had formerly served in Gladstone's cabinet, forwarded the relevant papers together with a doleful account of the incident to Cardinal Howard. Maintaining that the effect of the exchange had been 'most lamentable and most alarming, shattering the image which even the most bigoted Protestants' held of the unity and order of the church and causing Catholics to hang their heads in shame — indeed the greatest scandal since St Patrick — he begged Howard to refer the matter to the pope. And charging that the archbishop of Cashel was doing 'immense' evil in Ireland, he recommended that Croke be summoned to Rome. (Emly to Howard, 22 Mar. 1881, A.V.E.C.R.)

When Parnell came north in the following month to attend a Land League meeting in Hilltown, Dorrian and the bishop of Dromore sent letters of apology for non-attendance. Wishing the participants success, Dorrian explained that he wanted to see the Irish tenant farmers comfortably settled in their holdings and that he approved of every effort to root the people in the soil.[45] He was thereby giving support to the Land League at a time when Parnell had not given a definite opinion on the new Land bill.

That keenly-awaited bill had been introduced on 7 April. It conceded the long demanded three Fs — fair rent, free sale and fixity of tenure — and established a land court to fix rents at a fair level. The more moderate wing of the Parnellite party accepted it but the more determined wings both in Ireland and America grumbled at its inadequacy. The *Ulster Examiner* commented that it was not by any means satisfactory, referred to the 'cumbrous manner' in which some very important concessions were made, claimed that it was mostly concerned with guaranteeing the landlords' rights and noted that, as judicial rents were fixed on a fifteen year basis, those fixed in a time of prosperity could be too high in a time of adversity.[46] But as the debates in parliament neared an end its criticisms grew more strident: the bill had become 'a wretched, contemptible sham — a miserable compromise, the abject and cowardly surrender of liberal principles to landlord arrogance'.[47] Revd James O'Boyle conceded contemptuously that there was something in the bill but likened it to a halfpenny in the pound.[48] But he later insisted that the farmers should be the absolute owners of the land, and denounced Forster 'as the worst chief secretary that ever goaded Ireland to madness'.[49]

The bishops met on 26 April to consider the bill. They had already established a sub-committee which had taken the advice of distinguished lawyers on the terms on offer. Their resolutions accepted the good will behind the legislation, they considered the measures involved to be a real advance, and their proposals were designed to increase the confidence of the tenants in the even-handed administration of the new land courts. They advised that those who owed arrears of rent should not be excluded from the benefit of the bill, that the landlord should be obliged to prove that the rent was not fair, if he sought an increase, that a tenant under threat of eviction should be allowed the same time for the sale of his tenancy as was allowed for the non-payment of rent and that there should be an improvement of the condition of agricultural lab-

45 U.Ex., 26 Apr. 1881.
46 U.Ex., 9 Apr. 1881.
47 U.Ex., 26 July 1881.
48 U.Ex., 26 Apr. 1881.
49 U.Ex., 21 June 1881.

ourers.⁵⁰ When the bill eventually passed into law on 29 July, after interminable discussion in parliament, Parnell was faced with the difficult decision of giving it his support or agreeing with his left wing followers who wanted a rent strike. And as he played for time to test the new act in the courts, he courted the left wing by more provocative statements from the public platform. And it was for one of these, in reply to Gladstone's criticisms of the loyalty of his movement, when he taunted the prime minister with the failure of England's mission in Ireland, that he was arrested and jailed in Kilmainham for conduct likely to lead to a breach of the peace.⁵¹ There was an immediate and enormous outcry against this action.

On 14 October a meeting was held in St Mary's Hall at short notice, and large crowds, including at least ten priests, turned up to protest. A fortnight later another huge crowd gathered to inaugurate an anti-coercion union for the whole of Ulster, and was treated to a stinging attack on Gladstone by Michael Cahill.⁵² Between these meetings, more than thirty Belfast priests met on 24 October to register their protest at the imprisonment of Parnell, his fellow MPs, Dillon and Sexton, and other close collaborators. They passed resolutions expressing sympathy with the jailed leaders, objected to imprisonment without trial as a means calculated to drive people to seek redress unconstitutionally, and urged the tenants not to become involved in any action which would embroil them with the law as it was then administered; they each contributed £1 to the Prisoners' Fund.⁵³

Dorrian, who was not present on these occasions, found an opportunity for airing his views on the land question a short time later. The occasion was the inaugural meeting of the St Patrick's Club (a literary society based in St Patrick's parish) and his contribution was called forth by what he regarded as the excessive and injudicious comments made by the advanced nationalist, John Duddy, in response to a paper on the natural resources of Ireland. Duddy, criticizing the lecturer for not giving an opinion on the course to be followed in the midst of the great social and moral revolution they were then passing through, asked impassionedly if they were to be obliged to pass on to their descendants the heritage of slavery and misery which they had received. He feared the courage and manhood of Ireland were unequal to the occasion. The heart of the country was turning towards the great patriot archbishop of Cashel, who seemed to feel the difficulty of the situation but who seemed to lack the great characteristic of Stephen Langton, who

50 U.Ex., 30 Apr. 1881.
51 Lyons, *Parnell*, pp 164-9.
52 U.Ex., 29 Oct. 1881.
53 U.Ex., 25 Oct. 1881.

headed the barons in their confontration with the king and wrung from him the liberties that England needed at that time. Was there no Langton, Duddy wondered, to lead the Irish people when their sons were in prison? Then explaining that he spoke with every respect and veneration for the bishop who was present, he went on to charge the clergy, the recognized leaders of the people, with 'calling down the agitation' instead of encouraging the people to keep it on a moral and bloodless level. Consequently, the land question would be settled in bloodshed, unless the policy of passive resistance was fully applied.

Stung by this sweeping and undeserved reference to clerical inaction and angered by the threat of violence in Duddy's speech, Dorrian felt obliged to give moral guidance on the issues at stake. Conceding that Duddy held his views honestly, the bishop declared that, though it was not a suitable time to enter into a discussion of 'extreme points', if he were to do so, he would differ from him 'seriously, strongly, essentially, and from a moral point of view, unequivocally'. Admitting that passive resistance was a very powerful weapon when exercised legitimately, he pointed out that it must be used not against but in favour of morality, and if anything in its exercise was opposed in the slightest degree to what was moral, it ceased to be legitimate passive resistance.

He claimed that there was a great deal of good in the Land Act, though it was not all they could wish for, and by practical experience and honest endeavour the people would reap the advantages of it and the tenants would benefit by reductions of one third or one quarter of their rents. The bishops had wished to see a more favourable act but he was not prepared to go as far as Duddy, who claimed the purpose of the Land League was to abolish landlordism. The Land League had done a great deal of good and they all wanted to see every one own his holding, but even that would not abolish landlordism. For, if a man let a rood or half a rood to a labourer to plant cabbages, he became a landlord, and 'if the Father of the Faithful were to return again to earth, he would propound the doctrine of landlordism'. Defending the 'illustrious' archbishop of Cashel as he had defended the right to private property, Dorrian (who incidentally claimed that he himself was as advanced a patriot as anyone present) declared that he 'thoroughly endorsed every word written by that archbishop'. He then went on to encourage agitation on a constitutional and peaceful basis, even agitation by passive resistance, if it was not immoral, (though he did not offer further clarification of this point) and explained that he was obliged to make these comments not only in vindication of the honour of the archbishop but also to show that he himself was 'not afraid to walk' in Croke's footsteps.[54]

54 U.Ex., 8 Nov. 1881.

Since Croke had condemned the 'No Rent' manifesto immediately after its publication,[55] Dorrian's expression of full support for Croke's views made clear his stand on that issue. Apart from this reservation, he otherwise committed himself strongly to the Land League, while carefully admonishing his audience that all forms of intimidation and dishonest or immoral pressure on others should be avoided. He realized that he had made an important contribution to a public debate of engrossing interest, for he enclosed an extract from the *Ulster Examiner* containing the text of his speech in a letter to Tobias Kirby in Rome, to whom he explained that his views on the land question had been 'elicited quite by accident' and whom he assured:

> I am much nearer in accord with Dr Croke than with Dr McCabe. I am against the League Manifesto. It is said not to have been signed by Parnell. The arrests were very irritating and mischievous. I don't think the Irish will approve Mr Errington.[56]

In fact that meddlesome busybody had again set off for Rome, and in contrast with his previous visit, the English papers had reported his mission. Irish churchmen were understandably frightened that he might be more successful on this occasion, for, from a moral angle, the 'no rent' manifesto had placed the Land League in a far less defensible position than it had hitherto been. The prospect of English government influence on Irish ecclesiastical affairs and especially on episcopal appointments, with the certain diminution of respect and authority which the Irish church would suffer, filled them with the bleakest foreboding. And Errington was nothing if not persistent.

He arrived in Rome at the end of October 1881, fortified with a letter of introduction from Granville, the Foreign Secretary, to enhance his status at the Vatican.[57] While Granville felt that the mission might bring some benefits to the government in Ireland and had been ready to discuss closer diplomatic relations with Cardinal Howard during the previous summer, he never seriously got down to considering what price the British government would have to pay for this concession. Indeed all Granville was prepared to contemplate was diplomatic contacts on the cheap: an English agent having special

55 M. Tierney, *Croke of Cashel* (Dublin,1976), p.130.
56 Dorrian to Kirby, 8 Nov. 1881, A.I.C.R.
57 E. Larkin, *Roman Catholic church and the creation of the modern Irish state*, p.139. According to Sir Charles Dilke, a minister at the Foreign Office, Forster dispatched Lord O'Hagan on a secret mission to Rome about Ireland because he was not satisfied with the results obtained by Errington. (S. Gwynn and G. Tuckwell, *The life of the Rt. Hon. Sir Charles Dilke* (London, 1917), i, 375.)

status at the Vatican.[58] In the tense atmosphere then prevailing, any kind of recognition of an English representative at the Holy See would have aroused fierce suspicions among Irish churchmen about English influence in Irish ecclesiastical affairs. And British public opinion, in the heyday of imperial power, regarded its Protestantism as a liberating factor in the release of those national qualities of genius that led inexorably to greatness and would have considered the presence of a papal diplomat in London as an affront to national pride and as the restoration of a malign and retrograde influence in the capital of the empire; and it would have feared the danger of being embroiled in some cunning 'jesuitical' scheme concocted by the Holy See.

Errington had really nothing substantial to offer the Vatican; his constant activity was negotiating for some kind of condemnation of the land agitation and for public Vatican support for Archbishop McCabe's party. And when the pope announced his 'disposition' to create McCabe a cardinal — no unusual step given the precedent of his predecessor having the red hat — Errington reported this decision as a diplomatic triumph[59] and Granville thanked the Vatican authorities for their understanding and cooperation, fondly thinking that McCabe's promotion would significantly enhance his political power in Ireland. But further and real diplomatic successes eluded him.

Leo XIII held a consistory on 30 March and McCabe was among the six recipients of the red hat. The Propaganda authorities took advantage of his presence in Rome to ask him to submit a statement of his views on the needs of Ireland. The situation had deteriorated. With Parnell and the leaders of the Land League in prison, violence had increased and in the first quarter of 1882 more violent crimes were reported than in any other three month period in living memory.[60]

---

58 Errington himself assured Bartholomew Woodlock that the question of a nuncio in London did not arise; all that was proposed was the restoration of the semi-official relations that had existed until 1874, when an English agent acted on behalf of the government with the Vatican. (Errington to Woodlock, 16 Dec. 1881, A.C.D.A.)

59 Gladstone seems never to have entertained high expectations from Errington's mission. He told Granville he did not attach such vast importance to McCabe's getting a title which his predecessor had. All he wanted was Irish clerical support for the law and he felt the pope ought to want the same thing. (Gladstone to Granville, 6 Dec. 1881, quoted in E. Fitzmaurice, *Life of Lord Granville*, (London,1905), ii, p.286.) Gladstone later hinted to Newman that he should write to Rome to invite the pope to take action against troublesome priests but Newman replied that he was over-rating the pope's powers in political and social matters. (S. Dessain, ed. *Letters and diaries of John Henry Newman* (Oxford, 1976), xxx, 36-7)

60 Lyons, *Parnell*, p.177. 33 cases of homicide and firing at the person were listed as compared to 7 in the first quarter of 1881, and these were thought to be the work of agrarian secret societies which were given a freer rein in the absence of the leaders.

Accounts of this escalation of lawlessness were passed on to the Vatican. The ever-vigilant Errington ensured that such details reached those whom he judged sympathetic. As a result, Propaganda, at the pope's request, undertook a formal examination of the Irish problem, with a view to deciding what, if any, steps the Holy See should take.

Cardinal Nina, the former Secretary of State, was entrusted with organizing this investigation and he prepared a summary and analysis of the background to the Irish situation. In this he maintained that the Land League had been founded in the midst of famine conditions to protect tenants against the exorbitant demands of the landlords, but claimed that its purpose had been changed for the most part to the political one of obtaining a certain autonomy for Ireland, and for some people its goal had become revolutionary and communist. The way in which many of its supporters reacted to the Land Act showed that the protection of tenants was not their motivation. Nina then recalled the request that had been sent to Manning for information about the political involvement of clergy and his perceptive reply about the danger of the diminution of salutary clerical influence. In fact, the wrong kind of influences did gather momentum, for not a few people placed themselves under the direction of Protestant, non-believing and revolutionary agitators. Despite Roman exhortations, conflicting patterns of clerical behaviour continued and in the wake of reports of violent speeches by some clergy, the pope asked a commission of cardinals to study the issue, and he himself sent a further letter to the archbishop of Dublin in January 1881. Nina then addressed himself to the great and pressing anxiety of the Irish bishops: the fear that any action taken by the Holy See in the present circumstances could reflect even in part the influence of the English government — a fear which, he declared, if not eliminated, could weaken that lively sentiment of devotion which ever bound Ireland closely to Rome and to the person of the pope. But since the agitation had gone on and the response of the bishops and clergy was hampered by their attitudes to it, very pernicious consequences for the church were to be feared.

Nina then recalled that the pope had requested McCabe to make any proposals he thought would be beneficial to the Irish church to see if Rome could be of help. And he noted that among these were the suggestions that the meetings of the bishops should be invested with a quasi-synodical authority with all members being obliged to attend and observe secrecy; and that only those priests who were chosen by their bishops for their prudence and moderation should be allowed to participate in political gatherings.[61]

61. A.P.F., *Acta*, 250, ff 44v-46r. McCabe reported that priests frequently denounced by name in church those whom they deemed guilty of political misbehav-

Twelve cardinals, including Simeoni, the cardinal prefect of Propaganda, McCabe and Howard were present at the general congregation or meeting on 1 May 1882 where this whole issue was discussed. The decision reached, which suited all views among the Irish bishops, was to exclude any direct and public intervention by the Holy See. Even those bishops who were most critical of the Land League were very anxious to avoid anything that could be construed as a condemnation of it by Rome; a general condemnation of the use of violence for political ends was, of course, acceptable. The desire of the cardinals to support McCabe was shown by their acceptance *in toto* of his proposals: the bishops were ordered to meet each year to stem the evils affecting Ireland and all were obliged to be present, to remain for the full duration of the meeting and to observe the secret of what was discussed; priests were forbidden to devote their sermons to political questions and the bishops were to choose wise and prudent clergy who alone could participate in political meetings; moreover, the bishops were to examine the very grave disorders arising from the Ladies Land League. Errington would have been pleased with the decision about clerical involvement in politics, but the cardinals' final recommendation, that he should be officially advised to improve the condition of Ireland (presumably his political masters were intended) and that this should be made known to the bishops as a proof of the interest of the Holy See in their country, was rather a back-handed compliment to all his political intrigue of the previous two years.[62]

Dorrian, too, looked forward to an improvement in the conditions of the tenant farmers, in his Lenten pastoral of 1882. The Land Act, he suggested, was a step in the right direction and time and experience should make it easier to administer and more practical. Though no language could depict the turpitude and horror which agrarian outrages continued to excite, coercion, especially of the innocent, was not the proper response to the problem:

iour. As a result scandalous scenes frequently occurred and good Catholic families were obliged to stay from their church because of the danger they would incur in being present. He maintained that the involvement of the priests in the Land League and especially of the recently ordained, who often made the most violent speeches at the meetings, had done great harm. He explained that the state of the land laws had been very deplorable but when the question of remedying them arose it was taken in hand and managed by men of no position in the country, many of whom were without religion of any kind, save that of revolution. The Ladies Land League, he noted, went about inciting farmers to pay no rent. The foundress, Miss Parnell, was little better than an atheist and her English colleagues were professed atheists.

62 Ibid., ff 38r-41v.

as the blood that circles through the natural body becomes impoverished and leads to sickly eruptions, so we may not be surprised when we notice, in the social or body politic, evidences of irritation in the crimes by which we are appalled. And as the cure in the one case is by soothing and purifying applications so the cure in the other ought *not* to be irritation or coercion in the unjustifiable and strangest persecution of those who are looked upon and believed to be not only innocent of crime but as real and unselfish benefactors of their fellows.

Arguing that the ordinary law was quite adequate to punish the 'village ruffians', he claimed that the internment without trial of some of the best men in the country, many of whom were weekly communicants, was neither wise nor just.[63]

Gradually the unwisdom of their policy convinced the government that a change was necessary. Through intermediaries, Parnell made known to members of the cabinet his willingness to use his influence to put down outrages, if needy tenants were helped with their arrears and improvements made in the Land Act to allow leaseholders to benefit from it. Parnell was in fact happy to abandon the 'no rent' campaign, which had become an embarrassment, and Gladstone's cabinet was happy to release the Kilmainham prisoners, in the hope of bringing about more peaceful and stable conditions. The Chief Secretary, Forster, who wanted firm government and a stiffer dose of coercion, resigned and Gladstone promised not to renew the coercion act which was due to expire, but to replace it by tightening the ordinary processes of law. On 2 May Parnell, Dillon and their colleagues were released and for a very brief interlude a mood of optimism prevailed in political circles. But it was soon brutally shattered by the assassins' knives which cut down the new Chief Secretary, Lord Frederick Cavendish, and the Under Secretary, T.H. Burke, as they walked through the Phoenix Park on 6 May. The spontaneous and widespread sense of outrage created by this deed threatened to undo all the patient and conciliatory work that had preceded Parnell's release.

That release had been greeted everywhere in Ireland by enthusiastic meetings. On 5 May St Mary's Hall in Belfast was packed by cheering crowds who heard the chairman, Revd James O'Boyle, make a very bellicose speech. Declaring that the Irish race would

---

63 Dorrian papers, D.C.D.A.

only be satisfied with independence, he argued that nothing would be got from England that was not wrung from her. He insisted that he would not stoop to give thanks to England for freeing their political leaders, and, proclaiming his pleasure at the 'no rent' manifesto, he praised the prudent line adopted by Bishop Nulty of Meath, poured scorn on the attitude of Cardinal McCabe and taunted Croke with his cowardice on the issue. They wanted no one in Ireland, he claimed, other than the one who was prepared to go the whole hog with Michael Davitt. Turning then to Dublin Castle, he charged that it was a nest of vipers and that 'it would be well for Ireland if it were reduced to ashes tomorrow'. And with an emotional appeal to rousing martial verse be concluded by bidding them 'to be ready to go into the cannon's mouth, into the jaws of death, even into the jaws of hell' if necessary, for the liberties of their people.[64]

Had this heady rhetoric not been followed by the callous assassinations in Dublin, it might have been allowed to pass as an overexuberant, patriotic response provoked by the excitement of the occasion. But in the wake of the tragedy in the Phoenix Park, O'Boyle was severely censured by both the Liberal and Conservative papers in Belfast, and his performance must have caused serious embarrassment to his bishop and fellow priests. The quarterly conferences of the clergy were due to take place on 9, 10 and 11 May in Ballymena, Belfast and Downpatrick, and these occasions were used to pass strong condemnations of 'the cruel and barbarous assassinations', which, under Dorrian's signature, were given to the press.[65] Dorrian himself attended a large meeting of the influential citizens of Belfast, which was convened by the mayor in the council chamber to express abhorrence of the crime.[66]

A month after the Phoenix Park murders the bishops held their annual meeting in Dublin. It was conducted according to the synodical procedure prescribed by Propaganda, and the advice given by Rome to try to curb and moderate the intemperate political contributions of the clergy, especially those of the younger members of that body, was followed. An address to the younger priests, exhorting them not to give political sermons in church and to avoid participating in political activities outside their own parishes, was issued. But since Parnell had effectively killed off the Ladies Land League by starving it of funds shortly after his release from Kilmain-

64 N.W., 6 May 1882.
65 B.M.N., 10, 12 May 1882.
66 B.M.N., 11 May 1882.

ham, the bishops decided that it would be pointless and perhaps counter-productive to make any pronouncement on the matter.[67]

But this exercise of quiet prudence did not pass unchallenged. Rumours soon circulated that they had condemned the Ladies Land League, and to counteract them the ebullient Croke issued a denial in a letter to the *Freeman's Journal*. The ever-watchful Errington, who was probably still smarting from the paltry package he had received from Propaganda (of which an implied condemnation of the Ladies Land League was an item) wrote angrily to Rome about Croke's behaviour. Terming it 'outrageous', he charged that the good effects of Rome's efforts to cooperate with the British government, as evidenced by the instructions of Cardinal McCabe to have limitations placed on the political involvement of curates, was undone,[68] and a few days later, with his reason still in flight before his indignation, he reported that Croke's intervention would be regarded by the government as proof that Croke 'could with impunity slight the orders of the pope', which were therefore valueless; as a Catholic he was painfully embarrassed to see Rome, having given an order to a bishop to act in 'a Christian & moderate way' (presumably to condemn the Ladies' Land League) exposed to a rebuff.[69]

Though Pope Leo took no action against Croke, he sent another letter to McCabe, which was designed for public consumption. This was a natural follow-up to the decision of Propaganda counselling non-intervention in Irish political matters, for containing, as it did, impeccable sentiments about ensuring that their people should avoid the use of violence in striving for justice, abjure the activites of secret societies and assert their rights in a lawful manner, it did not give detailed instructions about the Irish political scene. The pope, of course, added the authority of his name to the bishops' injunctions (which already had Roman authority behind them) to their clergy, especially to the younger priests, to be moderate in word or deed and never to take any step that might appear wanting in prudence or the spirit of conciliation; and he concluded by repeating his confidence in the readiness of the British government to give justice to Ireland, reinforced as it was by the wisdom of thereby furthering the well-being of the whole empire.[70] Though the Irish bishops were not put under any obligations by the pope's advice, as they could answer that

67 F.J., 10 July 1882.
68 Errington to Smith, 11 July 1882, A.S.P.B.R.
69 Ibid., 14 July 1882.
70 I.E.R., 3rd series iii, (Dec. 1882), 764-6. The phrase used ('we are confident that the statesmen who preside over the administration of public affairs will give satisfaction to the Irish when they demand what is just') was sufficiently Delphic to permit the interpretation that the British government was being exhorted to act justly in the future rather than being commended for its behaviour in the past.

he was merely confirming their own appeals for the avoidance of violence, the very fact of his issuing a statement at all constituted something of an embarrassment, as it could be interpreted as indicating a Roman desire to nudge them along the path of duty. On the other hand, despite the pleasure of the government at Vatican support for peaceful pursuit of political activity, and the condemnation of secret societies, the letter offered no further serviceable tool for dealing with the Irish situation.

Howard, on his summer trip to England, had been commissioned by the Vatican to take soundings in political circles about diplomatic relations between England and the Holy See. To Errington's annoyance Granville suggested that a member of the British Embassy staff accredited to Italy be assigned to deal with the Vatican — a suggestion regarded by the Secretariat of State not only as objectionable but also as offensive. Howard also made contact with influential figures in the Conservative party and claimed to find the leadership of both parties favourable to the establishment of diplomatic relations, but was unable to report any real progress in achieving his goal.[71]

Though rumours of the establishment of diplomatic relations continued to trouble the Irish bishops[72] and Cardinal McCabe had been told to sell the idea to the viceroy in Dublin, (he was too well aware of the unanimous views of his episcopal colleagues to pursue this commission), no evidence has survived to indicate that the subject was raised during the *ad limina* visit of Dorrian and his three colleagues, MacCormack of Achonry, Gillooly of Elphin and MacEvilly of Tuam to Rome in November, 1882. Dorrian's visit was overdue; his last *ad limina* had taken place in 1867 and so fifteen years instead of ten had elapsed since he had presented a formal report on the state of his diocese.

71 Howard to Jacobini, 15 Sept. 1882, A.S.V., S.S. 1882, Rub.278, Prot. 50479, ff 20r-22v. On 28 Aug. the Secretariat of State wrote both to Howard and Errington discountenancing any suggestion of using the British Embassy attached to Italy for diplomatic relations with the Vatican. Howard was told that, if the situation could not be improved, it should not be made worse; Errington would be acceptable as a contact (*un anello di congiunzione*) at the Vatican, but Howard was entrusted with directing all his efforts to ensuring that Errington returned equipped with some kind of official document testifying to his position.

72 Jacobini to McCabe, 29 May 1882, Ibid., Prot. 49110, f.125rv. The anxiety of the bishops was shared by Cardinal Manning. When the politically astute archbishop of Westminster saw a report in the *Gazzetta d'Italia* from a London source about diplomatic relations, he promptly sent a firm denial to Cardinal Jacobini of having had any communication, direct or indirect, with the government on that subject. And he went on to say that no one around him was mixed up in such questions. Jacobini could draw his own conclusions from the finality of this assurance. (Manning to Jacobini, 21 Nov. 1882, Ibid., Prot. 51293, f.31rv.)

The bishops of Down and Connor, and Achonry, had their audience with the pope on 17 November, and their colleague, MacEvilly, the archbishop of Tuam, reported that they 'were enchanted with him — Dr Dorrian especially, who entertained him for half an hour with the photographs of all his new churches, schools & convents — and got at once on the most familiar terms with him. I enjoyed immensely his account of the audience — no one better deserves the comfort he derived from it'.[73] Kirby, the rector of the Irish College, who accompanied both sets of bishops on their visits to the pope, was also impressed with the paternal manner in which they were received and noted that the pope encouraged them strongly not to allow young ardent priests to preside at popular meetings but to ensure that this role was taken by prudent and experienced clergy who, whilst cooperating with their people in their search for justice, would guide them along the paths of order and legality.[74]

Though the bishops were to remain worried by rumblings of secret negotiations[75] which threatened an increase of British influence at the Vatican, the actual steps taken by Rome did not cause them much deep concern. On 1 January 1883 Pope Leo addressed yet a further letter to Cardinal McCabe thanking him and the other bishops for their acknowledgement of the last papal exhortation, encouraging them again to alert their people to the dangers of secret societies, whose crimes in recent months had continued to grieve him, emphasizing the importance of allowing only prudent and mature clergy to preside at public meetings, and commending the bishops for their zeal for Catholic education and for the preservation of the Catholic University. The pope, who was probably anxious to show his English critics that he was genuinely concerned by the continuing violence in Ireland, concluded his advice to the hierarchy by suggesting that seminarians should be trained in philosophy according to the mind of St Thomas.[76]

In May 1883, however, Rome took a step that caused very serious embarrassment to the Irish church. When permission was sought to sell Parnell's Wicklow property in the Landed Estates Court in

73 MacEvilly to McCabe, 20 Nov. 1882, D.D.A.
74 Kirby to McCabe, Ibid.
75 In E. Larkin, *The Roman Catholic Church and the creation of the modern Irish state*, pp 158-61, an account is given of an alleged exchange of letters between Cardinals McCabe and Jacobini in the London *Standard* of 27 Dec. 1882 in which Jacobini expressed the readiness of the Vatican to accept an English minister on the same basis as the minister who represented Prussia at the Holy See. Larkin regards these letters as authentic but there is no reference to them in the Dublin Diocesan Archives or in the archives of the Vatican or Propaganda, an omission which would be inexplicable if they had been genuine. They may well have sprung from the feverish imagination of George Errington.
76 I.E.R., 3rd series iv, (Feb. 1883), 126-7.

February 1883 to pay off mortgages then totalling £18,000, the Avoca branch of the Irish National League responded by initiating a national collection to relieve Parnell of this personal embarrassment. It gathered momentum slowly, until a letter written by Croke on St Patrick's Day appeared in the *Freeman's Journal*. In his most exuberant and ebullient mood Croke declared that the time had come to offer a national tribute to Parnell in repayment of the deep debt of gratitude owed to him for having won the right, (at the expense of incurring the cruel hatred of Forster, the Chief Secretary), for thousands of poor people to live and prosper in their native land. He was therefore pleased to devote himself to every movement which aimed at offering respect and service to Parnell and he proposed the formation of a national committee to appeal for subscriptions to the Irish race for this cause. The subscription list, he concluded, with a whiff of intimidation, would furnish an admirable means of distinguishing between those who did and those who did not belong to the Irish Parliamentary party, and would record the oft repeated truth that there was an ample and essential difference between practical patriots and those platform patriots and others, whether of church or state or of whatever class, who only made a profession of their patriotism.

While this threat of separating the sheep from the goats by taking note of public subscriptions to the fund quickly caused a stampede to the sheep's corner, it gave Croke's enemies the chance they were waiting for to denounce him to Rome.[77] The letter, accompanied by extensive glosses, was quickly forwarded to the Vatican. On the other hand, eight bishops — Butler (Limerick), MacCormack (Achonry), Duggan (Clonfert), Conaty (Kilmore), Conway (Killala), Fitzgerald (Ross), Power (Waterford) and Dorrian — most of whom had consistently supported Parnell and the Land League, quickly subscribed to the fund, joined the National Tribute Committee and found themselves in embarrassing company when Rome decided to take action.

What annoyed the Roman authorities was not so much the con-

---

77 Typical of the attack on Croke was the letter to Cardinal Jacobini from Henry Neville, the rector of the Catholic University, who had invested career prospects in the McCabe camp. Neville proceeded to blacken Croke's action by an unjust recital of Parnell's failings: a man without faith or morals, the close accomplice of Egan, Sheridan and other fugitives from justice in New York, a man who encouraged the non-payment of rents, the non-fulfilment of contracts, a man suspected of conniving at various outrages, and a recent visitor to Rochefort (the celebrated atheist) in Paris. (Neville to Jacobini, 15 Apr. 1883, A.S.V., S.S. 1883, Rub. 278, Prot. 52875, ff 51r-52v.) Cardinal Howard passed on a translation of the offending letter with comments on it.

tribution to Parnell[78], dismayed though they were by it, as the kind of moral compulsion Croke exerted on others to prove their patriotism by contributing to Parnell's support; and they also detected in the letter disrespect towards other high ranking ecclesiastics (presumably they had McCabe in mind).[79] So, in view of the comments of the Protestant press and the public declaration of support from bishops and priests, the pope asked Propaganda for advice, and the congregation recommended that Croke be summoned to Rome. Croke promptly obeyed the summons and had a lengthy interview with the cardinal prefect on 2 May. He defended his support of the Parnell fund as an act of charity, a just recompense to a man who had given up so much for his country, and maintained that at least twenty out of the twenty seven bishops in Ireland held the same views about Parnell as he did; moreover, his views enjoyed wide support all over Ireland and in America and Australia.[80]

The pope resolved that a letter forbidding contributions to the Parnell fund should be drafted in the congregation of Propaganda and submitted to a full meeting of the cardinals attached to that congregation on 7 May. The draft was passed on to him the following day and he decided that, with some modifications, it should be sent out in the name of the cardinal prefect to the Irish bishops, and that Croke should remain in Rome for some time. The ill-fated letter, which became known as the Roman circular, was issued on 11 May. It claimed that irrespective of the opinion held about Parnell and his objects, at least many of his followers had on occasions adopted a line of conduct opposed to the rules laid down by the pope in his letter to the cardinal archbishop of Dublin and to the instructions given to the bishops by the congregation of Propaganda, and accepted by them.

78 A.P.F., *Acta*, 253, ff 485r-491r. Parnell was described as a *noto agitatore*, a phrase which because of its nuances in Italian was a less than just assessment of his role at this time.

79 Ibid., Questa specie di morale coazione e lo stile stesso della lettera con allusioni certo poco riverenti e benevole verso illustri personaggi anche in dignità ecclesiastica destarono generalmente meraviglia e riprovazione.

80 A.P.F., S.O.C.G., 1021, ff 192r-194v. There is an account in Propaganda of the conversation between Croke and Simeoni, in which, for the most part, Croke defended himself but kept silent when charged with causing offence to the clergy by equating support of the Parnell fund with patriotism. Croke rebutted suggestions that his clergy were agitators, denied that he knew Parnell was with Rochefort and Clemenceau in Paris when the letter was published and pointed out that Irish newspapers were not known in Rome where attention was paid to hostile sources and to Errington, who, he claimed, had followed him to Rome to keep an eye on him. Errington had indeed done so, having first alerted the Vatican to the '*pénible impression*' created by Croke's letter in England and Ireland. Worse still, he went on, his example was seemingly followed by 'plusieurs autres Évêques, Mgr Butler, Évêque de Limerick qui a aussi écrit une lettre très imprudente, Mgr Dorrian, Évêque de Belfast et autres'. (Ibid., 5 Apr. 1883, ff 183r-184v.)

So, though it was not forbidden to contribute to the relief of distress, nevertheless

> the aforesaid, Apostolic mandates absolutely condemn such collections as are got up in order to inflame popular passions, and to be used as the means for leading men into rebellion against the laws. Above all things, such collections should be avoided where it is plain that hatred and dissensions are aroused by them, that distinguished persons are loaded with insults, that never in any way are censures pronounced against the crimes and murders with which wicked men stain themselves; and especially when it is asserted that the measure of true patriotism is in proportion to the amount of money given or refused, so as to bring the people under the pressure of intimidation.

Consequently, it was laid down that the Parnell testimonial could not be approved and that it was intolerable for any ecclesiastic, much less a bishop, to take any part in recommending or promoting it.[81]

In an account of this episode, written a year later in Propaganda, it was stated that the letter at first gave displeasure in Ireland because it was interpreted as an act favourable to England rather than an opportune and necessary provision for the good of Ireland, which had been called forth by the notorious proposal of an Irish archbishop; however, it did not fail to produce good effects, for if the subscription to the Parnell fund was continued by some clergy, ecclesiastics in general ceased to take part, at least publicly, in it, so that the energetic intervention of the Holy See helped to bring back even the most hot-headed supporters of Parnell within the limits of a just moderation.[82] A less accurate description of the effects of the circular could scarcely be imagined. Apart from its being perceived as a triumph of English machiavellian intrigue at the Vatican, it did not produce the results here attributed to it. On the contrary, Irish Catholic reaction ranged from disbelief to fury, and the only reasonable interpretation which most Catholics could put on the Vatican's forbidding what was seen as a simple act of charity, namely helping a man pay off his debts, was that English influences at the Holy See were so powerful and malign that they were able to deceive completely ill-informed Roman officials. The upshot was the opposite of what Rome intended: not only did the collection shoot up immediately, ultimately reaching £40,000 or more than twice what Parnell needed to clear off his debts, but the vast majority of the clergy was painfully embarrassed by this clumsy and insensitive

81 F.J., 16 May 1883.
82 A.P.F., *Acta*, 253, ff 485r-491r.

Roman intervention. The bishops who had contributed did not try to withdraw their subscriptions in deference to what they regarded as the mistaken directions of the circular. All they could do was sit out the furore in silence. Dorrian's clergy supported the stand he took (as indeed they had approved of his contribution to an appeal on behalf of Edmund Dwyer Gray, one of Parnell's MPs, the previous year)[83] and the rebuke from Rome did not at all damage his image with the vast majority of his people.

The sanguine Errington was overjoyed by the Roman circular and reported to Rome that the Protestant people of England, who had believed that the Catholic church was almost the accomplice of Irish crime, had entirely changed their views on seeing the pope exposed to attacks from the Irish party for having defended justice and condemned crime. Cardinal Howard, he enthused, had during his summer visit to England been warmly received by Gladstone, Granville and other ministers, and the issue of diplomatic relations had made great progress, though the difficulties in their way needed to be handled with caution.[84]

But a few months later the Holy See had the benefit of the cool restraining counsels of one who cast a much steadier eye on the English and Irish political scenes. Cardinal Manning spent five weeks in Rome in October and November 1883. He had not been consulted on Irish affairs for two years and had assumed that prominent figures at the Vatican had wished to exclude him, but, uncertain about whether the pope was aware of this or not, was very pleased with the six lengthy audiences which Leo granted him. Manning noted that he was free to speak on any subject and, apart from discussing the religious state of England and papal diplomacy with various European countries, they spoke 'most fully on Ireland and our Government'. Manning had an intuitive sympathy for the Irish poor, for the immigrants who were building up the church in England, and was strongly opposed to diplomatic relations which he foresaw would be directed through channels instinctively antipathetic to the Irish cause. He explained to the pope that Errington represented the English government and not Ireland[85] And as Errington ruefully reported to London, Manning had greatly aided

---

83 On 31 Aug. 1882 Patrick O'Kane, the parish priest of Downpatrick and vicar general of the diocese, in proposing the bishop's health at a conference of the clergy, remarked that Dorrian's munificent subscription to the fund being raised to pay the unjust fine on E.D. Gray showed his sympathy for a cause — a sympathy that was shared by the people of the diocese.

84 Errington to Cardinal Jacobini, 6 Aug. 1883, A.S.V. S.S. 1883, Rub. 278, Prot. 54233, ff 61r-62v.

85 Shane Leslie, *Henry Edward Manning, his life and labours* (London, 1921), p.387.

the Irish cause by claiming that papal policy to Ireland had been mistakenly based on false premises and reports, had consequently blundered and had received only rebuffs from the British government in and out of parliament.[86]

The pressure from the British Foreign Office had greatly eased as the political situation in Ireland had calmed down and crimes had diminished. And the sensitive political antennae of the Secretariat of State registered the weakening signals from Whitehall. Errington continued to ply his thankless trade with the same unquestioning selfrighteousness and breathless dedication, but without success. He strove might and main to have Henry Neville, whom he foresaw as McCabe's successor in Dublin, appointed coadjutor of Cork. Neville, the dean of the Cork chapter, and *alter ego* of the aged bishop, who had consistently wooed the right people, both in Dublin and Rome, seemed to have impressive credentials. But he had to share first place on the *terna* with the prior of San Clemente in Rome, and was strongly opposed by some of the Cork priests and by the influential bishop of Ossory. Moreover, the qualities that endeared him to Cardinal McCabe attracted Croke's most determined opposition and ensured a most damning report from the metropolitan of Cork.[87]

Cardinal McCabe wrote warmly to Cardinal Howard on Neville's behalf, suggesting that the candidature of his opponent owed its strength to the unsuspecting goodwill of Archbishop Kirby in Rome,[88] but, though Howard was a member of the congregation at which the appointment was made, he was unable to obtain it for his friend. The Munster bishops had voted seven to three in favour of Henry O'Callaghan, OP, who was subsequently appointed by the pope after Propaganda had refused to decide, and the pope had deferred his decision for two months.[89] This decision signalled a further defeat to Errington and even more so to his Irish patron, Cardinal McCabe, whose suggestion of translating O'Callaghan to Ossory was rejected by the Holy See. Croke and his friends were jubilant.

On the political front, meanwhile, Parnell, partly in appreciation

---

86 Errington to Granville, 19 Nov. 1883, cited in E. Larkin: *The Roman Catholic Church and the creation of the modern Irish state*, p.217.

87 Croke not only denounced Neville as the ecclesiastic *'maxime odiosum'* to the Irish people throughout the world but gave a stern warning of the danger of feminist power behind the episcopal throne in the shape of Neville's sister: '. . . mulierem superbam et dominatricem, quaeque inter notos aeque odiosa est ac frater ejus Reverendus. Quod si frater iste (quod avertat Deus) ad sedem Corcagiensem promotus fuerit, mulier haec Episcopa erit, nec minore gaudebit auctoritate tum in rebus ecclesiasticis, tum in profanis quam Episcopus ipse.' (A.P.F., S.O.C.G., 1019, ff 616r-617v.)

88 McCabe to Howard, 3 Feb. 1884, A.V.E.C.R.

89 A.P.F., *Acta*, 253, ff 146r-153v.

of clerical support remaining steadfast for his appeal despite the Roman circular, and partly to consolidate his own political authority, had made sure to improve his relations with the church. He took a step in that direction when he voted against Gladstone's Affirmation bill which would have allowed Charles Bradlaugh, the well known atheist, to take his seat in parliament by affirming rather than swearing the customary oath.[90] The hierarchy had protested strongly against this measure and Dorrian had telegraphed his opposition to it to Rome. This rapprochement convinced some of the more cautious bishops of the wisdom of going along with their braver amd more forward looking colleagues in thinking that Parnell's party could be trusted to protect their interests in parliament. And Parnell's increasing strength made him less tolerant of deviations from the party line which might annoy supporters, clerical or lay. When the National League in Belfast, under the chairmanship of the stalwart nationalist, John Duddy, proposed to organize a provincial convention in Belfast it received a stern, headmasterly reprimand from Parnell. He objected to two of the four resolutions which were to be proposed at the meeting: to the second because it smacked of land nationalization, which he had already dismissed as impractical and unpopular with tenant farmers, and to the fourth because it seemed to criticize the central organization of the League. When the Belfast committee proved intransigent and defended its right to maintain the fourth resolution on the grounds of democratic freedoms, Parnell refused to budge, ordered the Ulster branches of the League to withdraw and the planned convention collapsed.[91] Dorrian's reaction is not known but he can scarcely have regretted the humiliation of the inflexible and uncompromising Duddy, who, in the past, had resisted his appeals to cancel nationalist processions.

Duddy, however, succeeded in getting Michael Davitt to speak in St Mary's Hall on 18 December on 'Ulster and the new political situation'. But when the National League sent T.P. O'Connor, William O'Brien, Tim Healy and J.F. Small, all members of the Irish Parliamentary party, to a public meeting to discuss the redistribution of parliamentary seats, Duddy, the president, and Robert McMullan, the secretary of the Belfast branch of the National League, tried to prevent the meeting. They put up posters charging the speakers with coming to Belfast without an invitation, and, what was worse, with having ignored invitations to come during the previous three years. However, J.G. Biggar fought back, and got John P. Greene, the administrator of St Malachy's parish, to act as chairman for the occasion, and a large and enthusiastic crowd turned

90 Lyons, *Parnell*, p.253.
91 M.N., 30 July 1884.

up. To add to Duddy's humiliation, Dorrian invited all the MPs to dine with him 'as he strongly sympathizes with their objects in visiting the North'.[92] Though he did not attend the meeting, about twenty five priests were present on the platform, and Peter McEvoy, the curate of St Joseph's parish in Belfast, spoke. The resolutions called for ownership of the land by the cultivators and renewed support for Parnell and his party.

In fact very significant support and increased power and prestige had come its way a short time previously. At their national meeting in October the bishops had endorsed a proposal of Croke's which called on the party to bring before the House of Commons their resolutions on the training colleges, the treatment of convent schools and the subject matter for the courses in metaphysics at the Royal University, 'and to urge generally upon the government the hitherto unsatisfied claims of Catholic Ireland in all branches of the educational question. Naturally, those who had denounced Parnell and his fellows as the godfathers of agrarian crime resented this ennoblement of the party. Cardinal McCabe regretted the step[93] but Dorrian, who had long admired Parnell as an advocate of social justice, regarded it as a thoroughly welcome development. Nationalist papers suggested that the bishops could not have ventured to make such a move without papal approval and thereby implied that the pope had authorized it. In fact, the pope had not been consulted, and though Errington fumed about the bishops' action and claimed that the Lord-Lieutenant, Foreign Secretary and influential British opinion were outraged by it, the Vatican made no attempt to interfere.[94]

IV

Cardinal Manning's visit to Rome in 1883 had coincided with that of a group of American bishops, who had been summoned there to examine problems that had arisen in their rapidly expanding church, and to discuss the agenda for their third Plenary Council. The meeting had been successful, and, as Cardinal Angelo Jacobini reported, it had given the Roman officials an opportunity of knowing the circumstances and needs of the American church better, and at the same time had provided the American bishops with a chance of appreciating the very practical and prudent spirit animating Propa-

92 M.N., 29, 30 Dec. 1884.
93 McCabe to Simeoni, 18 Oct. 1884, A.P.F. S.C.(Irlanda), 41, ff 403r-404v. McCabe explained that as a result of the resolution Parnell was constituted the '*os et vicarius*' of the bishops in the British parliament, and the hierarchy had '*societatem incisse*' with the Irish Parliamentary party.
94 Errington to Smith, 21 Oct., 2 Nov. 1884, A.S.P.B.R.

ganda and of becoming more united to the Holy See, to Propaganda and to each other, as they discarded the prejudices that their geographical remoteness from Rome might have fostered. Leo XIII decided to extend the advantages of such contact, and, whether on his own initiative, or whether it was as a result of a suggestion from Manning, prompted by the Secretary of State, Cardinal Ludovico Jacobini, chose the Irish hierarchy both because it needed the special help of the Holy See and because the great majority of the people of Ireland were profoundly Catholic and loyal to Rome.

On 11 March 1884 Cardinal Simeoni passed on the pope's wish to Cardinal McCabe. Proposing that the meeting be held in September, he requested the archbishop of Dublin to suggest the names of colleagues who represented different provinces and different views among the hierarchy, and to indicate the most suitable topics for discussion. McCabe circularized the bishops about the agenda and recommended that the four archbishops and two others from each province — Ardagh and Meath for the Armagh province — and two who had special expertise should be invited. Among the subjects for their deliberations, he mentioned the possibility of formulating rules about the attendance of priests at political conventions. He also referred to the dissatisfaction of some bishops with the regulations governing priests' visitations of Christian Brothers' schools, the improvement of discipline and studies at Maynooth, and the regularization of ecclesiastical practices on the observance of feast days and the proclamation of banns for marriage.[95]

The meeting was postponed until the following spring. The bishops, including Dorrian, set off in April. McCabe had died in February, but his auxiliary was invited in his place. Before their departure the country was preoccupied with the forthcoming visit of the Prince and Princess of Wales. While many nationalists regarded it as inopportune (a view shared by Bishop Duggan of Clonfert), Croke recommended a courteous reception, even though they were not coming to inaugurate an Irish parliament or put an end to Orange ascendancy. Dorrian's counsel was restrained and laconic: 'no use in outpour of vinegar but dignity and calmness'.[96]

The episcopal delegation, consisting of three archbishops and fourteen bishops, including the auxiliary of Dublin and the coadjutor of Cork, reached Rome towards the end of April and the conferences began in Propaganda on 1 May.

In the previous autumn the cardinals of Propaganda had decided to abide by the decision taken at a general congregation in May 1882, which had concluded that it was not opportune to enter directly into

---

95 A.P.F., *Acta*, 253, ff 485r-491r.
96 F.J., 10 Apr. 1885.

the Irish political question, a decision which they found all the more relevant and acceptable in view of the greatly decreased level of violence in Ireland.[97] This spared any embarrassing discussion about the role of priests in politics and the enforcement by the bishops or observance by the clergy of the decrees of 1854 and the episcopal letter of June 1882.

On the basis of the other suggestions from Ireland, Propaganda had an agenda already prepared.[98] Part of it involved the interpretation and execution of Tridentine and post-Tridentine legislation in Ireland, about which Rome had in many cases already given official instructions — the reservation of the Blessed Sacrament in clerical residences, the administration of the sacraments, the proclamation of banns of marriage, uniformity throughout the country in observing fast days and holy-days of obligation, the granting of dispensations for mixed marriages, the role and powers of synodal examiners and diocesan chapters (consultors in those dioceses which did not have cathedral chapters), the maintenance and disposition of ecclesiastical property — and the Irish bishops were happy to accept the Roman rulings which, where possible, took sympathetic account of Irish customary usages.

The major issues concerned the length and state of the courses in philosophy and theology at Maynooth, and the spiritual direction and discipline of the students. Here the Propaganda authorities proved flexible and receptive to the bishops' views: they were willing to reduce the division of the college from four sections to three, each of which was to be placed under the supervision of a dean of discipline, and it was agreed that, when the bishops had drawn up rules for the college and obtained Roman approval, no changes were to take place without consulting Propaganda; they called for the appointment of two full-time spiritual directors and ordered minor seminaries to make similar appointments; they counselled the bishops to be careful about the books used in the seminaries and to ensure that the students were not exposed to improper material in classical authors or other works; they accepted a vote of the bishops which favoured the extension of the philosophy course to three years, and they specified the content and length of the courses in both departments; they endorsed the bishops' ruling about excluding Maynooth students from the Royal University, though young priests were permitted to sit its exami-

---

97 A.P.F., *Acta*. 253, ff 485r-491r.
98 Ibid., S.O.C.G., 1021, ff 330r-332r.

nations.[99] Regulations were laid down about the celebration of two Masses on Sundays, the confessions of nuns, and the procedure for canonical processes, and the bishops were ordered to make provision for the translation and circulation of papal encyclicals.

Propaganda was not prepared to reopen the whole issue of the Christian Brothers, which had been examined at length in 1878 and 1880, but it was agreed that, where all the trustees of a parochial school were Brothers, the bishop could in future appoint one trustee when a vacancy occurred; on the disputed issue of the priests' right to examine the pupils of the Brothers' schools in non-religious subjects it was made clear that an episcopal delegate could, after putting to the students questions in writing, depending on the results obtained, arrange for them to be examined. Moreover, the bishops were told that they could apply for the extension to Ireland of a rescript which the English bishops had won in the course of a struggle over their rights vis-a-vis religious orders. Children whose parents had a conscientious objection, certified by the parish priest, to a particular teacher were not to be compelled to attend that teacher's school, and the rule of compulsory attendance was not to apply to schools vested entirely in trustees. On one subject Croke displayed a delicate touch of diplomacy that would have drawn plaudits from the most experienced practitioner of that wily art: confronted with a request for the establishment of a Catholic newspaper in Ireland, he explained that the subject was so complex that the bishops present would have to consult their colleagues at home and other prominent clergy before taking further action.[100] The newspaper dropped quietly into the limbo of vague and remote promises.

Dorrian took seriously ill in Rome and could not attend the sessions held after 11 May. He therefore missed the discussion on the Christian Brothers, the subject which interested him most. He had no special expertise on the academic, disciplinary or spiritual standards obtaining in Maynooth, though the well-being of the college was very close to his heart. He is reported as having intervened directly only once, and that concerned the question of priests reserving the Blessed Sacrament in their own homes. Propaganda did not like this

99 The reports reaching Rome of the excessive intervention of some priests in politics had aroused Roman suspicions about the college in which most of them were formed. Moran, who had contributed to this anxiety by indicating that young priests who were involved in politics were seeking a substitute for the study which they were neglecting, replied on the whole favourably to a series of questions sent to him by Cardinal Simeoni in 1882. He assured Simeoni that the teaching of theology was orthodox, and that discipline was well observed but he claimed that the teaching of philosophy and Latin was weak, and recommended the appointment of a spiritual director. (Ibid., ff 107r-108v.)

100 A.P.F., S.O.C.G., 1021, ff 330r-332r, and 338r-343r.

practice but was prepared to tolerate it in cases of necessity where priests lived a long distance from their churches, or where there was a danger of the churches being profaned. In such circumstances oratories were to be provided in parochial houses. Dorrian explained that in the previous ten years or so, fifty presbyteries equipped with oratories had been erected in his diocese.[101]

In accordance with the decision of Propaganda taken before the bishops arrived, there was no formal discussion of political issues at their meetings. The subject came up during informal discussions and at the bishops' audiences with the pope. But with the decline in violence over the past three years and a more moderate tone in the speeches of the parliamentary leaders, the pressure on the Vatican to denounce clerical and episcopal 'sympathizers', or 'abettors', of crime had diminished. Papal intervention did not have to go beyond general exhortations about the necessity for avoiding the use of violent or evil means in the struggle for social or political justice. One issue of compelling concern to the bishops, and, indeed, because of its political overtones, to the country at large, dominated the background to these meetings — the appointment of an archbishop of Dublin.

Cardinal McCabe had died on 11 February. Because of his political views and the role he had played at national level, intense interest attached to the question whether or not a successor of a different calibre and outlook would be appointed — an interest as passionately felt by politicians as by bishops and priests. William J. Walsh, the president of Maynooth, a leading ecclesiastical intellectual and successful administrator, easily topped the *terna* or list of three names submitted by the parish priests to Rome, by obtaining forty six votes to the twelve and three obtained by his nearest rivals, Nicholas Donnelly, the auxiliary bishop, and P.J. Tynan, respectively. Walsh was already widely known at national level for his interest in the land and education questions. On both issues he had written to the newspapers, backing the popular line in defence of the tenants and in support of the claims of Catholics to equality of rights in higher education. His political sympathies were strongly in favour of the nationalist camp.

Walsh had not escaped Errington's suspicious attentions. To this tireless watchdog of political and ecclesiastical propriety he was quite simply a dangerous and untrustworthy man. Both the Foreign Secretary, Lord Granville, and the Lord-Lieutenant, Earl Spencer,

---

101 In one of the sets of surviving notes this remark was attributed to the bishop of Elphin and the further explanation, that this was all done at government expense, added. Dorrian would have been pained to think that his Latin syntax or pronunciation had given rise to such a ridiculous gloss.

disliked Walsh and would have liked to block his appointment, but could not find any hard evidence linking him with behaviour that would convince Rome of his unsuitability. Nor could they agree on a candidate of stature, whose political views they could trust, to submit to the pope in place of Walsh. Though the rest of the cabinet, apart from Granville and Spencer, did not become involved, the pope hesitated about making the popular choice until convinced, both by the repeated assurances of the bishops, who were in Rome, and by a judicious letter from Cardinal Manning recommending Walsh.

The decision was very well received in Ireland not only because of Walsh's acknowledged ability and national sympathies, but also because it was interpreted as a victory for Irish rights over English wiles. Walsh was summoned to Rome for his episcopal ordination and was gratified to find that the pope spoke to him in 'extraordinary confidence' at his audience. Leo revealed that the appointment resulted from the advice given in person to him by the bishops, and gave a firm assurance that Errington had become the chief victim of his own intrigues:

> The Holy Father was *very* severe on our friend Sir George. He gave orders not to admit him any more, and sent directions to the Propaganda and the Secty of State to give him no further encouragement. He merely did not ask them; he said 'to shut the door' against him.[102]

Dorrian's travelling companion, J.P. Greene, reported to Kirby that the papal decision had given great satisfaction and bound the pope more closely to Ireland.[103] The new archbishop held views on the land and university questions very close to those that had long been expressed by the bishop of Down and Connor. He believed that the fellowships of the Royal University should be dispersed among colleges other than University College, Dublin, and had questioned the wisdom of fixing the fellows' salaries at £400 per year instead of paying them a smaller sum and thereby increasing their number. He was also highly critical of the conduct of some members of the senate who were supposed to be representative of Catholic interests.[104] Walsh's new status gave his views greatly enhanced authority, and he soon became the recognized spokesman for the Irish church on all matters pertaining to education, but Dorrian was not destined for long to lend him support.

102 Walsh to Woodlock, 27 July 1885, A.C.D.A.
103 Greene to Kirby, 25 June 1885, A.I.C.R.
104 Walsh to Woodlock, 13 Apr. 1884, A.C.D.A. Two in particular — Francis Cruise and Lord Granard — drew his ire. He claimed that the Parnellite MPs would never have shown such disregard for Cardinal McCabe's wishes as they had done.

The appointment of Walsh was a happy end not only to the bishops' visit to Rome but also to the uncertainties and anxieties about the attitudes towards Ireland obtaining at the Holy See for the previous five or six years. It seemed to indicate that the cloud overshadowing Croke and his friends had at last been lifted, and the charges made by the Errington camp fully exploded. For Dorrian, who did not live long enough to experience any further stages in the land struggle, the choice of the popular candidate for Dublin must have seemed like the final victory for those who had striven to convince Rome of the justice of the tenants' case.

12

Celebrations and close

I

Dorrian took seriously ill in Rome on 11 May 1885. John P. Greene, the administrator of St Malachy's parish, who had accompanied him to the eternal city, cabled the news to Belfast and reported that his condition deteriorated so much on 12 May that the last rites were administered.[1] But on the following day he started to improve, and arrangements were made to begin the homeward journey a week later. They travelled slowly and, when they reached England, spent some days in Bolton with the bishop's cousin, a doctor. Though Greene remarked after their arrival home that it was a race against death, he added that Dorrian was stronger than before they set out, and that his cousin had predicted ten or twelve years further life for him, if he did not overwork.[2] A large meeting, representative of clergy and laity, was held in St Mary's Hall, before their return, to lay plans for a welcome for the bishop on his arrival, but decided, on account of his health, to postpone their reception and to convey their good wishes and esteem at the celebration of the silver jubilee of his episcopal ordination, which was due to be held later in the summer.[3]

This event occurred on 19 August. The public festivities began with a reception in St Malachy's College. The bishop was received by the staff and students and the president read a formal address eulogizing the contribution he had made to the development of the college and his struggle for 'a fair field and no favour' for Catholics in secondary and tertiary education. Dorrian, in reply, looked forward to the day when St Malachy's would become a university college for the north, and, though he expressed reservations about the operation of the Royal University, he pinned his hopes on a not-too-distant endowment for St Malachy's as a contributory college to it. The Intermediate Education Act got a more favourable mention. The

---

1 M.N., 16 May 1885.
2 Greene to Kirby, 23 June 1885, A.I.C.R.
3 M.N., 30 May 1885.

bishop disclosed that he had been consulted by a man who had played an important part in drafting the bill, and that he had passed on his approval of its terms, since it offered them the means of fair competition at that level.

The Catholic teachers of Belfast, represented by 47 men and 62 women, presented an address in Bank St. school. They thanked the bishop for increasing the number and enhancing the quality of schools under Catholic management. Acknowledging the improvements in the buildings, he paid tribute to the teachers' dedication and commitment.

The day ended with a public banquet in St Mary's Hall, where all available seats were filled (the balconies were reserved for the ladies) and many of the clergy and prominent laity of the diocese were present. The *Morning News* enthused that it was the most brilliant affair of its class ever held in the town. The hall was tastefully decorated with flowers, and throughout the dinner a band in the background played Irish airs. On behalf of the clergy, James Hamill, the parish priest of Whitehouse, read an address, which hailed the bishop's unwearying labours for the diocese and declared that the fruits of his zeal — the schools, the convents, the college, the churches — were the theme of universal admiration. On behalf of the laity, Peter Macaulay, a Belfast solicitor, read out an even more flattering account of the bishop's achievements. Dorrian was assured that, at the beginning of his ministry, Catholicity 'wore a pale and troubled aspect and the temples of God were few and far between in the land'. Since then an enormous change had taken place: 'in that comparatively brief interval there have sprung up on all sides, as though at the touch of the enchanter's wand, churches, presbyteries, convents, schools, monastery, reformatory, hospital, lecture hall, each of goodly proportions and prolific of benefit'. Having referred to the bishop's zealous discharge of all his pastoral duties, he then went on to salute his patriotism: 'a patriotism which recognizes to the full that the power of managing her own affairs, consulting for her own advancement, and safeguarding her own interests, is Ireland's heaven-ordained and inalienable right, which no man or nation may deny her or usurp'.

In reply to the clergy, Dorrian praised their zeal and co-operation but refused to accept any credit for their achievements other than that of having 'seldom if ever prevented a priest from doing a good act, or pushing on a good work'. He repeated this statement when responding to the address of the laity. He went on to speak in warm ecumenical terms of his relations (presumably at a personal level) with his fellow christians. Revealing that he had received very kind letters of congratulations on his jubilee from Protestants in Belfast, he declared:

it has been my good fortune to know and live in friendship with Presbyterians and Protestants with the greatest advantage to myself, and without the least slight of any sort to my convictions and faith. I have never met anything but fair dealing in that way and it is a proud thing for me to know that in struggling with Presbyterians and Protestants I have never been obliged to make the slightest sacrifice of any kind.

Then turning to his political views, he insisted that he never concealed his sentiments and had always held that 'no other country could manage our affairs better than we could ourselves', and he concluded by remarking that no superlatives could do justice to the generous Catholics of Belfast.[4]

The celebrations were, of course, more than a tribute of gratitude to the bishop: they were a public expression of self-congratulation by the whole Catholic community of the diocese, but especially that of Belfast. That community had begun to feel much more self-confident in recent years. The churches, schools and religious institutions were an outward sign of its increasing strength. Two or three decades earlier there had been little evidence of Catholicity among the public buildings of the town. Catholics were without influence in the business, professional and academic life of Belfast. Now they numbered over 60,000 and, with the recent changes in secondary and tertiary education, looked forward to providing a bigger share of the professional classes. It was not without significance that Edmund Dwyer Gray, one of the Parnellite MPs, was present and that a toast was proposed by Richard Marner, the former president of St Malachy's College, to the Irish Parliamentary party. The union of Catholicism and nationalism behind that party was almost complete, and the expectation that Home Rule would shortly be realized was very strong. Both Dorrian's achievements and his political views reflected the ambitions and satisfaction of his people.

Celebrations of such a kind are apt to degenerate into excessive hero-worship of their subject; speakers find the pull towards hyperbole almost irresistible. The subsequent disentanglement of the truth from its embroidery can be difficult.

But there is no gainsaying Dorrian's personal zeal, vision and energy. In 1866 he cut off Ballymacarrett from the parish of Holywood and brought all Belfast under his own immediate control as parish priest. In 1865 there were three churches, one religious community and a very inadequate diocesan seminary in the town; twenty years later there were six fine spacious churches (a temporary one at Ardoyne and an eighth being built), two male religious orders,

4 M.N., 20 Aug. 1885.

five orders of nuns, a flourishing seminary, handsome convents, homes for orphans and a hospital. The number of priests in the parish had trebled.

Since the ecclesiastical buildings in Belfast were imposing, the Catholic community of that town could easily be forgiven for thinking that little had been done throughout the diocese to restore the church before Dorrian's time. But if they thought so, they were mistaken. During Denvir's and Crolly's episcopates and from an even earlier date, the work of ecclesiastical reconstruction had gone on. Between 1835 and 1865 some thirty five churches were blessed and opened.[5] Many of them, and of those erected in the previous decades, were not capacious or impressive in appearance; their size and style were dictated by the limited means of those who paid for them. Consequently, some of them had to be replaced in Dorrian's time. But that does not detract from the work of the clergy of an earlier age, who ensured, as soon as they could, that their people had churches. Similarly, both Crolly and Denvir advised their clergy to take advantage of the national system of education. Before Dorrian's accession the number of schools under Catholic management throughout the diocese was impressive; again, Belfast was exceptional. Dorrian certainly encouraged his priests to equip their parishes with churches, schools and presbyteries and gave a boost to fundraising schemes by presiding at charity sermons and appealing for subscriptions, but, ultimately, the clergy were responsible for the building schemes in their parishes.

To deal with the social and educational apostolate in Belfast, he summoned several orders of nuns to his aid. The nineteenth century saw the foundation of very many female religious orders, and, beginning in France, this wave of founding new, or rejuvenating old, communities spread to Ireland before the famine. The Sisters of Mercy came to Belfast in 1854 and, a year later, established a convent in Downpatrick. No other religious order of women opened a house in the diocese while Denvir was bishop. Dorrian brought in five orders between 1870 and 1876. With the exception of the Sisters of the Sacred Heart in Lisburn, these were all assigned to work in

5 These were Cushendall (1836), Ballykilbeg (1837), Ahoghill (1837), Loughguile (1839), Glenariffe (1839), Carrickmannon (1839), Coleraine (1840), Cushendun (1840), Carrickfergus (1840), Dunloy (1840), Glenravel (1840), Drumaroad (1841), Lisburn (1843), Dervock (1846,1860), Bushmills (1846), Carnlough (1846), Rasharkin (1846), Newtownards (1846), Kilmore (1847), Magherahoney (1851), Portrush (1851), Bangor (1851), Saintfield (1853), Ballinderry (1853), Newcastle (1854), Culraney (1855), The Braid (1855), Kircubbin (1856), Donaghadee (1856), Larne (1859), Ballykinlar (1860), Ballymena (1860), Glenshesk(1863), Ballycruttle (1864), Aughlisnafin (1864). The church at Moneyglass was dedicated two weeks before Denvir's episcopal ordination.

Belfast. In covering the town with religious houses he was applying the same solution as many other Catholic bishops to the great social problems that confronted growing cities in the industrial age.

He also welcomed the spread of those devotional practices that were then receiving the encouragement and support of Pius IX. It has been claimed that the triumph of ultramontanism lay not in the declaration of papal infallibility in 1870 but in the interior transformation of Catholicism north of the Alps. Italian forms of piety, which placed more emphasis on the adoration of the Blessed Eucharist, on more frequenting of the sacraments, on devotion to the suffering Christ, to the Sacred Heart, to the Blessed Virgin Mary, to popular saints (such as St Joseph and St Anthony), and on processions and pilgrimages, spread widely. Many of these religious practices first became common in Italy under Pius VII. In 1825 Leo XII extended the Holy Year to the whole world, permitting the indulgence to be gained in cathedrals and churches everywhere. But it was Pius IX who gave the biggest boost to the devotional life of the church by extending these jubilee indulgences more frequently and by fostering the more popular religious exercises. In 1851 he recommended the perpetual adoration of the Blessed Eucharist, and in 1856 he extended the feast of the Sacred Heart to the whole church. Though the indulgences attached to practices of piety were at times sought after too mechanically, they attracted large crowds to the sacraments and non-liturgical worship.[6]

Dorrian made use of these devotions to animate the spiritual life of his people, and he encouraged and organized parish missions, especially when the jubilee indulgences could be gained. But before he succeeded to the see, some of these Italian forms of piety were spreading throughout the diocese. The Rosarian Society was founded at St Mary's Church in 1794 and the Belfast Christian Doctrine Society was established in 1834. Crolly's statutes of that year included questions for the parish priest to answer before parochial visitation about the number of confraternities in his parish. In 1837 Denvir obtained from Rome the customary indulgences for the Rosarian and Christian Doctrine Societies. In 1845 he indicated to Rome that the confraternity of the Blessed Virgin existed in many parishes, and noted that he had recently established one for the conversion of sinners. In 1850 the St Vincent de Paul Society was introduced to Belfast, and quickly made an important contribution to the social and educational needs of the town. By 1882 Dorrian was reporting to Propaganda that there were six different sodalities in the diocese. Consequently, he can be credited with encouraging missions and popular devotions, but their extension in Down and

6 R. Aubert, *Le Pontificat de Pie IX*, 2nd ed. (Paris, 1963), pp 461-4

Connor, as elsewhere, was ultimately part of a general devotional momentum that had been gathering pace for years. In the discussion, therefore, among historians of Irish Catholicism, as to whether there was a 'devotional revolution' after 1850 or a 'devotional evolution' from the first quarter of the century, the record of Down and Connor, despite the paucity of church accommodation in Belfast, favours the 'evolution' theory.

The transformation of ecclesiastical life in Belfast is Dorrian's greatest monument. It was about the pastoral neglect of the Catholics of that town that the most urgent complaints were made to Rome in the latter years of Denvir's episcopate. When Archbishop Dixon was at his wit's end trying to find some solution to the problems posed by his suffragan see, he suggested on one occasion that the administration of Belfast should be placed in Dorrian's hands and that Denvir might be allowed to retain control of the rest of the diocese. 'On that day when that will be done', he predicted, 'the Church of Belfast will clap her hands with joy, for her regeneration will commence'.[7] Dorrian fulfilled his predictions. Not only did he provide the necessary churches, schools, religious institutions, and increase the number of priests, Brothers and nuns, but he also led by example, sponsored all kinds of pastoral aids, such as clubs, societies, parish libraries and centres, and strove to ensure that these flourished under clerical, and ultimately episcopal, control.

Belfast grew more rapidly in the 1860s than in previous decades. The developments at the shipyards and docks attracted an ever-increasing number of workers. The Catholic population rose from 41,000 in 1861 to 55,000 in 1871. It was fortunate that Belfast Catholics had a leader, from 1865, who understood the problems of urban growth and the needs of a burgeoning and mainly poor population. By providing effectively for the needs of his own parish the bishop gave powerful example to the clergy throughout the diocese. While it is true that most of them would probably have built or rebuilt their churches and improved their schools, irrespective of their superior, Dorrian's encouragement and assistance must have added a greater urgency to their work. And his rearrangement of parochial boundaries also facilitated their task.

II

The jubilee celebrations turned out to be the bishop's swan-song. Illness struck him again in September, and, though he was able to attend the general meeting of the hierarchy in Dublin at the beginn-

[7] Dixon to Kirby, 31 Oct. 1863, A.I.C.R.

ing of October, he grew increasingly frail and feeble. On 30 October he attended three funerals, one in Belfast, one in Lurgan and one in Aghagallon, and his exposure to bad weather on these occasions brought on an illness. Nevertheless, he took his customary place in the confessional in St Malachy's Church on the following day. But he became so weak that he had to be carried into the adjoining presbytery, where the last rites were administered before he was moved to his own home. There, attended by his niece, who was a Sister of Mercy, he died on the morning of 3 November. The funeral obsequies were held three days later in St Patrick's Church. Archbishop McGettigan presided. The panegyric was preached by Bishop Logue of Raphoe, and five other bishops were present. Interment took place beneath the sanctuary of the church.[8]

By a remarkable coincidence, Patrick Dorrian, bishop of Down and Connor, died on the feast of St Malachy, the patron of the diocese. Malachy was a great twelfth century reformer, who restored the celebrated abbey at Bangor after its collapse in the wake of the Norse invasions. Appointed bishop of Down and Connor, his reputation for zeal led to his promotion to the primatial see, but he begged permission to resign that office and return to his beloved Down. He died at Clairvaux in the arms of St Bernard in 1148, and, with the leading churchman of Europe as his biographer, the fame of his sanctity spread quickly and widely and he was canonized in 1190. As his devoted son and successor, who had never spared himself in the service of his church, Dorrian could not have chosen a more suitable and fitting date on which to lay down the mantle of St Malachy.

8 M.N., 3-7 Nov. 1885, N.W., 4-7 Nov. 1885.

Bibliography

MANUSCRIPT SOURCES

ARMAGH
Armagh Diocesan Archives
Papers of Archbishops Dixon and McGettigan

BELFAST
Down and Connor Diocesan Archives
Papers of Bishops Crolly, Denvir and Dorrian

Public Record Office of Northern Ireland
Applications for aid for national schools
Minutes of Boards of Guardians
Legal papers of L'Estrange and Brett
Papers of Thomas O'Hagan

City Hall
Minutes of the cemetery committee of Belfast Corporation 1867-87

St Malachy's Presbytery
Minute book of the building committee of St Malachy's Church

DUBLIN
Dublin Diocesan Archives
Papers of Archbishops Cullen, McCabe and Walsh
Papers of Bartholomew Woodlock, rector of the Catholic University

National Library of Ireland
Butt papers
Croke papers
Larcom papers
Monsell papers
O'Hagan papers

St Patrick's Training College, Drumcondra
Minute books of the episcopal committee in charge of the college

KILKENNY
Ossory Diocesan Archives
Papers of Bishop Patrick F. Moran

LONGFORD
Ardagh and Clonmacnois Diocesan Archives
Papers of Bishop Bartholomew Woodlock

LOUGHINISLAND
Parochial House
Register of Baptisms and Marriages

NEWRY
Dromore Diocesan Archives
Papers of Bishop John P. Leahy

ROME
Vatican Archives
Papers of the Secretariat of State relating to Ireland

Archives of the Sacred Congregation for the Evangelization of Peoples (formerly Propaganda Fide)
Correspondence and recommendations of the congregation relating to Ireland

Irish College
Correspondence of Paul Cullen and Tobias Kirby, rectors of the college

St Paul's Basilica
Papers of Abbot Bernard Smith

Venerable English College
Papers of Cardinal Edward Thomas Howard

Christian Brothers' Generalate
Papers relating to the Irish province of the Christian Brothers

NEWSPAPERS

Belfast Morning News (Morning News)
Belfast News-Letter
Downpatrick Recorder
Freeman's Journal
Irishman
Irish People
Northern Star
Northern Whig
Tablet
Ulsterman

Ulster Examiner (Daily Examiner, Ulster Examiner and Northern Star)
Ulster Observer
Vindicator
Weekly Vindicator

PARLIAMENTARY DEBATES AND PAPERS

(i) *Hansard's parliamentary debates, 3rd series*

(ii) *Papers in chronological order*

Eighth report of the commissioners of Irish education inquiry, H.C. 1826-7 (509), xiii

Municipal Corporations (Ireland). Appendix to the first report of the commissioners of municipal corporations in Ireland, H.C. 1835, xxviii, pt 1

First report of the commissioners of public instruction, Ireland, H.C. 1835 [45,46], xxxiii

Second report of the commissioners of public instruction, Ireland, H.C. 1835 [47], xxxiv

Papers relating to an investigation held at Castlewellan into the occurrences at Dolly's Brae, on the 12th July 1849, H.C. 1850 [1143], li

Report from the select committee of the House of Lords appointed to inquire into the practical working of the system of national education in Ireland, 2 pts, H.C. 1854 (525), xv

Copy of correspondence between the commissioners of national education in Ireland and the committee of the Lancasterian industrial national school, Belfast, relative to the charges made by the Reverend Dr Denvir against the system and management of that school, H.C. 1856 (88), liii

Report of the commissions of inquiry into the origin and character of the riots in Belfast in July and September 1857; together with minutes of evidence and appendix, H.C. 1857-58 [2309], xxvi

Report to the Lord Lieutenant of Ireland by Messrs. Fitzmaurice and Goold, with the minutes of evidence taken by them at the inquiry into the conduct of the constabulary during the disturbances at Belfast in July and September 1857, H.C. 1857-58 (333), xlvii

Twenty sixth report of the commissioners of national education in Ireland for the year ending 31st December 1859, [2706] H.C. 1860, xxvi

Thirtieth report . . . for the year 1863, [3351] H.C. 1864, xix, pt ii

Thirty first report . . . for the year 1864, [3496] H.C. 1865, xix

Thirty first report . . . for the year 1865 [3713] H.C. 1866, xxix

Fiftieth report . . . for the year 1883, [c 4053] 1884, xxv

Copy of the memorial of the Roman Catholic prelates relative to national education in Ireland, and of the reply thereto of the Chief Secretary, H.C. 1860 (26), liii

Further correspondence relative to national education in Ireland, H.C. 1860 (206), liii

Copy of a letter on the subject of national education in Ireland, addressed to the Chief Secretary in the month of July last by certain members of parliament H.C. 1861 (212), xlviii

The census of Ireland for the year 1861 pt I, vol iii, Ulster, H.C. 1863, liv
Copy of revised rules recently sanctioned by the commissioners of national education:- Dissents from, or protests against the adoption of the above rules on the part of any of the commissioners of national education in Ireland, and given in by any of the commissioners to the board; and memorials to the Lord-Lieutenant against the recent changes in the rules and regulations, and replies, H.C. 1864 (157), xlvi
Returns, by counties and parishes, of the names of all the schools in connection with the board of national education in Ireland, (distinguishing vested from non-vested) in operation on 31st December 1862; name, profession and religious denomination of the patron of each school; name, religion, class, and year of training of head and assistant literary teachers, workmistresses and paid monitors of each school etc; days and hours set apart for religious instruction given in the school, and nature of same, as set forth in timetable in use or operation, for quarter ending 31st December 1862 and name or names and creed of the person or persons who impart it, 1864 (481), xlvii
Report made to the board of national education on the subject of convent schools in Ireland by Inspector Sheridan:- and letter or memorial to them from Baggot-street convent school, Dublin, applying for payment for training teachers and answers, H.C. 1864 (179), xlvi
Copy of resolutions of the education committee of the General Assembly of the Presbyterian Church in Ireland, transmitted to the Lord-Lieutenant and to the education board, relative to the recent changes introduced into the national system of education, 1864 (285), xlvi
Report of the commissioners of inquiry, 1864, respecting the magisterial and police jurisdiction, arrangements and establishment of the borough of Belfast; minutes of evidence and appendix, H.C. 1865 [3466], xxviii
Copy of memorials addressed to the Secretary of State for the Home Department by the Roman Catholic prelates in Ireland on the subject of university and national education in Ireland; and of the correspondence relating thereto; and memorials addressed to the Lord-Lieutenant on the subject of university education in Ireland, H.C. 1866 (84), lv
Correspondence between Her Majesty's government and the commissioners of national education in Ireland, upon the subject of proposals with respect to the training and model school contained in the letter of the Right Honourable C.P. Fortescue MP to the commissioners dated 19th June 1866:- minutes adopted by the commissioners in reference to these proposals; and memorandum or report upon the subject submitted to the commissioners by any of their inspectors or other officers, H.C. 1867 (225), lv
Statement issued by the elementary education committee of the General Assembly, in reply to the letter of the Right Honourable C.P. Fortescue MP, on the organisation and government of model schools, H.C. 1867 (226), lv
Copy of correspondence relative to the proposed charter to a Roman Catholic University in Ireland [1867-8], H.C. 1867-8 (288), liii
Copy of further correspondence relative to the proposed charter to a Roman Catholic University in Ireland [1868], H.C. 1867-8 (380), liii
Copy of declaration of heads of Roman Catholic colleges and schools and other persons lately laid before the prime minister (24 Mar. 1870), H.C. 1870 (153), liv

Royal commission of inquiry into primary education (Ireland), 8 vols. H.C. 1870 [C6 to C6-vii], xxviii

Copy of declaration of the Catholic laity of Ireland on the subject of university education in that country, lately laid before the prime minister, H.C. 1870 (140), liv

Copy of all minutes and proceedings from the 1st day of May 1866 to the present time, relating to changes of rules or of practice as to religious instruction: date when the certificate book of religious instruction was first brought into active operation, copy of such book, and copy of circulars to patrons and inspectors relating thereto; copy of query, if any, introduced into the form of inspector's report, with a view to record the observance or neglect of the rules as to the certificate book; and returns of all schools in which certificates have been used, etc., H.C. 1872 (416), xlvi

Copies of the declaration of the Catholic Union, forwarded by the president to the first lord of the treasury, in January last [1873] and of the resolutions of the Roman Catholic archbishops and bishops [18 Aug. 1869] referred to in that memorial and transmitted with it, H.C. 1873 (78), lii

The census of Ireland for the year 1871 pt I vol.iii Ulster H.C. 1874 [C 964. I to X], lxxiv

Copy of memorials from the council of the National Education League for Ireland, on the subject of inroads made and contemplated upon the fundamental principle of the national system of education in Ireland; and from the elementary education committee of the General Assembly of the Presbyterian Church in Ireland addressed to His Grace, the Lord-Lieutenant on the subject of non-vested training colleges, H.C. 1875 (201), lix

Copy of declaration of the Catholic laity of Ireland, on the subject of university education in that country, lately laid before the prime minister, H.C. 1878-9 (108), lvii

Copy of declaration lately present to the prime minister from the Catholic laity of Ireland, in favour of the University Education (Ireland) Bill, H.C. 1878-9 (264), lvii

The census of Ireland for the year 1881, pt I, vol iii, Ulster, H.C. 1882 [C. 3204] lxxviii

Copy of a memorial from the elementary education committee of the Presbyterian Church in Ireland on training schools, H.C. 1883 (181), liii

Copy of a memorial presented to the Lord-Lieutenant by certain Catholic bishops upon the subject of elementary education, and which was alluded to by the Chief Secretary in introducing a bill upon the subject, H.C. 1884-5 (229), lxi

PRINTED WORKS

Acta et decreta synodi plenariae Episcoporum Hiberniae habitae apud Maynutiam an. MDCCCLXXV (Dublini, MDCCCLXXVII)

Acta et statuta primae synodi dioecesanae, Dunensis et Connoriensis habitae die 15 Maii, A.D. MDCCCLXVII; statuta dioecesana in dioecesi Dunensi et Connoriensi observanda, et a RR.mo Gulielmo Crolly, episcopo Dunensi et Connoriensi edita et promulgata A.D. 1834 (Belfastiae, ? 1867)

Ahern, J., 'The plenary synod of Thurles', *Irish Ecclesiastical Record*, lxxv (1951), 385-403 and lxxviii (1952) 1-20
Akenson, D.H., *The Irish education experiment* (London, 1970)
—, *The church of Ireland: Ecclesiastical reform and revolution 1800-1885* (New Haven, 1971)
—, *A Protestant in Purgatory: Richard Whately Archbishop of Dublin* (Hamden, 1981)
Aubert, R., *Le pontificat de Pie IX* (Paris, 1963)
—, *Vatican I* (Paris, 1964)
Baker, S.E., 'Orange and green: Belfast 1832-1912' in *The Victorian City: image and realities*, ed. H.J. Dyos and M. Wolff, 2 vols. (London, 1973), ii, 789-814
Balfour, G., *The educational systems of Great Britain and Ireland* (Oxford, 1903)
Bardon, J., *Belfast, an illustrated history* (Belfast, 1982)
Barry, P.C., 'The legislation of the Synod of Thurles 1850', *Irish Theological Quarterly*, xxvi (1959), 131-66
Beames, M., *Peasants and power: the Whiteboy movements and their control in pre-famine Ireland* (Brighton, 1983)
—, 'The Ribbon societies: lower class nationalism in pre-famine Ireland', *Past and Present*, No 97, (1982) 128-43
Beck, G., (ed.) *The English Catholics 1850-1950. A century of progress* (London 1950)
Beckett, J.C., *The making of modern Ireland, 1603-1923* (London 1966)
Beckett, J.C. and Glasscock, R.E., (ed.), *Belfast, origin and growth of an industrial city* (London, 1967)
Bew, P., *Land and the national question in Ireland 1858-82* (Dublin, 1978)
Bowen, D., *The Protestant crusade in Ireland 1800-70: a study of Protestant-Catholic relations between the act of union and disestablishment* (Dublin, 1978)
Boyd, A., *Holy war in Belfast* (Tralee, 1969)
Brooke, P., 'Religion and secular thought' in *Belfast: the making of the city 1800-1914*, ed. J.C. Beckett et. al. (Belfast, 1983) pp 111-28
Budge, I., and O'Leary, C., *Approach to crisis: a study of Belfast politics 1613-1970* (London, 1973)
Campbell, A.A., *Belfast newspapers, past and present* (Belfast,1921)
Cannon, S., *Irish episcopal meetings, 1788-1882: a juridico-historical study* (Rome, 1979)
Carson, J.T., *God's river in spate: the story of the religious awakening of Ulster in 1859* (Belfast, 1958)
Castlereagh, Viscount, (Robert Stewart), *Memoirs and Correspondence*, 4 vols. (London, 1848-49)
Clarke, S. and Donnelly, J.S., (eds.), *Irish peasants, violence and political unrest 1780-1914* (Manchester, 1983)
Comerford, R.V., *The Fenians in context* (Dublin, 1985)
Connolly, S.J., 'Catholicism in Ulster, 1800-50' in *Plantation to partition, essays in Ulster history in honour of J.L. McCracken* ed. P. Roebuck (Belfast, 1981) pp 157-71
—, *Priests and people in pre-famine Ireland 1780-1845* (Dublin, 1982)
—, *Religion and society in nineteenth century Ireland* (Dundalk, 1985)

Corish, P.J., 'Cardinal Cullen and the National Association of Ireland' *Reportorium Novum*, iii (1862), 13-61
—, 'Political Problems 1860-78' in *A history of Irish Catholicism* ed. P.J. Corish, v, (Dublin, 1967)
—, *The Irish Catholic Experience* (Dublin, 1985)
Crispolti, C. and Aureli, G., *La Politica di Leone XIII da Luigi Galimberti a Mariano Rampolla* (Rome, 1912)
Crolly, G., *The life of the Most Rev. Doctor Crolly, Archbishop of Armagh: to which are appended some letters in defence of his character*, (Dublin, 1851)
Cullen, L.M., *An economic history of Ireland since 1660* (London, 1972)
—, *The emergence of modern Ireland 1600-1900* (London, 1981)
Cunningham, T.P., 'Church reorganization' in *A history of Irish Catholicism* ed. P.J. Corish, v, (Dublin, 1970)
Daly, M., 'The development of the national school system, 1831-40' in *Studies in Irish history presented to R. Dudley Edwards.* ed. A. Cosgrove and D. McCartney (Dublin, 1979) pp 150-63
Davitt, M., *The fall of feudalism in Ireland or the story of the Land League revolution* (London, 1904)
Dessain, C.S., et al (eds.) *The letters and diaries of John Henry Newman*, 26 vols. (London and Oxford, 1961)
Duffy, C.G., *My life in two hemispheres*, 2 vols. (London, 1903)
Fitzmaurice, E., *The life of Lord Granville*, 2 vols. (London, 1905)
Friedrich, J., *Ignaz von Döllinger*, 3 vols. (Munich 1899-1901)
Froggatt, P., 'Industrialization and health in Belfast in the early nineteenth century' in *The town in Ireland* ed. D. Harkness and M. O'Dowd (Belfast, 1981)
Garvin, J.L., *The life of Joseph Chamberlain*, i, 1836-85 (London, 1932)
Garvin, T., *The evolution of Irish nationalist politics* (Dublin, 1981)
Gwynn, S., and Tuckwell, G., *The life of the Rt. Hon. Sir Charles W. Dilke*, 2 vols. (London, 1917)
Hammond, J.L., *Gladstone and the Irish nation* (London, 1938)
Haywood, F., *Léon XIII* (Paris, 1937).
Healy, J., *Maynooth College: its centenary history 1795-1895* (Dublin, 1895)
Heatley, F., *The story of St Patrick's, Belfast 1815-1977* (Portglenone, 1977)
Hepburn, A.C., 'Catholics in the north of Ireland 1850-1921: the urbanization of a minority' in *Minorities in history* ed. A.C. Hepburn (London, 1978) pp 84-101
—, 'Work, class and religion in Belfast, 1871-1911' in *Irish Economic and Social History*, x (1983), pp 33-50
Holmes, F., *Henry Cooke* (Belfast, 1981)
—, *Our Presbyterian heritage* (Belfast, 1985)
Hoppen, K.T., *Elections, politics and society in Ireland 1832-1885* (Oxford, 1984)
Jay, R., *Joseph Chamberlain: a political study* (Oxford, 1981)
Jedin, H., (ed.) *Handbuch der Kirchengeschichte*, vi, (Freiburg-im-Breisgau, 1971-3)
Kavanagh, J.W., *Mixed education, the Catholic case stated* (Dublin, 1859)
Keenan, D., *The Catholic Church in Ireland in the nineteenth century* (Dublin, 1983)
Kennedy, D., *Towards a university* (Belfast, 1946)

Kennedy, L. and Ollerenshaw, P., (eds.) *An economic history of Ulster 1820-1939* (Manchester, 1985)
Kerr, D.A., *Peel, priests and politics* (Oxford, 1982)
Larkin, E., 'Church and state in Ireland in the nineteenth century', *Church History* xxxi (1962), 294-306
—, 'Economic growth, capital investment, and the Roman Catholic Church in nineteenth century Ireland' *American Historical Review*, lxxii (1966-7), 852-84
—, 'The devotional revolution in Ireland 1850-75', *American Historical Review* lxxvii (1972), 625-52
—, 'Church state and nation in modern Ireland', *American Historical Review* lxxx (1975), 1244-76
—, *The Roman Catholic Church and the creation of the modern Irish state 1878-86* (Philadelphia and Dublin, 1975)
—, *The making of the Roman Catholic Church in Ireland, 1850-60* (Chapel Hill, 1980)
Launay, M., *Le Diocèse de Nantes sous le Second Empire*, 2 vols. (Nantes, 1982)
Le Bras, G., *Études de Sociologie Religieuse*, 2 vols. (Paris, 1956)
Leray, F., *Au service des Ames. Un apôtre Le Père Jean Gailhac Fondateur des Religieuses du Sacré-Coeur de Marie* (Paris, 1939)
Lyons, F.S.L., *John Dillon: a biography* (London, 1968)
—, *Ireland since the famine* (London, 1971)
—, *Charles Stewart Parnell* (London, 1977)
—, and Hawkins, R.A.J., (eds.), *Ireland under the union: varieties of tension: essays in honour of T.W. Moody* (Oxford, 1980)
McCartney, D., 'The Church and Fenianism', *University Review*, iv (1967), 203-15
McClelland, V.A., *Cardinal Manning, his public life and influence 1865-1892* (London, 1962)
MacDonagh, O., 'The politicization of the Irish Catholic bishops, 1800-1850', *Historical Journal* xviii (1975), 37-53
—, *States of mind, a study of Anglo-Irish conflict 1780-1980* (London, 1973)
McErlain, J., *A statement of accounts and of a few facts of local interest presented to the Catholics of Ballymoney & Derrykeighan* (Ballymoney, 1881)
McGrath, F., *Newman's University, idea and reality* (Dublin, 1951)
—. 'The university question' in *A history of Irish Catholicism* ed. P.J. Corish, v, (Dublin, 1971)
McIlwaine, W. and Dorrian, P., *Correspondence between Rev. W. McIlwaine, incumbent of St George's Protestant Church, Belfast and Most Rev. Dr. Dorrian, Lord Bishop of Down and Connor with an introduction and notes by His Lordship* (Belfast, 1865)
Macknight, T., *Ulster as it is; or, twenty eight years experience as an Irish editor*, 2 vols. (London,1896)
MacSuibhne, P., *Paul Cullen and his contemporaries 1820-1902*, 5 vols. (Naas, 1961-77)
Macaulay, A., *Dr Russell of Maynooth* (London, 1983)
Malcolm, E., *'Ireland sober, Ireland free': Drink and temperance in nineteenth century Ireland* (Dublin, 1986)

Mansi, J.B., *Sacrorum Conciliorum nova et amplissima collectio*, lii (Arnhem and Leipzig, 1927)
Miller, D.W., 'Irish Catholicism and the great famine', *Journal of Social History*, ix (1975), 81-98
—, 'Presbyterians and "modernization" in Ulster', *Past and Present*, No. 80 (1978). 66-90
Moody, T.W. and Beckett, J.C., *Queen's Belfast, 1845-1949: the history of a university*, 2 vols. (London, 1959)
Moody, T.W., (ed.) *Ulster since 1800: a political and economic survey* (London, 1955; corrected impression, 1957)
—, *Ulster since 1800: a social survey* (London 1957; corrected impression 1958)
—, *The Fenian movement* (Cork, 1968)
—, *Davitt and the Irish revolution 1846-82* (Oxford, 1981)
Morrissey, T.J., *Towards a national university: William Delany S.J.(1835-1924), an era of initiative in Irish education* (Dublin, 1983)
Murphy, I., 'Primary Education' in *A history of Irish Catholicism*, ed. P.J. Corish, v, (Dublin, 1971)
Murphy, J.A., 'Priests and people in modern Irish history', *Christus Rex*, xxiii, (1969), 235-59
Norman, E.R., *The Catholic Church and Ireland in the age of rebellion 1859-1873* (London, 1965)
O'Brien, C.C., *Parnell and his party 1880-90* (Oxford, 1957; corrected impression 1964)
O'Hanlon, W.M., *Walks among the poor of Belfast and suggestions for their improvement* (Belfast, 1853)
O'Laverty, J., *An historical account of the diocese of Down and Connor, ancient and modern*, 5 vols. (Dublin, 1878-95)
O'Raifeartaigh, T., 'Mixed education and the synod of Ulster, 1831-40' in *Irish Historical Studies*, ix, (1955) 281-99
O'Reilly, B., *John MacHale, Archbishop of Tuam, His life, times, and correspondence*, 2 vols. (New York and Cincinnati, 1890)
O'Suilleabhain, S., 'Secondary Education' in *A history of Irish Catholicism* ed. P.J. Corish, v, (Dublin 1970)
P.R.O.N.I., *Problems of a growing city, Belfast 1780-1870* (Belfast, 1973)
Ramm, A., (ed.) *The political correspondence of Mr Gladstone and Lord Granville 1868-76* 2 vols. (Oxford, 1962)
Reid, T.W., *Life of the Rt. Hon. W.E. Forster* 2 vols. (London, 1888)
Rogers, P., 'The minute book of the Belfast Rosarian Society' in *The Down and Connor Historical Society's Journal*, viii (1937), pp 17-24
—, *Old St Mary's, Chapel Lane, Belfast*, (Belfast, 1941)
—, 'St Malachy's College, Belfast 1833-1933', *The Collegian*, ix (1933). 13-29
—, *Father Theobald Mathew* (Dublin, 1943)
—, *St Peter's Pro-Cathedral, Belfast 1866-1966* (Belfast, 1966)
Schmidlin, J., *Papstgeschichte der neuesten Zeit*, 4 vols. (Munich, 1933)
Snead-Cox, J.G., *The life of Cardinal Vaughan*, 2 vols. (London, 1910)
Soderini, E., *Il pontificato di Leone XIII*, 3 vols. (Milan, 1932-3)
Stewart, A.T.Q., *The narrow ground: aspects of Ulster 1609-1969* (London, 1977)

[Society of St Vincent de Paul], *Society of St Vincent de Paul centenary* (Belfast, 1950)

Steele, E.D., *Irish Land and British politics: tenant-right and nationality 1865-1870* (Cambridge, 1974)

—, 'Gladstone and Ireland' in *Irish Historical Studies*, xvii (1970) 58-88

Thornley, D., *Isaac Butt and Home Rule* (London, 1964)

Tierney, M., *Croke of Cashel: the life of Archbishop Thomas William Croke, 1823-1902* (Dublin, 1976)

Walsh, P.J., *William J. Walsh, Archbishop of Dublin* (Dublin, 1928)

Walsh, W.J., *The Irish university question: the Catholic case* (Dublin, 1879)

—, *Statement of the chief grievances of Irish Catholics in the matter of education, primary, intermediate and university* (Dublin, 1890)

Ward, I.E., 'Leo XIII, the diplomat pope', *Review of politics*, xxviii (1966), 47-61

Whyte, J.H., *The Independent Irish party 1850-9* (Oxford, 1958)

—, 'The influence of the Catholic clergy on elections in nineteenth-century Ireland', *English Historical Review*, lxxv (1960), 239-59

—, 'The appointment of Catholic bishops in nineteenth-century Ireland', *Catholic Historical Review*, xlviii (1962) 12-32

—, 'Political problems 1850-1860' in *A history of Irish Catholicism* ed. P.J. Corish, v, (Dublin, 1976)

Woods, C.J., 'Ireland and Anglo-papal relations, 1880-85', *Irish Historical Studies*, xviii (1972), 29-60

—, 'The politics of Cardinal McCabe, Archbishop of Dublin 1879-85' *Dublin Historical Record*, xxvi, (1973) 101-110

Index

Aberdeen, George Hamilton Gordon, 4th earl of 173
Alexander VI, pope 135
Allen, William 185
Amnesty Association 185, 186, 219, 222
Andrews, William Drennan 216
Anthony, St 373
Ardagh, bishop of (John Kilduff) 98, 175
Ardagh, diocese of 276, 317n
Armagh, archdiocese of 276, 317n
Artane Industrial School 285
Augustine, St 132

Ballast Board 22
Bankmore House 121, 122
Banner of Ulster 73
Barnabò, Cardinal Alessandro 107, 109, 111
Barry, Judge Charles, 316n
Beaconsfield, 1st earl of, *see* Disraeli, B.
Bedeque House 122
Belfast Academical Institution 61
Belfast, Frederick Richard Chichester, earl of 229
Belfast Academical Institution 61
Belfast Catholic Musical Association 128
Belfast Catholic Temperance Association 132
Belfast Charitable Society 62, 153
Belfast General Hospital 24, 27, 56, 60, 61n, 88, 228
Belfast Morning News 123, 193, 212, 214, 215, 216, 228
Belfast News-Letter, 133, 205, 224, 228; policy of 37, 193; and the Catholic Institute 146–9; Dorrian writes to 164

Belfast Observer 199
Belfast Reform Association 40
Bellarmine, Robert, St 135
Belvedere House 278
Bernard, St 375
Biggar, Joseph Gillis, and the founding of Home Government Association in Belfast 208, 221; contests Londonderry City 209; helps organize procession in 1872 222; advocates Home Rule 231–4, 239–40, 361
Blackrock College 315, 320, 322n
Blackstone, Sir William 35
Blake, A.R. 247
Blake, Michael, bishop of Dromore 36, 73
Blessed Sacrament, confraternity of 127
Blessed Virgin Mary, confraternity of 29
Bon Secours, Sisters of 122
Bowyer, Sir George 240, 328
Bradlaugh, Charles 361
Brady, Patrick, bishop of Dromore 67
Brannigan, Daniel Rogan 140, 149, 193, 195, 196
Brennan, Geoffrey 170
Brennan, Thomas 240
Brigid, St 13
Browne, James, bishop of Kilmore 98
Buggy, Kieran 63
Burke, T.H. 351
Butler, George, bishop of Limerick 324n, 334, 356, 357n
Butt, Isaac, lectures in St Mary's Hall 129, 232; acts as counsel for Dorrian in the cemetery dispute 155-7; founds Home Government Association 191–2, 219; defends A.J.McKenna 151, 198, 205 and Home Rule 207, 222, 225, 229 231,

233–6; and the university question 309
Butt Testimonial Committee 229
Byrne, Edward 206, 231, 310

Cahill, Revd Michael H. 212; career of 206; manages/edits the *Ulster Examiner* 203, 204, 214–15; attitudes of colleagues to 207; opposes the Whigs 213, 214, 216–17, 235–6; supports Home Rule 220, 224, 230–1, 234; backs the Land League 328, 333; opposes coercion 345
Cantwell, John, bishop of Meath 98, 175
Cardwell, Edward 251, 252, 253
Carlile, Revd James 252
Carlisle, George William Frederick Howard, 7th earl of 44
Cashel, archbishop of *see* Croke, Thomas William
Cashel, archdiocese of 129
Castleknock College 315
Castlereagh, *see* Londonderry, 6th marquess of
Catholic (bishops, church, hierarchy), and national education 245–6, 250–3, 259–60, 268; and university education 219, 302–18; and teacher training 275–9
Catholic and Celtic Society 128
Catholic Defence Association 223
Catholic Emancipation 26, 31, 33, 35, 37, 41, 45, 229, 249
Catholic Institute 121, 128, 168, 184, 262, 278, 282; controversy between Dorrian and members of 140–52; *Ulster Observer* and 193, 195, 197, 198
Catholic University, bishops seek charter for 174, 219, 303–9; progress of 301; Dorrian's views on 307
Catholic Young Men's Society 128, 224
Caton, Brother Lewis 286–8
Caulfield, Henry 37
Cavendish, Lord Frederick 351
Chamney, Robert 210, 211
Charitable Bequests Bill 45–7, 56
Charlemont, Francis William Caulfield, 2nd earl of 36

Christian Brothers 120, 365; establish a house and schools in Belfast 109, 116, 283–4; praised at Powis commission 265–6, 268, 284; and controversy with Dorrian 285–300, 320
Christian Doctrine Society 29, 39, 42, 127, 373
Church, Revd Charles 280
Church of Ireland 32, 211, 308; and disestablishment of 129, 181, 174–5, 181, 189–90, 219, 309; and national education 244
Clarendon, George William Frederick Villiers, 4th earl of 16
Clarke, Revd Patrick 195, 199–201
Clemenceau, Georges Benjamin 357n
Clogher, bishop of, *see* MacNally, Charles
Clogher, diocese of, 317n, 276
Clonfert, bishop of, *see* Duggan, Patrick
Cloyne, bishop of, *see*Keane, William and MacCarthy, John
Coates, Thomas 53
Colmcille, St 13
Conaty, Nicholas, coadjutor, (*later*)bishop of Kilmore 130, 198, 324n, 356
Conroy, George, bishop of Ardagh 130, 275
Convery, Revd Patrick 293, 295, 298
Conway, Hugh, bishop of Killala 324n, 356
Cooke, Revd Henry 39, 55, 80, 165; and mixed marriages 29n; politics of 32, 35, 189–90; challenges O'Connell 37, 39; funeral of 190; monument to 228–9
Corry, J. P. 227
Coulter, Revd John 73
Crawford, James Sharman 231, 236
Crawford, William Sharman 36, 53, 74, 210; and repeal 37; and land reform 40, 73; supports federalism 45
Croke, Thomas William, archbishop of Cashel 323, 333, 339, 345, 346, 360, 368; and agrarian distress 239, 347; supports Parnell and the Land League 240, 329, 338; and the Vatican 334, 357; and Archbishop McCabe 343; seeks support of Irish Parliamentary party 362

INDEX

Crolly, Revd George, student at Maynooth 16–17; curate in Belfast 30, 34, 39, 41, 52, 63; doctorate of divinity sought for 94
Crolly, William, archbishop of Armagh 14, 17, 28n, 62, 68, 119, 373; achievements in Down and Connor and transfer to Armagh 21, 26–7; and the Charitable Bequests and Queen's Colleges Bills 46–7, 54–5; and St Malachy's Church 51, 53; and tenant right 73; and national education 245–6, 271
Crozier, Revd John 257n
Cruise, Francis 316n, 367n
Cullen, Paul, archbishop of Dublin *later* cardinal 117, 197, 198, 263n; opposed to Denvir's joining the board of national education 89; tries to get Vincentians established in Belfast 90–1; favours appointment of coadjutor in Down and Connor 87, 92, 95–6; relays information on candidates to Rome 99–101; consulted about problems in Belfast 103–4, 106; and the resignation of Bishop Denvir 108, 110–11; and the workhouse system 158; and the National Association 173–9; and the Fenians 183–4, 186; and A.J. McKenna 197–8, 200–01; corresponds with Dorrian on national education 261; and the establishment of a training college 274–5
Cuming, Dr James 149, 302
Cunningham, Revd John 49, 198, 199n
Curoe, Revd Daniel 39, 50, 248n
Curtis, Patrick, archbishop of Armagh 68

Daily Examiner see *Ulster Examiner*
Daunt, W.J. O'Neill 173, 225
Davitt, Michael 237, 238, 239, 240, 324, 328, 331, 338, 341
Dease, Edmund 316n
De Courcy, John 13
De Grey, Thomas Philip, 2nd Earl 28
Delany, bishop of Cork 324n
Delany, William 311–2, 320
Dempsey, Charles J. 214–5
Denvir, Cornelius, bishop of Down and Connor 14, 17, 19, 21, 39, 40, 113, 114, 118, 121, 372, 373; career of 27; reports on state of the diocese 28–30; supports O'Connell and repeal 36–7, 43–5; and the Charitable Bequests and Queen's Colleges Bills 46–50, 55–6; and erection of St Malachy's Church 51–3; and Fr Mathew's temperance crusade 57; and the famine 60–2; criticized for diocesan administration 88–96; appointment of coadjutor to 96–102; refuses to involve coadjutor in diocesan affairs 102–08; resignation of 108–112; and Belfast riots 163, 167; and the National Association 174–5; and the national system of education 89, 93, 246–8, 271
Denvir, Revd Peter 73
Derry, apostolic administrator of, see Kelly, Francis
Derry, diocese of 317n, 276
Derry, John, bishop of Clonfert 102, 178
Devoy, John 238
Devitt, Richard 173
Dill, Revd J.F. 257n
Dillon, John 331, 338, 345, 351
Dillon, John Blake 173, 177–8, 180
Disraeli, Benjamin 215, 235, 307–8
Dixon, Joseph, archbishop of Armagh 193, 196, 374; informs Rome about situation in Down and Connor 87, 91–7; confirms plea of C.W. Russell to be excused episcopal appointment 99; consulted by the Sisters of Mercy about their financial problems 103–4; presses for resignation of Bishop Denvir 106–11
Döllinger, Johann 28n
Dolly's Brae 75–6
Dominican Fathers 118
Dominican Sisters 122, 280
Donnelly, Nicholas, auxiliary bishop of Dublin 363, 366
Donnelly, James, bishop of Clogher 225, 324n
Dorrian, Revd Bernard 14, 61, 247
Dorrian, Edward, 14, 48
Dorrian, Patrick, père 13, 14
Dorrian, Patrick, birth 13; education 14–17; ordination 17; supports the repeal movement 37–45;

controversy with Fr Spratt 57–9; and famine relief 60; leaves Belfast for Loughinisland 63–4; enlarges Tievenadarragh school 78; recommended for appointment as coadjutor bishop 97–101; appointment 101; episcopal ordination 102; concerned about debts on new convent and church in Belfast 103–05, 110; concerned about provision of school places for Catholic children 105–07, 111; succeeds to see of Down and Connor 112; extends St Malachy's College 115–17; reorganizes parish of Belfast 118–19; holds diocesan synod 119; visits Rome 121; rearranges parish boundaries 126–7; encourages missions and sodalities 127–8; pastoral letters of 131–3; engages in controversy with Revd W. McIlwaine 133–5; defends papal infallibility 136–7; and misunderstanding with the Passionists 138–9; and controversy over the Catholic Institute 140–52; and dispute about burial arrangements with town council 152–8; and reaction to trouble in Belfast 1862 163–4; at the inquiry into the Belfast riots of 1864 169–70; and the National Association 174–81; and the Fenians 184–7; and the *Ulster Observer* 193–4, 196–8, 200–2; and the *Ulster Examiner* 203–4, 210–11, 217–18; and Home Rule 224–5, 228–33; and attitude to Parnell 240–2; and attitudes to Whigs' educational policy 261–2, 305–6; on national education 263–7; and the establishment of a Catholic training college 275–9; and secondary education in Down and Connor 280–3; and the dispute with Christian Brothers 285–300; on the Royal University 312–22; on hunger and distress in 1880 325–7, 341, 350–1; and the Land League 331; on diplomatic relations between England and the Holy See 342; on the land question 345–7; attends meeting of Irish bishops and curial officials in Rome 363–6; celebrates silver jubilee of episcopal ordination 369–71; death 375
Dorrian, Rose, neé Murphy 13, 64
Dorrian, William 14
Down and Connor,(diocese, see), *see also* Crolly, W.; Denvir, C.; Dorrian, P.; McAlister, P.; McCartan, T.; McMullan, H.; McMullan, P.: 17, 27, 46, 97, 113, 124, 206, 221, 231, 276, 317n; priests serving in 19, 21, 37, 191, 201; state of diocese 28–30, 92; and the famine 62; coadjutor appointed to 97–102; succession of Dorrian to 112, 143, 259; reorganization of 118–30, 371–4; national education in 247, 255–7, 267–8, 273, 276–8
Down Classical Academy 280
Downpatrick Recorder 70, 76
Downshire, Arthur Hill, 4th marquess of 82n
Drew, Revd Thomas 79–81
Dromore, coadjutor bishop of, *see* Leahy, John Pius
Dromore, diocese of 276
Dublin, archdiocese of 277
Dublin Evening Post 194
Duddy, John 208, 221, 224, 231, 233, 333, 345, 361, 362
Dufferin and Ava, Frederick Temple Blackwood, 1st marquess of 226
Duffin, Adam 53
Duffy, Charles Gavan 32–4, 40, 179
Duggan, Patrick, bishop of Clonfert 225, 324n, 334, 356, 363
Dunraven, Windham Wyndham — Quin, 3rd earl of 262n
Dunville, Thomas 53

Ecclesiastical Titles bill 74
Egan, Patrick 356n
Elphin, bishop of, *see* Gillooly, Laurence
Elphin, diocese of, 276, 313
Errington, George, (*later*) Sir George 313, 360, 362, 366, 368; political mission in Rome of 335–8, 340, 348, 350, 354; reports on Croke 343n, 353, 354n, 357n; rebuffed by Vatican 367

Faloon, Revd Marcus 248n
Farrell, Brother Michael Stanislaus 293, 298

Fenians (and Fenianism) 237, 238, 240, 241, 325, 340n; and possible use of Catholic Institute 150–1; appeal of 173, 184–5; opposed by bishops 174, 182–3; Dorrian's views on 176, 185–6; release of 187–8, 215, 222
Ferguson, John 233
Fitzgerald, Revd Michael, archdeacon of Limerick 73
Fitzgerald, J.D. 262n
Fitzgerald, William, bishop of Ross 324n, 334, 356
Fitzpatrick, T.E. 203
Fitzsimons, Revd John 97, 98, 99
Foresters, 230
Forster, Edward, Chief Secretary 335, 344, 351, 356
Fortescue, Chichester 260
Freeman's Journal 230, 238, 356
Froggatt, Sir Peter 21n
Fullerton, Alexander George 123, 341n
Fullerton, Lady Georgiana 123, 341, 341n

Gallogly, Revd John 73
Gambetta, Leon 336n
Gillooly, Laurence, bishop of Elphin 175, 178, 278, 279, 324n, 354, 366n
Gladstone, William Ewart 181, 190, 192, 222, 225, 310, 348n; Dorrian praises policy of 186; releases Fenians 187; Land Act of 191; and university education 219, 224–5, 274, 308–9
Good Shepherd Sisters 121
Gosford, Archibald Acheson, 2nd earl of 36
Granard, George Arthur Hastings Forbes, 7th earl of 316n, 367n
Granville, Granville George Leveson-Gower, 2nd Earl 335, 337, 347, 348n, 359, 366
Gray, Edmund Dwyer 359, 371
Gray, Sir John 173, 180
Greene, Revd J.P. 235, 333, 361
Gregory XVI, pope 340
Grey, Sir George 260, 303, 304, 305
Griffith, Thomas 52, 53
Grimshaw, James 39, 45, 53

Hamill, Revd James 235, 370
Hamill, John 80, 122, 154

Hamill, Revd P.J. 224
Hanna, Revd Hugh 30, 63, 81, 82n, 83, 163, 212, 222, 270
Harbinson, William 187
Harkin, Dr Alexander 121, 310n
Hay, Lord John 180, 189
Heald, James 255n
Healy, T.M. 361
Henry, Revd Henry 139n, 282, 313, 320-2, 369
Henry, Mitchell 310
Henry, Revd P.S. 318n
Hicks-Beach, Sir Michael 275
Hill, Revd Robert 257n
Hincks, Revd Edward 36
Hoare, Brother James A. 283
Holland, Denis 193
Holy Cross College, Clonliffe 275, 315, 322n
Holy See (Vatican, Secretariat of State, congregation of Propaganda) 114, 139, 174, 367, 368; Denvir reports to 28–39; and the appointment of a coadjutor to Down and Connor 87, 91–102; and national education 89, 246, 249; and university education 46, 55–6, 302, 313, 315–18; and the question of Denvir's resignation 105–12; and Fenianism 186; and the appeals of the Christian Brothers 289, 295–6, 298–300; and agrarian agitation 323–5, 329–31, 334–43, 347–50, 352–60; and consultations with the bishops 362–6
Home Government Association 191, 219, 221, 225
Home Rule 207, 213–4, 328; gathers strength 219–36; Dorrian's attitude to 229, 231–2
Hopkins, Revd Gerard Manley 320
Houston, John 37
Howard, Cardinal Edward Henry 336, 343n, 347, 350, 354n, 359, 360
Hughes, Bernard 80, 105, 122, 128, 163, 224; and the Catholic Institute 149, 151; and the *Ulster Observer* 193, 195–6, 198, 200–1
Hugo, Victor 343

Independent party 173, 176
Inglis, Sir Robert 54
Intermediate Education Act 281, 282, 289, 290, 299, 311, 316, 369

Irish College, Rome *see* Kirby, Tobias
Irishman 193
Irish National Land League *see* Land League
Irish National League 356, 361
Irish People 174, 182
Irish Teachers' Journal 210

Jackson, Thomas 51
Jacobini, Cardinal Angelo 362
Jacobini, Cardinal Ludovico 313, 337, 340, 341, 343n, 355n, 356n, 363
Johnston, William 189, 227, 229, 235
Joseph, St 373

Kane, Sir Robert 316n
Kavanagh, Arthur 311
Kavanagh, James 198, 201
Kavanagh, Revd James 316n
Kavanagh, J.W. 269, 270, 315n
Keane, William, bishop of Cloyne 175, 178, 333
Kearney, Revd Thomas 30, 63
Keegan, Peter 121
Keenan, Sir Patrick 278
Kelly, Francis, coadjutor (*later*) bishop of Derry 73, 98, 209, 324n
Kelly, Thomas, bishop of Dromore 245
Kennedy, Patrick, bishop of Killaloe 46, 53
Keogh, William 173, 176, 221
Kerr, Owen 198, 198n, 203
Kerry, bishop of, *see* McCarthy, Daniel
Killaloe, bishop of, *see* Kennedy, Patrick
Killen, Revd James 73
Kilmore, bishop of *see* Browne, James
Kilmore, diocese of 276, 317n
Kirby, Revd Tobias (*later* archbishop of Ephesus) 107, 355, 360, 367; Cullen corresponds with 89, 108; Dorrian corresponds with 148, 175, 177, 180, 185, 241, 303, 321, 329, 333, 347; Dixon corresponds with 96, 106

Ladies Charitable Society 88
Ladies Land League 342, 343, 350, 352, 353
Land Act (1870) 191, 219
Land Act (1881) 344, 346, 349, 350, 351

Land League 327, 329, 340, 343, 350, 356; foundation of 239–40, 349; Dorrian favours policy of 242, 330–1, 341, 344, 346, 347; accused of association with crime 324, 332, 335, 337; defended by Croke 338
Langton, Stephen, archbishop of Canterbury 346
Larkin, Michael 185
Lavelle, Revd Patrick 183, 184, 186
Laverty, Revd Henry 313
Leahy, John Pius, bishop of Dromore 98, 99, 101, 113, 118, 324n
Leinster, Augustus Frederick FitzGerald, 3rd duke of 243
Lennon, Bernard 48
Lennon, Revd John 217
Leo XII, pope 373
Leo XIII, pope 127, 237, 323, 335n, 348, 359; meets bishops from Ireland 334; interest in diplomatic activity of 336; writes to archbishop of Dublin 340, 353, 355; approves letter on Parnell fund 357; invites bishops to Rome 363; appoints Walsh archbishop of Dublin 367
Lentaigne, John 262n
Liberation Society 181
Liberius, pope 135
Limerick, bishop of, *see* Butler, George
Logue, Michael, bishop of Raphoe 131, 324n, 375
Londonderry, Charles William Vane, 3rd marquess of 73
Londonderry, Charles Stewart Vane-Tempest-Stewart, 6th marquess of 216, 235
Londonderry, Elizabeth Frances Charlotte Vane, marchioness of 123
Loughinisland, parish of 65–9
Lynch, James, coadjutor (*later*) bishop of Kildare and Leighlin 275, 324n
Lundy, Peter 52
Lynch, Revd John 97, 98, 248n, 257n, 258
Lyons, Robert 316n

MacAleese, Daniel 206, 210
Macaulay, Peter 370
MacCarthy, John, bishop of Cloyne 324n, 334
MacCormack, Francis, bishop of Achonry 324n, 354–6

INDEX

MacEvilly, John, archbishop of Tuam, 324n, 330, 354–5
MacHale, John, archbishop of Tuam, opposes Charitable Bequests and Queen's Colleges Bills 45–6 48–9, 55; on papal infallibility 136–7; and the National Association 174, 178–9, and defence of Revd Patrick Lavelle 183; favours Home Rule 225; opposes meeting at Westport 238; attacks national system of education 246; opposes Land League 324n
Macknight, Thomas 209, 210
MacNally, Charles, bishop of Clogher 102
Macnamara, James 39, 44
Magee College 309
Magee, Revd Cornelius 257n
Magill, Hugh 36, 43, 47, 50, 52, 53
Magill, Revd Roland 73
Maglone, Barney 212
Magouran, James 48
Magouran, Peter 47
Maguire, Revd George 73
Maine, Sir Henry Summer 319
Malachy, St 375
Malcolm, Andrew 24
Manning, Henry Edward, cardinal archbishop of Westminster, and the university question 307, 309–10; explains clerical involvement in agrarian agitation 325, 330, 339, 349, 359; recommends Walsh for archbishopric of Dublin 367
Marner, Revd Richard 264n, 371
Martin, John 173
Masotti, Monsignor Ignazio 343n
Mater Infirmorum Hospital 122
Mathew, Father Theobald 56
Maxwell, Brother Richard 293, 295, 299
Maynooth College 93, 129, 306; Dorrian studies in 14–17; and the Royal University 312, 314; examined by bishops and Propaganda 364
Mayo, Richard Southwell Bourke, 6th earl of, 307–8
McAlister, Patrick, bishop of Down and Connor 139, 159
McAuley, Revd Bernard 36, 245
McAuley, Revd William 73
McCabe, Edward, archbishop of Dublin (*later*) cardinal 350, 353, 362, 363; and establishment of training colleges 278; and the Royal University 313, 314, 316n, 320, 321; opposes Land League 324n, 330, 338–9; and diplomatic relations 342; rebuked by Croke 343; created cardinal 348; supports Henry Neville for coadjutorship of Cork 360
McCance, William 53
McCann, Bernard 160
McCann, Revd Hugh 217, 257n
McCartan, Revd John (parish priest of Kilkeel) 67
McCartan, Revd John (parish priest of Saintfield) 67
McCartan, Revd Patrick 67–8
McCartan, Revd Paul 67–8
McCartan, Theophilus, bishop of Down and Connor 66-7
McCartan, Revd William 126
McCartan, Revd William 21n, 61, 68–9, 77
McCartan, William Stafford 67
McCarthy, Daniel, bishop of Kerry 324n
McCarthy, John George 310
McCashin, Revd Daniel 139n
McClean, Adam 51–2
McClure, Thomas 60, 189, 205, 213, 227
McConnell, John 167–8
McConvey, Revd Michael 159–60
McCourt, Patrick 193–4
McCoy, Frederick, 302
McCready, William 257
McDevitt, James, bishop of Raphoe 130
McDonnell, Charles 48
McDonnell, Revd Daniel 160–161
McDowell, Robert 35, 37–8, 53
McErlain, Revd John 124, 127
McErlean, Andrew 231
McEvoy, Revd Peter 362
McGettigan, Patrick, bishop of Raphoe 36
McGettigan, Daniel, archbishop of Armagh 98, 324n, 329, 375
McGreevy, Revd Edward 49
McHugh, Edward 199n, 208
McIlwaine, Revd William 82–3, 133–5, 212
McKenna, Andrew Joseph 121, 148–9, 151, 194–7, 207

McKenna, Revd Bernard 326
McKenna, Revd Francis 73, 160
McKenna, Revd John 83
McKnight, James 73
McLaughlin, Revd Henry 73, 126
McLaughlin, Peter, bishop of Derry 76–7
McManus, Terence Bellew 174, 183
McMordie, Hans 216
McMullan, Hugh, bishop of Down and Connor 67
McMullan, Matthew 193, 196
McMullan, Patrick, bishop of Down and Connor 67–8
McMullan, Robert 361
McMullan, Revd William, 21n, 61, 68, 69, 76, 77
McNaughten, Edward 217
Meath, bishop of, see Cantwell, John
Meath, diocese of 276, 317n, 363
Melbourne, bishop of (James Goold) 264
Mercy, Sisters of 76, 165, 264n, 278; establishment of convent and school in Belfast 88, 91, 103–4, 121–2, 280, 372, 375
Methodist Church 305
Methodist College 294, 298
Model Schools 93n 252, 260, 261, 274; foundation of 246–7; bishops opposed to 252, 257–8; models in Down and Connor 257–8, 264–5, 285–6
Molloy, Revd Gerald 312
Monahan, Henry, 262n
Monsell, William, (later 1st Baron Emly) 90, 220, 316n, 343n
Montgomery, Revd Henry 32, 36, 55
Moore, Revd M 257n
Moran, Patrick Francis, bishop of Ossory 343, 360; and St Patrick's Training College 275, 278; opposed to Land League 324n; and diplomatic relations 341–2
Morning News 217, 321, 370, 319
Moriarty, David, bishop of Kerry 136, 220
Morpeth, viscount see Carlisle
Morris, Judge Michael 316n
Mountmorres, William Browne de Mountmorency, 5th viscount 332
Mulcahy, Revd D.B. 128
Mulholland, Andrew 55
Murney, George 80, 140, 149

Murney, Henry 47
Murphy, Daniel, vicar apostolic of Hyderabad 100, 101
Murray, Daniel, archbishop of Dublin 17, 46–7, 55, 68, 244, 246, 248

Nardi, Monsignor Francesco 200n
National Association 173–81
National Education League of Ireland 271
Nazareth, Sisters of 122
Neilson, Revd James 14
Neilson, Revd Samuel 14
Nelson, Revd Isaac 172, 208, 221, 229, 231, 239
Neville, Revd Henry, rector of the Catholic University 311, 316n, 356n, 360
Newman, Revd John Henry (*later*) cardinal 301, 348n
Nicholas IV, pope 65
Nina, Cardinal Lorenzo 349
Nolan, J.P. 221
Northern Star 199, 202, 204, 207
Northern Whig 163, 164, 167, 196, 224, 235, 239; policy of 32, 37, 79, 193, 212; Dorrian replies to on temperance question 57–9; accuses Catholic clergy of apathy during riots 223; and controversy about Christian Brothers' schools 297
Nulty, Thomas, coadjutor (*later*) bishop of Meath 130, 175, 176, 178, 324, 351

O'Boyle, Revd Henry 313
O'Boyle, Revd James 333, 344, 351
O'Brien, Michael 185
O'Brien, Terence 195
O'Brien, William 361
O'Callaghan, Henry, coadjutor bishop of Cork 360, 363
O'Connell, Daniel 47, 49, 55, 63, 128, 165, 173, 176, 179, 180, 226, 229, 234, 340n; campaigns for repeal 34–5, 42–3; visits Belfast 37–9; Dorrian praises 41, 44–5, 230; opposes Queen's Colleges 54; monument to 164, 175
O'Conor Don, The (Charles Owen O'Conor) 311, 328
O'Connor, T.P. 361
O'Donoghue, The (Daniel O'Donoghue) 303

O'Donovan, John 302
O'Donovan Rossa, Jeremiah 186
O'Hagan, John 262n
O'Hagan, Thomas 209, 316n
O'Hagerty, Revd James 91n
O'Hanlon, Revd W.M. 24–6
O'Hea, Michael, bishop of Ross 175, 225
O'Kane, Revd Patrick 359n
O'Laverty, Revd James 53, 160, 217, 218
O'Loughlin, Revd Henry 114, 115, 159, 161
O'Mahony, John 181
O'Neill, John Bruce Richard, 3rd viscount 248n
Orangemen 33, 34, 41, 89, 118, 136, 146, 191, 212, 233, 315; and violence in Belfast 31–2, 81, 93, 169–71, 188; and O'Connell 37; and Dolly's Brae 74–5; and violence in Lisburn 83–4, 90
O'Reilly, Myles 173, 258
O'Reilly, Richard, archbishop of Armagh 67–8
Ormonde, James Butler, 1st duke of 136
O'Rorke, Alexander 158, 193
O'Rorke, Edward 36, 40, 44
O'Shea, Revd Thomas 73
Ossory, bishop of 313

Palles, Christopher 208–9, 224
Palmerston, Henry John Temple, 3rd viscount 181
Parnell, Charles Stewart 324, 327, 338, 345, 348, 351–2, 360–2; gets support from Belfast Home Rulers 233, 236, 239, 240; and agrarian agitation 238, 332, 333, 335; defended by Dorrian 241, 328, 331; and testimonial fund 355–8
Party Processions Act 222
Passionists 137–9, 140, 294
Peel, Robert 53, 54
Pigot, D.R. 262n
Pilot 55
Pius VII, pope 289
Pius IX, pope 121, 305, 336, 373
Porter, Professor J.L. 212, 318n
Ports and Docks Authority 80
Power, John, bishop of Waterford 324n

Powis Commission 150, 263–9, 272, 284
Powis Report 268–9, 274
Presbyterian Church, and national education 244–5; and training colleges 261, 275n
Preston, Thomas 262n
Prince and Princess of Wales 363
Propaganda, congregation of, *see* Holy See
Pye, Revd George 100, 101

Quanta Cura 141
Queen's Colleges 311, 313, 314; establishment of 46, 54–6, 301, 303–5; proposals to alter arrangements of 303–7, 309
Queen's College, Belfast 152, 294, 298, 301–2, 304–7, 317, 318, 322; Dorrian complains to Rome about 316
Queen's College, Cork 304, 305, 309, 322n
Queen's College, Galway 304, 305, 309, 322n
Queen's University 303–7, 311, 316

Raphoe, coadjutor bishop of, *see* McGettigan, Daniel 98
Raphoe, diocese of 276
Rea, John 210
Read, Daniel 193, 216
Read, Robert 193
Redington, Sir Thomas 316n
Reffé, Revd J.E. 320
Regium Donum 37, 79, 190
Repeal 34–45, 54, 63, 74, 175, 220
Repeal Association 50
Rerum Novarum 324, 327
Ribbonism 74, 75, 183
Richmond, D.C. 267, 268, 284
Rochefort, Henri 343, 356n, 357n
Roden, Robert Jocelyn, 3rd earl of 75
Rogers, Revd John 73
Rosarian Society 30, 127, 373
Rosemary Street Presbyterian Church 80
Ross, bishop of, *see* O'Hea, Michael and Fitzgerald, William
Ross, David 40, 55
Ross, William 122, 198, 200n, 201
Royal College of Surgeons 301
Royal Irish University 303

Royal University 282, 311–16, 318–22, 362, 364, 367, 369
Russell, Charles William 16, 17, 28n, 97–100, 113
Russell, Lord John 74, 147, 181
Ryan, James, coadjutor bishop of Killaloe 324n

Sacred Heart, Sisters of 122, 280, 372
Sadleir, John 173, 176
St Isidore's Franciscan Convent, Rome 67
St Joseph's Church 123, 125n, 127, 139
St Joseph's parish 223
St Kieran's College, Kilkenny 315
St Malachy's Church 88, 96, 103, 118, 121, 166, 228; building of 52–3; violence at 80, 93, 163, 170; Dorrian attached to 102; presbytery at 121, 123, 127, 375
St Malachy's College 114, 115, 129, 191, 287, 293, 294, 296, 298, 299, 300, 369, 371; establishment of 21; extensions to 116, 120, 291; affiliated to Catholic University 279–80; and the Royal University 312–13, 315, 317–22, 322n
St Malachy's schools 284
St Mary's Church 19, 20, 30, 40, 52, 88, 127, 128, 157, 163; building of 21, 31; rebuilding of 120, 123
St Mary's Hall, Belfast, establishment of 128; Isaac Butt lectures in 232; political speeches in 236, 239, 333, 341, 345, 351; Dorrian's jubilee celebrations in 369–70
St Matthew's Church 123, 127
St Patrick's Church, 19, 20, 51, 118, 245, 286, 326; building of 21, 52; rebuilding of 123; presbytery attached to 127
St Patrick's College 310
St Patrick's College, Carlow 315, 322n
St Patrick's Industrial schools 285n
St Patrick's Orphan Society 26
St Patrick's schools 23n, 284, 296
St Patrick's Training College 276
St Paul's Church 125
St Peter's Church 127, 293; building and opening of 102, 105, 110, 117–18, 283; cost of 125
St Vincent de Paul Society 88, 90, 92, 106, 107, 111, 121, 127, 373

Secretariat of State *see* Holy See
Sexton, Thomas 345
Sheridan, P.J. 356n
Simeoni, Cardinal Giacomo 329, 331, 339, 340, 340n, 350, 357n, 363, 365n
Sinclair, John 35, 37
Slattery, Brother James 289, 291, 292
Smith, Bernard, abbot 335 and 335n, 337, 343n
Smyth, Revd J.H. 257n
Spencer, John Poyntz, 5th Earl 366
Spratt, Revd John 57–8
Stanley, Lord Edward Geoffrey (*later*) 14th earl of Derby 36, 243–4, 263, 266
Starkey, Revd Patrick 73
Stephens, James 181
Syllabus of Errors 134, 135, 141, 205, 305
Synod of Drogheda 119
Synod of Thurles 119, 302

Tablet 55
Tenant League 176
Tennent, Emerson 31
Tennent, James Thomson 35, 37, 53
Tennent, Robert James 39
Terenure College 315
Tierney, Revd Mark 323
Todd, Revd Andrew 257n
Trent, Council of 134
Trinity College, Dublin 302, 304, 306, 309
Turnley, Francis 248n
Tynan, Revd P.J. 366

Ullathorne, W.B., bishop of Birmingham 117
Ulster Catholic Association 226
Ulster Catholic Publishing Company 199
Ulster Constitutional Association 36
Ulster Custom 72, 231
Ulster Examiner (*Daily Examiner*) 187–8, 227, 228, 233, 271, 310, 326, 347; supports Home Rule 192, 208, 232; launching of 202–4; Dorrian's connection with 208–9; opposes the Whigs 213–14, 216–17, 235–6; and the riots of 1872 222–4; and the Land Act 344
Ulsterman 92, 193

INDEX

Ulster National Education Association 261
Ulster Observer 121, 189; first years of 194–7; and the controversy over the Catholic Institute 146–9; and the riots of 1864 164, 166–7; and Fenianism 185, 187; closure of 198–200
Ulster Times 37
University College, Dublin 315, 320-21, 367

Vatican *see* Holy See
Vatican Council 135–7
Vaughan, Herbert, bishop of Salford 342
Vicinage House 21
Vincentians 90, 91, 96, 274–5, 276, 278
Vindicator 50, 53, 57, 59, 193; launching of 32–3; policy of 34, 36, 37, 45; and O'Connell 39, 40, 55
Volunteers 33, 53, 120

Waldron, Laurence, 262n
Walshe, James, bishop of Kildare and Leighlin 324n
Walsh, Revd Luke 49
Walsh, Revd Peter 136–7
Walsh, William J. president of Maynooth, (*later*) archbishop of Dublin 316n, 319n, 320, 322n, 323, 366–7
Ward, Judge Michael 13
Warren, Michael, bishop of Ferns 324n
Waterford, bishop of *see* Power, John
Watson, William 80, 81, 140
Watterson, Revd Edward 217
Weekly Observer 199
Whately, Richard, archbishop of Dublin 244, 249, 252
Wodehouse, John, 3rd Baron Wodehouse (*later*) earl of Kimberley 261, 303
Woodlock, Bartholomew, rector of the Catholic University, (*later*) bishop of Ardagh), and finding an editor for the *Ulster Observer* 193–4; and the Catholic University 274–5, 307, 317n; and the Royal University 312–14, 320–1; opposed to the Land League 324n

Young Ireland 54, 63
Young, Revd Samuel 73